U Nu—Saturday's Son

U Nu
Saturday's Son

by U Nu

Translated by U Law Yone

Edited by U Kyaw Win

New Haven and London
Yale University Press
1975

Library of Congress catalog card number: 74-79835
International standard book number: 0-300-01776-6

Designed by Sally Sullivan
and set in Baskerville type.
Printed in the United States of America by
The Murray Printing Co.,
Forge Village, Mass.

Published in Great Britain, Europe, and Africa by Yale
University Press, Ltd., London. Distributed in Latin America
by Kaiman & Polon, Inc., New York City; in Australasia
and Southeast Asia by John Wiley & Sons Australasia Pty.
Ltd., Sydney; in India by UBS Publishers' Distributors
Pvt., Ltd., Delhi; in Japan by John Weatherhill, Inc., Tokyo.

Dear San San Nu, Maung Thaung Htike, Maung
Aung, Than Than Nu, and Cho Cho Nu:

Your father, U Nu, once known as Tartay, Saturday's
Son, was a revolting character who through the most
stringent efforts made a man of himself. Thus in his
life he was guilty of much wrong but also credited
with some good. If this book should lead you to avoid
your father's mistakes and to improve on his virtues,
the task of writing it will have been worthwhile.

                                                    U Nu

Contents

Acknowledgements

U Law Yone, whose friendship I have treasured since our beloved Burma gained independence in 1948, translated *U Nu—Saturday's Son* from the Burmese. As founder and editor of *The Nation*, Burma's premier English-language daily until it was silenced by the military regime in 1964, he has been a constant critic. His paper adopted as its motto, "Let me make the newspapers of the land and I do not care who makes its laws," from Thomas Jefferson.

It is my fervent hope that he will someday write his own account of the conception, birth, and first three decades of the national life of independent Burma.

Professor U Kyaw Win, whom I met for the first time in July 1955, when he was a graduate student in Washington, D.C., edited the manuscript. With a singular commitment to excellence, he laboured many hours, day and night, over the task. His perceptive mind and liberal use of the red pen brought the manuscript to its final form.

To these two persons I wish to express my heartfelt thanks for a task done so well by intoning the age-old Pali word *thadu*.

I, and I alone, accept responsibility for the substance of the autobiography.

U Nu

Costa Mesa, California
4 January 1974

*Mahawthada, from an etching on an antique
Shan saber, drawn by Alban Law Yone.*

Translator's Note

The manuscript of this book was sent round the world before it
fell into this translator's hands. Given only thirty days in which to
complete a work of this nature, only someone acquainted with the
author, and his thought processes, would have attempted it. If the
English version lacks scholarship it cannot be blamed on shortage
of time; the author himself makes no pretensions to scholarship in
the Burmese language.

Nevertheless, the translator regrets he has been unable to convey
the essence of earthiness, directness, and simplicity in the original
prose. He has made only one contribution, by prevailing upon the
author to alter the spelling of classical Pali words according to the
way they are pronounced in Burma—in the tradition of Shway Yoe
(Sir James George Scott) in his book *The Burman*.

Although this book is pure autobiography, a curious device has
been used whereby the authorship has been made to devolve upon
an older man called U Nu, after whom the man who was to become
prime minister of Burma was named. Recounted here are the life
and times of a spirited Burman forced to change roles almost over-

night, from rebel to government leader. Its theme is perhaps that to be a good Buddhist is to be a good democrat, and that the guiding principle in the unavoidable use of force, in the service of king and country, is defined in the life of Mahawthada, the embryo Buddha, a model on which U Nu still strives to fashion his own life.

U LAW YONE

Goldsboro, North Carolina
15 July 1973

Guide to Burmese Forms of Address

There are no family names in Burma as we know them in the West. Children are given individual names. Even though there may be up to three syllables in a person's name, it is really only one, preceded by a title. The use of the names Maung Nu, Ko Nu, Thakin Nu, and U Nu may at first seem confusing to non-Burmese readers, but in fact these names all refer to the same person. The title in each case signifies the relationship of the addressor to the addressee. *Maung* is a prefix used before the name of a boy; *Ko* is used for students and for young men in their twenties; and *Thakin,* meaning "lord," is a title used by members of the Dobama Asi-ayone (Our Burma Association), a revolutionary political party. *U* (pronounced *oo*) is a prefix tradition endows upon a man when he has attained stature because of age, education, or status in life. The corresponding prefixes for women's names are *Ma* (for young women) and *Daw* (for older or married women). There are no patronymics in Burmese, and women retain their maiden names after marriage. The titles *Saya* (teacher) and *Bo* (officer or leader) are also used frequently in the text, and the names of non-Burmans are preceded by the appropriate titles or prefixes in their own languages. Hence male Karens are addressed as *Saw* or *Mahn,* Shan and Kachin chiefs are addressed as *Sawbwa* and *Duwa,* respectively, and the Shan title *Sao* (lord) also appears occasionally. In Burmese custom it is rude to address a person without using the appropriate prefix, except between close friends and family members.

Namo Tatha Bagawataw Arahataw Thamma Thambhodatha. (Homage to the Blessed One, the Exalted One, the fully Enlightened One.)

Prologue

My name is Maung Nu. I studied up to the ninth standard, Anglo-vernacular,[1] when I left school to help run my parents' drapery store in the Wakèma bazaar.

Around 1905, two local personages, U Po Chan and U Shwe Gon, formed the Ponnya Kawthanla (Friendship) Association, which attracted to itself a considerable number of religious-minded youths. Shortly after I joined up, I became fast friends with one Ko San Tun. I was eighteen, pushing nineteen; Ko San Tun was five years older.

Ko San Tun's widowed mother had entrusted him, at the age of five, to the Kungyangon Monastery in Minbaing quarter of Wakèma town. At ten, Ko San Tun donned the yellow robe of a *koyin* (novice) and received instruction until he had mastered

---

1. Public schools established by the British in Burma; in these schools both English and Burmese were compulsory.

1

the nine stanzas of the Thingyo. At eighteen, he reverted to lay status. At the time he and I enrolled, almost simultaneously, with the Ponnya Kawthanla, Ko San Tun had no regular employment. He cooked for his mother, fetched and carried, and helped her with her work at a grocery shop.

At ease with contemporaries, Ko San Tun was respectful towards elders. No one needing a helping hand, irrespective of whether he was a close friend or a stranger, ever found Ko San Tun tardy. He was a good speaker who had formed the habit of interlacing his words with scriptural quotations. His manly attributes, in form and content, were such that he soon caught the eye of U Shwe Gon, our vice-president. Indeed, U Shwe Gon became to enamoured of this prodigy that the moment the association's work was done— sometimes as a prelude to it—he would put on a performance for our benefit.

"Hi, Po San Tun,[2] tell us about Sinbyushin,"[3] he would command, finding ready compliance.

Did he want a refrain from one of U Ponnya's[4] compositions? Ko San Tun at once broke into melody.

"Say, Po San Tun, how did the saying 'fearful of the tiger, supplication is made to the Shingyi[5] spirit, only to discover him the greater of two evils' originate?" And there and then would follow an explanation.

Broach the subject of *Tha-ti Pa-htan,* and Ko San Tun would be launched on a discourse on the four disciplines of mental awareness. Whether the subject be fortune-telling, or native medicine, or astrology, Ko San Tun was always at hand, displaying if not the wisdom of the expert at least the knowledge of the practitioner. Knowledge and experience were in short supply at the association. Some were knowledgeable enough, but they lacked Ko San Tun's brashness or his articulateness. U Shwe Gon might call on them by name, but they could not spring to it. They preferred to sit with heads lowered and make funny faces.

Finally these many considerations impelled U Shwe Gon to take

2. Po is a term of endearment usually used by an older person in addressing a younger male.
3. Lord of the White Elephant, a prominent king in Burma's historical past.
4. A famous Burmese poet and playwright.
5. A guardian spirit believed by many Burmese to possess immense powers.

Ko San Tun into his house, to apprentice him as a petition writer and clerk, and, after a year of close association, to give him in marriage his own sister-in-law, Ma Saw Khin.

On Saturday, 25 May 1907, corresponding with the full moon of Nayon, 1269 of the Burmese Era, Ko San Tun came to our drapery shop about eleven o'clock. He looked depressed. He poured himself a cup of tea, drank it, and announced, "Ma Saw Khin was delivered of a baby at eight this morning." My mother asked eagerly, "What is it?"

Tun: A boy.

Mother: That calls for a celebration. But looking at you, Maung San Tun, I get the impression you are somewhat unhappy.

Tun: Today is Saturday and, Aunt, you must have heard that a first child born on such a day stirs up woe like fire. It is inevitable that the mother or father should perish.

Father: Oh, Maung San Tun, you're so full of modern learning, I'm surprised you subscribe to Hindu beliefs. Have you ever heard of the Buddha's preaching that besides *kutho kan* and *a-kutho kan,* which are the two kinds of volition (good and evil) governing sentient beings, there are also the influences of the planets, such as Saturday, Sunday, Wednesday, or *Yahu?*

Tun: No, I haven't.

Father: Then, why accept false beliefs? Do not cling to them, for they can only cause you misery.

Mother: Since you have this obsession, why don't you do this? I remember as a child my father saying that if the first to arrive is a Saturday-born, the father must carry a sword and cross back and forth over the child seven times, to ward off the evil.

Father: That's a lot of rubbish.

Mother: Don't talk like that. Everyone is not a bigot like you. Some people get obsessions and you can't just say, "Don't have them."

So fearful was Ko San Tun that he took Mother to heart, and, carrying a sword on his shoulder, he hopped over his newborn child not seven times but seven times seven.

Four years passed, during which time Ko San Tun and Ma Saw
Khin went in fear and trembling, but neither died. The truth of
course is that there is no connection between a first child being
born on a Saturday and the destruction of his parents, but, as far
as the couple was concerned, they firmly believed they owed their
continued existence to the sword-carrying, child-leaping trick, and
consequently they were greatly indebted to my mother.

The Saturday-born not only did not harm his parents, but a
circumstance arose when he was three that might lead one to believe he brought good fortune. Ma Thein Tin, a daughter of U
Shwe Gon and Daw Kyi, won the second prize in the St. Leger
sweepstakes. It amounted to over forty thousand rupees, a not
inconsiderable sum in those days. Out of his love for his Saturday-
born nephew, U Shwe Gon used the money to provide the capital
for Ko San Tun and Ma Saw Khin to open a yardage shop in the
bazaar. This freed them from their dependent status at the parental
home and set them up as the owners of a small business.

However, although the Saturday-born did no harm to his parents,
he did not fail to afflict himself. His conduct took shape in relation
not to his birth but, I presume, to his environment. *Bagyi*[6] U Shwe
Gon loved his nephew to distraction. He spoiled him in every way,
so much so that if in playfully tossing the child in the air the latter
should urinate into his face he would chortle with delight. Once,
in his descent from space, the child kicked out and dislodged one of
his uncle's teeth. To give in to such an extent was bad enough,
but U Shwe Gon went several steps further. He would encourage
the child to insult callers and the ward would respond by greeting
a guest with, "Hey, big beast." The Saturday-born progressed in
bad manners and learnt to use abuse and invective, from which
the wives and sisters of the grown-ups addressed were not spared.

"Push out your midriff," the uncle would encourage, and the
Saturday-born would make the lewd gesture.[7] This, of course,
did not endear him to the people around, but there was U Shwe
Gon's influence to consider; besides, no one was prepared to take
issue with a child; so they had to grin and bear it. Next, however,

6. Big uncle, i.e., the eldest brother of either of the parents.
7. The Burmese consider this gesture so insulting that when an army officer used
it during World War II he was shot dead by a soldier.

the rudeness that had been reserved for guests and intimates was extended to passers-by.

Again, let me illustrate these environmental influences: there was a *wut* association started by Ma Saw Khin when she was a spinster. As a religious devotional group, its membership comprised about twenty neighbours, both married and unmarried women. Some of U Shwe Gon's followers, young blades of the town, took advantage of Saturday's readiness to do as he was bid and instigated him to annoy the girls by pinching their bottoms, pulling their hair, spitting at them, and even kicking them. Ko San Tun and Ma Saw Khin strongly disapproved, yet, because of U Shwe Gon, they could not chastise the offender. The wut association was in this troubled state when one day, encouraged by a prankster, Saturday put a lighted candle to a woman's shawl. The wearer, who was none other than the head of the group, was enveloped in flames and narrowly escaped being burnt to death. The night they extinguished the fire, the wut association expired.

Eventually the volume of protest registered by all who had suffered affront found expression in a single contumacious phrase: "*Tartay*,[8] Saturday's Son." The town of Wakèma rang with it.

It was not vouchsafed to Bagyi U Shwe Gon to go on pampering his nephew. When Saturday was only four years old, his uncle succumbed to the ravages of old age. Not long thereafter, Ko San Tun was in my shop.

Tun: Maung Nu, have you been made aware of the distinguished title our ward has conferred on my son?

Nu: Do you mean "Tartay, Saturday's Son?"

Tun: No other. So, what is there to add? In our language "tartay lan" is the ultimate, the final stage, as when one has reached the far shore of vileness, wickedness, dirtiness, and uselessness. My son at four is already "tartay." He will be confirmed as "lan" very soon, next year for sure.

Nu: Ko San Tun, I've been meaning to tell you a long time but have so far desisted because I didn't want to hurt your feelings. But since you have opened the subject, I'll begin by asking you if you're aware that everybody detests your son.

8. A scoundrel, in colloquial Burmese.

Tun: That I'm well aware of. (*He joined his palms and raised them in veneration over his head.*) May my benefactor rest in peace. But he was the one that spoilt the child.

Nu: Well, the old man is out of the way. It's not too late to correct the child.

Tun: Yes, but the old lady remains. She is not as bad as the other, but she refuses to have the boy chastised. Beating is out of the question. And if Ma Saw Khin or I were even to scold him she would get upset and go without food. That's the situation.

Nu: You people can't go on in this reprehensible manner. The whole quarter hates your son. I'm going to tell you something, now that I have the opportunity. Don't get angry. Don't even question anyone about it; just lock it in your heart. You know Ko Mya, your next-door neighbour? Well, every time your son spots him he comes out with filthy words or lewd gestures. So, last month, Ko Mya coaxed the boy to the beach and tried to drown him. When Ko Mya thought he had had enough he lifted the boy's head above water and asked him if he'd mend his manners. "Take me home, mother-fornicator" was the answer he got. Your son had his head pushed down four or five more times, but each time he came up for breath there was foul abuse until other bathers intervened. It was not that they didn't want the little beast destroyed, but Ko Mya was reminded in time he'd be up for manslaughter. Ko San Tun, since you're an old friend, let me put it bluntly. I don't blame Ko Mya. You'd have done the same in his position.

Tun: Yes, Maung Nu, I don't hold it against Ko Mya. I'm more concerned about reforming my son.

Nu: I don't say one must not indulge one's own nephew, or son, or grandson. But there are limits. Other people's rights and feelings have to be respected. Look at Ma Ma's children.[9] Father loves them very dearly. He denies himself so they might eat the best. Within his means he sees that the grandchildren appear in public wearing decent clothes and suitable ornaments. But when it

9. I.e., Maung Nu's older sister's children. An elder sister in a family is addressed by her younger sisters and brothers as Ma Ma, while an elder brother is addressed as Ko Ko.

comes to behaviour toward strangers he enforces discipline. They are taught to bow respectfully when passing elders; they answer questions respectfully; they do obediently as they are bid. If ever they are wilful or disrespectful, he corrects them sternly on the spot.

Tun: That's a very good example which I must try to emulate. I'm much obliged to you. But today I have another favour to ask.

Nu: Yes?

Tun: My son goes to school next year. According to the Manipuri astrologer Saya Kyu, who cast his horoscope, the boy's name is Tun Min. I don't like that. I'd like my son to be admitted to school under another name.

Nu: What's the name you prefer?

Tun: I like the name Nu.

Nu: For what reason?

Tun: Since opposites attract, my son being so rough, so wild in spirit, I wish to name him Nu[10] to turn him gentle and civil.

Nu: (Laughing) A name is not a monopoly, Ko San Tun. You don't need my permission to call your son by my name. You may use it, if you wish. But I doubt that calling your son gentle will make a gentleman of him. If one could turn out according to desire, everyone would be named Rich and the world would be full of wealthy people.

Tun: But you are my dearest friend. Don't you feel that too has something to do with my wanting to name my son after you?

Nu: Here, Ko San Tun, I also would like a favour of you.

Tun: Name it. Whatever is in my power is yours.

Nu: It's just a matter that intrigues me. There are many in Wakèma here who have more money and influence than you. But their children, until they reach maturity, live in obscurity. Your son is only four, and already the whole town knows him. I find that most interesting.

Tun: How odd! Tartay, Saturday's Son should evoke not interest but revulsion.

10. Meaning "tender," or "gentle."

Nu: Oh, the bad in your boy is incontrovertible. But put it aside for a moment. Isn't it remarkable that he should already have caused a public furor at his age?

Tun: I'm not exactly amused by this phenomenon. I've thought of running away from Wakèma and have even consulted my wife.

Nu: Just let me continue, Ko San Tun. If you will permit it, I wish to start writing a book under the title *Tartay, Saturday's Son*.

Tun: Amalay! I was wondering what you were leading up to. For goodness' sake, please don't do this to me. With my hands joined in supplication I beg of you. If you so require, I'll kneel with an offering.

Nu: Do let me finish, Ko San Tun. Your son is four. He has a long way to go. It is possible he may change for the better.

Tun: Do you honestly believe he can change in the future?

Nu: Because he is so young, it is too early to predict. If I say he will change for the better I may be proved wrong. By the same token, if you say he will remain bad throughout life, you may be proved wrong. So let's do this: from you, from Ma Saw Khin, from his family, friends, acquaintances, and teachers I'll gather as much information as I can about your boy. I will personally observe him and keep notes. At an appropriate time I will commit the compiled notes into writing as his biography, which will be shown to you.

Thoughts raced through Ko San Tun's mind. Painfully aware as he was that his son was in general disfavour, he could not help but suspect that Maung Nu too must dislike the boy. He, of course, would not wish to drown him, like Ko Mya, but to keep a record of the boy's misdeeds could be a form of refined punishment. Could this be the purpose of the project? He decided not. Maung Nu could not hate the son of his best friend.

You don't mean you're going to publish such a book?

That's up to you. When the manuscript is ready I'll donate it to you.

You won't print it without my permission?

I promise.

Thus, over the years, this biography has come to be written, slowly, based on notes personally compiled by me. As each chapter took shape, Ko San Tun was given it to read. He objected to some of the material as being likely to injure his son's reputation. He also requested that certain chapters be omitted because of the stark situations portrayed in language that decent people would consider unsuitable reading.

I could not accommodate him. Only violence done to truth could have justified changes or omissions. There is no one who is perfect. There are good points and bad, and both have to be recorded if a life story is to be factual. Ko San Tun was not altogether satisfied with this explanation, but he did not press the point.

In January of 1948, Maung Nu became prime minister of Burma. Years later, in finally giving his permission for the biography to be published, U San Tun reiterated his former objections to certain parts of the book that might portray the subject, now in a position of respect, in a bad light. But I insisted facts were facts and U San Tun acquiesced.

U San Tun's heart suddenly gave out in 1951, about two hours after I had seen him. I had just completed a portion of the manuscript and was able to read it to him. Stricken with palsy, he could no longer articulate words. But he was able to smile and nod his head.

May the gentle readers of this book be able to peruse it in soundness of mind and body.

1

Flaming Youth

EARLY CONCUPISCENCE

Ko San Tun loved his son and heir to distraction. If anyone complained of Maung Nu being spoiled, he would shift the blame onto his benefactor U Shwe Gon, or U Shwe Gon's wife. In fact Ko San Tun and Ma Saw Khin both pampered the child. Whenever he was put out with his son, Ko San Tun's expression would harden. If further aggravated, he might raise his voice and even throw things, but his displeasure seemed directed at others rather than at the culprit. He might even leave the house in high dudgeon, but when he returned he invariably brought a gift for the boy, sometimes even a whole sack of groceries, to cook him something special.

As the vendor of robes and priestly paraphernalia, Ko San Tun was just a small businessman. He was by no means rich. But by depriving himself and practising small economies he was able to acquire a horse-drawn carriage for Maung Nu. In a town like Wakèma, with its narrow streets, Ko San Tun's phaeton was an extravagance. The only other carriage was one owned by tycoon U Pe Gyi, and in his case it was a necessity. He lived at one end of the town and, with advancing age, the only way he could commute to the monastery he had endowed was by buggy. Ko San Tun's only purpose was to give his son delight. He named the horse *Mine Pyauk,* or "Miles Fade." It proved to be as stubborn as the boy and needed to be dragged out of the stable for each day's run. A dimwit called Saw Hlaing was the only one who could coax it to get between the shafts.

Ma Saw Khin's method of dealing with her recalcitrant son was somewhat different. She would pick up a stick or raise her hand in a gesture of severe chastisement, but always the blow came to rest gently. Maung Nu's cousin, Ma Thein Tin, would poke fun at her. "Don't beat him so hard," she would say with simulated alarm. "You're liable to tear him apart."

In 1912 Maung Nu was placed in the local middle school. He showed no special aptitude but was not a dunce either. He was to remain in the lower half of the class and to secure just sufficient marks to make the pass list. However, from the time he entered school he stopped insulting people. This prompted me to go to U San Tun, to inquire if he had taken note of the change in the boy.

U San Tun, I think the cessation of bad language and lewd deportment is truly remarkable.

Is it a strange phenomenon?

Well, if evil were inherent in him, he certainly would continue to be offensive. The fact that his manners have undergone this change encourages the belief that previously he was playing a role suggested by his uncle. It is still too early to say, because he is only five, how he will eventually turn out. His character will develop according to the company he keeps. I'd like a little more time to watch him grow.

From the age of five until he was nine, nothing unusual developed. At nine, Maung Nu found himself in the fourth standard, with a widening circle of friends, both in the school and among those in the quarter. Of the latter, one Pan Yee was destined to play a strange role.

Pan Yee had been a boathand but had contracted malaria and been left in Wakèma Hospital to recover when his schooner sailed away. Discharged from the hospital, Pan Yee had been hired by Ko San Tun as a cook. He was fifteen years older than Maung Nu.

Pan Yee was a hard worker—what the people in the ward called a fellow with a "light derrière."[1] He cooked, fetched water, laundered clothes, kept the premises clean, watered the garden, and carried lunch to Ma Saw Khin in the bazaar, besides taking Maung Nu and his younger brother, Maung Oo, to school and bringing them home. After his many labours, he was wont to drink a little in the evenings. The household did not approve, but they overlooked it.

It happened that the Ponnya Kawthanla, or Friendship, Association held a festival about this time. Pan Yee exerted himself, performing chores of various kinds, and was rewarded by U Lu Galè, an officer of the association, with what remained undrunk in a bottle of "White Horse" scotch whisky. Pan Yee hoarded it in his room. Then, one night, a famous monk from Mandalay arrived to preach, and everybody in the household went to hear him, except the aunt Daw Kyi, who was hard of hearing, and the two boys.

At nine o'clock the boys were expected to go to bed. Pan Yee took them to the lavatory, and, after their ablutions, induced Maung Oo to go to sleep. Maung Nu, however, he gently touched with his finger and led into his room, locking the door after him. There Pan Yee picked up a cucumber and with practised hand cut the tip off one end. Next the vegetable was washed and sliced. Finally, the whisky was brought out and he poured a few drops for Maung Nu to drink. To make it palatable he added lime and sugar. Maung Nu did eat of the cucumber and drink. Thereafter, Pan Yee and he were friends.

The risk of discovery prevented Pan Yee from sharing his liquor with Maung Nu as often as he might wish. But whenever the elders were out of the way the light touch with the finger would signal the way into his room. The whisky was soon gone, but there was a local brew, a rice wine called *gazaw* which, when diluted with lime juice, was not too harsh to swallow.

Familiarity led to connivance. Soon, at his mentor's instigation, Maung Nu was stealing money from his mother's shop. It might be one or two rupees, or four or five—even as much as ten rupees—and the thieving went on with regularity, two or three times a week. The stolen money had to be surrendered in full to Pan Yee,

1. The Burmese regard the size of the buttocks as an indicator of a person's diligence—the heavier the derrière, the lazier the person.

who once asked Maung Nu if he wanted a special treat for himself. The latter said he could do with a ball and a penknife.

It was apparently never intended that Pan Yee should use part of the stolen money to gratify Maung Nu. If they could steal the money, they could come by the ball and the knife by a similar trick. There were eight entrances into the Wakèma bazaar, four each from the east and the west. At each of these entrances there was a stall run by a Chulia, which sold an assortment of goods. Pan Yee, in his daily rounds of the bazaar, observed the stall next to Ma Saw Khin's yardage shop. Chulias, being Moslems, opened their shutters only after 1:00 P.M. on Fridays. The particular stall that Pan Yee had in mind, in common with others of its kind, was not a permanent structure, but a sort of lean-to extending from the main wall of the bazaar. The shutters were detachable and at closing time had to be put singly into place before the last two could be latched together and padlocked. With the passage of time some of these shutters had shrunk or warped and, if sufficient pressure was applied, gaps could be widened enough to let a boy's hand through. Pan Yee had noticed that rubber balls were displayed suspended in a net from the ceiling; the penknives were more directly approachable. So, early on a Friday morning, Pan Yee stood on a stool with Maung Nu perched on his shoulder. With some exertion on their part, the ball was successfully lifted. The knife required even less effort. Maung Nu was thrilled. He did not know that theft was punishable in this life with imprisonment, in the next with hell. He urged Pan Yee to arrange for more of the same adventure, but then Maung Nu's cousin, Ma Thein Tin, had taken to supervising his homework in the mornings, and of necessity, the Chulia's stall could be raided only between six and six-thirty on Friday mornings, when it was closed. Thus it was only every two months or so that they could repeat the shoplifting expedition.

Three more thefts, and they were found out. Friends of the Chulia discovered them in the act, and Maung Nu's parents were told. Thus, Pan Yee had to shift ground.

Along the strand in Wakèma there was a Chinese shop selling cold cuts. The meats were arrayed around a tray and the buyer could point to his fancy. The seller was an opium addict, and if

Pan Yee and Maung Nu spent an anna and dallied over the food they could generally steal off the tray right in front of the drowsy Chinese. Pan Yee said that palming food in this fashion bespoke daring and dexterity. Maung Nu was filled with bravado.

Pan Yee's brain proved fertile in yet another adventure. He let a piece of baited twine down, in a loop, to the ground beneath the kitchen. Chickens from neighboring yards came to eat the few grains of rice in the loop and were trapped. Maung Nu's task was to collect the birds, which were then killed and cooked, to go nicely with gazaw. The only good that resulted was that there was no longer any need to steal from the drowsy Chinese in the night bazaar.

It was also during a drinking session that Pan Yee suggested to Maung Nu that he should start playing the husband-and-wife game.

"How does one play it?" asked Maung Nu.

"Why, you damn idiot! You do it this way." Pan Yee proceeded to tell him how to do it.

Maung Nu was deeply impressed. He had long looked upon Pan Yee as an extraordinary companion, replete with wonderful ideas. Now, with a new intentness, he asked: "With whom does one play this game?"

There were two maids in the house, one about twenty years old, the other a child of nine. They can be called Mai Sein and Hla Kyway. Their real names do not matter.

On the very next day, Pan Yee piled curry into Hla Kyway's plate. "You listen to me, and I'll feed you like this every day," Pan Yee promised. He gave her a small coin, which gladdened her even more. For three or four days he continued these favours. Then came Saturday, with Ko San Tun and Ma Saw Khin at the store, Daw Kyi asleep, Ma Thein Tin and Mai Sein out shopping, and Maung Oo outdoors playing marbles.

Hla Kyway and Maung Nu were led into Pan Yee's room and told, "Now you play at being husband and wife." He lifted the corners of the unwashed mosquito net under which he slept and let the children in. There, in the rancid atmosphere of the cheerless room, the little drama was enacted. But however thoroughgoing Pan Yee's instructions might have been the execution fell short of adult reality; it remained juvenile make-believe.

One day, while sweeping in the bedroom, Pan Yee spotted currency notes and silver coins to the value of a hundred rupees. The money belonged to Maung Nu's uncle, Ko Ba, a teacher. Actually, it was school fees which he had brought home because the clerk had left ahead of him before closing time. Pan Yee told Maung Nu to steal the money for him, and it was readily done. Then followed the confrontation.

Maung Oo, did you take the money on the desk?

No, uncle, I did not.

Maung Nu, did you?

I did.

Where's the money now?

With Pan Yee.

Pan Yee, where's the money you took from Maung Nu?

I don't know what you're talking about.

The child admits to giving you the money. Stop lying.

I'm not lying. Hey, Maung Nu, what nonsense are you fabricating? (*Looking fiercely at Maung Nu*) Did you give me any money?

Yes, I did.

Pan Yee was told to confess, otherwise it would go hard with him. But he continued to profess his innocence until the police were told and a sergeant arrived to investigate. At the police station, three or four vicious blows in the solar plexus brought about a confession and the return of the money. Pan Yee was subsequently dismissed from his job.

Shortly afterwards, Mai Sein and Ma Thein Tin being in the kitchen, the following conversation took place.

Tin Tin,[2] I'm relieved Pan Yee has been sent away. He's a wicked man.

Oh!

Yes, he took Maung Nu into his room and fed him drinks.

2. A term of endearment for Ma Thein Tin. Burmese nicknames are often made by doubling one part of a person's name.

When was that?

It's been going on for a long time.

Why didn't you report this at once?

I was sorry for Maung Nu. He would have been caned.

That was very irresponsible of you.

But that's not all. There's much worse you should know. Pan Yee spoke bachelor words to me. He frequently told me to go to his room at night when the grown-ups were asleep. Each time he suggested this I abused him by reviling his mother.

I wish you'd told me in time.

One day he snatched my hand in the kitchen. I wasn't going to stand for it. I reviled his mother and slapped his face. He called me a bitch and threatened to unleash Maung·Nu under my mosquito net. Sure enough, two days later, there was Maung Nu in bed with me. It was past midnight. When he embraced me I woke up with a start and pushed him away. When I realised it was not a dream I said, "You little beast, what are you up to? Go back to your own bed, or I'll shout for Tin Tin to hear." Maung Nu went away.

I suppose Pan Yee must have sent him.

I'm sure of it.

The moment Maung Nu came home from school that day, he was summoned. Ma Thein Tin was an extremely strict person, with no nonsense about her. She did not hesitate to inflict punishment, whether it be with knuckles to the head, or a pinch on the thigh, or a cane applied to the behind. The brothers Maung Nu and Maung Oo feared neither father nor mother, and as for their senior aunt, Daw Kyi, she was inconsequential and could be neglected in any reckoning. But Ma Thein Tin they dreaded.

Maung Nu, did you drink Pan Yee's liquor?

I did.

How often?

Frequently.

I'm told you sneaked into Mai Sein's mosquito net. Is it true?

Yes, it is.

Bring me the feather duster.

(*Here Mai Sein interposed*)

Please, Tin Tin, he's only a child.

You keep out of this. Maung Nu, fetch me the feather duster.

To the accompaniment of admonitions that he must never repeat those offences, the cane was applied five times across Maung
Nu's back. Maung Nu feared Ma Thein Tin. But neither the birch-
ing, nor the thigh pinching, nor the head knocking was able to get
a whimper out of him.

When Daw Kyi learnt of the chastisement, she was appalled.
Seeing the stripes on her beloved nephew's behind she wept.

A SCHOOL STRIKE AND ITS AFTERMATH

In December 1920 the first Rangoon University Students' Strike
occurred. The movement spread to the high schools and the middle schools, and Maung Nu was involved. He was then in the seventh standard at the Wakèma Anglo-Vernacular School, at age
thirteen.

Subsequently, it began to be noticeable that a change was taking
place in Maung Nu, in speech and deportment. Observers believed
that the speeches and exhortations made by the strike leaders, coming on top of the books on freedom and independence he had read
in the national school he began to attend,[3] and the study made of
the lives of freedom fighters, must have made deep impressions on
his mind. It is probably true that his character was changing, but it
was not a complete metamorphosis, in that he did not turn over
a new leaf. In word and action he displayed that which was commendable as well as facets that were reprehensible.

A relative summed him up about this time in the following
words: Man has two principal organs, the brain and the heart. In
some cases, these develop uniformly; in others the brain develops

---

3. After the 1920 students' strike, many schools were set up quite independently
of the British colonial government. These were called national schools.

faster than the heart; in yet others the development of the heart outstrips the brain. Maung Nu falls into the third category.

Because his heart was expanded out of proportion to his brain, what most people would regard as trivial or inconsequential would affect Maung Nu profoundly. In such a situation, before the brain had had a chance to size it up and determine its trivial or fruitless nature, Maung Nu was wont to speak out or to act. And since his words and actions sprang out of a resolve to disregard consequences, a decision once made was not easily alterable. It was only after it was carried out, when the brain had had time to weigh and assess, that the error would become apparent to him and Maung Nu would be seized with contrition. He would then make a firm resolution to reform, but, with heart the master of his mind, no matter how much he tried he could not overcome the tendency to act first and think afterwards. Thus there was to be a profusion of errors first and recriminations afterwards, a pattern that was not restricted to the period when he was thirteen or fourteen but was to persist into adulthood. If there was any change, it was this: the proclivity to act hastily according to the dictates of the heart was there, but it would be tempered by lessons that the wisdom of advancing years was to bring. In his youth, Maung Nu was oblivious of *kutho* and *a-kutho,* merit and demerit, of good and evil, or crime and punishment. Consequently, these did not enter into his deliberations at all. Later, however, the teachings and instructions of his beloved father as well as Saya Deedok U Ba Choe[4] were to bear fruit. Consciousness of good and evil was then able to restrain his propensity to act in haste and repent at leisure.

Instances abound of Maung Nu following headlong the path determined by his heart.

The school strikes had hardly begun when Maung Nu one day announced to a group of four or five friends that they should shave their heads, divest themselves of clothing except for their

4. U Ba Choe was called "Saya" (teacher) as a mark of respect and "Deedok" (owl) after the Burmese journal of the same name, of which he was managing editor. In 1946 he became a member of the Governor's Council and was assassinated along with General Aung San.

longyi (sarongs), which they would wear drawn up and tucked between their buttocks, put on cloth shoes of Chinese manufacture, and, seizing a rock in each hand, advance into the marketplace. His friends agreed with alacrity, with the exception of Tun Yin. This boy was a dandy who used cosmetics and plastered his hair down. He wore his clothes long, obscuring his ankles. To tuck up his longyi, sacrifice his well-parted hair, and expose his body in the market full of girls was unthinkable to him. But Maung Nu had made up his mind and Tun Yin, feeling extremely foolish, had to comply.

On another occasion Maung Nu interrupted a conversation by saying he had drunk liquor but had never tried hard drugs. He urged his friend Maung Han to procure some cocaine. Some of his other friends objected, saying cocaine could lead to hallucinations, but Maung Nu was adamant. When the cocaine was brought they repaired to Gani's teashop and everyone rubbed cocaine on their lips which then swelled, impairing their speech. "No good," was Maung Nu's verdict.

Next, having experimented with liquor and cocaine, Maung Nu thought of opium. He said he had to try it once. Disregarding all objections, he led the group into a den but, fortunately for the objectors, the atmosphere was repellent. One look at the torn mats, the grimy pillows soaked in perspiration, and the dregs encrusting the opium pipes and Maung Nu was filled with nausea. They left hurriedly.

☆   ☆   ☆   ☆   ☆

Another day a gang of four or five Burmans was seen attacking an Indian at the jetty. Maung Nu, who happened to be passing by, got off his bicycle and went to the rescue. Among the hoodlums was the brother of Yan Shin, the notorious gangster who held sway beyond the Wakèma cemetery. Others belonged to the Po Chit gang, with whom none of the townsfolk cared to tangle. Maung Nu knew nothing of this state of affairs. He was unaware of a recent incident when Po Chit waylaid police sergeant U Ba Myit near the Kungyangon Monastery and left him for dead. He had not waited to find out who was in the right or in the wrong. His heart simply prompted him to wade into the uneven fight. If the gangsters had not known that he was U San Tun's son, he might not have got off lightly.

Next, there was the incident at the coal shed. Maung Nu was with a friend when they were stopped by Aung Thin, the bully from Ywathit across the river. Aung Thin was two years older than Maung Nu, stronger and taller. Also he was extremely quick tempered. When angered he used hands, fists, knees, and heels with devastating effect. When therefore he demanded of Maung Nu's friend why he had not returned his book, the friend was petrified. Maung Nu knew nothing about the lent book or why it had not been returned, but he did not like the threatening tone of the bully, so he said to his friend, "Don't give him back his book." He received a resounding punch in the jaw for his trouble and was reeling about under a barrage of blows when his groping fingers found a piece of clinker. This he was able to bring down on the temple of his tormentor before he blacked out.

☆   ☆   ☆   ☆   ☆

In connection with the nationalist political agitation in Burma at the time, the British government in 1921 sent out the Whyte Commission to determine if Burma was fit for Dyarchy.[5] The General Council of Buddhist Associations (GCBA) decided to demonstrate against the commission, and when its members went into the countryside the demonstrations followed them. En route to Bassein, the commission touched in at Wakèma in December 1921. The moment the steamer tied up at the jetty, Maung Nu's group went into action, creating a din that was to reverberate through the town. The order that came from the organisers was that the demonstrators were to confine themselves to beating on tin cans, but Maung Nu, a creature of the heart, could not contain himself and flung a soda bottle at the steamer. It broke into fragments against the side. For this Maung Nu was arrested and detained for a period.

☆   ☆   ☆   ☆   ☆

In 1922 Maung Nu passed the eighth standard. He had no intention of continuing with his studies and in fact placed no value

5. For a further discussion of Dyarchy in Burma, see Chapter 5, esp. note 4.

on education, but his parents—the father, in particular—wished him to proceed and, if possible, to become a barrister. Accordingly, Ko San Tun arranged for him to enter the Rangoon National School which had been set up in the Thayettaw Kyaungdaik Monastery.

A few days before Maung Nu's departure from Wakèma, a feast was held honouring the Buddha and eight of his disciples in the house of a friend, *Kalama*[6] Ba Maung. During the ceremony Aye Maung II (to differentiate him from another Aye Maung) beckoned Maung Nu outside with the customary touch of the finger and said, "Maung Nu, you're going to school in Rangoon. I want to give you a most excellent farewell." This, it transpired, was a visit with a girl newly arrived from Einmè.

First, Maung Nu had to enter a lane and station himself beneath a window. Then Aye Maung II threw down to him a new tafetta jacket of his which they took to a Chinese on Payagyi Road and pawned for four rupees.

The experience with the Einmè girl was his first completed sexual act. It was very different from the husband-and-wife game he had played with Hla Kyway at Pan Yee's instigation. Maung Nu's mind was a turmoil of emotions. He was filled with gladness and satisfaction, also wonder.

In May 1922, Maung Nu entered the Myoma National High School in Rangoon. The school could not afford a building of its own, so, with the approval of the monks, classes were held in a monastery in a large square which is still known as Thayettaw Kyaungdaik. Initially the school administration maintained a boarding house in Hlèdan, a few yards from the square. But after six months they could no longer afford the separate establishment and Maung Nu moved, with the other students from the provinces, to one of the monasteries. Discipline was laxer there than it had been at Hlèdan.

One night, a large fire broke out in East Rangoon and Maung Nu stood on the street watching the flames and the smoke against the skyline. Suddenly, to a friend by his side, Maung Nu said, "Do you know where the prostitutes live?" The man said he did. But when Maung Nu asked to be led to the brothel, the man said,

6. Ba Maung was nicknamed Kalama ("Indian woman") because he looked like an Indian woman to his friends.

"Kid, I'll show you the way because that's what you want, but you must promise never to reveal my name." On the way, they stopped at a Chinese restaurant. Maung Nu did not know how to measure drinks. He would have filled himself with liquor but the friend restricted him.

It never entered into Maung Nu's mind that drinking liquor was a sin or that cohabiting with a prostitute was evil. He did not have the intelligence. To be able to order a drink at a Chinese restaurant in a big city like Rangoon, and to have a fling with a prostitute in a whorehouse, was to him to be a man of the world. He was so full of himself that he even thought of initiating his friends into the rites before they went home for the holidays.

Thereafter, whenever he was in funds and in congenial company, Maung Nu made it a rule to drink at a bar and sleep with a prostitute. This unrestrained habit brought its consequences. In 1923 he contracted a disease which a friend told him was gonorrhea. A swelling developed in the groin and his friend said it was a manifestation of the same disease. With his help, Maung Nu went to Mogul Street and bought a bottle of medicine at the Benjamin Pharmacy which he thought sounded like Balsam of Copeba. The friend applied ice to the swelling.

The mind of youth is a strange thing. It is difficult to evaluate it. Under medication, with ice between his thighs, Maung Nu's spirit was one not of degradation but almost of emancipation in which he felt he could revel.

The exams over, Maung Nu returned to Wakèma for the holidays. On 13 April, the eve of the Thingyan Water Festival,[7] Maung Nu went out with four or five friends, all wearing funny clothes. They soon found themselves in a Chinese noodle shop, drinking country liquor to excess. Water throwing was out of the question. Finally, their longyi loose and dragging, their bodies naked and unsightly, they collapsed in their own vomit, and Maung Nu had to be carried home unconscious by relatives.

The days of the Water Festival came and went, and Maung Nu remained comatose. His parents, greatly distressed, used concoctions of *ekarit* root and lemon juice, and anything else sug-

7. This ancient festival, during which the Burmese douse each other with water, runs annually from April 13 to 16.

gested by neighbours for antidotal effect. Finally Maung Nu came round, but it was feared he might go on another binge, so Ko San Tun proposed that he should go and rest at his granary in Talaingsu village. Maung Nu said he would go if he was allowed to take some of his friends along, and this was agreed to. Lying across the river from Wakèma, Talaingsu proved to be a pleasant spot. Behind the two granaries stretched a banana plantation. There was a two-storey house allocated to the boys. Ko San Tun had told his cousin Ko Ba Waing, "Keep these fellows happy, and don't let them cross the river." The house was well provisioned. Ko Ba Waing seemed to have misunderstood his cousin. He interpreted the injunction as meaning that so long as they were happy, and so long as they did not go over the river, they were to be given whatever they desired.

Two days later, when Maung Nu expressed a wish to go to Wakèma, Ko Ba Waing restrained him, saying his father would not like it. "Then, find me something to drink," Maung Nu requested, and a bottle of country spirits was produced. Emboldened, Maung Nu inquired, "What's the woman situation? Can't you procure one for us?" So a woman was found to keep the young man happy. She proved to be thirtyish, unprepossessing, and badly made up, with her *thanaka*[8] smeared anyhow on her cheeks. But however repulsive she was, the boys were sex-hungry. Like a pack of hound dogs in the month of September, they were stirred by the presence of a bitch. No time was wasted. They cast lots and took turns at the woman. Among the five friends present, Maung Nu drew lot number five.

The following day, Ko Ba Waing announced that the country liquor sold in shops was unsatisfactory and that he would distill his own. He brought an empty kerosene tin and filled it half full of water into which he soaked a quantity of jaggery. It was then buried for three days under a pile of paddy and allowed to ferment. The whole was afterwards cooked over a still, the steam being pushed against the well-scrubbed bottom of an aluminum pot. The condensed product then settled into a china bowl and proved to be a most potent brew. With the experience of the

8. A sweet-smelling paste made by grinding on a flat round stone the bark or root of *Murraya paniculata,* a flowering shrub of the citron species.

drinking bout during the Water Festival fresh in their minds, the boys did not drink to excess but kept steadily to the dosage as measured out by Ko Ba Waing and generously diluted with sugar water.

For ten days, until they returned to town, the boys kept to the following routine: they rose at seven, swam in the river and dove from the bridge; they pelted all who walked along the bank with mud balls; they separated into two groups and staged mock battles. When they were tired, they went home and feasted on liquor and the food Ko Ba Waing had cooked. Then they drew lots and had their fill of the same middle-aged woman, who, except for time off for food and bath, and a coffee break, was given no respite. At five in the afternoon, the woman was sent home.

Barely two days after his return to Wakèma, Maung Nu found he had developed a chancre. One of his friends was similarly afflicted. They sought advice and were told to use hydrogen peroxide and to sprinkle Chinese snuff over the sore. Before it could heal, Maung Nu was back in Rangoon, where he was immediately sent to a doctor. He was given six injections of neosalvarsan. From Chindooroy's Clinic he obtained a compound called Shwe Ba mixture. A knowing friend then counselled prudence for the future. He explained the harmful effects of venereal disease, not only upon the person contracting it, but also on his progeny. The same person who had shown the way to the brothel, seeing Maung Nu thoroughly alarmed, expressed contrition at having led him astray, but Maung Nu would not exculpate himself. He said he had already been initiated in Wakèma, and that if it had not been that particular friend there would have been found another equally obliging. "The fault is mine alone," he admitted. The friend begged of him to stop going to brothels. "Take a wife if you can't contain yourself," he suggested.

Having listened to your warnings, I'm frightened.

Then, will you give me a promise never again to frequent those houses?

I won't promise; but I'll think about it.

Why don't you deflect your sexual urges into other channels?

In what direction?

Take up boxing; join a soccer team. You'll lose the urge to chase women.

The very next day, Maung Nu went into training. He boxed and played soccer. He skipped rope and worked out on the parallel bars; he sprinted. His wayward thoughts diminished; so did his carnal desires.

From the moment he arrived at the Myoma National School Maung Nu's zeal to appear as the champion of the oppressed grew. Because his heart overruled his head, he scarcely paused to find out if those he championed were in fact oppressed or ill-used. Similarly, if a student was reputed to be unfair to others, Maung Nu never stopped to inquire if the reputation was deserved but must needs resolve on instant confrontation. In these quarrels and fights he did not always come out the winner, but no matter how bitter the defeat or humiliation he never learnt his lesson. Come what might, he was in there, pitching.

There are endless anecdotes that illustrate picaresque conduct, but three will suffice. In 1923, the British government decided to recognize the national schools. These then broke apart into two factions, one accepting the recognition, and the other repudiating it. The monks of the Thayettaw Kyaungdaik Monastery having rejected the government's offer, the national school housed there had to move its senior classes and boarders to a British army barrack facing the western slopes of the Shwedagon Pagoda. Thus, at age sixteen, Maung Nu was a tenth-standard student living and studying in this barrack. Everyone there respected Saya Tint, the boarding master, who cared for them conscientiously, but he was at the same time a strict disciplinarian. One night a twenty-year-old student from Ngaputaw, for the minor infraction of returning from leave half an hour late, was severely caned in the study hall. That night the boarders were afraid to breathe.

It happened that Saya Tint had to go home to a sick father and his place was taken by Saya Ba Kyaw, his assistant. Although Saya Ba Kyaw refused leave to everyone else, he permitted a favourite student to attend a play at the Jubilee Hall, where Po Sein was acting. Maung Nu, on receiving this intelligence, stationed himself outside Saya Ba Kyaw's door and announced in a loud voice that he was going to the Po Sein *pwe*[9] and would permit anyone who so desired to go along with him. He made the same announcement in the dormitory, but only Thein Maung, a boy from Thongwa, risked going with him. They did not get to the Po Sein pwe but went to the Shwedagon Pagoda instead and returned about 11:00 P.M.

Meanwhile, an enraged Saya Ba Kyaw got the boarders to turn out for a roll call, marked Maung Nu and Thein Maung absent, and dismissed the rest.

The truants, for their part, knew they would be called up. The plan was for them to charge the boarding master with injustice, and then, if he got tough, Thein Maung was to beat him on the head with a stick while Maung Nu punched his face. Then, before the authorities could expel them, they would leave. But, contrary to their expectation, they were not summoned the next day, nor the day following, which led them to conclude that the teacher had chosen not to make an issue of it. However, the day Saya Tint returned from Minhla, Saya Ba Kyaw's favourite came to invite Maung Nu and Thein Maung to appear before him. At first, Maung Nu merely told him he was not coming, but when he came back ten minutes later with a more urgent summons Maung Nu said, "Buzz off! If I see your face again I'll slap it." A while later, a senior student called Maung Galè was sent to fetch them. He was a good friend of theirs, and he persuaded them to go before Saya Tint and explain how Saya Ba Kyaw's unfairness had led them to do what they did. Maung Nu went first; Thein Maung followed, with a piece of wood hidden in the folds of his longyi. It was a rod that had become dislodged from the veranda, and it was to be the means of implementing their previous resolve if things got rough.

They found Saya Tint pacing the floor of his office. He wore a set expression. Propped against the wall was a stout Tavoy cane.

Maung Nu, where were you on that night?

9. Any kind of staged performance, dance, musical recital, or festival.

At the Po Sein pwe.

Thein Maung.

Yes, sir.

Were you along too?

Yes, I was.

Did you have anyone's permission?

No.

Do you admit your fault?

No.

Why not?

If Saya Ba Kyaw's pupil could go to the pwe, so could other students.

Don't drag Saya Ba Kyaw into this. If he is guilty of wrong-doing he will be dealt with separately. You are here to explain your conduct. Are you or are you not at fault?

No.

Any student who goes to see a show without permission is guilty and must be punished.

We will not submit to a beating.

And why not? What is so special about you? Are you being raised on a diet of gold dust?

We never said we were. But we will not take a caning.

If Saya Ba Kyaw was unfair, your duty was to wait until my return and report the matter. Do you think it was smart to take the law into your own hands?

Maung Nu had nothing to say to this, but his gaze did not waver. In the end they were dismissed with a last warning.

Other incidents occurred about this time, the memory of which in later years was to provoke many a smile. In 1924, for example, there was a leakage of question papers, so the tenth-standard examination was twice postponed. Maung Nu, marking time, realised that he had been kept moving from place to place in preparation for the finals. First, as already described, he had been shifted to the barracks formerly occupied by British troops near the Shwedagon Pagoda. Six months later, he had had to move to the Gurkha barracks on Prome Road. And now he was housed at No. 1 Voyle Road.

At this time, the new school term had already commenced. Among the fresh arrivals was a Sino-Burman from Moulmein. Maung Nu, who merely boarded at the place pending examinations, was not acquainted with him, but one day a friend came to tell him that the new student, a large boy, had a gargantuan appetite and was eating everything in sight, including other people's leftovers. When Maung Nu heard that the sweepers were being done out of their food he determined to punish the glutton. But it was not easy to tackle a big boy. Maung Nu had to station himself on a table so that he might take a flying kick at the Sino-Burman. Maung Nu's friend, Maung Han, also joined in the fray. Afterward, when the melee was ended, it became clear that the new boy, although a big eater, was a very fine character. He had been to the headmaster to apprise him of his appetite and had offered to pay double for his food. The headmaster, however, had permitted him to eat all he wanted without extra charge. Furthermore, it was not true that the servants were going hungry. There was so much over and above normal requirements that a quantity of leftovers had to be thrown into garbage bins every day. When Maung Nu learned of these facts he blushed with shame. The next day Maung Nu was called up before Headmaster U Ba Lwin. Maung Nu admitted his guilt and expressed contrition. He took five lashes with good grace.

A brush with his own father was even more amusing. U San Tun had come back from Mandalay with a potted croton of which he was inordinately fond. He kept it on a shelf, apart from other plants, and would water it with a silver bowl. One day, Maung Nu, after gargling, spat out the water on the precious plant. U San Tun beat his breast until it resounded, and berated his son. It had been an unthinking act on the part of Maung Nu, but now he deliberately filled his mouth with water and deluged the croton. U San Tun spoke not a word but, with a pained expression, he fetched clear water and tenderly washed each bespattered leaf.

Realising the wrong he had done, Maung Nu grasped his father about the waist in contrition. They entered the house that way, swaying in playful contention. As a sign that all was forgiven U San Tun wrestled with his son until both were spent and covered with perspiration. Then they went to sleep in each other's arms.

☆　☆　☆　☆　☆

When heart takes mastery over mind, things tend to happen as a result of suppressed desires being set free. One day, for some unexplained reason, Maung Nu went home to Wakèma. While asleep on the steamer, he dreamt that he was being married to Ma Aye Kyaw, daughter of Daw Ein Nyein of Wakèma. Maung Nu had seen Ma Aye Kyaw but had never spoken to her, let alone shown any interest in her. At this time Maung Nu had never been in love with, nor paid court to, anybody. But when he awoke he recalled the events in the dream. There was a lingering coldness in his breast as he realised his suppressed desire for the girl. It was not in him to ponder deeply, so he confessed his love in a letter which he posted before he returned to Rangoon. He had expected Ma Aye Kyaw to respond in a week, but when four weeks elapsed without bringing a reply Maung Nu composed another letter and mailed it from Rangoon. He was not disappointed in any way. He took to learning a popular song by the great U Po Sein that began with: "'Tis your husband Maung Sein, with sweetness in his words." Then, when the holidays arrived, he harmonised with his friend Maung Han and they sang the song with gusto every night, pacing up and down in front of Ma Aye Kyaw's house.

Back in Rangoon, Maung Nu pined for three days and was on the verge of composing another letter when a fellow student, a cousin of Ma Aye Kyaw's, came waving a letter. A quick reading told Maung Nu the letter was from Ma Aye Kyaw all right, but it was addressed to the cousin, not to him. His heart sank when he got the message. The girl was imploring her relative to prevail upon Maung Nu to stop writing her. She was already betrothed and would soon be marrying another. Maung Nu's love letters were causing her embarrassment and might be misunderstood by the elders. With a sickening smile Maung Nu could only tell the cousin

that with him it was not a prank but the real thing. He was in love
with the girl, he declared, but under the circumstances he was
sorry he had bothered her. It would not happen again.

Well, it was his first love and it had not prospered. He was forced
to realise that love could not be a one-sided affair. It had to be
reciprocated. Lying on his bed, after the cousin had left, he sought
solace in the song he had memorized. The tune brought back those
many nights of serenading when exposure to the cold air had afflicted his feet and his stomach and yet he had kept going until the
barking of a dog unleashed had cooled his ardour. Still other re-
pressed feelings of a similar nature were soon to surface in impetuous Maung Nu.

☆   ☆   ☆   ☆   ☆

Maung Nu was a poor scholar. In those days, however, examinations were not too exacting, and he found no great difficulty in
passing those that were set haphazardly. But the tenth standard was
a government examination and it presented a real problem. His
friends had already decided he would be failed and his teachers
had made similar predictions with complete unanimity. As for
Maung Nu himself, he had never reflected on the advantages of
higher education. He certainly had no aims in life in regard to jobs
and professions. Success or failure caused him no concern. If he
failed the examination, he would simply leave Rangoon and go
home.

About the middle of January 1924, the school held preliminary
examinations. This was in the nature of a test run. Those who
made the grade would be presented for the finals in March. One
day before the list of examinees was published, the students were
required to bring the fee of twelve rupees. Those who made the
list would appear before the government examiners. Those who
did not could get the twelve rupees refunded and go home. A
teacher having hold him that he had failed the preliminary, Maung
Nu was prepared to be sent home, but that evening the faculty
entreated the headmaster to stretch a point, and permission was
reluctantly given for all the students to take the government examination.

When the results of the finals appeared, two students who had
failed the preliminary passed: Kyaw Sein of Moulmein made the

A list, and Maung Nu graduated in the B. Equally surprisingly, Maung Thein of Ngathainggyaung, who had topped the list in the preliminary, was failed!

GETTING TO KNOW GIRLS

The passing of the tenth standard affected Maung Nu not at all, but his father, U San Tun, went into paroxysms of delight, relatives, friends, and comparative strangers being asked to dinner to celebrate the occasion. He himself cooked the food and, when it came to the chicken curry, his exuberance was such that he mixed every kind of condiment, coconut milk vying with cow's milk, and both blended with chilli. When some of the guests seemed to balk, U San Tun pressed them to eat hearty, claiming that his creation was the celebrated "friendship stew."

In entering the University College of Rangoon University, Maung Nu entered into a new world. The buildings were elegant and in marked contrast to the old monastery and the army barrack that he had called school. At the Myoma campus the students had seemed quite ordinary, but now at the university there were student luminaries who excelled at English, mathematics, history, chemistry, physics, and law. There were debaters, soccer players, boxing and tennis stars, and other outstanding athletes; in fact a majority of the students seemed possessed of qualities that merited emulation.

The new environment was bound to bring about changes in Maung Nu. Whereas formerly he had been indifferent to learning, he now began to develop a thirst for knowledge, and along with it he began to think about a future career. He had already been exposed to Shakespeare, but in an abridged form and as a textbook. As such his interest in the Bard had been slight. But here, in the library, were his entire works to select and savour at leisure. He fell in love with Shakespeare, imagined himself as a playwright, and began to experiment with blank verse. In particular the sonnets that he composed, in imitation, filled him with immense satisfaction.

In that year, Prome and Tagaung Halls sported rival soccer teams. Saw Duwun was captain of Prome and Ba Shin of Tagaung Hall. Maung Nu found a place as left half for Tagaung. The sonnet writer could not resist the temptation to parody Saw Duwun, and his effusions, sometimes posted on the notice board, never failed to provoke the victim to anger.

One full-moon night an Indian beating on a drum in the distance caused vibrations in Maung Nu's breast. He immediately wrote a sonnet called "Under a Mayan Tree," which he took to a tutor to read. The tutor was an urbane individual. He said nothing to discourage or humiliate the would-be poet. He merely remarked that diligence would bring success. Thus encouraged, Maung Nu read Bernard Shaw's *Julius Caesar* and *Candida* on the recommendation of the tutor. He then made up his mind that when he wrote his own plays he would do so in prose.

Once, browsing through the library, Maung Nu came upon Cervantes's *Don Quixote,* and there and then he decided that his plight was not dissimilar to Don Quixote's, in his self-importance and in the delusion that he could right all the wrongs of the world. Such a person could not be called mad, but he was strange and his exploits were provocative of mirth. As he continued to read, Maung Nu was seized with irresistible laughter. He was greatly taken with the book.

Maung Nu had barely been a month in college when he spied a large dog trying to bully a smaller animal out of his food. In the unequal fight the small dog was bitten and rolled over again and again. Picking up two rocks Maung Nu soon settled the dispute, but so angry was he that he continued to chase the large dog after he had run away from the punishment. Now, having read Cervantes, he tried to be less quixotic—to curb his natural inclinations in regard to speech, deportment, and emotions. Nevertheless, during that first year, he was to experience another affair of the heart.

There was a girl called Tin Tin Myint in Wakèma whose father, U Khin, was a retired superintendent of police. She was one of five sisters, all of them good looking. Maung Nu had been with Tin Tin Myint in the same school from the first to the seventh standard, but she was prudish and discouraged any attempt at friendship on the part of the boys, none of whom dared to speak to her. During the school strike of 1920, Maung Nu left to join the national school, but she remained in the Anglo-vernacular school, and the two had not met since then.

The Tazaungdaing Festival of 1924 brought them face to face. Seeing Tin Tin Myint again, Maung Nu experienced a surge of great tenderness, but although he might be reckless in other regards he was a bit of a coward in love. Not for him was the direct approach—an open declaration by word of mouth or by letter personally tendered. He fell back on the post office. There was no response, however. Undaunted, Maung Nu continued to pay court by mail. Between November 1924 and March 1925 he must have written no fewer than thirty love letters. Thirty-six years later U Nu, in a conversation with Chief Engineer U Kyaw Sein, Daw Tin Tin Myint's brother-in-law, was to confess that during his heedless youth, as a young bull with its halter broken, he had pestered Tin Tin Myint with an avalanche of thirty love calls. He asked her, through U Kyaw Sein, to forgive him. Daw Tin Tin Myint was still unmarried at that time. She appeared to detest the other state.

☆ ☆ ☆ ☆ ☆

In 1925 Maung Nu passed the junior Intermediate of Arts and the Part B examination in one go. He was eighteen years old. College reopened the beginning of June, so in order that they might have some free time in town Maung Nu and his friend Ko Tun Tin returned to Rangoon a week early. Ko Tun Tin was a good student. He was two years older than Maung Nu and already in the junior B.A. class.

First they went to worship at the Shwedagon Pagoda; then they took in parts of the town and were at the cinema by three-thirty in the afternoon. Dinner at six-thirty was at a Chinese restaurant. Liquor having been consumed, the two discussed a visit to a brothel. Since they had imbibed the conventional wisdom in college, they were not venturing out unprotected. They chose condoms.

At the brothel each selected a woman of his choice. Maung Nu's selection was considerably older than himself. She was about twenty-five, dark complexioned and not pretty. But in his eyes she was pleasant enough. He liked his women tall rather than short, and her height pleased him. He found her very attractive.

What's your name?

Ma Khin Myint (*not her real name*).

Are you from Rangoon?

No.

Where do you come from?

From Taikkyi.

How did you get here?

There was no immediate answer. Instead, she kept her head lowered in order to hide her tears. Maung Nu, who had never seen a woman weep at such close range, was quite overcome. When Ma Khin Myint raised her head there were still traces of tears round her eyes.

"I don't belong in this class. My husband took a lesser wife who goaded him to mistreat me and finally to drive me out of the house. I came to Rangoon to look for work. Lack of food and lodging drove me into this," she explained.

Maung Nu was filled with pity, and also rage that the husband should have been so cruel. Why had she given ground? Why hadn't she stood up to the mother-fornicating bully? If she had struck back the coward would have cut and run. Maung Nu fairly exploded with righteous indignation.

Where would a woman find the courage to strike back? Maung Nu could only wish that he had been present at the scene. He would have put up a show worth watching. It was only the scent of Ma Khin Myint's powder that brought him back to reality.

On the way home, on the road, entering the school building, and in bed, the sight of Ma Khin Myint's tearful face haunted him. It was as though it had been imprinted on his iris.

The next day, after lunch, Maung Nu went to Ko Tun Tin's room and suggested another visit to the brothel. Ko Tun Tin put down the book he was reading and accompanied him. The brothel was not as busy by day as by night. They lingered for quite some time.

The following afternoon Maung Nu was again at Ko Tun Tin's room proposing another visit with Ma Khin Myint.

Maung Nu, isn't this overdoing it?

I'm about to take Ma Khin Myint.

Take her? What for? What as?

To be my wife, of course.

That's impossible.

Why is it impossible?

Because she's a whore, that's why.

Can't one marry a whore?

Maung Nu, are you really serious?

I've made up my mind.

Then I object.

I've quite decided.

For about two minutes Ko Tun Tin stared at the wall. Then he declared he was not ready to go just yet. He had some writing to do, but would be free to go around 1:00 P.M.

When that hour struck, Maung Nu found Ko Tun Tin's door locked. Stuck into the latch was a note saying he had been called away but would join Maung Nu in town "at the appointed place." When Maung Nu reached the brothel there was no sign of Ko Tun Tin, or of Ma Khin Myint either. Having already struck up an acquaintanceship with the pimp, Maung Nu inquired of him where the missing persons were to be found. The answer he received was that they were both present and together in a room the pimp indicated with his chin. Maung Nu had chosen to forget that Ma Khin Myint was a prostitute, at every customer's beck and call. Others had enjoyed her favours ahead of him; still others would do so after him. He of course wanted to make an honest woman out of her, and he felt betrayed that she should still be profligate. What should he do now? Burst into the room? Tear the place apart? Shout obscenities?

Before he could make up his mind, the silence was broken by a male voice. It was Ko Tun Tin speaking:

Do you know Maung Nu?

Of course I do.

Ma Khin Myint, do you love Maung Nu?

I don't fancy him that much.

Ma Khin Myint, would you marry Maung Nu?

No, I wouldn't marry that kid.

Ma Khin Myint, are you in love with me?

I adore you.

The duet had gone far enough. Maung Nu stomped out of the house. But he did not go far. Not long afterwards Ko Tun Tin emerged, and Maung Nu charged at him, his umbrella at the ready. An Indian in Thirty-sixth Street tried to block him off and got thrown down for his trouble. This was the signal for other Indians to crowd around Maung Nu and restrain him from carrying out his design, while Ko Tun Tin looked on pityingly. "You're mad at me now," he said, "but you'll thank me for this one day." Maung Nu was incoherent. All he could blurt out was a dire threat and a warning to the other to look out.

Then, in a childish way, still struggling to extricate himself from a sea of Indian arms, Maung Nu demanded the return of his cuff links. Ko Tun Tin had lost his pair some time before and Maung Nu had given him gold ones as a replacement. These Ko Tun Tin now calmly removed from his shirt and surrendered to an Indian.

Back in his hostel, Maung Nu slammed the door after him, bolted it from the inside, jumped into bed, pulled down the mosquito net, and covered his head with a blanket. He wept tears of mortification.

It took Maung Nu two weeks to forget Ma Khin Myint and rediscover his sonnets. Gradually he began to realise how much he was in Ko Tun Tin's debt. The public scene he had caused over a common prostitute filled him with shame. Finally came the moment when he was able to go to Ko Tun Tin and offer an abject apology, which was accepted along with the restoration of the cuff links.

Maung Nu did not need to be told that Ko Tun Tin had gone ahead to enlist the pimp's support in the plot to disillusion Maung Nu. The pimp proved only too willing, since he stood to lose what seemed to be a sound investment if Maung Nu should prevail upon the girl to give up her profession. In fact, if Maung Nu, instead of losing heart, had returned to the brothel for a showdown, he would have been roughed up. He could count himself very lucky.

☆ ☆ ☆ ☆ ☆

About a month later, Maung Nu went to see a play at the Jubilee Hall. Beside him sat a Parsee girl of striking appearance. Next to her was her sister, also a beauty, and then their parents, elderly folks. Maung Nu noticed that the girl by his side was tall and slender, with bewitching eyes. She was obviously a person of refinement, perhaps a little older than himself, withal an uninhibited and friendly type. Since Maung Nu was without a programme she gave him her copy, saying she would share her sister's. She asked him whether he knew the scenario of *The Admirable Crichton* and, when he confessed he did not, gave him a brief rundown before the curtain went up. Then, after each act, she would draw him into a discussion of the various parts and the manner of their rendition. Maung Nu was eager to contribute, but he found his English inadequate, the Parsee girl's being so perfect. With nods and smiles he could only encourage her to go on, and he thought the play ended too soon. She bade him goodbye. "Wasn't Crichton perfectly admirable?" were her parting words.

Maung Nu stared after her car until it drove out of sight, then started to walk home, still savouring her perfume. Every fibre in his being tingled at the thought of her, the curvature of her body, the expression in her eyes, the melody in her voice. It was four in the morning when he completed his sonnet. But where was he to send it? It had been on the tip of his tongue to inquire after her name, but he had not found the courage. Not that she would have denied him anything, he felt. She had seized every opportunity to give him information. It was just that he had been an idiot. He could have kicked himself.

He was able to keep his longing bottled up for two days. On the third, the lid flew open. The friends to whom he confided said Rangoon was full of Parsees and without a name they despaired of being able to trace the girl. "You're such a fool," they said, and Maung Nu felt more of one than ever.

Then followed a search for his heart's desire. He drew a blank at the cinemas, in Fytche Square, at the Royal Lakes. Then the

Gymkhana Club staged a revue called *Say When,* at the Jubilee Hall. Maung Nu went there two nights in a row, but she was not there. He had pined for a month when his friend Hla Maung brought an address for a Miss Homasjee. The sonnet went to her with a note suggesting a meeting. No reply came in weeks. Maung Nu complained to Hla Maung, who chided him. Genteel persons could not be rushed. There were such things as propriety, maidenly reserve. Maung Nu was advised to persevere. Three more letters were dispatched, at decent intervals. When they failed to elicit any response, Maung Nu decided he would go to her door. "Show me the way," he beseeched Hla Maung. When at length the latter could no longer put him off, he admitted through peals of laughter that he had lifted the name out of the telephone directory.

Once, in the past, Maung Nu had faked love letters to his friends Maung Shein and Tun Yin. They were in a girl's handwriting and were made to look like replies to the boys' importunities. When the unsuspecting swains appeared to keep the tryst Maung Nu and his companions doused them with water in the dark. "Retribution" was Maung Nu's conclusion after his latest episode.

☆ ☆ ☆ ☆ ☆

In his senior Intermediate of Arts year, Maung Nu took to drinking more than ever. Each Saturday night like-minded students would foregather in his room and open a bottle of Johnny Walker whisky. The contents would be poured into a basin to which was added a soft drink called Vimto. The concoction was served with ice and everyone drank to his heart's content. Ordinarily, Maung Nu did not smoke, but he cultivated the habit, resorting to cigarettes in the ratio of one puff to each sip of liquor. Other students might get inebriated, but they were generally able to keep a hold on themselves. Not so Maung Nu, who, when he got drunk, disgraced himself. When Prome and Tagaung Halls held a joint Christmas party, attention was centred not on the stage, where an *anyein*[10] was being danced, but upon Maung Nu in his cups. There, in the middle of an audience comprising D. J. Sloss, principal of the college, the wardens, the professors, and men and women stu-

10. A dance recital performed by one or more *danseuses,* assisted by two male jesters. The danseuse sings to accompany her dancing.

dents, Maung Nu passed out and had to be carried to his room. Along the way a tightly laced shoe somehow left his foot. It was found by the janitor.

Since his arrival at the university, Maung Nu had been consumed with an ambition to excel at public speaking. He envied students with the ability to thrust and parry in school debates, and he strove to become proficient himself. Three or four opportunities were lost because he could not pluck up enough courage to face an audience. Although he took a vow to starve himself for a day if he did not meet the next challenge, he found, when the time came, that he was shaking with fright as though possessed by a *nat*.[11] Then came the debate on the motion "The pen is mightier than the sword," and in this Maung Nu resolved to participate, even if he perished in the attempt. All the principal speakers were girl students who were not seasoned debaters in their senior year but freshmen making their debuts. He took a solemn vow that if he failed to state his case logically and convincingly, if he allowed himself to be vanquished by the opposition, he would go without food for four days.

Speaking for the motion was Cissy Aung Gyi, a girl of Maung Nu's age. She had a sweet face and, because she wore her hair bobbed, looked little older than a child. Unruffled and unhurried, Cissy made her points. Hers was not a brilliant speech by any means, but she was lucid and competent. Three other girls followed her at the lectern and held their end up with commendable poise. When the debate was thrown open to the audience Maung Nu sprang to his feet, but that was all he could recollect. Everything else was in a haze, as if he were peering through water. It was said that, in some fashion, he opposed the motion.

Anyway, the ice was now broken and Maung Nu gave himself up to rejoicing. Along with this elation, however, appeared a recrudescence of an old familiar complaint, and this was brought about by none other than Cissy Aung Gyi, of the Debating Society.

Cissy had a face that lacked distinction except that her lips were permanently curled into a smile. She was slim—almost too thin, as

11. A spiritual being, or god.

though she might have something physically wrong with her. Bobbed hair, too, might strike one as incongruous when worn with Burmese dress. What then was her appeal to Maung Nu?

Maung Nu had had to force himself to enter the debate, but because of stage fright he failed to acquit himself creditably. Cissy, on the other hand, had been cool and collected. Her speech could have been prepared in advance, of course, but her rebuttals could not have been rehearsed or preconceived. Maung Nu's eyes and ears convinced him the girl had gumption and a clear mind. Certain foods brought on certain fevers. Maung Nu knew this, and with equal certitude he knew the malady that would afflict him when, through a process of osmosis, that which beguiled his senses pierced the citadel of his heart.

Past experience had taught him that writing love letters could be unrewarding, so now he bided his time thinking up another stratagem. An opportunity presented itself one afternoon at a Burmese movie house. Cissy Aung Gyi was there with two other girls. There was a long queue. Should he nip in quickly, buy three tickets, and present them to the girls? This idea was squelched when he imagined how foolish he would look were the girls to refuse the tickets. Well, he could offer to buy the tickets for them, but what if they said, "No thanks, we'll do it ourselves." He had heard of men students trying to act familiar and being snubbed in public. It might be wiser to keep his distance, ready to help if needed. The girls ignored his presence, waited until the crowd had thinned, then went in and bought their tickets. Throughout the show, Maung Nu was wracked by self-recriminations. He should have offered to help, he told himself, even at the risk of being spurned. His motives were pure; he need not have feared rebuff. Besides, he believed he had caught Cissy in a sideways glance, almost imploring help. That night he lay tossing in bed while the damsel who had caused him so much distress was elsewhere, blissfully asleep.

Instead of the usual outpourings of the lovelorn, Maung Nu's message to Cissy Aung Gyi, when it came to be written, fell somewhere between a story and a play. Composed in blank verse, it told the tale of the Lady Cissy, the peerless beauty, lofty in mind and spirit, who dwelt in a jungle fastness. Her castle was surrounded by a garden, the approaches to which were guarded by goblins. Since there were a thousand of them, the youth called Nu could only gaze on the lady from afar, his heart consumed with love of her. Release for him could only come if she, in her mercy, commanded him to come into her presence, immediately lifting all barriers and restraints that separated them. Maung Nu did not know how the poetic would judge his verse, but he himself was extremely pleased with it. Nevertheless, when it came to delivering it to the person concerned, his nerve failed him. He dropped his masterpiece in the letter box.

If his affection was returned, the reply should come in a week, he reasoned. When three weeks of silence passed, he was sure the letter had been lost in transit. These things had been known to happen. He wrote her a second time and, after several weeks, a third. In the end, he took counsel of Pagan Ko Ba Gyan,[12] who opined that the girl must already have a lover. Maung Nu was inclined to the view that she just simply did not care for him. In any case, he stopped writing letters.

The university finals were held in March. Cissy was the first to leave the hall, followed by Maung Nu and Ko Ba Gyan. The girl walked about thirty yards, stopped and about-faced. Ko Ba Gyan urged Maung Nu to go forward, but Maung Nu panicked and ran into an adjoining building. When Ko Ba Gyan caught up with him, Maung Nu, who had made up his mind that his quest was hopeless, explained that he dreaded the prospect of being snubbed over the letters.

"If she reproaches you, all you have to say is 'That's fine; I shan't write again; thanks.' You're bold in everything else, but when it comes to women you're a funk," Ko Ba Gyan scolded him. Then, still complaining that Maung Nu was hasty in love and hasty in retreat, Ko Ba Gyan threatened to tackle Cissy himself. But the lady had gone.

Ko Ba Gyan suggested tracking Cissy down at the Ladies' Common Room. This was a famous rendezvous, and after classes students of both sexes could be seen standing about the room in pairs. But there Maung Nu would not go. In eight years of college life he never had a date in the vicinity of this room. He had in fact entered the portals of the Inya (Ladies') Hall once, but merely as a compan-

12. Ko Ba Gyan was called "Pagan" after the Burmese town from which he came.

ion to Budalin Ko Thein Pe[13] who wished to call on his friend, Ma Thein Nu of Mandalay. He would have liked to have gone on his own, but always he was unnerved by the prospect of visiting a women's stronghold.

When college reopened for the June term of 1926, Cissy was not there. Maung Nu's inquiries elicited the information that she had contracted a lung disease and died. Fate was to decree that the news should prove to be false and that the two should meet again under strange circumstances.

SCHOOL EXAMINATIONS

When the March vacation arrived in 1926, Maung Nu went home to Wakèma. It was while drinking with friends one day that he learnt that he had failed the last examinations. Previously, when he was in high school, he had taken such things casually, but now he had set his heart on higher learning, with hopes of continuing his studies in England. The news was a setback to his contemplated career as a playwright and novelist, preferably in the English language. He was shaken more than he betrayed to his drinking partners.

That night he dreamed that Principal Sloss had published a supplementary list of passes and that his name was on it. He dreamed it again and again. Thereafter he avoided his companions and displayed a disinclination to meet even the other members of his family. Five days later he moved out to a cottage his father owned on the fringe of town. He kept the gate locked and would emerge only late at night, an iron walking stick in his hand. One midnight he was on the road outside the courthouse when it suddenly came to him that he had failed because of his immoral conduct. The moment he realised this, he made a vow that he would not drink liquor for the next five years.

Although Maung Nu strongly believed that he had failed because of his drinking, there may be other considerations that should also be taken into account, including the following. In the Intermediate of Arts course, Maung Nu had taken logic, ancient history, and modern history. Ancient history was taught by Saya David. A Mad-

13. Ko Thein Pe was called "Budalin" after the town from which he came.

rassi by race, Saya David had compiled for the benefit of his students notes from various publications. In order that these notes might be copied rapidly by the class, he taught a kind of speed-writing, or shorthand. Thus "therefore" became ∴ and "because" was written ∵; "century" was O, and so on. Because he himself had taken such pains with these notes, Saya David wanted his students to stick close to the text. But Maung Nu was a nonconformist, with the result that he usually scored only one out of ten in the weekly tests. For the final examination Saya David required his students to enter their home address on their answer paper and to provide sufficient postage so that he could mail them the results. When Maung Nu's answer paper reached him, he found it marked one out of a hundred, and beneath the score Saya David had written this remark: "For pity's sake."

Whatever the influence of such incidents on his overall examination results, however, Maung Nu himself was convinced that his failure was a direct result of his drinking, and thus he took very seriously his vow to abstain from intoxicants.

AN INQUIRY INTO BUDDHISM

After he had taken the vow, he had a serious conversation with his father. Asked if there was a hereafter, U San Tun said yes.

Besides human beings and animals that we can see, Father, how many other sentient beings are there, that we cannot see?

There are *byamma, nat,* very miserable beings called *pyaittar* and *ah-thu-ra-ke* and beings in hell. Of all these beings, byamma are the highest. Nat come next. Below nat are human beings. Beings in hell, animals, pyaittar, and ah-thu-ra-ke are called beings of the four nether regions.

Father, can you prove that there are byamma and nat?

The Buddha never preached anything that could not be proved.

Father, I want to see a nat.

Son, for this you need extrasensory insight, called Abain-Nyin. The Buddha has taught how this can be acquired. Once it is acquired, you will not only see but also hear nat and byamma.

You can also look back upon past existences, what your mother was in a former life, even how Toe Pwa, our dog, came to be what he is.

Father, is it very difficult to acquire this insight?

Not if you have faith, diligence, and a good instructor.

What have beings in hell, animals, pyaittar, and ah-thu-ra-ke done in their previous existences in order to deserve rebirth in those four nether regions?

In their previous existences, they were beings that committed one or another of these ten sins:
1. Killing
2. Stealing
3. Committing adultery
4. Telling lies
5. Setting one person against another
6. Using rough and abusive words
7. Indulging in useless talks
8. Coveting what belongs to others, such as property, fame, influence, beauty, a wife or husband etc.
9. Having an evil desire to ill-treat or destroy others
10. Failing to believe in the law of causation and effect[14]

Beings in hell, animals, pyaittar and ah-thu-ra-ke had committed one of the above sins in one of their previous existences.

Father, what should I do, if I want to be reborn as a nat after death?

You must:
1. Refrain from killing
2. Refrain from stealing
3. Refrain from committing adultery
4. Refrain from taking intoxicants
5. Refrain from telling lies
6. Refrain from using rough and abusive words
7. Refrain from indulging in useless talk

---

14. According to the law of causation and effect, one's actions in this life determine the nature of one's existence in the next. For example, a person who commits murder may be reborn after death as an animal of some kind.

8. Refrain from coveting what belongs to others

9. Refrain from having evil desires to ill-treat or destroy others.

10. Refrain from doubting the law of causation and effect.

Those who refrain from committing the above sins will be re-born, after death, as either nat or human beings.

Father, what should I do if I want to be reborn as a byamma after death?

You must have *zan* up to the time of your death.

What is zan, father?

Roughly speaking, zan means extraordinary mental concentration on an object. The Buddha prescribed methods for achieving this extraordinary mental concentration.

Father, what manner of being is a Buddha?

It is He who through His own efforts, and without a teacher, is able to come to understand the Four Noble Truths, namely, suffering, the cause of suffering, the end of suffering, and the way to the end of suffering.

How did our Gautama Buddha obtain omniscience?

Over four aeons and a hundred thousand worlds ago, Gautama Buddha was born as Thumeida, a rich man. He gave up his wealth and became a hermit. Not long afterwards, he met Dipingara Buddha. If under the Buddha he had become a monk and practised *wipathana*[15] meditation he would have become a saint. He would have freed himself from the scourges of old age, death, and separation. Thumeida, however, because of his great compassion, did not wish to enter *Neikban* (Nirvana) alone. He wished to save all beings and attain Neikban together with them. He therefore made the wish before Dipingara Buddha that he might be born a Buddha. The Buddha, with his power of prescience, foresaw that the hermit Thumeida would become a Buddha. So the Buddha ordained that his wishes would be fulfilled. Thumeida practised the ten parami through successive existences for four aeons and a hundred thousand worlds. He became a Buddha in this world.

15. Buddhist meditation whose aim is to uproot defilements such as greed, anger, and false belief in matter and mind.

I too would like to become a Buddha. Is that possible? I wish to save beings.

Of course, it is possible.

Don't say that lightly. I am not a good person. I've killed, fornicated, lied, and drunk.

These are not important. These are human frailties. The important thing is to realise the error of your ways and to avoid them in the future.

Are you saying that for my peace of mind? Can you cite scriptural text to support what you've just said?

When it comes to religion, I don't speak carelessly. The paya-alaung Mahawthada,[16] for the defence of his king and country, killed enemies and committed other sins as well. In another existence, as the hermit Haritasa, he committed adultery with the queen while the king was in battle. And in yet another existence, when he met the future Seinzamana, who was to try to discredit him later, he was a drunkard. However, there was this distinction. From the time of their dedication as paya-alaung to the time of attainment of Buddhahood, the paya-alaung, throughout four aeons and a hundred thousand worlds, believed implicitly in the doctrine of kan, of causation and effect. In some existences they went wrong, but because of their great faith they were able to recognize their errors and become righteous. In none of these existences were they beyond self-correction.

I do so want to be a Buddha, father. Tell me the ten parami.

They are: (1) *dharna* (chastity), (2) *thila* (restraint of body and mouth from doing or saying what is sinful), (3) *neikkhama* (renunciation), (4) *pyinnya* (wisdom), (5) *wiriya* (diligence), (6) *khanti* (forbearance), (7) *thitsa* (truth), (8) *adeiktan* (resolution), (9) *myitta* (love), and (10) *upekka* (passionlessness). Again, there are three classes of parami, low, middle, and high; to forsake wife,

---

16. A *paya-alaung* is a being who, through the accumulation of massive kutho, has been recognized by the Buddha as a future Buddha and has been consecrated. Mahawthada was one of ten paya-alaung who are well known to Buddhists.

children, and possessions is to earn low parami; to suffer the loss of an eye or a limb is to gain middle parami; to make the supreme sacrifice of life is to attain high parami.

U San Tun went on to interpret the thila parami in order to illustrate the three classes of parami:

Let us say you've been abducted. The kidnappers compel you to drink. You refuse though you are deprived of your family (low parami); you have your eye gouged out (middle parami); you are killed (high parami).

Next, as an example of khanti parami, U San Tun related the life of the embryo-Gautama in a previous existence, when he was known as the hermit Khantiwardi. The king, while out hunting, fell asleep. When he awoke, he found that the queen had gone to pay her respects to the hermit. In anger, he had the hermit bound and whipped. The latter was able to practise forbearance (low parami); he maintained this forbearance even though he was torn limb from limb (middle parami); and when he was about to be executed he forgave everyone (high parami). Continuing, U San Tun said:

The paya-alaung, from the moment of consecration until the attainment of Buddhahood, had to go through countless existences amassing the ten parami up to the highest level.

What is consecration?

The abodes of men, nat and byamma are full of beings who dedicate themselves through a wish to become Buddha. The Buddha does not give his sanction merely because of the dedication or the expression of a wish. It is only in the case of an individual who has acquired massive kutho through countless worlds that the Buddha will declare that that individual will become Buddha in such and such an existence. The future Buddha will be named, as also his disciples. From this moment of nomination or consecration, the aspirant becomes a paya-alaung and he has to fulfill his parami through four aeons and a hundred thousand worlds.

In that case, it is most difficult to become a paya-alaung, let alone a Buddha.

That is right, son.

Father, it doesn't matter how long it takes. To be a Buddha is to be able to relieve the distress of all sentient beings.

I'll say Amen to that.

Tell me, father, why haven't you talked about religion with me before? I might have avoided much sin.

U San Tun struck his breast until it resounded. He pointed out that he had, on innumerable occasions, broached the subject of the law of causation and effect, of hell and the Four Noble Truths, but had been cut short every time. He said: "You either said you did not believe in these or simply forbade me to speak. If I continued, you walked away. Now that you've taken the initiative I'm over-joyed."

Having won an admission from his son that he had erred in the sight of the Buddha, the Assembly, and his parents, and that he had wronged human beings as well as birds and animals, U San Tun pointed out that there was a right moment for some persons to change and that he had failed in the past to change his son because the right moment had not yet come. U San Tun also said that the Buddha, unlike ordinary persons, always waited for that right moment, when he chose to make his conversion.

Leading Maung Nu before the family altar, his father made him sit in a respectful manner before the images of the Buddha. He got him to worship the Three Noble Gems[17] with humility. He recited the Five Precepts[18] which Maung Nu repeated after him. Finally, with fingers joined in adoration, Maung Nu vowed, through application of mind and body to their fullest extent, that he would dedicate himself to acquiring the ten parami in their thirty layers and prayed that he might one day become the true Buddha.

U San Tun wanted to ask his son to turn to him for absolution, but he hesitated because if, as in the past, Maung Nu were to react in an unseemly manner, the momentum towards change and virtue would be lost. Thus it was Maung Nu himself who faced his father and made obeisance. U San Tun wept tears of joy.

17. The Buddha, the Law, and the Assembly (of monks).
18. The Five Precepts urge restraint from killing, stealing, committing adultery, lying, and taking intoxicants.

TOWARDS REFORM AND VIRTUE

Just because Maung Nu had made the wish to become a Buddha, it did not necessarily follow that he would be one some day. Let alone becoming a Buddha, it would be no easy matter to find an existing Buddha and to get him to consecrate one as a paya-alaung. Maung Nu's action had been taken on the spur of the moment, upon hearing his father's admonitions. As he found more time to reflect on the inevitability of death, old age, and separation, and the ceaseless rounds of cares and tribulations in the circle of endless rebirths he was frightened. Others before him, intimidated by the prospect of so much toil and suffering, had abandoned the Buddha-wish and settled for the attainment of *a-ra-hat*-ship[19] that would bring release from the woes of thanthaya. No one can say that Maung Nu, who had begun to entertain such grave fears, would not renounce the Buddha-wish and decide to concentrate his call into a single existence.

The immediate results of having made the wish were edifying. One night his conscience was troubled by the recurring vision of birds he had destroyed. There was a cock he had snared, tied to a post, and killed with a blow to the head. The death had been a lingering one, and afterwards he had got Pan Yee to cook it and eat it with him. The hen he next killed was feeding with a brood of chickens. He had used a broken brick on that occasion. Although he did not get to eat that bird, others did.

As contrition swept over him for the enormity of what he had done, he slapped himself on the cheeks, gathered up his slings and catapults, and cut them up with a knife. The airgun he dismantled, throwing away its parts. Remorse over the suffering he had caused birds and beasts soon began to manifest itself in another way. When he looked at the dishes laid before him at meals he would be overcome and refuse to eat meat. These moods lasted four or five days, or two or three months, later even two to three years. Even when he grew weak and faint and his eyes blurred the doctor could not prevail upon him to go back to a meat diet.

The next thing he learnt to avoid was the accidental destruction of animals. It became a habit with him to walk with his eyes on the

19. The major insight that can uproot mental defilements.

ground, so that try as he might he could not look ahead or straight for any length of time. Then he took to rescuing insects fallen in the water or caught in webs. In others this might be regarded as trivial but Maung Nu made a big thing of it.

Maung Nu recalled his father saying that, in regard to theft, it was immaterial whether the stolen article be large or small, valuable or cheap. Taking it without the permission of the owner constituted theft. Often, in orchards, his friends might climb trees and pluck mangoes, guavas, or *mayan* fruit, or knock them down for fun. But without the permission of the owner, or the presiding monk, Maung Nu would now touch neither fruit nor flower. Even in regard to toothpicks, put out for all who ate in restaurants, Maung Nu would ask for permission before he reached out for more than one.

His scrupulous care in regard to accidental taking of life and in regard to another's property, and his concern for animals generally, put him in mind of a tale told by his father. There once lived a certain Zabuka who, for transgressing against a saint, went to hell. When he had completed his term, his a-kutho kan remaining in residual form, he came back as a man but one so debased that he fed on excreta and went naked. Whenever others were likely to see him he would open his mouth, hold one foot up, and explain that he was such a righteous person he ate only air, that he went without clothing because his devotional exercises were rigorous, and that he could not put both feet on the ground lest he destroy the world. Then Zabuka met the Buddha, found the path of truth and salvation, and became a saint.

Whenever he thought about Zabuka, Maung Nu would smile to himself. Many unknowing people must regard his own fastidiousness and his concern for animal life as hypocrisy or—worse—as the wily tricks of a Zabuka trying to gain the good opinion of others.

Before returning to college, Maung Nu asked his father what he thought of consorting with prostitutes. Did one go to hell for it? Before he answered the question, his father said he would like Maung Nu's own views to be stated. So Maung Nu said he thought there was no wrong in it. The prostitute named her price and the customer paid it. He did not mistreat her nor deprive her of her honour since it was already lost. As for the sexual intercourse itself, there was nothing shameful in it. Bad people indulged in it, but so did good people, and so did gods. What they did to their heart's content after paying the price of pleasure did not deserve punishment in hell.

To start off with, U San Tun said in reply, prostitution was a problem that could not be treated superficially. If his son felt he could not do without a woman, he had only to say so and his father would arrange to find him a wife before he went back to school. "Don't ever go to a prostitute," he said and added quickly, "Have you by any chance contracted venereal disease?" Maung Nu confessed he had, twice. "Then, get it totally cleansed from your system," U San Tun advised. "Otherwise your children and their children will be in trouble."

U San Tun went on to discuss the social and religious aspects of prostitution. He pointed out that some of the women in brothels did not get there voluntarily. Agents would go to villages and lure the girls with promises of work or clothing or jewellery. The pleasures of Rangoon and the cinemas were held out as bait. When they succumbed, they were sold to pimps who starved, beat, and threatened them into submission.

Not all prostitutes were professionals. Some of them came from the districts to visit and to buy some merchandise. They might be short of cash for the return home, or they might wish to buy something fancy. Others might want a fling in the absence of the family. It might be true they were doing a temporary stint for four, five, or ten days, and willingly at that. But in most cases they had husbands.

Finally, U San Tun explained, there were the so-called respectable establishments, where the owners had some ostensible means of support. They were wage earners or in business. To them would come secret offers from ordinary women needing spending money, clothing, or jewellery. Others were upper-class women used to having gold and diamonds. These, having been lost at gambling or pledged with the pawnbroker, had to be accounted for before the husbands got suspicious. Or the women might hanker after larger gems. So they put themselves up for high bids which Burmans could not generally meet. Their rich clients were Indians and Chinese.

All this was new to Maung Nu and he thought awhile. Then he asked whether sleeping with a married woman could result in going to hell. Yes, said the father, that was where he was bound for. He would remain there a long time and if he was reborn as a man he would be a *nabon pandok*. This he would define as a kind of homosexual. The person was born with male genitals, but he was not a manly man. He had to suck another man's penis or submit to anal intercourse in order to find the virility to approach a woman. He was altogether a debased person.

Father, I've been with a married woman.

When?

Remember the time you sent me to the other bank? To the granary?

Whose wife was she?

I never found out. He was in jail for robbery. Left his wife with Uncle Waing, and when I asked for a woman he produced her.

Why, the rotten son of a bitch!

Leave him be, father.

But U San Tun could hardly contain himself. He shouted to his servant, "Hey, Saw Hlaing. Get Ba Waing out of my granary!" Maung Nu had to grab him bodily to restrain him.

Maung Nu asked one last question: "What if the customer did not know the woman had a husband?" U San Tun said he would still go to hell. A man bitten in the night might think it was a harmless watersnake, but that would not prevent the poison from the viper doing its work.

Apparently satisfied, Maung Nu thanked his father, took all the blame for the goings-on at the granary, and extracted a promise that the uncle would not be punished. The talk between father and son proved to be of benefit as far as Maung Nu was concerned. From that moment he stopped consorting with prostitutes.

Since having made the Buddha-wish, moral discipline loomed large in all of Maung Nu's thinking. What the body did, the lips spoke and the mind thought, these were the essence of morality. He put himself on guard against breaches of this discipline.

Lying and talebearing, which headed the list of infelicitous speech, had not been among Maung Nu's shortcomings. But he was aware of the need to correct himself in regard to coarseness of speech and the habit of mouthing trivial and inconsequential words. His frivolous manner and the spirit of levity he displayed on all occasions had often drawn rebuke from his cousin Ma Thein Tin. She said he reminded her of Bandu, a beggar, whom a minor stroke had reduced to a shuffling, blithering idiot, uncoordinated in speech and movement.

With the need for restraint and self-improvement Maung Nu began to choose his words, eliminating those he considered trivial and wasteful. If despite his vigilance frivolity crept into his speech he would stop in the middle of a sentence. The imperfections remained, but Maung Nu did show improvement and a continuing effort in that direction.

In regard to liquor, having been an addict himself he realised, now that he had given up the habit, what a disgusting spectacle a drunk made of himself. Man had reason; animals did not. When a man became intoxicated he lost his reason and reduced himself to the status of an animal.

Maung Nu recalled the story told him by his father of two friends, the first of whom tried to induce the second to commit with him murder, theft, and rape. The second man resisted these attempts as well as a further suggestion to bear false witness against another. So the first man said, "Let's have a drink," and the other obliged because he did not want to seem unfriendly. Then they both went out and committed all four crimes together.

Maung Nu's original vow was to abstain from drink for five years. In fact, for seven years he did not touch a drop. By this time he had become a teacher. Then came his transfer from Thongwa to Pantanaw, and the older pupils who helped him pack asked for a drink of toddy (fermented palm juice). Maung Nu started to drink himself but stopped after two sips. Later, during the Water Festival in Wakèma, his old drinking partners opened a bottle of whisky and made a sherbet. Maung Nu recoiled after the first taste. He was never able to drink again.

One other change wrought by Maung Nu's having made the Buddha-wish was to be seen in his attitude towards his parents and elders. As a child and throughout his life he had been spoilt by the family. They gave in to him in every way, so much so that his younger brother Maung Oo, product of the same womb, who was not similarly pampered, nursed a grievance against the parents. Preferential treatment at all times and the withholding of corporal punishment when it was deserved had made for a certain arrogance and disrespect in Maung Nu's manner. But now it was noticeably altered. However late in the night, Maung Nu, on coming home, would go to the foot of his parents' bed and *shikhoe*[20] them. When he came home from school, and before his return, he paid his respects in the same manner to all the older members of the family. He took care of his parents and massaged them when they were tired. In his relations with his father, he had recourse to him as to a dear friend. Everything was open and above-board between them. There was a new respect on the part of the son, particularly in regard to religious instruction.

Whenever he recalled past misdeeds, Maung Nu used to exculpate himself by throwing the blame on someone else. He deceived himself that he had done much wrong because he was too young to be able to distinguish right from wrong. The killing of birds, the thefts, and the sexual experiments were laid at Pan Yee's door; it was Pan Yee who had taught him to drink; and it was his uncle U Ba Waing who had brought the married woman. But now he recognized he had been a moral coward. He hated himself for blaming others when he alone was guilty of: (1) taking the lives of birds, (2) stealing money, merchandise, and food, (3) sexual impurity, (4) drinking spirituous liquor, and (5) disobedience toward his parents.

To record these wrongs, and confess his guilt, Maung Nu vowed to write them down each day in his diary for one hundred and eight days. This vow was kept and was renewed on two subsequent occasions.

---

20. A Burman Buddhist shikhoes (pays homage to): (1) the Buddha, (2) the Law (of Buddha), (3) the Assembly, (4) his parents, (5) teachers, and (6) those who are older than he. The proper way to shikhoe is to observe the "five touches": both knees, both forearms from elbow to palm, and the forehead touch the floor simultaneously.

2

Settling Down

When Maung Nu returned to University College in June 1926, he kept his vow to eschew alcoholic drinks. In March of the following year he passed the Senior Intermediate of Arts examination, and he believed this success was a result of his resolution. While it is impossible to say whether or not this was true, it can be seen that other factors were involved, just as there may have been several factors involved in his failure of the year before. This year Saya David was gone. In his place was Dr. Aspinall, an Englishman, who had a different style. He discussed the lessons with the class and considered some contrary opinions "interesting." In the weekly tests Maung Nu now often scored some seven points out of ten, and never below five. This was probably a reflection of the kind of latitude displayed by Dr. Aspinall.

When he got to the Bachelor of Arts course, Maung Nu maintained his unorthodoxy. Let us see how he consequently missed being flunked in the finals by a finger's breadth.

He had chosen English literature, Burmese literature, and philosophy as his courses. In the philosophy course, Saya Ross taught psychology, and Saya Saunder ethics. In Ko Nu's second year these Englishmen retired and their places were filled by Indians: Saya Mazumder and Saya Banerji. Maung Nu got along all right in psychology, but he found much to argue over in ethics. Saya Banerji seemed to like argument and challenge. Among his five students he

often selected Maung Nu to visit him at home and partake of re-
freshments. Banerji was partial to French toast and cocoa. Maung
Nu would join in and then be drawn into discussing Burmese and
Indian politics. Sometimes, on the subject of ethics, Banerji would
exclaim, "I can appreciate your views, but if you put them in your
answers you're done for," often adding the warning that a professor
from abroad would come as external examiner and that he, Banerji,
would be powerless to help.

Despite these warnings, when the finals came, Maung Nu answered in his usual free-wheeling style. Banerji took one look at the
answer book, muttered "Just as I thought," and invited Maung Nu
to see him at home. There he was introduced to the external examiner, who was no other than Dr. Sarvepalli Radhakrishnan, the
man destined one day to become the president of India. After a
few words had been exchanged, Saya Banerji said, "Maung Nu
here holds views somewhat at variance with what is contained in
textbooks. You might find them interesting." With that he reached
out for Maung Nu's answer book and placed it in Dr. Radhakrishnan's hand. The professor started to read and soon his brow wrin-
kled. Ten minutes passed and a smile appeared, then grunts of
"H'm, h'm." Finally he laid down the book and asked: "Maung Nu,
what's all this you've written?" Maung Nu grinned. "Exactly what
you've read, Professor," he said. "Weird," Dr. Radhakrishnan pronounced, "Except that I can't say definitely that you're wrong."
Saya Banerji was more pleased than Maung Nu that he had been
passed.

In his B.A. class Maung Nu found a new love, only this time it
was writing plays. Class work was neglected and the new love pampered. He took to writing long plays and was so engaged a fortnight
before examinations. His friend Ko Khin Zaw, thinking he was
cramming, entered his room to find him doing something else.
"You'll fail because of this," Ko Khin Zaw grumbled, and he left
taking the incomplete act with him.

Maung Nu's plays were not good ones. It was hard to call them
plays because they were devoid of action. They did not hold one's
interest and were as wearisome as an exchange of views. Maung Nu
himself thought the world of his plays. He even entered one for the
Prince of Wales Prize. This literary award had been funded by the

government of Burma to commemorate the visit of Edward, Prince of Wales, and was the highest honour among the scholastic and literary community, carrying with it a cash prize of a thousand rupees. When his entry was rejected he charged the selection board with jobbery.

There were points of similarity, one might note, between Maung Nu and the night watchman Po Myaing. This Po Myaing was a shiftless person, somewhat light in the head. He would not settle down in a job but drifted around with his calves serving as props to his house, as the saying goes. Maung Nu's father, U San Tun, took pity on him and appointed him night watchman at his granary. Po Myaing requested a *pattaya,* a native xylophone, which he intended to play to keep himself awake, and this was granted. Po Myaing did not know how to strike a single note, but from the moment he got the instrument he never left it alone. Except for periods of sleep, meals, and visits to the toilet, he was at the pattaya, striking up a cacophony. From time to time he sang some discordant notes. "Maung Nu," he boasted one day, "You can search the whole of Wakèma without finding my equal." Those whose duties kept them at the granary could not sleep because of the din, but they could hardly complain against U San Tun's appointee.

The trading season brought U San Tun himself to the scene. He put up with the racket the first night but in the morning told his durwan to sing and play softly. But as the evening shadows fell, the sound of Po Myaing's "music" rose in crescendo, so the next morning U San Tun confiscated the pattaya. Po Myaing then went into decline; he locked himself in his room and refused to eat. When he began to rave in bed, U San Tun quickly restored the pattaya and sent for the doctor.

Maung Nu was not crazy like Po Myaing, but writing plays was to him what pattaya playing was to Po Myaing. A pretty woman, moonlight, a spring or a babbling brook, a glade or a hilltop would set him off, and if prevented from writing he too would go into decline and be positively ill. But the moment he started to write the distemper would leave him, the tautness in his nerves and veins disappeared, and he would be filled with a sense of well-being. He would begin writing after dinner and work till midnight, then wake up from time to time to fill a bedside book with notes.

Perhaps Maung Nu differed from Po Myaing in only one respect. Durwan Po Myaing died in the unswerving conviction that he was a great musician, the like of whom was not to be found in the length and breadth of Wakèma. Maung Nu, on the other hand, got to read more books and more plays, and gradually, as, with the single exception of the obscure *Duwun Magazine,* all other magazines and journals sent back rejection slips, the realisation began to sink in that his output was pretty shoddy.

FROM LEARNER TO TEACHER

In May 1929, Maung Nu graduated with a Bachelor of Arts degree. He would have liked to have entered the journalistic world with both feet, but he realised that in his case accomplishment did not keep pace with ambition. While he hesitated—and since he did not wish to be a government servant—he enrolled in law school. He had attended law classes only three days when he received a telegram calling him away to Pantanaw. There his uncle suggested that he should become the headmaster of the national high school. Maung Nu was then only twenty-two years old; he had never intended to be a schoolmaster, but the school committee members all wanted him and he acquiesced, withdrawing himself from law school.

Maung Nu had hardly been a fortnight in Pantanaw when his many relatives began sounding him out on the prospects of marriage. Did he have a sweetheart—an intended bride? He disclosed that he was not engaged to be married, and that he had no one in view. When he inquired why they were so interested, he found that they were intent on getting him to settle down with a local girl who was none other than Ma Mya Yee, the youngest daughter of U Aung Nyein, the school superintendent, and his wife, Daw Nyi Ma. Maung Nu had jokingly asked his aunt whether Ma Mya Yee was pretty and was told he could decide for himself when he saw her.

In the year that followed, Maung Nu hardly found the opportunity to look at Ma Mya Yee at close range. He managed to find excuses on three or four occasions to call at U Aung Nyein's, on school business, but he had only glimpses of the girl as she flitted

about from room to room. It would have been too obvious if, in
the midst of official business, he had allowed attention to wander
from father to daughter.

Maung Nu knew Ko Ohn Maung, Ma Mya Yee's eldest brother,
who had been in college with him. He thought he might see the
sister if he called on the brother socially. But Ko Ohn Maung proved
most uncooperative. He would receive his caller in front of the
door and talk to him there. Maung Nu felt unwelcome. Here was
a person who would one day woo and win another's sister. Yet
when it came to his own sister, he was strangely insensitive and
mean. Maung Nu was so hurt he decided he would not visit there
again. Even on the occasions when his path led past the house he
would not look at it. Once, when his aunt asked him if he had
looked upon Ma Mya Yee, he said no with such a lack of enthusiasm that she did not pursue the subject. Maung Nu himself was
convinced the fates did not favour a match, so he stopped thinking
about Ma Mya Yee.

Maung Nu's career as a teacher was less than successful. A schoolmaster has to have great patience, a headmaster even more. Maung
Nu was a short-tempered person, so it was not long before he found
himself at odds with the staff. It was not that there was an open
quarrel; it was just that Maung Nu was officious and the teachers,
who had their own problems raising children through successive
years as though they were tender plants, resented Maung Nu's
superior attitude. Since they were men of refinement the teachers
avoided any exchange of words that might elevate their differences
with the headmaster to a quarrel, but they were dissatisfied and this
in turn caused the school committee great distress.

The clash of temperaments was to extend beyond the teachers
and reach the inspector of schools. This official, who was the government head of the division for education, had, in his annual in-
spection of Pantanaw the year before, advised those teachers who
had not yet passed through the Teacher's Training College to so
qualify themselves. It happened that Maung Nu had a teacher on
his staff who possessed the highest qualification—a diploma in
teaching—but was disappointingly inefficient. Everybody knew
about this, but, whereas the others had tolerated him for ten years,
Maung Nu's disillusionment was complete within one. He consid-

ered him not only inefficient but lazy and would have dismissed him if he could. It was in this mood that he wrote in his annual report that, in his experience, some teachers who still lacked paper qualification were more able instructors than some others who had undergone training—in more specific language, that a diploma did not make a teacher. Since this ran counter to what he had laid down, the inspector of schools felt insulted. It was well known that he had it in his power to make his displeasure felt. Government recognition of the school could be withdrawn or, at the least, the school grant could be cut. The committee was again greatly troubled.

The cause of their tribulations was soon in trouble himself. That March, as was customary, there was the Shwemyindin Pagoda festival just two miles out of town. Many came from neighbouring places and the school, in order to attract more pilgrims, held its annual sports meet. Inevitably a drunk got into the crowd and began to get offensive. As a reformed alcoholic Maung Nu was irritated by this particular form of annoyance and he found himself taking a running kick at the drunk. The man collapsed in a heap and was removed from the scene. This was the end of the affair as far as Maung Nu was concerned, but the other held a grudge. A month later, as Maung Nu stood outside a food shop waiting for his aunts inside, he was recognized by a man in an adjoining house. This was the person who had been drunk and disorderly. Maung Nu was severely beaten from behind and, although he was able to get a blow in with his walking stick, he came off second best in this encounter. The side of his head had been split open, necessitating several stitches. Friends and relatives were incensed. They insisted on a complaint being filed with the police, but Maung Nu refused to press charges. To him it was simply a case of tit for tat. However, if he could view the incident with equanimity, the school committee could not. To them it was unheard of, and unthinkable, that a person they had raised to a position of respectability should make a public exhibition of himself in a common brawl. Like a cane held over a fire they were being consumed by a heat they were powerless to control. When therefore at the end of the year Maung Nu resigned to go back to law school they were so relieved they did not even keep up appearances by pretending they would have liked him to continue for another year.

THE AFTERMATH OF A PATRIOTIC SONGFEST

In 1930, Maung Nu had been back in law school less than two months when he fell in with a "thakin," as members of the nationalist Dobama Asi-ayone (Our Burma Association) were known. The thakin's passion in life was the Dobama Song. This composition, later to become the national anthem, had been sung only three or four times in public and was therefore quite new. This thakin friend told Maung Nu he was desirous of singing it at the university, and Maung Nu, making light of the fact that the authorities were dead set against the thakins as well as their song, said rather casually that he would make the arrangements. Having talked it over with some of his friends at Thaton Hall, where he was in residence, Maung Nu went to see Principal Sloss. Not finding him in his office, he went to his house. It was around 4:00 P.M. and the attendant said his master was asleep. Maung Nu found a piece of paper and wrote on it that he proposed to hold a singing session that evening at seven. He asked that they be allowed to sing the Dobama Song. When he returned after an hour to inquire of the attendant, the latter said Mr. Sloss had read the note and torn it to pieces. He had then gone away to play tennis. If Maung Nu had not been so naive, he would have known that it was simply not done to beard the lion in his den. The other students stood in awe of Principal Sloss and would not have dared to visit his house, let alone write a chit to him. But all that was in Maung Nu's mind was his promise to his thakin friend, and this he would proceed to implement. The thought of cancelling the recital just did not occur to him. Instead he went to Professor U Pe Maung Tin, the warden of Thaton Hall, who readily gave his assent. That night the song was sung with great gusto and reverberated through the hall and its surroundings.

In two days the Rangoon press had reported the event, with a translation of the lyrics. The Criminal Investigation Department (CID) of course found out who had arranged for it to be sung at the university, who came, and who among them were political diehards and extremists. It stood to reason that a copy of the CID report reached the principal. At any rate, Maung Nu found a notice stuck on his door which demanded his presence in the principal's office at two the following afternoon. It was customary for such notices to be affixed to the notice board in the hall, so the singular treatment accorded to Maung Nu led to speculations that he might be expelled. Maung Nu himself tore up the notice and to show his indifference waited until two days later before presenting himself.

In five years of residence, Maung Nu had met the principal three times. The first was in 1924, when, as a member of the victorious Tagaung Hall soccer team in intercollegiate competition, he had been asked to dinner in the Commissioner Road office of Mr. Sloss. The latter had also donated the silver cup.

The second occasion was in 1926 when Maung Nu was approaching the senior Intermediate of Arts examination. The practice was for the students to pay a fee and then apply for registration. Maung Nu had paid the fee but failed to register. When his name did not appear on the list he protested to the bursar and was sent to see the principal. Mr. Sloss listened to his complaint, then wrote a message to the bursar, keeping Maung Nu waiting. There were chairs in the room but Maung Nu was not invited to sit down. However, since he was at fault for having failed to register he endured the discomfort of standing meekly for fifteen minutes until the reply from the bursar arrived. Mr. Sloss's verdict was, "Your fee has been paid. You'll have to go to the registrar and see what he can do. I can't help you." He also added the observation that he never met a stupider student in the university. Maung Nu had seen the registrar as directed and easily obtained registration.

The third encounter was really one in passing. Since coming to college Maung Nu had noticed with distaste that the students were in the habit of saluting the faculty members. Whether they were professors, lecturers, or demonstrators, they expected the students to raise their hands in salute. Maung Nu was all for respecting teachers, but in his opinion the proper way would have been to join hands in a Buddhist *shikhoe*. A salute was a monstrosity, one which he sternly discouraged in his friends, he himself never subscribing to it. When therefore Principal Sloss's car passed them one day and the hands of his two friends flew up to their heads, Maung Nu had beaten them down with great and sudden asperity. The car was passing very slowly and Principal Sloss from close proximity had turned his head to look in consternation at Maung Nu.

Now he was face to face with the principal and was being taken to task for having sung what after all was a patriotic song. Asked what his excuse was for failure to appear on the appointed day, Maung Nu said he had been engaged in some important business.

Did you get permission to sing the *Dobama* Song?

Yes, I did.

From whom?

From the warden of Thaton Hall.

Are you not aware my permission is needed for all campus activities?

Maung Nu replied that he was aware of that fact, then proceeded to explain how he had tried to meet the obligation. The clincher of course was Professor U Pe Maung Tin's permission. Without it, it might have gone hard against Maung Nu. As matters stood, he was dismissed with the warning that severe action would be taken if there was a recurrence of political activity on university premises.

Ten days or so later, a tutor came to summon Maung Nu to the principal's office. Mr. Sloss had this counsel to offer: The country was flooded with lawyers—more than the demand warranted. Therefore, if Maung Nu really loved his country he should engage in tasks that could really serve the national interest. Mr. Sloss thought the Co-operative Department in Burma was one such fruitful field. He pointed to the co-operatives in Britain and Europe which were making spectacular headway. In Burma, the department had languished because the Burmese were not interested. Since he considered Maung Nu to be suitable, he had suggested his name, for consideration for the post of assistant registrar, to Mr. Dunn, the finance commissioner, and to Mr. Fogarty, the registrar of co-operative societies. These officials had evinced a desire to meet him. Principal Sloss telephoned them for an appointment. At a subsequent meeting, when Maung Nu still had reservations about joining government service, Mr. Sloss pointed out that it might be government service but it was a department that served the people's interests—not one opposed to them.

Returning to his room, Maung Nu pondered the problem. Although he had a distaste for government service, the fatherly advice

was such that it would be churlish to go against it. At the same time
he was shamed by the prospect of seeing his name emblazoned in
the annals of history as one who had weakened when cajoled with
a job offer. If Principal Sloss had taken a hard line, he would have
been prepared to strike back, even at the risk of expulsion, but the
kindly approach made it impossible for him not to reciprocate in
some tangible form. He therefore wrote out a letter thanking the
principal for his fatherly interest but begging off the co-operative
job because he was not inclined that way. He had also lost interest
in law, he wrote, and therefore wished to discontinue his law studies
at the same time. Thus it was that Maung Nu departed the law
school for the second time.

Next, Maung Nu went to live with a friend in Kalabusti, on
Stockade Road (now renamed Theinbyu Road). He thought of
joining a newspaper but recoiled from the idea of being a salaried
employee. He could write a book, but that would be a play and
few people liked his plays. In the meantime, his mother had begun
to worry about him because she considered Rangoon a dangerous
place to live in, full of strange things, so if he was not doing anything she wished he would come home and marry a girl she approved of and had selected for him. In response to her many importunities U San Tun had to write to his son saying that his mother
wished to be able to see him, and not be separated. The girl who
had taken the mother's fancy was indeed of good moral character
but, in the eyes of Maung Nu, not of sufficient pulchritude, so he
would not go home to marry her.

It was during this period of indecision that Principal Sloss wrote
to Maung Nu asking to see him. As he went to the interview, Maung
Nu could not help wondering how Mr. Sloss had come by his address. Anyway, he was to learn that his former principal had not
given up on him. He still wanted him to take the co-operative job.
After six months he could count on being deputed abroad for further studies. That would give him two years in England and a year
in continental Europe. On his return he would be in a position to
be of real service to his country and would be assured of promotion. Maung Nu wanted to go abroad. In ordinary circumstances
he would have been eager to win a state scholarship, but because
of the clash he had had with the principal he now had serious mis-

givings. He gave the lame excuse that his mother would not like him to travel. To this Mr. Sloss replied that he would be pleased to write Maung Nu's father to explain to his mother how beneficial further studies would be both for him and the country. On his way back home Maung Nu found himself wishing that Principal Sloss would take him for a ne'er-do-well, with no appetite for work, and give him up as a lost cause.

Ten days later U San Tun arrived in Rangoon, bringing with him Mr. Sloss's long letter. He said he was much gratified and Maung Nu's mother approved of his going abroad. Principal Sloss had shown such goodwill that it was incumbent upon him to prove he was not ungrateful. Maung Nu was sufficiently influenced by this as to go to Mr. Sloss and accept his offer. The necessary forms were obtained and Maung Nu filled in the original under the supervision of a beaming principal, who told him it was all right for him merely to sign the remaining three copies, which his staff would prepare for him. In this application there was a column for the principal's remarks, in which ordinarily he would write "Forwarded" to the appropriate authority, but in Maung Nu's case Mr. Sloss took the trouble to append a powerful recommendation.

State scholars were selected based on the results of an entrance examination which Maung Nu was to take in December. This, however, was a nominal affair, the real power to choose being vested in a board. Mr. Sloss was a member of this board, and insofar as university students were concerned his decisions always prevailed. As the examination approached, Maung Nu's uneasiness increased. In the last few days he constantly pictured his friends mocking and jeering at him. He could hear their voices saying he had gone over "to the other side." Finally, with heart triumphant over mind, Maung Nu undid everything by staying away from the examination.

COURTSHIP AND AN ELABORATE ELOPEMENT

About the end of 1930, on a visit with relatives in Pantanaw, Maung Nu was conversing with his aunt, Daw Daw Myaing, outside her yardage shop when a girl passed by. Daw Daw Myaing detained her saying, "Mya Mya, I'd like a word with you." As they sat talking a few feet away from him, Maung Nu took stock of her. The first thing he noticed was that she was decked out in her finery as though she was bound for a social function; the next, that this Mya Mya was none other than Ma Mya Yee, the youngest daughter of U Aung Nyein. He had heard from relatives that Ma Mya Yee, whether going only to the market or to a social event, was not content until she had done her hair in style and set it off with blossoms. The report had it that she smeared her entire body with sandalwood paste and powder and cologne, over which she wore her favourite perfume. As far as exterior ornamentation was concerned, she was certainly sporting all the family jewels, making it certain that she was the same Ma Mya Yee whom he had previously seen only too seldom and for such fleeting moments. Now he was able to pass judgment in his mind: she is indeed very pretty.

Even now it would not do to stare at her. The survey had to be conducted through stolen glances. The first of these already showed she was beautiful; the second, she possessed a certain dignity; the third, she was lovable. After her departure, Daw Daw Myaing said, "Don't you know her? Her father is U Aung Nyein, your old school superintendent." Maung Nu acknowledged he had seen her before but never at close quarters. He himself then left.

But to his cousin, Ma Tin Tin, Maung Nu confided that he was smitten and wanted Ma Mya Yee for his wife. When she suggested that he should go to the father who, after all, was his former superintendent, Maung Nu confessed that as headmaster he had run afoul of U Aung Nyein and the latter hated him. "He's not going to agree to the match; he won't agree even to see me," he said. This brought her to his side. She deprecated the old man's attitude and encouraged him. "After all, you're not a nonentity," she stated. Maung Nu pleaded that he simply did not have the courage. He would like her to speak in his behalf—not to U Aung Nyein, but to the daughter. "Tell her I love her" was his urgent request.

Ma Tin Tin thought she needed a little time to consider the matter, but Maung Nu could brook no delay. "You're an old maid," Maung Nu argued. "You don't know what it is to be in love. I can't wait." So saying he wrote a letter telling Ma Mya Yee he loved her from the moment he saw her at the yardage shop, and that he trusted she would return his love.

When his cousin returned in an hour Maung Nu asked her excitedly whether she brought a reply and promptly received a rebuke. Did he think it was as simple as buying a bowl of noodles over the counter? Maung Nu remained another five days in Pantanaw hoping to hear from Ma Mya Yee. During this period his cousin saw her three times, but all that she was able to convey was the fact that she had accepted the letter but would say nothing in reply. Back in Rangoon, Maung Nu let a week go by and then wrote again to Ma Mya Yee through his cousin, begging her for an answer. During the month that followed the pressure in his love barometer dropped fifty percent. Was he to go through life always disappointed in love? Well, he would write one last letter, which was no sooner said than done. Ten days elapsed and the postman put him on tenterhooks by delivering an envelope which obviously contained another as an enclosure. He laid aside his cousin's note and hastily tore open the other letter which began with a term of endearment: "Ko Ko Nu!" The instant he read this a big ball of joy hit the pit of his stomach with such resonance as to almost tear it wide open. If this sounds like hyperbole it must be remembered that all of Maung Nu's previous romances had been one-sided affairs. He had written to a host of women, more numerous than those listed in these pages. Many names have been omitted because they conjure up no special memories. In the case of still others discretion and concern lest unnecessary embarrassment be caused have kept them secure in the recesses of Maung Nu's memory. But it is true to say there was nothing faintly resembling a response to the innumerable *billets-doux* he had penned. So here, at last, with the spell broken, nothing he said or felt could be called exaggeration.

Maung Nu read the letter over and over. Still not content, he bore it in triumph to his bed and reread it several times. He must have looked like a monkey who accidentally discovered a pocket watch. Had she addressed him as Ko Ko Nu under the tutelage of his dear cousin? Or had she been reading novels and been influenced by the mores of lovers? Perhaps she had overheard the nearest and dearest to him in Pantanaw call him by that name. Whatever the reason, the fact remained she had given his ego a great lift.

At this time Maung Nu was substituting for an assistant editor on a Burmese daily, the *Thitsawaddy*. He took his precious letter to work in his jacket pocket. But as he reached the front door he transferred it to his shirt pocket, next to his heart, a handkerchief stuffed over it to guard against loss. Before any editorial work could be done he felt impelled to reread it again and again. It was borne in upon him then that his previous adventures had not prospered simply because of fate. His love *kan,* he mused, was a wondrous thing. The Buddha, however, had taught about wisdom, or understanding, and effort, or application. Kan did not stand alone. Whatever the kan, no self-respecting girl would find it easy to respond to a proposal brought by the mailman. She would feel inhibited whatever her secret feelings might be. Energy or effort was certainly not lacking on Maung Nu's part, but all along he had failed in understanding female psychology—how a normal, self-respecting girl would react in the situation created by him through the mail. If, instead of enlisting the support of his cousin, Maung Nu had relied on the postal service, he could not have conquered the citadel that was Ma Mya Yee. He would have been compelled to lift the siege and retreat as usual.

In April of 1931 Maung Nu met Inspector of Schools U Po Kya at a social function; this led to the offer of a job. U Po Kya said that the headmastership of Thongwa National School was vacant. The salary would be small and even irregular, so he would have to be prepared for a certain amount of hardship. Maung Nu said he could take the hardship but he was doubtful, in view of his Pantanaw experience, that he could make a go of a similar job in the teaching profession. The inspector told him he knew of Maung Nu's past exploits, some of which were quite creditable. In any event, the Thongwa post was a temporary one and the committee was clamouring to have someone sent to them quickly. Maung Nu went.

From his cousin Ma Tin Tin, Maung Nu heard that Ma Mya Yee's parents had made up their minds he was a thoroughly irresponsible character and it would be impossible to win them over. So, when his school recessed in October at the end of the Buddhist Lent, Maung Nu appeared in Pantanaw, ready to abduct Ma Mya Yee. The cousin blamed him for springing it on her in his usual hasty fashion, but he was able to plead his case and the young couple met by stealth in her house.

Maung Nu's initial problem was how best to address her. Her

relatives called her Mya Mya. Mya ("emerald") would denote a greater sense of intimacy, such as a lover might be expected to profess. When she arrived, however, he had decided on Ma Mya Yee on the theory that when poling a big boat it was advisable to use old-fashioned regulation strokes. He had planned to tell her a myriad of things, but at the sight of her he trembled in every limb and all he found himself saying was "When I return to Thongwa, come with me." He found her restrained and sensible. There was nothing she would like better, she said, but he would have to give her a little time—about one month. He besought her not to keep him in suspense longer than a month, and she gave him a promise. Ten days after he reached Thongwa, her message came: she would be waiting for him on the second waxing of Tazaungmon—two days after the full moon in November.

Maung Nu arrived for his elaborate elopement one day ahead of schedule. But by then the whole of Pantanaw had been mysteriously alerted by the rumour that something of this nature impended. It behooved him to snatch her quickly as she left the parental roof and carry her off to relative safety. Ma Tin Tin's folks were in Pathwè, two hours' journey by motor boat; they could hole up there until the hubbub died down. The arrangement was for Maung Nu to take the public transport to Wakèma, where small motorboats were on hire, find a Johnson Seahorse and be back in Pantanaw by 8:00 P.M. Around 2:00 A.M. Ma Mya Yee would leave her house and join him in the dark. In the event, however, it proved to be one more of those best-laid plots that nearly went awry. Maung Nu, impatient to be back, took a boat an hour ahead of time from Wakèma, but at the entrance into Pantanaw creek the outboard motor failed and he drifted with the tide. At precisely the hour when he should have been meeting his affianced bride, Maung Nu was back in Wakèma hamstrung by a faulty motor. He arrived in Pantanaw more than twenty hours late for the appointment. There he learnt that, in his absence, his cousin Ma Tin Tin had substituted for him and taken Ma Mya Yee to Pathwè.

The waterway to Pathwè being clogged with water hyacinth it was not until 2:00 A.M.—twenty-four hours behind schedule—that Maung Nu was finally able to present himself at the Pathwè home of U Po

Yin and Daw May who, together with his cousins Daw Lay and Ma Tin Tin, were awaiting his arrival. U Po Yin invoked the choicest blessings on the eloping couple, and the company departed after ceremoniously depositing them in the bedroom. Alone at last.

Mya.

Yes, Ko Ko Nu.

I love you very much.

PEACE WITH THE PARENTS-IN-LAW

When U Aung Nyein first learnt of his daughter's disappearance he was moved to wrath. Husbands must be at a premium, he thought, for Ma Mya Yee to have succumbed to the likes of Maung Nu, whom he had long judged to be a brittle, unsteady type. However, as the saying went, unwanted baskets and utensils might be thrown away, but no parents could discard errant sons and daughters. Within a few months, Ma Mya Yee's parents informed cousin Ma Tin Tin that their daughter should come home and that they were reconciled to the idea of receiving Maung Nu as their son-in-law.

When the couple eventually emerged from Pathwè, to go through the motions of restoring Ma Mya Yee to parental care, Maung Nu had misgivings not about the parents but about Ko Ohn Maung, the inhospitable brother. Would he again be barred at the door? But Ko Ohn Maung greeted him with a smile and made him welcome.

In May of 1933, when the Pantanaw National High School reopened, Maung Nu found himself the new superintendent. U Aung Nyein was not so greatly enamoured of him, but he disliked the idea of his daughter moving out with him. The school committee acquiesced because they did not want to tangle with U Aung Nyein, and Maung Nu himself thought he had better behave and be accommodating for at least a year. In 1934, having lived quietly and trouble free, he was able to resign and return to the university to resume his law studies, leaving his wife with her parents in Pantanaw. He realised the outlook for his twice-interrupted law course was less than propitious and he often caught himself wondering how he would fare this time.

EARLY ASSOCIATION WITH AUNG SAN

Ko Nu had been less than a month in law school when he became friendly with Ko Ohn,[1] a tutor from Thaton Hall. Ko Ohn in turn had three friends whom he wished Ko Nu to meet. When the meeting took place in Ko Ohn's room, Ko Nu, who found himself considerably older than the others, let the others do the talking. The first, Ko Kyaw Nyein,[2] was an easy conversationalist with a good sense of humour. The second, Ko Thein Pe,[3] also had a natural flow to his words, but without any frivolity. The third, Ko Aung San,[4] hardly spoke at all; he just sat and stared. The meeting broke up after an hour, but they were to come together with increasing frequency at places appointed by Ko Ohn. For some unaccountable reason, the group met one night less than fifty feet from the principal's office. It was a dark spot and they could not see each other's faces—very dramatic and conspiratorial, except that there was no conspiracy and nothing that was ever discussed was secret. Long after he left the university Ko Nu tried, without finding any rational explanation, to figure out what the purpose of that mysterious meeting might be—whose bright idea it was.

A QUARREL WITH PRINCIPAL SLOSS

Shortly before the October holidays the vice-president of the Rangoon University Students' Union (RUSU) left school, necessitating a by-election when the university reopened. The five-man group put up Ko Nu, who was returned unopposed.

Near closing time in December an important notice was issued under Principal Sloss's signature, instituting preliminary examinations. Only those students who passed these could take the regular examinations in March. Obviously the new measure was motivated

1. After independence, U Ohn served as ambassador first to the Court of St. James's and then to the Soviet Union, where he was for some time dean of the diplomatic corps. Later he became an adviser to Prime Minister U Nu.
2. After independence U Kyaw Nyein became deputy prime minister.
3. U Thein Pe subsequently became a Communist Party leader.
4. Bo Aung San, who became a general during World War II and was assassinated in 1947, is known as the George Washington of Burma.

by Mr. Sloss's desire to improve performance. He wished to improve the standards at the university and the quality of his students. It was already a matter of record that great strides had been made under Principal Sloss's guidance, but he wanted to see Rangoon University universally acknowledged as preeminent in the British Empire.

While designing measures that called for more studying on the part of the students, the principal did not spare himself. All the students, whether they hated or loved Mr. Sloss, would have had to admit that he was an extremely hard worker. However, because of the atmosphere prevailing at the time, everything the white man did was "imperialistic" and suspect. The preliminaries were thus seen as an instrument of oppression.

A demand immediately arose to call an emergency meeting of the student body and this was done in the Union Hall. Condemnatory speeches were made, and as the students became more inflamed they began to talk excitedly about striking. Senior students intervened at this point, and at their suggestion it was decided to send the president of RUSU to the Principal; he was to report back to the student body before the Christmas holidays. The president, not daring enough to go alone, proposed two of his colleagues to be sent along with him. However, the president and two of his colleagues who were deputed to confer with the principal caught cold feet, so by the time the holidays arrived nothing had been done. The mass meeting had assigned no specific task to Vice-President Ko Nu, but when he saw the president and his committee dodge the issue he decided to step in. He sent Ko Kyaw Nyein to the principal and waited in the Mess Hall for the outcome. When Ko Kyaw Nyein returned, it was to report that Mr. Sloss had banged on the table and said he would not be intimidated by groups or individuals. The preliminaries would be held as ordered.

During the meal Ko Nu did some hard thinking, as a result of which he hit upon a plan. Several times, before he unfolded it, he made as if to abandon it, because essentially it was dishonest, but in the end he decided to go through with it because it was for the general good. For the sake of the students he would roast in the lowest reaches of hell.

After lunch he called his five-man cabal together and told them the president and his cohorts, like Po Tha Wa's bull,[5] had charged off at a tangent and something would have to be done. He then revealed his secret plan, which was agreed to. Ko Ohn knew an editor at the *Mawriya;* Ko Nu knew someone at the *New Light of Burma.* To these newspapers the cabal repaired and planted stories saying that Principal Sloss had defied all Burmese political parties and their leaders. Ko Nu's group was well aware that Mr. Sloss's statement had been addressed to them and the Students' Union; the distortion was done deliberately for greater effect. The next day the stories appeared under bold headlines and Principal Sloss was moved to protest. But the newspapers concerned would not retract, nor would they print Sloss's letter.

As the next move, Ko Thein Pe was sent north and Ko Nu went south to hold mass meetings. Ko Thein Pe was known only in Monywa and Budalin, just as no one outside of Wakèma and Pantanaw knew Ko Nu. As they themselves knew, there was no public interest in the grievance they were about to air, with the result that only a few of their friends came to the meeting. In fact one would have had to take an oath to satisfy the townsfolk afterwards that such a meeting had taken place. Nevertheless, token affairs though they were, telegrams were sent to the waiting Ko Kyaw Nyein and Ko Aung San in Rangoon confirming that "Sloss, Get Out" resolutions had been passed. When the *Mawriya* and the *New Light* got the stories they dressed them up to look like huge mass meetings instead of the cockfight audiences they really had been.

Back in Rangoon Ko Nu and Ko Thein Pe addressed a mass meeting on the slopes of the Shwedagon Pagoda. The colonnade chosen was a venue for large meetings. On some occasions the crowds were so thick they overflowed to nearby covered causeways. But on this occasion, since the public's attention had not been caught, there were some thakins from the Dobama Asi-ayone and perhaps a hundred other persons. Principal Sloss, however, was sufficiently alarmed to send barrister U Soe Nyun,[6] a member of the University Governing Board, and Bursar U Tin to explain his side

5. This proverbial bull was very good at making bold displays but would run away the minute a fight started.

6. U Soe Nyun became Burma's first ambassador to the United States.

of the dispute, but the audience consisted of Ko Nu's invitees, and Sloss's men could make no impression. The "Sloss, Get Out" resolution was passed.

The five-man group had planned the Shwedagon meeting as the first stage of the offensive; the next stage would inevitably be a strike. Fortunately for them, the newspapers gave them good coverage and the university gave in. That evening the Governing Board met in emergency session and the preliminary examinations were cancelled. But Principal Sloss demanded that Ko Nu and Ko Kyaw Nyein be expelled. A member, barrister U Thein Maung,[7] objected, saying the expulsions would touch off student protests. As a compromise Vice-Chancellor Dr. Set was asked to meet with the students and obtain a signed statement from Ko Nu and Ko Kyaw Nyein that they would no longer instigate student unrest. Dr. Set was commissioner of the Rangoon Corporation, and the meeting with him took place in his office. The ringleaders refused to sign, despite the fact they had won their point in regard to the preliminaries. Dr. Set sent them away to reconsider their decision and report back at two in the afternoon. Ko Nu and Ko Kyaw Nyein remained obdurate: expulsion was preferable to the signing of the pledge. Dr. Set shook his head, called them troublesome and ended the interview.

This success did not turn Ko Nu's head. He realised that he had been able to take an unbending attitude and still win because the British were respecters of the law. In the absence of the rule of law other imperialists, whether they be capitalists, socialists, or fascists, would have eaten him alive.

MEET THE RUSU PRESIDENT

At the next RUSU elections, Ko Nu was returned unopposed as president. Characteristically, he caused an incident on the very first day. After the election of the RUSU executive committee, the student body had to be invited in for the inauguration. As the meeting convened and the general secretary announced "The President!" everyone rose to his feet. Ko Nu entered and his first words were: "This is all rubbish; in future when I enter nobody stands." Then

7. U Thein Maung later became a chief justice of the Supreme Court in Burma.

he removed his *gaungbaung*[8] and threw it on the table. This conduct gave offence to the committee who, following the general meeting, convened an executive session and censured Ko Nu. They pointed out that the procedure of introducing the president by the general secretary, as well as the mode of dress and deportment, were written in the constitution and had been traditionally adhered to since the formation of RUSU. "You have no right to break precedent," they scolded him. "We stand up to honour not you but the presidency."

Ko Nu was unaware of these requirements. During his terms of office as vice-president and then as president, he did not appear to have read the constitution from beginning to end even once. So he just sat and grinned while his fellow office-holders passed a resolution commanding him to obey the rules. At the next mass meeting Vice-President Ko Raschid[9] read out the stricture and President Ko Nu entered, wearing his gaungbaung.

During his term of office Ko Nu was often on the dais making speeches. What he spoke about he himself does not recall, but, according to one or two sources, out of every five speeches he made, four castigated the practice of saluting the authorities.

A month after Ko Nu was elected president, Principal Sloss went home on leave. In his absence, the acting principal received an application for leave from a Pantanaw student. The application was unusual because it lacked precedent. Day students went home or stayed away at will; boarders usually told assistant wardens or tutors, and Ko Nu himself, whenever he was nostalgic for his wife or his daughter, born in 1934, absented himself. If students wished to keep up attendance they got a friend to answer the roll call.

In the particular instance alluded to, however, the acting principal asked the student why he wished to go home, why the leave application was based on a letter from a sister rather than the parents, and so on. There were no racial overtones, no intention to insult or annoy; the acting principal was merely taking a parental interest in a sixteen-year-old student. But Ko Nu, when he heard about this, immediately jumped to the conclusion that here was white imperialism browbeating a Burman. He dashed off to the

8. Traditional men's headgear.
9. U Raschid served in several capacities in the Cabinet in independent Burma.

acting principal to ask for leave. If he was asked the reason he
would say a letter had come from home. The clincher would come
when asked to produce the letter: Did the tutors in Oxford and
Cambridge dare demand to read such letters? What did happen was
slightly different from the mentally rehearsed act. The conversation
went:

I'd like to go home. Please give me leave.

What's your reason for wanting leave?

I received a letter from home.

All right, you may go.

Nonplussed, Ko Nu could only gape at the acting principal.

THE COST OF CREDULITY

One day Ko Nu found himself in the offices of the *Deedok Journal,*[10] speaking with a thakin from the Dobama Asi-ayone. The subject of conversation was the well-known monk U Ottama who, the
thakin charged, had lost his nationalist zeal and turned corrupt.
There was a party led by five old-time politicians called "Nga-bwint
saing" (Coalition of Five Parties) which had paid the Reverend
U Ottama one thousand rupees for addressing each political rally
in their behalf. The thakin urged that on the forthcoming National
Day Ko Nu should mount the rostrum and condemn U Ottama
as a traitor. The thakin said he would be doing the same at a
Fytche Square rally. When the thakin left, Deedok U Ba Choe,
managing editor of the *Deedok Journal,* warned Ko Nu to be careful not to do anything because the thakin was an unreliable character. But Ko Nu had made up his mind to "expose" U Ottama.

Properly speaking, the RUSU was not a political association and
had no business interfering in Burma's politics. Even if the rules
permitted, Ko Nu should not have taken a position until he had
personally investigated the charges against U Ottama. Then, if the
charges were found to be true, it would still be incumbent upon

10. A nationalist weekly in Burmese. For some time before the Japanese occupation of Burma it led a very strong anti-Japanese campaign.

Ko Nu to consult with the committee and get their approval before he mounted the rostrum. Ko Nu fulfilled none of these obligations. He had made a unilateral decision.

This propensity for making rash judgments often made him ridiculous. Those knowing of his overcredulousness took advantage of him. His friends might warn him he was too quick to believe and should be more on his guard, but he resented such advice. To him, to be told he was too quick to believe was no different from being told he was gullible or stupid. His own image of himself being one of prescience, with the flame of genius burning in his soul, he took advice for insult.

On National Day, the quadrangle outside Union Hall was filled with eminent guests from the city, reporters, and undergraduates. At this ceremony President Ko Nu gave vent to all that the thakin leader had told him. He levelled all kinds of accusations against the Reverend U Ottama and condemned him out of hand as a traitor. At the Fytche Square rally, which was being held simultaneously, the thakin leader responsible did not even mention U Ottama by name.

U Ottama was a national hero who had suffered imprisonment and atrocities and who had first opened the eyes of the country and put it forever in his debt. When they heard his accusations and sweeping indictments, the students—particularly the members of the executive committee—were moved to anger against Ko Nu. The next day the newspapers pounced on Ko Nu. "Base," "inhuman," and "ungrateful" were some of the adjectives used.

A FIENDISH TATTOO ON TIN CANS

Before the end of his term of office as RUSU president, Ko Nu had another interesting clash with Principal Sloss. With the approach of the March finals, the students took to their books with a vengeance. But in the warden's house outside Sagaing Hall there was the sound of revelry by night, almost every other day. This prompted Ko Kyaw Myint, a Sagaing student, to protest and the warden bawled him out. That very night when the singing and merrymaking at the warden's were at their height, Ko Kyaw Myint collected some friends and beat a fiendish tattoo on tin cans. Subsequently, acting on a report made by the assistant warden, the principal suspended Ko Kyaw Myint for a year.

Ko Kyaw Myint, thinking to himself that rustication was preferable to expulsion, would not tell Ko Nu. He was packing his bags quietly when Ko Nu, told of the incident by someone else, arrived. Ko Kyaw Myint was extremely reluctant even to discuss the case, but Ko Nu wasted no time. "You're surrendering without a fight," he charged, and, suspension order in hand, he led Ko Kyaw Myint to a barrister in the city. The advice they received was that a direct complaint should be filed in court, demanding damages from the principal for the anguish caused by his unjust order. The next day the principal called Ko Kyaw Myint to say, "Stop the suit and I'll rescind my order."

RUDENESS ON THE RAMPAGE

Then came the close of the academic year and the annual meeting of the RUSU. This time the ceremony was truly imposing. Present were the prime minister of Burma and members of the Cabinet, members of the Legislative Council, puisne judges of the High Court, barristers, and other prominent citizens. Ko Nu's presidential speech began with commendable restraint and in the middle it still observed the proprieties, but it trailed off into a diatribe. His obsession about students saluting the faculty was brought out with virulence. From being merely spirited he became uncontrollably aggressive so that when it came to the part about the sixteen-year-old student and his leave application, he blurted out: "If the principal had asked to read my letter from home I'd have kicked him right out of his office." It was an unfortunate speech, and although it met with student applause Ko Nu realised, when the hysteria left him, that he had put on a shameful exhibition. There came to him with poignancy the words of Mr. Justice Brown, one of the guests, who had sidled up to him with the laughing remark: "You had a good case over that letter but your presentation was bad. The judgment goes against you."

The faculty did not ask to read private letters at Oxford and Cambridge. This Ko Nu knew. What he did not seem to realise was that at those universities students also do not threaten professors with physical violence.

EXPULSION AND THE STUDENT STRIKE

Following the annual general meeting, classes were closed to enable students to prepare for the final examinations. Ko Nu, having spent his time in extracurricular activities, decided he would catch up on his reading and began turning the pages of law books. He savoured the moment of contingent success. The impediments to his first two tries at law had disappeared; now he was within reach of his law degree. Three days went by and a letter arrived from the principal's office. Another offer of an assistant registrar's job, no doubt. To accept this offer would send him floating in the spittle of the students. Ko Nu smirked. He opened the letter. It was not an offer of anything but an expulsion order. He stared at the book open before him. "Miss Law," he said, "I love you, and because I do I've come back to you three times. But it's like the popular refrain:

> The two of us, each
> the other desires.
> But the outsider cometh
> And with him ruin.

He closed the manual, saying goodbye. Then he went to bed and slept. When he awoke, his first thought was of the commotion the letter might cause on the eve of finals. He decided he would tell no one. He burnt the paper, changed, and went to the cinema.

The news of course was out. Some students learnt about it from the principal's office, and within twenty-four hours it was known throughout the campus. A delegation of student leaders headed by vice-president Ko Raschid arrived and at once began reproaching Ko Nu. Why had they not been told? they demanded. They brushed aside Ko Nu's excuse that he did not want to disturb the students so close to the examinations. "This is not a personal matter; it is the concern of the entire union," they asserted. "We're not going to take it lying down."

Ko Nu pleaded with them in vain. They surprised him by saying not only he but Ko Aung San also was getting sacked.

"Whatever for?" Ko Nu inquired.

"In his magazine there is an article entitled, 'Hellhound at

Large,' aimed at a member of the faculty. The authorities want to know who wrote it and Ko Aung San won't tell."

So that was that. The RUSU executive committee met and resolved to boycott the examinations. Then an emergency mass meeting was convened and the resolution of the executive committee was read out. As vice-president Ko Raschid finished reading, the air was rent with shouts of "Strike! We will strike!"

OUTSIDE THE IVORY TOWER

The 1936 University Strike lasted four months. The authorities yielded to the extent of readmitting expellees Ko Nu and Ko Aung San, agreeing to form a University Inquiry Committee to look into the students' complaints, and incorporating suitable provisions in the University Act. The strike was then called off, but Ko Nu and some other students did not return to classes. They chose to leave the university.

With two of his friends, Ko Hla Pe[11] and Ko Tun Ohn,[12] Ko Nu began working on a project to set up a national university. He also apprenticed himself at the *Deedok Journal,* where he wrote a number of articles, and began to concentrate on play writing. Since his long plays were not popular with the reading public, their publication in the *Deedok* would have hurt its prestige. Consequently, Ko Nu produced one-act plays, all of which editor U Ba Choe, with unfailing good humour, published. After a year at the *Deedok Journal* Ko Nu founded the Nagani (Red Dragon) Book Club. A small room was found in the western wing of the Scott Market at a cheap rental, and the bookstall became a busy meeting ground for politicians with ill-digested views, students, and ordinary book buyers.

The Nagani was modelled on the Left Book Club of Victor Gollancz in England. It proved an immediate success. In addition to the monthly list of popular books, Ko Nu was able to add, once every two or three months, a supplementary list of special publications. Very soon the *Nagani Journal* made its appearance and the

11. U Hla Pe later served as a deputy minister and minister of defence in U Nu's Cabinet after independence.

12. U Tun Ohn later served as commissioner of the Corporation of Rangoon after independence.

Nagani Daily (newspaper) was projected. But it never saw the light of day. The Second World War arrived instead in 1942, and Thakin Nu (he had become a thakin by then) and others were imprisoned on charges of sedition and obstructing the war effort.

In Ko Nu's place, Ko Raschid was elected president of the Rangoon University Students' Union for 1936-37. He was succeeded by Ko Aung San for 1937-38, in which year the Inquiry Committee completed its work and accepted the more important of the students' demands.

In due course the Inquiry Committee's recommendations reached the government headed by Dr. Ba Maw, which then prepared to pass them through the legislature. The students were overjoyed.

At this time there occurred a series of riots involving Buddhists on one side and Moslems on the other. There was considerable knife play and many deaths and injuries resulted. One day Ko Nu, conversing with a friend on the upper floor of the Scott Market, was distracted by shouts emanating from Twenty-fifth Street. A Buddhist monk, out begging, was being assaulted by a Moslem. It was only when Ko Nu and his group appeared on the scene that the assailant broke off his knife attack and escaped up a flight of stairs. The monk, suffering from severe head wounds, was placed on a rickshaw and Ko Nu himself accompanied him to the hospital.

Returning from the hospital, Ko Nu found the crowd excitedly discussing the attempt on the monk's life. The Nagani Book Club had become a hotbed of radical views. Upon one man stating that it was the Buddhists who were bearing the brunt of things, another joined in with the assertion that Dr. Ba Maw was in league with the sons of Missiri Khan of Tseekai Maung Taulay Street and was leaning to the side of the Moslems. This was a perfectly baseless charge. There was no reason why Dr. Ba Maw should lean in the manner alleged. But gullible Ko Nu accepted it completely. He did not wish the Buddhists to suffer at the hands of the Moslems, nor vice versa; all he wanted was a speedy end to the riots, with the government dispensing justice impartially. Therefore, once he had got it into his head that Prime Minister Dr. Ba Maw was aiding and abetting his Moslem friends, he could not rest for thinking of ways and means of ousting the Ba Maw government.

One day, while several schemes were churning in his mind, Ko Nu went to visit with friends near the Rangoon Central Jail. On his return he saw, near the General Hospital, a pushcart containing the corpse of a murdered dock worker. A Moslem was alleged to have struck him with a lance. Seeing the body covered with blood, Ko Nu conjured up a vision of Dr. Ba Maw which prompted him to act swiftly. At the university, finding Ko Aung San absent, Ko Nu composed a statement and left it in the RUSU office with instructions that copies be sent to Dr. Ba Maw and the newspapers. The statement denounced Dr. Ba Maw for siding with the Moslems and causing the deaths of Buddhists and demanded his resignation forthwith. Students in their thousands were to be required to sign this statement.

That evening Ko Aung San and a group of students appeared at the Nagani Book Club.

Ko Nu, your arrangements are poor. I have a better idea.

What is it?

In a day or two, the Ba Maw government will be introducing the University Bill in the Legislative Council. We will say we don't want this bill and call on members to oppose it. If Dr. Ba Maw proceeds with the bill over our protests it is probable his government will fall. If he holds back, he will be denied the kudos which he expects through passage of the University Act. This act has been a source of great pride to him.

Yes, I agree. Yours is a better plan.

The very next day Ko Aung San and his executive committee invaded the Legislative Council and flooded it with pamphlets calling on members to oppose the University Bill. Dr. Ba Maw was forced to withhold the proposed legislation. This caused a stir at the university, and resentment mounted against the RUSU executive committee. A mass meeting, which was heavily attended, was held in the central dining hall. Speeches were made in violent denunciation of the RUSU executive committee and demanding: (1) that an emergency meeting of the entire Students' Union be at once convoked, and (2) that at the meeting a resolution be passed expressing no confidence in the members of the executive committee and dismissing them. Both of these proposals were adopted without dissent.

Following this incident, Ko Aung San and some of his colleagues on the executive committee went to the Nagani Book Club. They told Ko Nu that the students were in an uproar and that their demands for an emergency meeting would have to be met, at 5:00 P.M. that very day. Since they were going to be thrown out, would it not be wiser to resign before the vote?

This seemed to Ko Nu to be a defeatist attitude. The battle had not even begun. Fight it, and you might lose, but you might also win. It was far better to have two possible outcomes than just one, and an adverse one at that.

"Have no fear; fight the scoundrels. I'll fight by your side," Ko Nu told them.

The student leaders having departed, Ko Nu prepared for that evening's meeting of the union. He was no longer a member of the union. Would it be proper for him to attend? It was possible that ex-presidents earned the right to be perpetual members, but he could not be certain. He had served as vice-president for six months, as president for a year, but he had not once read the constitution. Failure to acquaint himself with relevant literature had been one of his shortcomings. His mind raced to an earlier time when he proved unequal to the challenges of a similar situation.

It was shortly after he had left law school as a result of singing the Dobama Song in Thaton Hall. He read in the newspapers that the Rangoon University Students' Union was calling a mass meeting to pass a resolution in support of dominion status for Burma. Burmese political leaders were even then at a round table conference in London seeking such a measure, and a RUSU resolution would strengthen their hand. Ko Nu, who wanted no part of dominion status but only complete independence for Burma, decided he would attend the mass meeting and oppose the resolution. His companion on this expedition was Saya Tint, a former master from Myoma National High School. As they were about to leave the house, Saya Tint, putting on his shoes, broke the laces, which he regarded as a bad omen. He cautioned Ko Nu to be careful with his speech.

The mass meeting was held not at union headquarters but in the gymnasium. In vain Ko Nu tried to ascertain why the site had been changed. On the dais were ranged members of the union executive

committee. As the proceedings commenced, someone moved a resolution that the entire union support the demand for dominion
status in the British Commonwealth. Three or four others stood up
to second the resolution. Then the president asked if there was
anyone wishing to oppose it and Ko Nu, with finger upraised,
ascended the platform. He said he rejected dominion status and
would not be satisfied with anything less than complete freedom.
But he had scarcely uttered fifteen words when he was cut short.
A member of the executive committee had risen on a point of
order. He said Ko Nu was not a student and had no right to speak.
The president then rang a little bell twice and ordered Ko Nu off
the platform. Ko Nu argued that it was a national issue which concerned everybody and that as a Burman it was his privilege to state
his views. The shouted reply he received was that he was out of
order and that he could air his views elsewhere, whereupon thirty
or forty among the crowd called upon him to stop disputing the
president's decision and to get out. Not a single voice was raised in
Ko Nu's favour. Confused and angry, Ko Nu was unable to continue
and had to leave the meeting amidst cries of "Shame!"

Moments passed in reminiscence. This time, however, Maung Nu
determined, he would not be shouted down. "Let them throw me
out, if they dare," he said to himself. "For the sake of my friends
I'll brave shouts and insults."

Long before the appointed hour, before the doors could be
opened, the student body could be seen milling about the place.
The moment Ko Aung San declared the meeting open, Ko Nu took
the rostrum. He capitulated point by point the ulterior motives that
had impelled the moves of the proposed no-confidence motion. The
crowd that had come to support the motion was completely swayed
in the opposite direction. Within ten minutes it was giving bent to
catcalls and cries of "Shame!" and "Get out!" but they were directed,
not at the speaker, but at the instigator of the ouster move, who sat
silent and unbelieving. As Ko Nu proceeded, supporters of the
executive committee and the sudden converts rose en masse in
various corners of the hall and, pointing their fingers at the hapless
student leader now completely shattered by the fickleness of the
audience, demanded his immediate withdrawal. Finally, as pande-
monium reigned, the student bowed out.

PLUNGING INTO POLITICS

His term of office over, Ko Aung San left the university and for a time no one knew where he had gone. But one afternoon he appeared at the residence of Ko Nu and Ma Mya Yee, who had joined her husband in Rangoon and lived with him in a house on Stockade Road.

Ko Nu, shall we join the Dobama Asi-ayone?

I shan't.

And why not?

I don't wish to enter politics.

You can't just dodge issues like that.

I'm not avoiding anything.

Those who should be in politics and refuse to be are ducking something.

I have no taste for politics.

And yet you were vice-president of the Fabian Party.

That was because Deedok U Ba Choe had proposed me in absentia. I resigned as soon as the election was over.

The taste for politics develops as you go along. It grows on you.

Po[13] Aung San, I've been observing you. You are a good judge of character, but it seems you've completely misjudged me.

Indeed! What are you?

I'm an exponent of the one-shot deal.

What exactly does that mean?

Let me put it this way: for a politician, politics is a full-time job. He lives it every moment of the day, while he sits or stands or walks or lies down. It absorbs him completely. With me, I must have a cause for concern before I can act. The action done, I no longer wish to see anybody. I want to withdraw into a corner, there to think, to dream, and to write a little.

13. A term of endearment.

What are you prattling about? Is now the time to be dreaming and scribbling?

This gave Ko Nu pause. But he continued.

Po Aung San, why don't you do this? You and your political friends go ahead and join the Dobama Asi-ayone. Then, when you have a fight on your hands, call me and I'll join in. If I fall in battle that will be the end of me. But if I survive I'll find a nook to dream and compose in. Don't let me be a politician in perpetuity.

After independence you can do what you like. Till then you must be a politician. There are no ifs or buts about it. We'll go this very moment to join up.

There ensued two hours of argument on "to be or not to be." Finally:

Po Aung San, we're both tired, so let's leave it at that. Give me a little time, one month's time, to reflect.

That's a waste of time. Let's go now.

Ko Nu thought it would be uncomradely to refuse Ko Aung San's request outright, so he decided to comply. As they were about to board the bus it occurred to Ko Nu that he would feel too self-conscious using the prefix *thakin* (lord). But Ko Aung San cut him short. "Would you rather be styled *kyun?*" he asked, citing the Burmese word for vassal.

The Dobama Asi-ayone was discovered meeting in one room on upper Phayre Street, hard by the railway station. The place was dimly lit by a single kerosene lantern of the kind used by night watchmen. The electricity had been cut off because of unpaid bills. Within the room sat the president, Thakin Hteiktin Kodawgyi, and three or four other thakins. Ko Aung San said he wished to join the association. Ko Nu said nothing. The president issued two membership cards to Ko Aung San. Each of these cost four annas. Ko Aung San paid eight annas. Henceforth the two men would be known as Thakin Nu and Thakin Aung San.

3

Nationalist and Buddhist

DOBAMA POLITICS

In those days, Thakin Aung San and Thakin Nu were well known among the students, but the political world knew little about them. When they joined the Dobama Asi-ayone they brought to that organisation support from the student masses, but it could not be said that they brought much public support. The one who contrived to gain the most public endorsement was Thakin Kodaw Hmaing, who was revered by the people as a true patriot, respected for his rectitude, and venerated by priest and layman alike for his eminence as a man of letters. Through the machinations of Thakin Thein Pe, he became the patron of the Dobama Asi-ayone which, in turn, used his influence to propagate itself.

In 1938 the Dobama Asi-ayone split; one half became known as the Thakin Kodaw Hmaing faction; the other as the Thakin Ba Sein faction. The Asi-ayone headed by Thakin Kodaw Hmaing included Thakins Hla Baw, Lay Maung, Hteiktin Kodaw Gyi, Mya, Tin, Aung San, Than Tun, Soe, Hla Pe, Nu, and others. After the split, Thakin Hla Baw became president and Thakin Aung San general secretary, with Thakin Than Tun as joint general secretary. Its headquarters were moved from Phayre Street to Pazundaung Yegyaw Street.

Among these men, Thakin Hla Baw was noted for his honesty, generosity, and patriotism; he was universally loved. He also had a habit of speaking plainly and directly.

Thakin Aung San, as general secretary, was stationed at headquarters. He was assisted by three young men, Thakins Tin U, Thet
Tin, and Hla Maung.

The joint general secretary, Thakin Than Tun, was a teacher at
the Moslem High School in Kandawglay. He devoted his spare
time to running the headquarters together with Thakin Aung San.
The two could be best described as an architect (Aung San) and an
engineer (Than Tun). Thakin Aung San was bilingual and spoke
and wrote in English and Burmese with facility. Thakin Than Tun
excelled in Burmese and worked faster in this medium. Both were
voracious readers. Thakin Aung San had a communications problem. It was not that he was testy or quarrelsome; he simply refused
to pretend where his likes and dislikes were concerned. If he was
displeased, he would turn away his head or pick up something to
read. If someone he disliked should address him, he was apt to
ignore him. Thakin Than Tun was of a different calibre. He was
relatively smooth and easy at public relations. Thakin Aung San
might on occasion give vent to anger; Thakin Than Tun was ever
a controlled person. Thakin Than Tun was economical with words;
Thakin Aung San, when the mood seized him, would discourse for
hours, giving others little chance to interrupt. Two examples may
be cited of the latter's idiosyncracies, one when he was Burmese
defence minister under the Japanese; the other when he became
president of the Anti-Fascist People's Freedom League.

As defence minister, General Aung San went to live near the
home of a secretary,[1] making it incumbent on the latter to call on
him. Knowing of the minister's propensity for long conversations,
the secretary chose five in the afternoon, judging that he would be
dismissed soon afterwards, before the dinner hour. But the general
had come home early hungry and, by the time the secretary arrived,
had already eaten his food. When nine o'clock struck, the secretary
tried to take his leave, giving as his excuse that he was afraid he
had kept the general from his dinner. It took but one minute for
General Aung San to pause and reassure the secretary in regard to
dinner. Then he resumed the conversation where it had been
broken off and talked nonstop until eleven. By then the poor secre-

1. The highest bureaucratic post in each ministry was that of the permanent
secretary, who worked just under the appointed minister.

tary was more troubled by a full bladder than an empty stomach and tried to beat a hasty retreat. General Aung San saw him to the gate, where he lingered for another forty-five minutes, until the secretary, almost sobbing, muttered an apology and fled.

The second instance was General Aung San's performance, as president of the Anti-Fascist People's Freedom League, at a Central Committee meeting. His speech lasted over six hours.

Thakin Soe was another interesting character. As a member of the Dobama Asi-ayone executive committee, he was the one closest to Thakin Nu, to whom he confided many a secret. (Thakin Nu has not divulged these confidences to this day.) Thakin Soe was a strange-looking man. He smiled often, but the odd thing about his face was that even when he laughed his eyes were stern and forbidding. Like Thakins Aung San and Than Tun, he too was a most literate individual. His mastery of communist literature was more impressive than that of the other two. Politicians tended to regard Thakin Soe as a man of violence; actually, although he would not hesitate to use violence when the occasion called for it, he was at the same time capable of kindness and gentleness. He knew how to respect other people, paying honour where honour was due. There was a politeness inherent in him, a source of popularity wherever he went. During the conflict between the thakins and Dr. Ba Maw's Sinyetha (Poor Man) Party, Thakin Soe alone remained on good terms with the Sinyetha. He was a skilful violinist and had a good voice, singing both popular and classical songs.

Thakin Lay Maung, Thakin Mya, and Thakin Tin were some of the original thakins who were present at the founding of the Dobama Asi-ayone. They fashioned it into an instrument for the gaining of independence. Thakin Lay Maung had a natural reserve; Thakin Mya was known for his patience; and Thakin Tin had a facile way of explaining complexities to the man in the street. The Dobama Asi-ayone included many other notable characters, but space precludes listing all of them.

Thakin Nu, given as he was to gaping, dreaming, and composing, and having found a new interest (which will be more fully explained later in this chapter) was an infrequent visitor at the Dobama headquarters. He might attend a committee meeting, or go to see Thakin Aung San, or hand in a contribution, but in the main he stayed away. His political duties were few, confined generally to field trips at the behest of the general secretary.

One of Thakin Nu's political rallies was to be in Pyawbwè, where feelings between the thakins and Galon[2] U Saw's followers were running high. U Saw at this time was minister of forests. There had been an earlier incident (probably at Pegu) during which Galon U Saw's arrival was greeted with the beating of tin cans by the thakins, and U Saw's men had charged them with staves and poles. The Dobama Asi-ayone had since then ordered that U Saw should be confronted everywhere he went with a tin can parade. U Saw in turn went on record saying such demonstrators would be beaten with long sticks.

Thus when U Saw decided not long afterwards to visit Pyawbwè in response to an invitation by his supporters, the thakins girded for action. Pyawbwè was a thakin stronghold, and they promised to give the visitor a deafening reception, to which U Saw's men countered with the threat to strike down the disturbers. As tensions mounted, the authorities realised the civil police would be unable to cope with the situation. They brought in the military police, with a detachment of horses. The thakins demanded leadership of the Dobama Asi-ayone headquarters and Thakins Nu and Ba Yin (of Dallah) were deputed.

They arrived in Pyawbwè a day in advance of U Saw and were told excitedly of the thakins' plot to get even with the galon storm-troopers. Not all the thakins would be beating drums; some would lie in wait with knives, and when U Saw's men charged with sticks the thakin rearguard would cut them down. This of course was in contravention of Dobama policy, which then laid down that violence was to be avoided and the struggle against the British pursued with peaceful means.

Thakin Nu accordingly told the thakins they must be prepared for a beating and must not retaliate. If they disagreed with this policy they could stay away. The Pyawbwè thakins then expressed the wish that he should explain the party line to their supporters in Mindan quarter. When Thakins Nu and Ba Yin arrived there, they found it to be the centre of the knife industry, where the best

2. U Saw and his followers were called Galon after a very powerful bird in Hindu mythology.

sword blades were manufactured. The thakins here were truculent. "Four cuts to the enemy's one" was their motto. They refused to remain passive in a fight. "Then, stay away," they were told, and they complied.

Pyawbwè railway station faced the highway running north and south. By eight o'clock in the morning, one hundred thakins of the "Tin Can Brigade" were gathered there. This front line was flanked by Thakins Nu and Ba Yin. Behind them stood several rows of thakins and thakinmas (female thakins) and their supporters. The Mindan thakins had not stayed away after all but were out in force, making up the rear. They carried umbrellas, in which were concealed sharp blades. But Thakin Nu did not know about this at the time.

As the thakins lined up to the left of the road, U Saw's galons occupied the right, facing them. They had their staves out but were clever enough to use them as standards topped with flags and pennents.

At 9:00 A.M., as U Saw arrived in his long, white carriage, the thakins gave tongue through loud speakers, mocking the minister. "Galon" is the Burmese version of *garuda,* the mythical bird that carried Vishnu, but U Saw was being branded a "lada," or vulture. As the cheerleader called out "Lada U Saw," the crowd shouted, "Not wanted!" The din increased as U Saw, flanked by supporters, strode up from the station. This was the signal for empty tins and ironware of all kinds to come into play. The noise was overpowering. Those holding the long sticks ground their teeth in exasperation, but not a single banner-waver crossed the road, completely policed as it was by troopers carrying rifles and on horseback. As U Saw passed down the line, it needed just one hothead to touch off a riot. Then knives would have flashed and guns gone off. Many would have been trampled by police horses. U Saw, however, passed unmolested.

U Saw addressed a meeting at a cinema house. The thakins did the same in another. In the evening, Thakin Nu and others went to the house of Thakin Htay, the local president, and had been there some time when U Saw's supporters appeared outside. They chanted, "Cooringhee Ideology, Not Wanted!" This was in retaliation for the tin can demonstration, the insinuation being that the drummers were not Burmese but Cooringhee coolies.[3] Thakin Htay immediately seized a lance and went after the enemy, but it was dark outside, and he did not even see his assailant before he was attacked and knocked out. This touched off a counterdemonstration by the thakins outside the house of U Hpyo Tha, U Saw's main supporter, which Thakin Nu had the greatest difficulty in quelling.

Then there was the time when he was sent to mollify the oilfield workers who had become disgruntled with the Dobama Asi-ayone. With him was Thakin Soe. Arrived at their destination, they learned with disquiet that the workers' complaints were more deeply rooted than they had thought. Thakin Nu therefore took the precaution of warning Thakin Soe in advance to be patient and diplomatic.

The meeting took place in a monastery building. The instant Thakin Soe got up to speak, there was an interruption. Thakin Khin Zaw, then either the general secretary or an executive committee member of the Oilfield Workers' Association, without so much as a by-your-leave, approached the chair and began sauntering up and down the aisle. If the purpose of his singular action was not clear enough, his accompanying remarks expressed disgust with the Dobama Asi-ayone. To a man of Thakin Soe's disposition this proved intolerable. He bounded to a nearby stand holding up an amplifier and wrenched from it an iron rod.

Crying out, "What are you doing, man?" Thakin Nu reached him just in time to try to wrest the weapon from him. Even after Thakin Nu's expostulations, Thakin Soe clung to the weapon until he was allowed to continue with his speech. There was of course a commotion, with many leaving the place or milling about. The workers were in a vile mood, and the sight of Thakin Soe, pouting and aggressive, did nothing to improve matters. Fortunately, there was no bloodshed. But it was touch and go.

INFLUENCE OF THE *Payeik*

Unlike other thakins, Nu very seldom went to the party headquarters. A new interest, which his colleagues in the Dobama Asi-ayone considered a fad, was keeping Thakin Nu, the gazer, away

3. South Indians imported by the British for menial labour. They were in the habit of merrymaking to the accompaniment of drums.

from party work. In fact this "fad" was something quite serious that happened in his life, and thus it should be explained in detail.

Three years before he became a thakin, Ko Nu, as he was then called, happened to visit Kyaung-ama-chaung village near Moulmeingyun. There he saw a man who had been struck dumb late in life because, as the villagers related it, he had chanced to cut a tree and the custodian *nat,* or spirit, had been affronted. The man had grown children, and up to the time of his paralysis had talked normally. Now he could only blather *"nè-nè, nè-nè,"* and point to the woods as towards a scene of tragedy.

On his return to Rangoon Ko Nu mentioned this incident to a group of friends gathered at the *Deedok Journal* and expressed a keen desire to help the unfortunate woodcutter. They told him it was voodooism, or *payawga,* and that Deedok U Ba Choe was an expert on this subject.

Deedok U Ba Choe's prognosis was that the payawga could be lifted by someone who had drunk fetish water called *inn.*[4] He signified his willingness to administer one of several inn in his possession. Maung Nu learnt that there were the inn of the four great elements, and the *a-hta-ya-tha inn* and the *weikza mayeikdi inn.* The first two he could drink straightaway, but not yet the weikza mayeikdi. The reason for the discrimination was that it was an inn of great potency and the oath that went with it was fearsome in the extreme.

Pressed on what this oath consisted of, Deedok U Ba Choe said the wording ran like this: "I solemnly promise that from this moment onwards I shall abstain from adultery and spiritous liquor; should I be guilty of breaking this oath, may I vomit blood and die on the spot."

Ko Nu said that he foresaw no hardship in taking this oath, but what were the benefits in drinking the inn? He was told that the custodian nat would be bound to help inn drinkers by giving them

4. *Inn* derives its power from the sacred texts of the Three Noble Gems—the Buddha, the Law, and the Assembly. These are required to be committed to writing on special paper manufactured in the Shan State of Maingkaing (paper of Western manufacture cannot be used). Various masters illustrate the inn in different ways, using numerals, symbols, zodiac signs, graphs, and squares in a recognisable pattern. These papers are then reduced to a fine ash and administered, mixed with water, at appropriate times.

the power over payawga for as long as the oath was honoured; the moment it was broken, its curse would strike.

The exorcism of payawga, it was explained, was a relatively simple matter. By chanting over a cup of water the Nine Glories (of the Buddha) it would be filled with magic, and the sprinkling of this water would rid the sufferer of payawga. The a-hta-ya-tha inn and weikza mayeikdi were so miraculous mere proximity would suffice to drive out the evil spirit. Breaking the oath, on the other hand, was to invite certain disaster. The curse of the first two inn would not be more than maiming or insanity, but the third inn resulted in death.

Although Ko Nu kept insisting that he was ready to swallow all three inn, Deedok U Ba Choe would not indulge him. He pointed out that the year before a pupil of his had badgered him so much that he gave him the weikza mayeikdi. Shortly afterwards the man slept with the wife of a fellow worker in a Dallah rice mill, coughed up blood, and died.

Undeterred, Ko Nu said he would drink the weikza mayeikdi, in preparation for which he examined the inn already prepared by U Ba Choe. These were marked in letters and numerals. Number nine for example denoted the Nine Glories of the Buddha, number six the Six Glories of the Law, number four the Four Noble Truths, and again the number nine, the Nine Glories of the Assembly. The meanings of the acronyms *sa-da-ba-wa, ta-tha-nya-kha, ka-pa-da-wa, ya-ga-ba-da,* and so on, were explained according to the definitions of the sages.

Consequently one night, at about 11:00 P.M., U Ba Choe led Ko Nu to a corner of the Shwedagon Pagoda and administered the a-hta-ya-tha and the weikza mayeikdi inn, after Ko Nu had solemnly sworn that he would not commit adultery and that he would refrain from drinking intoxicants. Beginning the next day he was to drink regular doses of the four-elements inn. This was a compound and had to be drunk separately as earth inn, air inn, fire inn, and water inn on successive days and in rotation.

Deedok U Ba Choe then spoke to Ko Nu in adjuration: "Maung Nu, it is possible to plant a tree by throwing a seed into the ground. You must have seen mango and neem trees that have come up this way. But the good gardener does not grow them this way. He prepares the soil, pours water over the newly planted seed, and feeds it manure. He raises the earth around it from time to time and puts up a fence to keep off animals and poultry. Such a tree flourishes and bears good fruit. In the same way, the recitation of the rosary and incantation of the *payeik*,[5] the observance of the Eight Precepts within predetermined periods of nine, ten, thirty, thirty-seven, and forty-five days, and penances such as the avoidance of eating meat are good methods for increasing the powers of the inn. Give to these devotional exercises your concentration and a calmness of spirit. The Great Payeik contains eleven *thok*. If you cannot recite all eleven daily, you should at least recite the *Mingala Thok,* the *Yadana Thok,* the *Myitta Thok,* the *Khanda Thok,* the *Artanatiya Thok,* and the *Pokbanhna Thok*. On the days of the sabbath, which should be prolonged as much as possible, it is permissible to eat meat but more meritorious to eat vegetables. By these means, increase the power and efficacy of the inn."

The next day Ko Nu bought his beads and prayer outfit at the Shwedagon Pagoda and began to practise all that U Ba Choe had taught him. His waking moments were spent in prayer, meditation, and inn drinking. He adopted a system of alternating seven days of normal living with seven days of sabbath,[6] which he later prolonged to nine-day periods and finally to forty-five days at a stretch. He observed sabbath throughout the ninety days of the Buddhist Lent, from the full moon of Waso to the full moon of Thadingyut, which roughly corresponds to the period from the full moon in July to the full moon in October. When he was observing the sabbath he did not eat anything after noon each day.

With the inn drinking, the rosary, the payeik, and the sabbath becoming established as a way of life, Ko Nu was, for the greater part of the day, to be found sitting on the floor before the altar. As the hours and days of immobility before the altar continued,

5. The *payeik,* or *wut,* is a collection of eleven sermons, or *thok,* of the Buddha which will protect believers against evil and therefore must be chanted daily.

6. Strict religious observances, or *U-paw-tha-hta thila,* in which the Buddhist refrains from killing, stealing, having sexual relations, lying, drinking intoxicants, eating any solid food after noon, enjoying any form of amusement, using scents, and resting upon luxurious couches or beds.

Ma Mya Yee could not restrain herself from poking gentle fun at
him. From making faces and giggling she carried her teasing to
the point of open laughter. Then she began calling him names
such as "the great spiritualist and diviner," all of which he studiously ignored; but one day he took umbrage and walked out of
the house. He was gone only about an hour, but he had cooled
down sufficiently to return in search of his wife. She was lying
in bed and greeted his return with a look of great relief. She confessed that during his absence she had been overcome by an intense
desire to take her own life. What actually brought about this suicidal urge no one was able to fathom, but the fact remained that
thereafter Ma Mya Yee took no more liberties with her husband.

Of the three religious observances that followed on his initiation
to the inn rite, the rosary, the sabbath, and the payeik, the payeik
was the form that most inspired him. In three years he ceased imposing on himself prior constraints in regard to the rosary, although
he said it whenever possible. Likewise, he would no longer commit
himself to keep the sabbath for a minimum of a hundred and fifty
days as he used to. But he increased the frequency of the payeik
invocations. However busy he might be, he found time to complete
these devotions. Even if he fell asleep through fatigue, he instructed
someone—frequently his wife Ma Mya Yee—to wake him before
the day was done. He also learnt to snatch "forty winks" at a time
so that after a brief moment of rest he could wash his face and go
back to the payeik.

The order of the payeik went like this: At its commencement
the nat and the *byamma* were invited to hear the word of the
Buddha; next the sermons that the Buddha preached on earth were
recited. Since the preachings of the Buddha were intended for the
relief of suffering, they held a special appeal for the nat who in-
habited not only this world but other worlds in the universe as
well. These gods, thirsty for the Buddha's Law, were in constant
search of a place where it might be defined. Thus when Thakin Nu
invoked their presence at the start of the payeik they flocked to
listen. Convinced on this point by lay and religious teachers whom
he venerated, Thakin Nu was always glad to be able to recite the
words of the Buddha, which alone could end the cycle of rebirth,
old age, suffering, and death. With his adoption of the payeik as

a regular devotional offering, his gladness turned to unspeakable joy that he had transported himself to becoming a missionary in the realm of the gods.

When recitation of the payeik became habitual, Thakin Nu was to undergo a strange metamorphosis. In his ardour for the missionary life, he learnt to differentiate between *thathana dayakar,* or donors for the faith, and *thathana pyu,* or workers for the faith. The former were the pillars of religion who donated money, robes, medicines, and alms food and endowed monasteries; the latter, the preaching order capable of constructing the law. The donors were free to have carnal knowledge of their own wives; but the preachers were severely restricted. If they were ordained monks the strictures were total: a man who became a monk on the day his daughter was born was precluded from touching the day-old baby. If he did so, under the *wini* rules of discipline he would be placed under interdict. As for sexual intercourse, the moment the monk's penis entered a woman's vagina, even by so much as the breadth of a grain of rice, he incurred damnation and ceased to be a monk. In these cases, the Buddha had taught, the offenders could never again be ordained, for as long as they lived.

Laymen who aspired to the missionary life were under an obligation to be celibate like the monks. Although he had not yet embraced such a calling on earth, Thakin Nu considered himself a worker for the faith in regard to the celestial world. Each time he approached the sexual act he could see, in his mind's eye, his congregation of nat and byamma warning him to desist. There were occasions when he told himself such things were delusions and completed the sexual act. But afterwards he had strong feelings of guilt, and he would know no peace until he was able to find solace in the glorious mysteries of the rosary.

In course of time he confided his dilemma to his wife, Ma Mya Yee, and sought her advice as to whether he should take the vow of celibacy. In her frank manner Ma Mya Yee said men and women got married "for this very business." If his religious convictions were such that he had to renounce the joys of marriage though, she would not stand in his way but would instead help him fulfill his *parami.* At this time, Thakin Nu was not absolutely certain in his mind that he wished to go through with his conversion. The visions of nat and byamma that caused him such distress as to impede him on occasion might be ephemeral. Thus he postponed the decision to become a celibate.[7]

The payeik was Thakin Nu's refuge and his mainstay. From the time he was a student at the university, his life was beset with many problems. The largest of these problems occurred later and involved his country, when its fate was tottering at the edge of a cliff, and his person, when death was averted by a hair's breadth. On such occasions Thakin Nu, being human, naturally suffered loss of morale. Then, leaving everything aside, he would don a white cotton prayer cloth, cover his torso with a white cotton shawl, and enter the altar room. With the calmness induced by fifteen minutes spent in meditation, he would concentrate on a recitation of the payeik, with results best portrayed in the following movie scene.

A battle sequence: Bodies are strewn about, many dead or dying. The fighting has been severe and the survivors, bereft of food and water, are stretched out here and there, dispirited and too tired to move. In this atmosphere a lone drummer raises his two little sticks and beats the reveille on a sidedrum. It is as though life is injected into the recumbent soldiers, who find their feet, at first slowly and unsteadily, but are soon marching in order, their fatigue overcome.

Such was the effect of the payeik upon Thakin Nu's morale. It acted like a drumbeat that renewed his strength, confirmed his faith, and revived his hopes.

If truth must be told, the religious regimen of inn drinking, the rosary, and the sabbath originated with U Nu's ambition to gain mastery over witches, ghosts, sorcerers, and devils. He wanted the power to overcome the evil spirits. Gradually, however, this ambition faded, and the truth dawned on him that the inn water, the sabbath, the beads, and the payeik were fortifications to keep him strong against the follies and indiscretions of his youth.

Among his political friends, Thakin Nu's obsession with inn drinking and other religious observances often gave rise to ridicule. One man in particular asked him provocatively what he saw in

7. U Nu's later decision to renounce sexual congress is discussed in Chapter 10.

fasts and abstinence and the mumbling of prayers; he was told, "You can take liberties with me, but never speak lightly of devotional exercises, because I don't like it."

His friend apologised handsomely but added that he still wished to know what possible good could come of counting beads, chanting verses, drinking oath water, and eating leaves. If he could be convinced they held benefits he might try them himself. Thakin Nu replied:

The advantages are many.

Thakin Nu, don't tell me of what's going to happen in the next existence. We are men of the world. We don't understand about the life hereafter.

Let me confine myself to the here-and-now. You don't just drink inn water. You have to swear before the Buddha that you will not touch any woman other than your wife and to refrain from liquor. If you break this oath you vomit blood and die. If you keep it, it becomes impossible for you to commit adultery or get drunk. Consequently, (1) you don't waste time on women and drink, (2) you don't waste money on them, (3) you don't run the risk of losing your character, (4) you don't bring distress to your wife and children because of your bad name, and (5) you don't, if you are a leader, expose your followers to aspersions of guilt by association with a bad man.

But Thakin Nu's friend was not on the same track as himself. Like mercury and iron, they were elements of a different nature. Thakin Nu believed in a future world; his friend did not. Thakin Nu believed in moral law; his friend did not place much value on it. Thakin Nu considered adultery and drunkenness sinful; his friend did not. Furthermore, he did not believe in hell. To him the five benefits that Thakin Nu was at pains to expound must have appeared ridiculous. He was not prepared to argue with someone who had no sense of humour where his religion was involved. He merely looked pityingly at Thakin Nu.

WAR AND THE FREEDOM BLOC

Shortly after the outbreak of World War II in September 1939, Thakin Aung San came to Thakin Nu's house on Stockade Road and suggested that the time was ripe to agitate for Burmese independence. Thakin Nu agreeing, Thakin Aung San said he wished to confer with Dr. Ba Maw. On the appointed day, Thakins Aung San, Than Tun, and Nu went to call on Dr. Ba Maw. The latter had only recently been brought down from the office of prime minister, and of course the thakins were partly responsible for his defeat in the Legislative Council. In these circumstances, although the leaders could thus meet over a national cause, there was still bad blood among their followers.

The leaders of Dr. Ba Maw's Sinyetha Party and the thakins conferred among themselves several times and decided to form a Freedom Bloc. This was a brainchild of Thakin Aung San's which Dr. Ba Maw christened Htwet-Yat Gaing (a pun on a mystical sect and singularly appropriate because it combined the words "out" and "stand" and could thus be rendered in English as the Standouts). In the Freedom Bloc were Dr. Ba Maw's Sinyetha Party, the Dobama Asi-ayone, and such individuals as barrister U Tun Aung, U Ba U of Mandalay, and Karen leader Saw Pe Tha.

The Freedom Bloc's purpose was to tour the countryside carrying the message to the people that it would support the British war effort only if the British government made a declaration promising independence to Burma after the war; otherwise it would oppose it. Thakin Aung San, as general secretary, deputed Thakins Soe and Nu to represent the Dobama Asi-ayone on these field trips.

A countryside meeting was convened in Tharrawaddy shortly thereafter by the Dobama Asi-ayone, and a resolution giving effect to the Freedom Bloc's policy as described above was drafted by Thakins Aung San and Than Tun. It was moved by Thakin Nu and carried without dissent.

Thakin Nu also participated at a Jubilee Hall meeting of the Standouts where, in the presence and hearing of Rangoon's citizens, speeches were made calculated to bring the British government into disrepute. There were thus two police complaints against Thakin Nu, and his arrest was believed to be imminent.

Thakin Aung San had reason to believe that, along with Thakin Nu, he and all other thakins would soon be arrested. He told Thakin Nu that it would be impossible to direct political activities from jail; he would therefore evade arrest, go abroad, and continue the fight for independence until it was won.

Thakin Nu had a close friend in one Saya Ko Tun Shwe, whom he introduced to Thakin Aung San. Ko Tun Shwe in turn brought in his own friend, Saya Chit, who was destined to become a top leader of the Communist Party. Together they hid Thakin Aung San out of reach of the police. Subsequently, Saya Ko Tun Shwe, Saya Chit, and others were able to make the arrangements to leave Burma by stealth.

For moving the Tharrawaddy resolution, and for his Jubilee Hall speech, Thakin Nu was sentenced to two years in jail—one year for each offence. He was not released at the end of this term but continued under detention under the Defence of Burma Act. Thus Thakin Nu and other political detainees escaped from Mandalay Jail only when the Japanese troops were approaching the city.

4

Under the Japanese

Having escaped from Mandalay jail, Thakin Nu and his friends found signs of great excitement at the first village they entered. Men and women, boys and girls were out on the street, talking animatedly. Soon two monks appeared and the villagers, unrehearsed, fell in behind them in a procession obviously headed for Mandalay. Two old women distributed sprigs of *thabyeban* (eugenia) and these were seized with practised ease even by those balancing bowls of rice and fruit on their heads. Other old women, with scarves round their breasts, as though bound for a place of worship, were dancing madly to the strains of a popular ditty that is sung whenever the victory flower appears. All were exulting in the thought that Burma would at last be free.

The air was thick with rumours: The Japanese were arriving as friends. They had the same war aims as the Burmese; they were ready to die for Burma. The most persistent rumour was that a Burman prince rode in the Japanese vanguard.

Thakin Nu met some of these same people later that afternoon. They were no longer marching in procession but straggling back in clumps of three or four. They had obviously met with some Japanese but did not seem inclined to relate their experiences. Pressed by Thakin Nu for details, a surly voice said, "The Japanese commander was less than grateful for our rice. When he took his hand out of his pocket it was to greet us with a hard slap in the face." And then he broke out laughing.

The face slapping had apparently been the prelude to a work detail that involved clearing logs and endlessly drawing water. Finally, the Japanese had, without so much as a "thank you," taken not only all the rice and curry but the bowls as well.

By now surliness in the speaker had given way to sheepish grins and loud guffaws. Thakin Nu thought to himself that, whatever one might say, there could be nothing much wrong with Burmans who could see the funny side of things in the most trying circumstances. But from that moment onwards the news spread rapidly from one village to another that the Japanese were a coarse, hard crowd.

DR. BA MAW FORMS A GOVERNMENT

Some time elapsed, and Thakin Nu was invited by Dr. Ba Maw to join the Preparatory Committee which was to fashion the form and content of the Burma government. Thakin Nu's initial reaction was to refuse, but Dr. Ba Maw had his name on his list and would not be gainsaid. He pointed out to Thakin Nu that, along with Bo Aung San and Thakin Than Tun, he must equip himself for responsibility and leadership. Dr. Ba Maw, as a much older man, would soon shed his mantle but only upon a successor he had trained. He was willing to be Thakin Nu's mentor.

Thakin Nu's rejoinder to this was that Dr. Ba Maw should go ahead and train Bo Aung San and Thakin Than Tun, but he himself was "not interested in that kind of thing."

"And, pray, what does interest you?" Dr. Ba Maw queried, and this drew the admission from Thakin Nu that all he cared about was writing.

Dr. Ba Maw brushed this aside with laughter. "I thought for a moment it was something serious," he said, continuing, "but writing is just a phase that all youngsters go through. I was mad about it myself once. But it passes."

The upshot was a compromise. Thakin Nu would serve on the Preparatory Committee, but implicit in this acceptance was agreement on the part of Dr. Ba Maw to drop him when the government was formed. The next day they all went to the Japanese army headquarters in Maymyo.

Since the time he first took up politics, Thakin Nu never felt
so miserable as he now did. He had known both hunger and thirst
but his lot, on the whole, had been a happy one, and even the
deprivations of life in prison had not dampened his spirits. Now
he had a fine house to live in and a car to call his own, but what
with worry for himself and worry for his people he never had a
moment's ease. His was a case of a golden dome above and a hollow
belly within, as the saying goes.

It occurred to Dr. Ba Maw that Thakin Nu had perhaps suffered
a loss of esteem in the eyes of the Japanese military police because
of a visit he had made to China in 1940 as a member of a Burmese
goodwill mission. Therefore it would be necessary for Nu to re-
deem himself by making a public pronouncement of Japanese
probity and invincibility. Thakin Nu was to develop the theme
of an East-West conflict in a historical context, with the Russo-
Japanese War of 1905 as the fifth in a series of confrontations.
Dr. Ba Maw himself dictated an account of these five wars, and
Thakin Nu sallied forth to do justice to his thesis. The occasion
chosen was the East Asia Youth Conference, presided over by Ko Ba
Gyan. At the end of the lecture, when questions were invited, up
spoke an Arakanese lawyer: "Will Japan give Burma independence?"
Thakin Nu felt vexed. What was the man up to? He must know
the room was full of Japanese spies and informers. "Of course they
will," he replied. The lawyer was on his feet again. "I don't believe
a word of it," he said. The emotions Thakin Nu felt were mixed:
he could not help admiring the man for his courage, but there was
also pain at the thought of what the military police might do to the
intrepid lawyer.

☆   ☆   ☆   ☆   ☆

About two months after the formation of the Preparatory Committee, Dr. Ba Maw received approval for the setting up of a
Burmese government subordinate to the Japanese command. As it
was to take effect from 1 August, Dr. Ba Maw had to appoint his
Cabinet before the end of July. In accordance with the previous
arrangement in Maymyo, Dr. Ba Maw agreed to omit Thakin Nu's
name. By this time the extent of Japanese perfidy in regard to the

future of Burma was widely manifest, and a Burmese resistance movement had already started, almost from the very first days of the Japanese occupation. General Aung San and Thakin Than Tun had begun to organise for the tasks that lay ahead, and were indefatigable in bringing about reconciliation between Burmans and Karens.

Thakin Nu's being excluded from the Cabinet, logical though it might have been in the light of the "gentlemen's agreement" with Dr. Ba Maw, did not fail to arouse the suspicions of the Japanese spies, and at a dinner given by the Japanese commander-in-chief, Colonel Nasu asked pointedly if it meant that Thakin Nu did not wish to collaborate with the Japanese. On the contrary, Thakin Nu assured him, it would mean full-time participation in the promotion of good relations between the Burmese and the Japanese.

UNDER THE KEMPEITAI

With his coming into power, Dr. Ba Maw fused his own Dama[1] organisation with the thakins' party. The result was the Dobama Sinyetha Party, an amalgam of the words meaning "We Burmans" and "Poor." The latter word did not signify "proletariat" or the industrial working class but simply meant people without any means. Nevertheless, such was the atmosphere of suspicion that the very title gave rise to conjecture, and the Japanese, through their agents, were soon inquiring if "sinyetha" was synonymous with "communist." Communism was the special bugbear of the dreaded Kempeitai, or Japanese military police, which went to great lengths to gather reports that might somehow incriminate individuals, either as communist sympathisers or as malcontents whose disenchantment with the new order might be expected to lead to trouble. In addition to Burmese agents and special newspaper reporters appointed by the military command, Japanese soldiers were found to be mingling with the people, castigating the Kempeitai and deploring injustices against the communists. They dug little verbal canals into which the responses of the naive, the innocent, and the unsuspecting might flow. Thakin Nu, like many

1. A *dama* is a medium-sized cleaver or hatchet.

others, was continually finding such traps set before him, but he managed to escape the ordeals by water or electrodes, the nail plucking, and the emasculation that others less fortunate than he had to endure.

Even as he felt besieged and beset by the Japanese Inquisition, Thakin Nu was startled out of his wits to discover that the Kempeitai had closed in on the thakins in Toungoo. All the thakin leaders were in custody, except one who had been executed by the Kempeitai chief. Upon receiving this news Thakin Nu sent Ko Hla Maung to Colonel Hiroaka, while he himself sped to the Japanese headquarters to see Colonel Nasu, the chief of staff. He found General Aung San already there. Since the message from Toungoo explicitly said that all the arrested men had been condemned to death, the first step was to send a reprieve order by wireless. Colonel Nasu rose to the occasion. An aide was dispatched to wait on Major-General Matsuoka, commander of the Kempeitai, and an appointment was made for Thakin Nu to see the major-general. By the time this interview took place, Thakin Nu had learnt that Colonels Nasu and Hiraoka had prevailed upon the Kempeitai to stay the executions in Toungoo. But the matter was far from ended. At Colonel Nasu's suggestion, Thakin Nu went to Toungoo to clear up the misunderstanding.

Everyone knew Bo Saing-gyo, the head of the Kempeitai in Toungoo. The interpreter from the Japanese War Office who accompanied him told Thakin Nu that Bo Saing-gyo was more of an ogre than a man, and the description was not exaggerated. Bo Saing-gyo was angry even in repose. With him, to suspect was to torture. One of his suspects, accused of theft, was strung up on a beam, his collarbone broken. The next day the real thief was caught, and the innocent one was fortunate to get out alive. If time hung heavy on him Bo Saing-gyo would look out into the street and arrest the first passer-by. The pedestrian was expected to know that the kicks and blows he received were delivered in fun.

If the thakins in Toungoo remained alive, it was largely owing to the pluck and pugnacity of Thakin Than Pe, who would not break under torture. Repeatedly beaten and kicked in the head, twice rendered unconscious, he still refused to sign a confession which would have been a death warrant for all the thakins. Thakin

Than Pe, with a blindfold over his eyes, was actually on his way to execution when the stay order arrived. By the time Thakin Nu arrived in Toungoo his friends had already been released.

On the evening of 30 July 1943, Dr. Ba Maw summoned Thakin Mya, Thakin Than Tun, and Thakin Nu to Government House. Thakin Nu was asked if he had quite made up his mind not to enter the government, and he said, "Yes, long ago." Wearily, Dr. Ba Maw explained to the company that he had done everything in order to persuade Thakin Nu to accept office but had failed. He reminded Thakin Nu of their visit to Singapore, which he intended as an indoctrination tour in preparation for Thakin Nu's entering the Foreign Office.

"Look at him," Dr. Ba Maw complained to Thakin Mya. "All he wants is to be a writer." Thakin Mya only smiled.

"Yes," Thakin Nu said. "But after we got to Singapore and I had listened to what you had to say, I realised what we were losing in you as a writer. To tell the truth I admire you more now as a writer than as a statesman, and if you were to give up politics and take to writing it would be a great gain to Burmese literature."

The meeting ended on this amiable note and Thakin Nu went home. But then the top thakin leaders descended on him and bitterly reproached him. It was just like him, they complained, to make decisions without thought of consulting them. They too would like to stand aside and ignore the call of duty. One said that he had a good mind to resign, if only to get even with Thakin Nu. Another taunted him with the charge that it was mere pretence, that he was playing hard to get. Assailed on all sides, Thakin Nu's defences weakened and crumbled. He held out the white flag in unconditional surrender, and Thakin Mya, General Aung San, and Thakin Than Tun appointed themselves an allied victory council to make the capitulation complete. The choice lay between the Home Office and the Foreign Office. It was General Aung San who opined that the Foreign Office was the more important of the two, so the following day Thakin Nu went to Dr. Ba Maw and accepted this portfolio.

AN EMBARRASSING INCIDENT

The cars of Cabinet ministers came equipped with a flagstaff, and regulations called for flying the national flag whenever a minister was riding in the car. Thakin Nu regarded this as ostentation and refused to display the flag, to the immense sorrow of his faithful driver, who felt demeaned in the eyes of his peers. At length Thakin Nu gave in, and up went the flag. The first time out with the flag flying, a Burmese policeman saluted smartly and Thakin Nu called out to the driver, "Hey, you're quite right; we are more important with a flag." But a little further on, a Japanese military policeman ordered the car to stop. It seemed a Japanese general was expected to pass that way at any moment. Thakin Ba Hein, who was riding with Thakin Nu, had been to Japan and spoke the language fluently. "This is the foreign minister," he said, "on his way to office."

"Is that so?" replied the policeman, "Good, good; then you can just stay where you are." So there they sat, covered with shame, in full view of the Kamayut police station. Just then a breeze sprang up and, when their flag fluttered before it, Thakin Nu felt even angrier and more ashamed. It was all because the wretched driver would not leave well enough alone. He vented his anger on the hapless man and shouted to him to drive straight home. Nor would he ride in the car that day, but went to his office by rowing across the lake.

LEAVING THE FOREIGN OFFICE

After a year at the Foreign Office, Thakin Nu asked Dr. Ba Maw to let him resign or transfer to another department. As foreign minister, besides sending telegrams, he was expected to greet foreign visitors upon arrival and departure. He found all this very trying. Among friends he was capable of talking freely and volubly, but in the presence of strangers he was often tongue-tied. Prior to the university strike in 1936, he had found it hard to eat if there was a stranger at the table. General Aung San, notorious for his rudeness when displeased, could nevertheless be the life and soul of a party; Thakin Than Tun was quite the cleverest mixer among them; even Thakin Mya, despite his quiet ways, moved easily and

got things done. As for Dr. Ba Maw and U Tun Aung, they ex-
uded charm on every festive occasion. Thakin Nu thus found himself relying more and more on U Tun Aung to deal with visitors.

In many respects life at the Foreign Office was pleasant enough.
In Assistant Secretary Ko Myo Min and a cadet in training, Ko Htin
Fatt, he found congenial company and a dedication to the advance-
ment of the arts and sciences that was stimulating. The truth was
that he found the Japanese attitude towards his office degrading.
In independent countries, a deputy minister or permanent secretary
could summon a foreign ambassador. But he, as foreign minister,
was obliged to go to the Japanese embassy if he had anything to
discuss. The Japanese ambassador had called on him twice: once
upon his arrival in Burma, and only once more since then. On all
other occasions he had sent a deputy or subordinate. The ambassador made a habit of going over the minister's head direct to Dr. Ba
Maw. The position had become intolerable to Thakin Nu.

Not long afterwards Thakin Nu was transferred to the Greater
Burma Department but, owing to some disagreement, he moved
on again to the Information Department. At his first press conference he discommoded his audience of Japanese reporters by saying
something like this: "Burma and Japan are geographically far apart.
We are even further apart spiritually. When the war began, Burmans had a great respect for the Japanese and looked up to them in
every way. Your former commander-in-chief, General Iida, has
acknowledged that Burmese support contributed to the success of
the Burma campaign. In the short time that has elapsed since then,
95 percent of our population has lost its fervour, and something
radical will have to be done if Japan's good image is to be restored.
It is not enough for the Japanese to proclaim 'We're on the side
of the Burmans.' If they want true Burmese regard they must
change their whole attitude. So long as your military police continue to be so rough and your traders so greedy there will be no
accord between us."

Thakin Nu did not know if he was expected to talk a lot of
nonsense about Burma doing its best to help Japan win the war.
In any case, having said what he had said, platitudes about the war
effort would have come as an anticlimax. It was left to Secretary U
Tun Sein to somehow mollify the Japanese by explaining that the

minister was a blunt man who liked to speak his mind, but that underlying the outburst that day was a passion for improving relations between the Burmese and the Japanese. The cover-up was not totally effective. Major-General Ichida, successor to Isamura, had reservations which he brought to the attention of Dr. Ba Maw.

THE RESISTANCE

Thakin Nu, although his thoughts were charged with hatred for the Japanese, was incapable of expressing them other than in words. It took a man of action like Thakin Than Tun to find ways and means of getting rid of the Japanese. First he sent a secret mission to the Chinese army, which failed because the Burmese messenger contracted malaria on the journey. Next, he turned to India, and Thakin Nu was made privy to his plans only after initial success. One Thakin Tin Shwe had accompanied Ko Thein Pe in their escape overland to India and had returned with letters from Thein Pe and Comrade Joshi, the general secretary of the Communist Party of India. Thakin Than Tun now appeared, with Thakin Tin Shwe in tow, to announce to Thakin Nu that Thakin Tin Shwe was to rejoin Ko Thein Pe in India, this time taking Ko Nyo Tun with him. Although Ko Nyo Tun was a young Arakanese living in a hut in Thakin Nu's own compound, Thakin Nu had known nothing of what was going on under his nose. All he could manage to say to Thakin Than Tun was: "You're a slick worker."

GENERAL AUNG SAN LEADS AN UPRISING

One night a conference was held at Thakin Nu's house. Present were members of the thakin inner circle: General Aung San, Thakin Mya, Thakin Than Tun, and Thakin Chit. The general read out a long proclamation he had prepared entitled "Rise and Attack the Fascist Dacoits!" Everyone present signified approval and support, whereupon it was decided that the Burmese army would print the proclamation and send copies of it to revolutionaries everywhere for the widest possible circulation. From that day forward the Burma Defence Army linked itself indissolubly to the resistance and spearheaded the uprising that would follow.

Events moved fast thereafter until one day, in March 1945, General Aung San, Bo Let Ya, Thakin Than Tun, Ko Kyaw Nyein, and Thakin Soe arrived at Thakin Nu's house to apprise him of the latest situation. Thakin Soe alone was carrying a weapon, a tommy-gun. Thakin Than Tun produced a flimsy piece of paper with English writing on it. According to this message, Thakin Than Tun was to rendezvous with an English major called Carew near Toungoo. It would not be possible for him to return to Rangoon, so Thakin Than Tun would have to go underground.

Once Thakin Than Tun disappeared, General Aung San and Thakin Nu would have to follow suit. Than Tun's meeting with Carew was fixed for 18 March, so on that day Thakin Nu would go into hiding, leaving his family in Bo Let Ya's care. For Thakin Nu to take up arms was out of the question. When it came to shock action he would be worse than useless, because he would be a hindrance to the others. Since the purpose of his disappearance was simply to put him out of harm's way, Thakin Soe's plan was to use his wireless to make arrangements for Thakin Nu to be airlifted to India or elsewhere beyond reach of the Japanese. Three or four days later Thakin Soe sent a messenger to pick up Thakin Nu's bags in preparation for his departure.

When the time came for Thakin Nu to vanish, he hesitated. Just recently he had been discussing the general situation with Dr. Ba Maw, and the latter had told him even the Japanese had noticed how close they were to each other—that Nu, a thakin, was more in his confidence than one of his own party. The thought of leaving, without a word of warning, a man to whom he had pledged his loyalty went against Thakin Nu's grain. So when Bo Let Ya arrived to spirit him away, he asked him to wait a couple of days.

This sort of procrastination was characteristic of Thakin Nu and is best illustrated by an incident that took place long before in Pantanaw. A neighbour, Khin Maung, had managed to pin down a cobra that had come to raid his chicken coop and was hollering to Thakin Nu to bring out his big gun. Thakin Nu responded quickly enough, but then the injunction "Thou shalt not kill" prevented him from pulling the trigger. At the same time he recollected the saying "Fate won't save you from pricks if you tread on thorns." If he spared the snake, would it not bite men? While he struggled with indecision the snake struggled free and escaped.

In his present dilemma U Nu decided he must confide in Dr. Ba Maw. Dr. Ba Maw heard him out; then, with gaze averted, he sighed deeply before he spoke. He said, "I suppose you'd better go into hiding. As things are, I'm hardly in a position to protect you, and before long it will be as much as I can do to protect myself. So there you are! If you wish to go into hiding, do so. As for any sort of pledge made to me I free you of it."

"But if I go into hiding, won't the Japanese be doubly suspicious of you?" Thakin Nu asked.

"They won't trust me any more because you remain," was the retort.

In his kindly way, Dr. Ba Maw adjured Thakin Nu to be careful in trusting others. People were apt to tell all under military police interrogation. Thakin Nu bowed deeply to Dr. Ba Maw and said farewell, as though for the last time.

But again that evening, when Bo Let Ya came to fetch him, he was not ready to leave. He told Bo Let Ya to go ahead and send for him from Pyapon. It was just as well Bo Let Ya did not tarry because at dawn the following day the military police raided his house.

Bo Let Ya kept his trust and sent a reliable man to guide Thakin Nu to safety, but before then Ko Hla Maung and Ko Kyaw Nyein had persuaded him to stay. They pointed out earnestly that if he went away Thakin Mya would be unable to cope with the Japanese, besides which Thakin Nu's presence would be essential at the time of the Japanese retreat if the Burmans whom the Japanese were holding were to be saved.

Only a few days later, Thakin Nu was called out of bed at two o'clock in the morning. With a start he recognised the voice of a Japanese summoning him downstairs to see Major Takashita. Saying to himself, "Now they've got me," Thakin Nu threw on some clothes and woke up Ko Chit, who was sleeping in the same room. Downstairs, standing at the door, were the major, an interpreter, two military policemen with fixed bayonets, and another in Burmese dress. The major held a note written in English, apologizing for the lateness of the hour but asking him to go at once to the Japanese army headquarters as they feared for his life. Simultaneously, that same night, Dr. Ba Maw and all the other ministers received the same message offering them protection. According to the Japanese, Dr. Ba Maw was so much against Japanese soldiers entering his house that he would not tolerate them even for his own protection. So this time the Japanese had acted without consulting him.

THE JAPANESE WITHDRAW

On 22 April Dr. Ba Maw met with his ministers. Thakin Nu, who saw him alone ahead of the others, was told the Japanese were withdrawing and would abandon Rangoon on the following evening. Dr. Ba Maw would be leaving Rangoon with the Japanese, but Thakin Nu was not expected to do so since he did not seem to get along with the Japanese. However, he must not tell this to the other ministers. Thakin Nu at once rejected this advice. He would accompany Dr. Ba Maw, as he was certain there would be many thakins caught and held on the Moulmein side for whose safety he held himself responsible. He announced this decision to the other ministers when they came in. The only thing Thakin Nu refused to do was to leave the confines of Burma.

Some of the ministers followed Thakin Nu's example and accompanied Dr. Ba Maw to Mudon, a small town near Moulmein. There, on the evening of 14 May, Dr. Ba Maw called all the ministers to his house and read them a letter from the Japanese ambassador telling them of the atomic bomb, the entry of Russia into the war, and the Japanese intention to surrender. Thakin Nu was thrilled to know that the war and all its dangers had come to an end but saddened at the same time by the thought that thirty resistance leaders had been executed only ten days before.

The ambassador's note warned the ministers that the news was very secret as it had not yet been communicated to the troops, and Dr. Ba Maw impressed this on his hearers. However, Thakin Nu felt compelled to confide in his wife. There had earlier been an assassination attempt on the life of Dr. Ba Maw, which the Japanese had been at pains to hush up but which had all but shattered Ma Mya Yee's nerves. So, as soon as he got home, Thakin Nu whispered to her, "Ma Mya Yee, the Japanese have surrendered; the war is over." She was overjoyed. But it was not because the war had ended; it was because this was the first time in her life that Thakin Nu had told her a political secret.

5

Independence at Last

In pursuance of his original resolve, Thakin Nu, as soon as the war was over, bethought himself of writing the books he had always intended; thereafter he would apply himself to the study of religious books and enter the missionary field.

In vain did General Aung San point out that the fight for independence was not yet over. Other friends too might argue that his departure from politics was premature; Thakin Nu remained obdurate. He collected his reference books and departed for Moulmeingyun. But there, while Thakin Nu was writing his book *What is Marxism?* incidents occurred that might seem to have reinforced the views earlier expressed by friends that Thakin Nu was like an old boxer going into retirement, who, at the sound of music, would be caught flexing his muscles.

In mid-October, 1945, Sir Reginald Dorman-Smith, who had been governor of Burma, returned from Simla. He conferred with the leaders of various political organisations. The Anti-Fascist People's Freedom League (AFPFL),[1] through General Aung San, demanded seven seats if the Cabinet was to be made up of eleven ministers. If the Cabinet was enlarged to fifteen, the AFPFL wanted eleven places. When Sir Reginald offered only two portfolios the

1. The AFPFL was a united front initiated by General Aung San, Thakin Than Tun, and Thakin Soe during World War II. Its principal aim was to mobilise the entire country to fight against the Japanese fascists and to struggle for independence.

AFPFL rejected it. Tensions rose and things came to a head when, in May 1946, a raid was made on the People's Volunteer Organisation (PVO)[2] stationed at Tantabin, near Insein, and the police shot three PVOs in an AFPFL demonstration that followed.

There was seething unrest in the country and Thakin Nu, in Moulmeingyun, put aside his books and wrote a long letter to Sir Reginald Dorman-Smith, the gist of which was that the old Burmese politicians were dead tigers, and that the governor had no option but to accede to General Aung San's demands, since he alone commanded the support of the people.

A week later Thakin Nu received a telephone call summoning him to Government House. There he explained to the governor the situation in the country and the political temper of the people and recommended that General Aung San be sent for. The governor agreeing, General Aung San and Thakin Than Tun went to meet him and to repeat their former demands. At this time, Sir Reginald said that he was about to resign because of poor health, but that he would carry the proposals to Britain.

Before his departure, Sir Reginald wrote to his successor, Sir Henry Knight, that General Aung San "is Burma's popular hero and without any shadow of doubt he has the biggest personal following of any man in the country . . . . His League does possess the only nation-wide organisation . . . . I think he is out for peace and tranquility. He has enough sense to realise that an uprising can only mean added misery."

Following the meeting between the governor and General Aung San, Thakin Nu's political friends besought him not to return to Moulmeingyun. Although he did return to his books, his purpose wavered.

Soon, however, there developed a rift between General Aung San's group and the Communist Party of Burma led by Thakin Than Tun, which filled Thakin Nu with gloom. One morning, Thakin Nu saw a demonstration of peasants in town. As they marched, they were shouting slogans, among them "Burma's Chiang Kai-shek, Not Wanted!" Thakin Nu realised that the peasants of Moul-

2. The PVO was a semi-military organisation formed by ex-officers of the Burmese Defence Army, which disbanded after the war. General Aung San was president of the PVO.

meingyun would be incapable of such gratuitous insults to General Aung San; they must have been instigated by Thakin Than Tun's group in Rangoon. He thereafter left immediately to put matters right with Thakin Than Tun.

Thakin Than Tun listened to Thakin Nu's expostulations, that not he nor Thakin Nu nor anybody else but only General Aung San could organise the country, and that any attempt to discredit General Aung San was contemptible. For his own part, Thakin Than Tun was able to adduce reasons why he disagreed with General Aung San on policy. The reasons were in the main political, but Thakin Nu could not help knowing that there was also a clash of temperaments. Thakin Than Tun was a person who could keep his composure at all times. Not so General Aung San, who, because of his forceful nature, at times seemed to be hectoring or shouting Thakin Than Tun down.

Thakin Nu recalled that he had faced a similar situation during the Japanese regime. The members of Dr. Ba Maw's Cabinet and some political leaders were then engaged in the task of drawing up a Constitution. They met in a cabana beside a swimming pool. Thakin Nu was not interested in the discussions, which had to do with the powers of the president, so he kept to himself, reading a book or doodling. At any rate, Thakin Than Tun had made proposals that General Aung San found distasteful, so, in characteristic fashion, he shouted them down. This woke Thakin Nu from his reverie and, noticing how charged the atmosphere was, with one participant overwrought and the other silent and sullen, he commiserated with Thakin Than Tun and entered the debate on his side.

The following morning, General Aung San came to Thakin Nu's house and asked him not to attend the meeting that day. Asked the reason for this strange request, General Aung San said, "Because I don't wish to quarrel with you." Thakin Nu said, "Then don't yell at Thakin Than Tun." This brought a smile to General Aung San, who was careful not to raise his voice at the meeting. Thakin Than Tun consequently brightened up, and Thakin Nu did not have to inject any more remarks.

Thakin Nu did not consider it politic to air Thakin Than Tun's personal troubles, but he did explain to General Aung San the political reasons for his dissatisfaction. He admonished General Aung San to compose his differences with Thakin Than Tun. When there was no immediate response, Thakin Nu was constrained to ask, "Do you remember the tiff you had with Thakin Than Tun during the Japanese regime?" and this brought a laugh from General Aung San.

As it turned out, Thakin Nu's efforts to bring peace between General Aung San and Thakin Than Tun were unavailing. Thakin Nu could only console himself with the thought that he had at least tried. Again his political friends pleaded with him not to go back to Moulmeingyun, and for the second time he wavered.

Having completed *What is Marxism?* Thakin Nu sent it to a local press in Moulmeingyun to be printed. Because of lack of staff, Thakin Nu had to go daily to the press to correct proofs. In his spare time he commenced another book, *What is Heroism?* About the end of August he heard that the new governor, Sir Hubert Rance, had arrived. Sir Hubert was the man Supreme Commander Lord Louis Mountbatten had handpicked to cope with the explosive situation in Burma. Lord Louis, whose military skill was surpassed only by his political acumen, had convinced himself that Great Britain's postwar policy towards Burma should be one of magnanimity. Accordingly, as soon as the war ended, he brought his enlightened views into play.

For a considerable period Burma found herself under a military administration, during which British officers arrested and arraigned thakin political leaders in various places. Indeed, some of the prisoners had been convicted and executed before Lord Louis Mountbatten was able to put a stop to the harsh repression. His firmness in enforcing his policy of generosity and accommodation resulted in the freeing of Burmese politicians accused of collaboration with the Japanese. It also won for Lord Louis the respect and admiration of General Aung San and all those in the AFPFL. Sir Hubert Rance, then, was the instrument chosen for the implementation of a policy conceived and elaborated in advance at the headquarters of its designer. Once in Rangoon, he promptly sent for General Aung San and other politicians for consultation. On 26 September he agreed to General Aung San's terms and the AFPFL leaders joined the Cabinet. This filled Thakin Nu with satisfaction, but if he had been able to see into the future he would have been less jubilant.

RECALL TO POLITICS

Not long afterwards, Myanma Alin U Tin,[3] who was treasurer of the AFPFL, and who was very close to Thakin Nu, wrote to him to point out that, now that many AFPFL leaders had joined the government, the headquarters was understaffed. Thakin Nu had therefore been elected vice-president, and he was required to come to Rangoon immediately. When Thakin Nu demurred, saying that he was busy writing books, another letter arrived compelling him to come. U Tin said Thakin Nu need devote only two hours a day to the AFPFL; the rest of the time he could continue to write. The call could no longer be ignored, so Thakin Nu collected his "pocket army," which by now included wife Ma Mya Yee, daughter San San, and sons Thaung Htike and Maung Aung, and reported to Rangoon.

General Aung San was extremely pleased that Thakin Nu had arrived. But there were no conventional greetings or expressions of pleasure. He merely sat awhile near Thakin Nu and, with a single exclamation, "H'm," pulled out a piece of paper which he laid before Thakin Nu. On it was written, "The power conferred upon me by the executive committee to use the funds of the AFPFL in my discretion I hereby transfer to Vice-President Thakin Nu as of today." As soon as he read it, Thakin Nu realised that it was not in General Aung San's power to make such a transfer. He could only propose the measure and seek sanction from the executive committee. But it was General Aung San's way of showing his regard and his confidence, and Thakin Nu laid it aside. Not long afterwards, General Aung San called on Thakin Nu, bringing his wife Daw Khin Kyi with him. During that visit, Daw Khin Kyi placed in Thakin Nu's hand a cigarette tin. It was very heavy. Thakin Nu opened the lid, to find it full of gold coins. They had been donated by various people for General Aung San's use. These coins remained forgotten in Thakin Nu's possession until 1951, when they were discovered by Thakin Nu while rummaging among

3. U Tin was the managing director of *Myanma Alin,* or *New Light of Burma,* which was a very prestigious newspaper before World War II. After independence U Tin became minister of finance.

his possessions. He then consulted Daw Khin Kyi and, with her approval, donated them to the Meditation Centre.

It had been Thakin Nu's intention to support himself by writing. He felt that working for two hours a day for the AFPFL did not deserve any remuneration. But from the moment he arrived at headquarters, he scarcely found time to recite his religious verses. All day long the office was invaded by politicians bringing the country's problems. They came early in the morning, during meals, and at night when he was asleep.

One day, a meeting of the AFPFL executive committee was being held upstairs at General Aung San's residence, when the general's aide-de-camp, Bo Tun Hla, arrived with the intelligence that someone had shot at Galon U Saw. Thakin Nu turned to U Kyaw Nyein and said, "Hey, Kyaw Nyein, who do you think did it?" U Kyaw Nyein said he did not know. The next evening, Thakin Nu accompanied General Aung San to the hospital to inquire after U Saw's condition. As he got ready for the visit, Thakin Nu said he believed it was the Communists who had attacked U Saw. "What do you think?" he inquired; the general said he did not know. In the hospital they found U Saw with his eyes bandaged. He knew they were there, but he could not see them.

From the time he arrived at headquarters, Thakin Nu witnessed the clash between General Aung San's government and the Communists. It was never claimed that the Communists should support the government. They were free to criticise the government within the AFPFL. This being a united front, the Communists were also free to influence other elements in their favour. If they thereby secured a majority in the league the government would have to do its behest. In actual practice, the Communists not only objected to and strongly criticised General Aung San's measures in the AFPFL, but when they lost in the league they carried their objections and their denunciation of the government in the columns of their paper, the *People's Journal.* General Aung San frequently warned the Communist leaders in the AFPFL about this, but to no avail. Thakin Nu then took to explaining the constitutional aspects of their infractions to the Communists, but the attacks in the *People's Journal* became more frequent and more savage. Inevitably, the executive committee of the AFPFL, in mid-October 1946, expelled the Communist Party. At the beginning of November the action of the executive committee was ratified by the Central Committee.

Following the Communists' departure, Thakin Nu summoned AFPFL Secretary General U Kyaw Nyein to confer on a subject that seemed to him to be of great moment. This took place about the middle of November. Thakin Nu recounted how, in 1917, the British government had introduced in India the reforms known as Dyarchy.[4] Burma was then left out because it was considered that she was still unfit for Dyarchy. It was only in 1923, after much agitation, that Dyarchy came to Burma. Now again this year (1946), a British Cabinet mission had gone to India to enter into discussions with Indian political leaders. The British Parliament had already made public the fact that after independence India could freely elect to stay in the British Commonwealth or to leave it. As far as Burma was concerned, however, only a White Paper had been issued and there was no notification whatever in regard to independence.

Thakin Nu went on to compare the activities of India and Burma during the period of the Second World War. Both countries had given Britain trouble. Burma had joined with Japan in assailing Britain. Subhas Chandra Bose, the Indian leader, had likewise collaborated with the Japanese. If the Japanese had been successful in invading India there might have been millions more like Bose. Since their positions were so similar, it was invidious that only one country, India, should have been promised independence. Thakin Nu asked:

Do you know why the notification has been made only in regard to India?

Why?

Because of the fact that the "Quit India" resolution was adopted in 1942, following which Indians, both men and women, staged violent demonstrations, inviting arrests by the thousands and tens of thousands. In 1945, with the war won, British authorities released most of the detainees, but the 1942 "Quit India" resolution

4. Under Dyarchy, elected representatives of the people were invited by the governor to take charge of some of the departments in the administration; real power continued to be vested in the British governor.

was not dropped. The Indians prepared to go on until independence was achieved. The British were mindful of the fact that the end of World War I gave rise to strong feelings about independence, culminating in violence, bloodshed, arrests, and general unrest. This is what led to the dispatch of the British Commission to India in May of 1946 and the declaration regarding independence.

From the above Thakin Nu drew the inference that Britain would feel compelled to make a similar declaration in regard to Burma if the Burmese, after serving due notice, were to adopt the Indian tactics. Thakin Nu went on, "The Indians had Mahatma Gandhi. We have General Aung San, who, like him, is able to mobilise the whole country. I should therefore like to get a resolution passed and to enter into the fight for independence. I want you to carry this message to General Aung San."

As U Kyaw Nyein was about to go, Thakin Nu called him back to add: "Oh, Kyaw Nyein, if we decide to fight for independence, we must strike now. The Burmese public is extremely fickle, and, if we delay, the political leadership now in the hands of the AFPFL can pass to the Communists. In this I am not exaggerating. I have been in politics a long time and I can gauge the temper of the people, so tell the general I am not saying this in jest but in all seriousness. For myself I want an independence secured by the AFPFL—not one granted by the Communists."

Thakin Nu was at pains to ensure through U Kyaw Nyein that his proposal was clearly understood. He broke it down into two parts: (1) The British government was to be required to make a declaration by 31 January 1947, that Burma would be granted independence within one year; and (2) if this was not done, the AFPFL members of the government were to resign, and engage in non-violent civil disobedience.

When adopted as a resolution by the AFPFL, the demand would be transmitted to the British government and also made public. Preparations and necessary arrangements would be made for the civil disobedience campaign. If the British government met the demand, there would be no need for the campaign; otherwise, it would be launched.

Having carried this message to General Aung San, U Kyaw Nyein returned after three hours and said that an executive committee meeting of the AFPFL would be held that same evening. When the meeting convened, Thakin Nu moved the resolution, and U Kyaw Nyein seconded it. Three or four members spoke in opposition, and the rest did not speak. They seemed to be waiting for a cue from General Aung San. The latter, for his part, had apparently come prepared to listen to what everybody had to say before he would commit himself. He was aware that if he agreed to the proposal, everybody else would; and they would similarly follow his cue if he rejected it.

Thakin Nu, with only one supporting vote, waxed eloquent over his proposal. There was a strangeness in his make-up, also a measure of contrariness and an obstinacy that were clearly evident on this occasion. By 11:00 P.M., with fatigue setting in, someone proposed that the threat to resign and wage civil disobedience should be omitted, the demand being confined to the declaration by the British government by 31 January 1947 that independence would follow within one year.

"A worthless suggestion," Thakin Nu said, rejecting it out of hand. "I'd rather have no resolution at all." When midnight struck, General Aung San adjourned the meeting until the following day.

Prior to the next day's meeting, General Aung San went to confer with Thakin Nu. He agreed that if the latter's suggestion were not adopted independence as an issue would be submerged. The problem was how to avoid violence in the civil disobedience campaign, since the introduction of violence would disrupt the movement entirely. In that event, the prospects for independence would dim.

When the meeting took place that evening, it proved unnecessary for Thakin Nu and U Kyaw Nyein to speak. For an hour General Aung San patiently explained the salient features of what had become the cause. He said if priority was not given to the issue of freedom it could be lost sight of. He deemed it insufficient that there should be merely a demand for independence within a year of 31 January 1947, without a statement specifying what the consequences of noncompliance would be. Without the threat of direct action, the demand would either go into a file or into the waste basket. When no one contradicted him, the general proceeded to explain that resistance, although imperative, was no easy matter. When Mahatma Gandhi introduced civil disobedience in India, he laid down that it was to be waged in a nonviolent manner. When some people went against this dictum Gandhi discontinued civil disobedience. The temper of the Burmese people was a fragile thing. The AFPFL would have to watch and see how far they could resist without becoming aggressive. The moment violence broke out, it would be necessary to suspend civil disobedience. Following this, the resolution was adopted unanimously. A public declaration of it was made, and the British government notified.

At the end of November 1946, U Kyaw Nyein came to Thakin Nu with a message from General Aung San. It transpired that the British government had invited General Aung San and company to go to Britain for consultation, and that the general had agreed to go. When pressed as to whether the issue of independence was on the agenda, U Kyaw Nyein admitted that there was no specific issue; it was just an invitation to meet and confer. Thakin Nu at once objected, pointing out that in the case of India the British government had made a declaration of intent in Parliament before the Cabinet mission was dispatched to discuss the specific issue of independence. In that declaration, made in May, it was clearly stated that India had the choice of staying within the Commonwealth or breaking away. Failing such a provision, Thakin Nu opined, the British government's invitation should be refused. When U Kyaw Nyein explained that the AFPFL government had already accepted the offer and informed the governor accordingly, Thakin Nu realised that the matter had gone quite far; nevertheless he directed U Kyaw Nyein to carry his objections back to General Aung San. When the executive committee met that evening, all agreed that Thakin Nu's objections were valid, but the fact remained that the invitation had been accepted and it would be improper to retract. Still Thakin Nu was intractable. The honour of Burma and the prestige of the AFPFL were at stake. It might appear to the world that the British had merely to beckon and the AFPFL would get up and go, not knowing what they were going to Britain for. He insisted that the Indian precedent be followed, failing which he wished to go on record as having lodged his serious objection. When there was a reluctance to renege on the undertaking given to the governor, Thakin Nu proposed that he be deputed to call on the governor. This being agreed to, Thakin Nu went with U Kyaw Nyein to Government House. Sir Hubert Rance proved to be a high-minded person. He listened sympathetically to what Thakin Nu had to say and promised to convey his message to the British government.

On 20 December 1946, the British prime minister, Clement Attlee, said in the House of Commons, "We do not desire to retain within the Commonwealth and Empire any unwilling peoples. It is for the people of Burma to decide their own future. . . . The day to day administration is now in the hands of Burmese members of the Governor's Executive (Council). . . . For the sake of the Burmese people, it is of the utmost importance that [the march toward freedom] should be an orderly—though rapid—progress."

Since the above declaration was deemed eminently satisfactory, the AFPFL executive committee gave its sanction to the AFPFL leaders in the government to proceed to London. But the matter, of course, could not rest there. A committee meeting had to be convoked to consider the agenda. Thakin Nu had only one point to make, comparing the Burmese situation with India's experience. The British Cabinet Commission and the Indian leaders having discussed the granting of independence, it had become necessary to hold a general election. The party that won would form the government to which the British would transfer power. Then the Constitutional Rules Act would be written. In accordance with these procedures the general election was held in November 1946. Since India was a vast country the general election was completed only in December. It was held under the 1935 Government of India Act.

If now agreement on independence for Burma were to be reached with the British government, it would become necessary to hold a general election, and the likelihood was that it would be held under the provisions of the Government of Burma Act of 1935. Thakin Nu said he had ample reasons for opposing such an arrangement. Those who referred to the Government of Burma Act of 1935 as the Ninety-one Departments Act knew that, although Burmans were nominally in charge of many departments, the real power was in the hands of the British governor. The act therefore was of no benefit to the nation; it merely satisfied the aspirations of the office-hungry and was the subject of derision on the part of old and young alike. Thus, reference to that act would raise suspicions as to the validity of the independence to be granted. In principle, the prospect of historically linking the precious independence, which Thakin Nu valued as life itself, with a British enactment which he had denigrated and scorned all through life filled him with horror. Furthermore, under the 1935 act, not all of voting age could vote. There were property and tax qualifications which the voter had to meet. Thakin Nu wanted these restrictions removed, and only the minimum voting age retained.

To sum up Nu's objections: (1) It was undesirable to hold elections under the Government of Burma Act of 1935, returning members to a Legislative Council. (2) What was needed was the type of elections held in countries on the eve of independence, with a universal franchise, returning members to a Constituent Assembly. (3) In order to accomplish this, it would be necessary for the British government to bring in a new act as enabling legislation.

In response to Thakin Nu's statement, some of the committee members pointed out that the British would be unlikely to make a departure from the 1935 act since that was the vehicle for the holding of elections in India. But Thakin Nu insisted on having his way and, with the permission of the committee, again went to see the governor, taking his trusted U Kyaw Nyein with him. By chance, Sir Gilbert Laithwaith, the British constitutional expert, who was staying with the governor, was also present at this meeting. He too pointed out that the Indian elections had been held under the 1935 act and that a similar procedure would have to be adopted in Burma. Still, Thakin Nu was adamant, and he instilled into the minds of the AFPFL executive committee the conviction that, if the British did not agree to elections to a constituent assembly, the Burmese delegates should break off the negotiations and return home. In doing so, Thakin Nu was banking heavily on the popularity and prestige of his friend General Aung San. He believed it was entirely possible that under General Aung San's leadership the British could be got to yield.

The Socialist Party, for its part, agreed unanimously to Thakin Nu's proposals. Since only Cabinet members had been invited to

London, the Socialists moved that their president, Thakin Mya, should resign as home minister, and be replaced by Thakin Nu so that the latter could be included in the mission. General Aung San, however, was of the opinion that, in case of a breakdown in Britain, it would become of paramount importance to begin civil disobedience, in which case Thakin Nu's presence would be required at home to organise it. He gave a promise that if elections to a Constituent Assembly were denied he would break off the negotiations and return to Burma.

Before the mission returned to Burma, Thakin Nu received a cable from U Kyaw Nyein that filled him with joy. The message had consisted of only one word: "Orange." That was the code adopted in advance to signify success. In case of failure the message would have read: "Lemon."

PREPARATIONS FOR INDEPENDENCE

Following the Aung San-Attlee Agreement, notification was made that there would be a general election to the Constituent Assembly in April 1947. Convinced that anyone having the support of General Aung San would be elected, very many AFPFL members sought his endorsement. The allocation of seats for Burma proper was 182, but over 500 applicants came forward. Some were coaxed with soothing words to withdraw, but others held on stubbornly and sometimes had to be shouted out of AFPFL headquarters. The sifted list of candidates was distributed among the members of the executive committee.

Two days before the executive committee met to consider this list, General Aung San appeared at headquarters.

Thakin Nu, I don't find your name in this list.

That's correct.

Are you not going to enter the election?

No, I'm not.

Oh, go on. You have to enter.

I don't wish to.

I've considered you for the post of speaker in the Constituent Assembly.

That makes me all the more unwilling.

Why so?

If I became speaker I should never be able to quit politics.

General Aung San was visibly upset. Whether he thought, here is Thakin Nu trying to bolt politics instead of sticking with his colleagues, or whether he was disappointed that he, Aung San, had shown a special regard for Thakin Nu which had not been reciprocated, will never be known; but he raised his voice and Thakin Nu, who felt he was being coerced, raised his. Guests and some of the staff came running to see what was amiss. They saw General Aung San leave in high dudgeon and Thakin Nu slumped in his chair, cancelling all appointments.

Shortly afterwards a messenger came to call Thakin Nu to the telephone. He said General Aung San was at the other end.

Hello, that you, General?

Please enter the election.

I told you I will not.

The country is doomed.

Obviously what he meant to say was that, if the people best qualified to serve refused to come forward, the country was doomed. The way he banged down the telephone emphasised his words.

The Constituent Assembly differed from the Legislative Council in that it was charged with the duty to draw up a Constitution under which the new government was to function. Such an opportunity could hardly come even once in a lifetime. The office of speaker carried immense prestige. Thakin Nu was not unmindful of the honour and not averse to accepting it. He knew, too, that there were many others more qualified than himself, and that General Aung San in selecting him had been moved by personal affection. What deterred him was the knowledge that he would be in politics for keeps.

When the general election did take place, the AFPFL won 171

seats out of a possible 182; the Communists won 7 and the rest went to independents.

With the Constituent Assembly scheduled to open on 9 June 1947, General Aung San sent out invitations for a meeting of the newly elected members for the middle of May. Although intended for members of the Assembly, Thakin Nu was also invited as vice-president of the AFPFL, but he did not once attend the conference because he felt the others were quite competent to discharge their task of constitution making, and also because he was counting the days when he would be relieved of his duties at headquarters. But then a matter arose which compelled his attendance.

In drafting the Constitution General Aung San disliked on principle any mention of religion. Some members wished to include religion in some form or other, while others openly desired that Buddhism be made the state religion. But because General Aung San held extremely strong views on the side of exclusion, no one dared broach the subject. However, while the conference was taking place, some prominent monks and Buddhist leaders made an appeal in the newspapers that Buddhism be written into the Constitution as the state religion. When these newspaper articles were brought to his attention General Aung San, in the midst of a speech before the conference, snapped, "I can't be getting up to look every time the dog barks." The general obviously directed his barb at the newspapers, but the newspapers of course deflected it towards the monks. Consequently there was much anguish in Buddhist circles, and the governor, Sir Hubert Rance, in his concern sent for Thakin Nu.

The governor said he had received reports that the words spoken by General Aung San before the conference had made the monks and Buddhist leaders unhappy. Since the matter could not be disregarded, he expressed the wish that Thakin Nu intervene. Sir Hubert produced a copy of the Irish Constitution, which stated that Catholicism was the religion professed by the majority but that Protestantism also had its adherents. He thought that Buddhism might be included in this guise in Burma's Constitution. The difficulty was that none of the members dared to introduce the subject, and, even if they did, General Aung San would not listen. That was where Thakin Nu came in. Thakin Nu took the Constitution of Ireland and headed for General Aung San's residence. When the Constitution was drafted for Burma, members were surprised to find religion included in it.[5]

When the Constituent Assembly ended, members went back to their respective constituencies. U Khin, the member for Mergui, started home on the steamer *Sir Harvey Adamson* which was lost at sea, everyone on board perishing. Shortly thereafter, General Aung San was at AFPFL headquarters to suggest that Thakin Nu should stand in the by-election to fill U Khin's vacancy. Thakin Nu asked for a little time to consider and was told: "Don't consider; just enter."

Thakin Nu reminded him that it was the general himself who had pressured him to join the Dobama Asi-ayone. He had not been given any time then to weigh and consider; this time he wished to think before he decided. Thakin Nu tossed the matter over in his mind, but could reach no decision. Then one evening the general appeared once more. "You have until tomorrow to file your candidacy," he said to Thakin Nu. "Have you not finished considering?"

Well, General Aung San was a person to be reckoned with. He had been able to bring independence to Burma and was the country's national hero. He would have to be regarded in this light, not merely as a fellow worker from student days at the university. Furthermore, he was now Thakin Nu's leader, and his request to enter the by-election was tantamount to an order. Thakin Nu found in his head an answer to the dilemma, but it took him a while to formulate it in words. "I shall enter the by-election, but six months after independence I will leave politics," he said at last.

Apparently satisfied, General Aung San left with the words, "Six months after independence is a long time."

The following day Thakin Nu signed the application and it was carried by an agent by air to be filed in Mergui. General Aung San's prestige secured the seat for Thakin Nu without opposition. It did not seem to occur to anyone that under the election law candidate Thakin Nu was required to sign the application before a magistrate

5. Section 21: "(1) The State recognises the special position of Buddhism as the faith professed by the great majority of the citizens of the Union. (2) The State also recognises Islam, Christianity, Hinduism, and Animism as some of the religions existing in the Union at the date of the coming into operation of this Constitution.

in Mergui. It was possible that his action in signing it in Rangoon and sending an agent to file it in Mergui was in contravention of the law. Whether he could have signed before a magistrate in Rangoon and then deputed the agent was also questionable. Because of the time factor it might have been impossible to sign in a Rangoon court.

By the time Thakin Nu was declared elected to the Constituent Assembly it had been in session for three days, with the Socialist Thakin Mya in the speaker's seat. Thakin Mya now resigned and joined the government as a Cabinet minister, and Thakin Nu was elected speaker. The first day in office he mused: Because of General Aung San I changed from Ko Nu to Thakin Nu; because of him, from a writer I became a politician; and because of him I am on this dais. I wonder what I shall be next because of this general. A member seeing him with a smile on his face might well have thought: He pretended he didn't want to be speaker, but look at him now—as pleased as Punch!

On 16 June 1947, a motion was proposed by General Aung San in the Constituent Assembly declaring Burma to be a sovereign independent state. Since many members signified their intention to speak in support of the resolution, the motion had to be tabled at the close of day until the following morning. During the intervening night the *sawbwa* (chief) of Maingpun came to the AFPFL headquarters. With him was another leader, probably Sao Wunna, representing the Karen State. They raised with Thakin Nu the question of the status of Burma's minority ethnic groups.[6] The Maingpun sawbwa told Thakin Nu he could not support General Aung San's resolution unless there was express provision that the Shan State could leave the Union of Burma if it so desired. Failing this, the declaration of sovereignty and independence for the Union of Burma would have to exclude the Shan State. Since the agreement signed in January 1947 by British Prime Minister Attlee and General Aung

6. Under both Dyarchy and the Government of Burma Act of 1935, the minority ethnic groups living in the hill areas of Burma, including the Shans, Chins, Kachins, and Karens, were not permitted to send representatives to the Legislative Councils. Instead they were governed by the British under the Frontier Administration, which was separate from the administration of Burma proper.

San stipulated that the hill areas had the right to decide whether or not they would join with Burma proper, Thakin Nu immediately notified General Aung San of what the Maingpun sawbwa had said.

General Aung San's Cabinet next conferred with the Shan representatives. The Karenni representatives were also present. In view of the fact that: (1) the Shan State and the Karenni State, from the commencement of British rule over Burma, had had separately defined borders, (2) it was desirable to include the Shan State and the Karenni State within the Union of Burma, and (3) it was necessary to pass General Aung San's resolution in the Constituent Assembly and communicate it to the British government within a day or two, the Cabinet agreed to the Shan and Karenni demand for the right of secession. The Shan and Karenni representatives agreed not to exercise this right within the next ten years.

General Aung San's resolution was duly adopted by the Constituent Assembly, after which it became necessary to draw up the Constitution of a sovereign and independent Union of Burma. The whole assembly could not embark upon this task, so it appointed a Constitution Drafting Committee. The assembly then adjourned *sine die* in about the middle of June. At the end of June, Thakin Nu was invited to Britain and he left together with U Kyaw Nyein. There were also some Socialist delegates in the group, including U Ko Ko Gyi.

The day after their arrival, Thakin Nu and U Kyaw Nyein called at the office of the secretary of state for Burma and met with Lord Listowel and Deputy Minister Mr. Arthur Henderson. As soon as the Burmese entered the room they noticed that the seating arrangements were such that a single chair faced three other chairs. Thakin Nu was walking towards the row of three chairs when he was invited by Mr. Henderson to take the single chair. When he found himself facing the light, with U Kyaw Nyein and the British Ministers on the shaded side, he felt he was under scrutiny. Lord Listowel was courteous but spoke very little. It was Mr. Henderson who engaged in a friendly discourse, the gist of which was that Burma should elect to remain within the British Commonwealth, because thereby Great Britain and Burma would be mutually benefitted. A dominion government was entirely independent and sovereign. By embracing this status in the British Commonwealth of Nations, Burma would not be subject to British influence. He made a full exposition of his standpoint.

Although Thakin Nu had been fighting against the British for many years in order to win independence, he thought very highly of the British and was much attached to them. He liked the British character and was much impressed by their respect for law while they were administering Burma. He was also a lover of English literature.

Because he held the British in such high regard, Thakin Nu was touched by Mr. Henderson's words. Nevertheless, it was his mission to point out there were two reasons why certain leaders of the AFPFL, headed by General Aung San, could not agree to dominion status. A dominion might have sovereign power, but it was required to recognise the British monarch, and this would come up against the rising tide of nationalism in Burma. Secondly, the moment the AFPFL opted for dominion status, the Communists would shout from the housetops it was not the true independence hoped for by the Burmese, that the AFPFL has sold Burma to the British, that if, with public support, they became the government they would immediately withdraw from the British Commonwealth and declare the country entirely free and sovereign. If the Communists then redoubled their efforts, with this battle cry, much of the public support now behind General Aung San might swing to the Communist side. For this reason, too, the AFPFL leaders could not accept dominion status and were moved to declare themselves completely independent.

The British leaders were men of high ideals and good intentions towards Burma. Although they would have preferred to see Burma stay in the Commonwealth, they did not obstruct her wishes to keep out. They assisted in securing a smooth transition for her sovereign independent status. In order that the Opposition Conservatives in Parliament might not be obstructive, they suggested that Thakin Nu's delegation should meet the Conservative leaders. Accordingly Thakin Nu called on Lord Salisbury, Mr. R. A. Butler, and other Conservative Members of Parliament.

After the discussions with Lord Listowel and Mr. Henderson, Thakin Nu conferred with Prime Minister Attlee, who told him that General Aung San would no longer be deputy chairman in the Executive Council, but the prime minister of Burma. He said the governor would soon be apprised accordingly.

THE ASSASSINATION OF AUNG SAN THE HERO

Thakin Nu could not take the cold in England. He fell ill there once, and again in Rangoon on his return in the middle of July. On the evening of 18 July 1947, General Aung San came to call. Thakin Nu told him of Mr. Attlee's arrangements to have his designation changed from deputy chairman to prime minister. General Aung San stayed an hour and then left. The two men were fated not to meet again in this world.

At eleven o'clock the following morning, Myanma Alin U Tin telephoned to say that General Aung San and some of his ministers had been assassinated. Thakin Nu rushed to the Secretariat and, discovering that the bodies had been removed to the General Hospital, followed thither. As he looked upon the corpse of the friend who had been with him only the previous evening, he was choked with tears.

Everything had happened so suddenly that Thakin Nu was at a loss what to do next. He had not been able to recover enough from the impact of the sudden blow to worry about the fate of the country and Burmese independence now that General Aung San had been removed. It was about 1:00 P.M. when he arrived back at his residence on Lowis Road. There he was told that the leaders of the AFPFL awaited him at the adjoining headquarters of the People's Volunteer Organisation. As Thakin Nu appeared there, Thakin Tin greeted him with the words, "The whole nation will be in trouble if U Saw is appointed in General Aung San's place. You must see the governor so that you will fill the general's position." Thakin Nu, who usually reacted to politics as a worm to salt, did not hesitate for a single moment. Yes, he would see the governor and do what was required. The executive committee passed the necessary resolution and, upon Thakin Nu's insistence, agreed to record the provision that, with the expiry of six months after independence, he would be allowed to resign.

As he emerged from the emergency meeting, there was a telephone call from the governor. At Government House, before Thakin Nu could open his mouth, Sir Hubert Rance invited him to become prime minister and to form a government. Thakin Nu was relieved his mission had been accomplished without any difficulty. Before he left, Sir Hubert recommended that a compassionate grant of one hundred thousand rupees be made to the widow of each martyr.[7]

7. Assassinated with General Aung San were six other members of the Governor's Council (Thakin Mya, U Ba Choe, U Razak, U Ba Win, Mahn Ba Khaing, and the sawbwa of Maingpun) and two additional government employees.

6

An Amateur in Office

"Some are born great, some achieve greatness, and some have greatness thrust upon them." Thakin Nu clearly fell into the third category. He did not have any special gifts at birth and strove for no qualities to fit him for the office of prime minister; circumstances alone put him there. If at the time of General Aung San's death either Thakin Mya or Deedok U Ba Choe had been spared, it would not have been possible for Thakin Nu to assume the premiership. Thakin Nu himself, as vice-president of the AFPFL, would have proposed the name of either one or the other of these leaders and got him elected. As the Burmese might say, Thakin Nu found himself above the shrubbery only because a wild ox flung him up there.

A few days after his fortuitous elevation, Thakin Nu took stock of himself and the situation he was faced with. Other prime ministers he knew had considerable experience of general administration or some department of it; others at least had had an opportunity to study and learn before being called upon to take responsibility; also they might have had the good fortune of inheriting a government machine in which the switches worked and the lights came on. In his case, he had no special bent for administrative work, no experience whatsoever, and no opportunity to have acquired any. The kind of machine he was expected to operate was a sorry object, almost cannibalised by the Japanese occupation and further ruined by political infighting in its aftermath.

The ravages of war had been great, but even more frightening was the potential for greater destruction. To the guns issued and seized from the Japanese add those discovered in caches and buried underground, and again add the weapons brought in by the Allies, and it could be seen what a formidable array of armaments had fallen into the hands of incipient rebels. Actual statistics were lacking, but, counted as units, the guns flooding the country were many many times in excess of the total number to be found in all one hundred years of British occupation.

Thakin Nu saw before him a derelict, with leaks in its gas tank and radiator, and punctures in front and rear tyres. He, who had never learnt to drive and had seen a motor car only once or twice at a distance, was expected to take the wheel and drive it over the worst road imaginable.

When he examined himself, he found a creature of the heart, forever acting upon impulse and racing ahead of reason. What to others might seem of slight import was often magnified by his emotional nature, and he had the habit of speaking out or deciding precipitately. There was a stubborn streak that made him stick to a decision once made—even a hasty one. Later, when reason was able to catch up and reassert itself, he might realise his errors and be truly repentant—that is, until hit by the new wave of provocation, reaction, and remorse.

He was forever contending with himself for mastery over his quick temper. When he was teaching English in high school he drove himself hard, spending time at home to prepare the day's lessons which he then took to class with enthusiasm. The zeal and fervour he put into his work he expected to find in his pupils. If, in addition to lack of concentration, a pupil were caught distracting others or clowning, the master would see red and punch his ears. Afterwards he would be sorry and would be impelled to coax the boy. But it was improper both to strike the pupil and soothe him afterwards, so he would carry his beads in his jacket and count them whenever he was irritated. But there would always be the irrepressible prankster to provoke him beyond control, when out went the fingers and bunched into a fist.

When he became prime minister, Thakin Nu was sufficiently under the influence of religion to be able to restrain himself against physical violence. But daily mundane matters persisted in acting as stimuli to his quick nature, and his emotional reactions, compounded by an obstinacy that made him stick to decisions, continually gave rise to recriminations. He had made mistakes as a common individual and as a teacher, but the resultant mischief or hurt affected only a few; now he was in a position to harm the whole country. This recurring fear could only be overcome with the thought that he was committed to serve only a limited time. As a traveller in the dark longs for the first ray of light, Thakin Nu longed for the six months of independence to pass.

For Thakin Nu, to gape, to dream, and to write was to be. In ordinary times he might have continued being what he was. But the times were far from ordinary. The country was stunned by the loss of its beloved leaders. It was flooded with guns in the wrong hands. The Communists that the AFPFL had expelled had the guns used in the wartime resistance. Through collusion on the part of a British officer, U Saw's men had two hundred Brens. Of the two, U Saw's was the more imminent threat and Thakin Nu set about removing it. Thanks to the police and the People's Volunteer Organisation (PVO), most of the Brens were recovered. If U Saw, rather than Thakin Nu, had become prime minister, these guns would undoubtedly have been put to nefarious use. This one fact alone should bring home to the country what a debt of gratitude they owe Sir Hubert Rance.

When the threat posed by U Saw[1] had been effectively quelled, Thakin Nu turned his attention to the Communists. He met with Thakin Than Tun:

> Thakin Than Tun, I presume your task of building an earthly paradise is going to be a difficult one.
>
> It won't be easy.
>
> An earthly paradise is not a concomitant of independence? In other words, it does not follow automatically?
>
> No.
>
> You are not alone in wanting your earthly paradise. While you were shouting about it, we, too—I and everyone in politics who

1. U Saw was at this time secretary of the Burmese Communist Party. He was put on trial for the assassination of General Aung San and his fellow-martyrs, and he and a few of his henchmen were found guilty and hanged.

has the good of the people in mind—have been making promises. What do you say to building it together? What would you say if I said, "Thakin Than Tun, help me."

I'd say yes.

As a first step they agreed, following this talk, that they would tour the country and stop the cult of killing. If they could not put a stop to it in time, politicians would start to fly at one another and the country would run blood.

Since being expelled from the AFPFL, the Communists had been cast in the role of enemy. Now the leaders of both organisations were going to work together, so the followers had to meet before Thakin Nu and Thakin Than Tun went anywhere, and when they arrived the two groups merged to give them a rousing reception. "Unity" was the common cry of the people and "Unity" was the word that appeared on posters and placards. Thakin Nu's theme at these rallies was that guns and politics did not go together. Burmese history was replete with instances of fathers killing sons, sons killing fathers, and brothers killing each other. The net result was slavery. "So," he would say, "let the politicians of today turn away from the gun and go to the people for what they want."

In homes, in rest houses, on the move in motor cars, Thakin Nu told Thakin Than Tun there was reason to expect that one day the people would give power to the Communists. The Communist Party had some very good organisers. The people were quick to change; they might support one organisation today, another tomorrow. In the democracies, political parties were given turns at governing. He also pointed out that the appeal to the people of the AFPFL was the appeal of General Aung San. With this attraction gone, there was no need to resort to arms to seize power from the AFPFL. "Have a little patience," he would counsel Thakin Than Tun, "power cannot keep running fast enough to escape you."

The second step in Thakin Nu's plan was to match the action to the words. It would not be difficult to get ten AFPFL leaders to resign their seats in Parliament, and to permit the Communists to win the seats thus vacated. Then Thakin Than Tun could be the leader of the Opposition. In this manner adversaries would forsake the battleground and instead air their differences in the legislature. It would be verbal warfare, but with a rich taste and a flavour all its own. He would let the Communists savour it at the most opportune moment.

THE COMINFORM'S NEW MILITANT LINE

While Thakin Nu planned and waited, the world was not standing still. A political measure introduced in faraway Europe was to send Thakin Nu's castle crashing to the ground. The move was the outcome of the organisational meeting of the Cominform in Poland in September 1947, and the presentation there of the new left, or militant, line by Andrei Zhdanov. According to this, the newly independent countries of Asia, as well as those with early expectations of independence, were fair game for organisations of the left, particularly the communists. The method of takeover was armed insurrection.

With no inkling of what this portended, Thakin Nu was still trying to find accommodation with the Burmese Communists, still devising ways and means of finding unity. Before he left for Britain in October 1947, he had at least four meetings with the Independence Celebrations Committee and gave them instructions that there should be Communist representatives on the main committee and various subcommittees. He personally told Thakin Than Tun of these arrangements and pressed him to have delegates ready to serve on these committees.

On 17 October 1947, there was signed in London a document that has come to be known as the Nu-Attlee Agreement. It contained fifteen paragraphs, the most significant being the statement that the British government recognised Burma as an independent sovereign state. The ceremony ushering in independence was held in the Legislative Assembly Hall in Rangoon at 4:20 A.M. on 4 January 1948. Among the distinguished guests were many from abroad. Thakin Nu could be seen craning his neck to look for a face among them. With immense satisfaction he found whom he was looking for—Thakin Than Tun.

His pleasure, though, was shortlived. The fire lit by Andrei Zhdanov less than four months before was to spread to Burma and reduce it to a heap of burning debris. The independence celebrations were hardly over when Thakin Than Tun responded to the invitation of the Cominform to attend a conference in Calcutta. With him was one Goshal, a man of Indian parentage and therefore generally classified as an Indian; but Goshal was born in Burma, weaned on Burmese water, educated in a Burmese school, and was a Burmese citizen. He not only had a Burmese name, Ba Tin, but was fluent in Burmese, his speech being without any trace of a foreign accent. He was a sensible person who was well liked in the Communist Party. Thakin Nu met him on several occasions but did not know him as intimately as he did Thakin Than Tun. But from what little he saw of him the impression was gained that Comrade Ba Tin was Thakin Than Tun's superior in intelligence.

During the war, when Thakin Nu was in Mandalay Jail, he heard one day that Goshal and four or five Indian politicians had been arrested and placed in the same jail. They had been less than two days in their cells when they disobeyed the chief jailor and were brutally beaten up by the wardens. Some heads were broken and Goshal was left with a fracture in one hand. The chief jailor in question was notoriously cruel, with a record of atrocities that included maiming and even death. Not satisfied with what his wardens had done, the jailor recommended more severe punishment for the hapless detainees, and the superintendent ordered Goshal and the other Indians to be flogged. They were given twenty lashes each and were fed on gruel in solitary confinement for a month. This being so excessive, Thakin Nu went to see the superintendent, whose name was Davenport, and charged him with injustice. Davenport's reaction came as a bark: "Don't stand in my path; get out!" and Thakin Nu was left struggling in the arms of the wardens.

This then was the same Goshal now with Thakin Than Tun at the Calcutta Conference. The date was February 1948, just a few weeks since Thakin Than Tun had stood among those celebrating Independence. With a host of delegates from India, Europe, and the British Commonwealth, the Calcutta Conference discussed the new, militant line enunciated by Zhdanov and reaffirmed its principle. Several speakers excoriated the AFPFL. This did not surprise Thakin Nu, who had expected the Communists to do their worst by condemning both his party and himself; but he was not prepared for the virulence of Thakin Than Tun's attack: The Nu-

Attlee Agreement was a worthless document giving birth to a sham independence, he said, and if the running dogs of Anglo-American imperialism struck one blow, the thousands of Burmese Communists and the ten thousand of their shock troops would strike two. To this was added the proud boast that, with a new united front to be formed, the AFPFL government, the creature of capitalist expansionism, would be overthrown in 1948 and real independence for Burma achieved.

The moment Thakin Nu read this account in the newspaper he was overcome with rage. So this was the man who was going to walk hand in hand with him bringing about the earthly paradise. He, Thakin Nu, was the swain awaiting his marriage at the end of the Buddhist Lent, and here was his affianced bride parading in front of his house, shouting aloud to the neighbours what a sucker he was, and gleefully announcing her choice of another! For once his control broke. Forgetting his station in life and who he was surrounded with, the volcano of his youth, long thought to be extinct, erupted: "Mother-fornicating Russians. They give the order and our miserable Communists obey. Our Communists think Stalin loves them. Speaking about love for the Burmese, Stalin comes nowhere near General Aung San, even when the latter is baring his penis and pulling the foreskin back!"

Following their return to Burma, Thakin Than Tun and Goshal concentrated on the campaign to discredit the Nu-Attlee Agreement as the purveyor of a sham independence for Burma. Their loud cries of protest, increasing each day in vehemence, were a prelude to the full-scale armed insurrection that they were about to launch under Russian instigation. Home Minister U Kyaw Nyein went to tell the prime minister:

I have a top secret document. I don't want you to question me where I got it.

Wait a second. What's all this about?

This is a presentation made by Goshal in their politburo, on armed insurrection.

How did you get hold of it?

If you press me for names I'll have to reveal the source, and the information I've been getting from the Communists will dry up.

Ummah! You don't trust even me?

I have a man planted in the politburo.

Aw . . .

Again insisting that the prime minister should not compel him to divulge the identity of the informer, U Kyaw Nyein handed over the document: "The Current Political Situation and Our Programme." Then he spoke:

The Communists are going to rebel for certain. It won't do for us to be indecisive.

What do you plan to do?

While the Communists are grouped together in Rangoon, we must raid them and pack them off to jail.

This is a serious matter. I'd like some time to think it over.

I've stated my views. The decision of course is yours.

U Kyaw Nyein was a man who did not allow the grass to grow under his feet. For example, at the start of World War II, when the Allied troops were withdrawing from Mandalay, he and his companions in the anti-British underground were at Kabaing, near Madaya, a short distance away. One day, while U Kyaw Nyein and two companions were walking towards Mandalay, a car overtook them and an Allied soldier sprang out, a Tommy gun in his hand. Whether the soldier was acting on suspicion or had somehow identified them as the underground will never be known. In an instant U Kyaw Nyein, who is slight of build, had thrown his arms around the soldier and was commanding his companions to shoot. One of his men, *Taingchit* Ko Thein Pe,[2] had a revolver, but he hesitated because he was not prepared for the sudden emergency. He fired just in time. Another moment and they would all have been mowed down.

Kyaw Nyein, I'd like to let the executive committee know about the Communist rebellion.

That would be the proper thing to do.

2. *Taingchit,* meaning "patriot," was the name of a newspaper owned by Ko Thein Pe, who should not be confused with *Budalin* Thein Pe.

You could then explain about your plans.

What plans?

Your scheme to seize the Communists *en bloc* and detain them in jail.

Hah! That will never do. There are representatives of the Asian Youth and the People's Volunteer Organisation on the committee. If they know, Than Tun and Goshal are bound to find out.

All right, you needn't discuss plans.

A QUARREL WITH THE PRESS

While the AFPFL government was being sorely tried by the Communists, a problem concerning a top Socialist leader was thrown into Thakin Nu's lap. Thakin Tin, minister of agriculture, was planning a trip to Tharrawaddy, then a notoriously insecure area. Thakin Nu, hearing about this, detailed an officer and ten men for the minister's protection, with strict instructions not to let him out of their sight. Some time after Thakin Tin's return to Rangoon, a letter was received by one of the prime minister's friends which alleged that Thakin Tin had taken a married woman into the bungalow and raped her. With the letter was a photograph of the woman. The letter being brought to Thakin Nu, he called up the officer of his security unit who had accompanied the minister and questioned him. The officer reported in detail the movements of his charge. He said he had slept in the same room as the minister and accompanied him even to the toilet. No such incident as that reported could have taken place without his knowledge. Thakin Nu decided it was a joke in rather bad taste.

But three days later the same photograph was on the front pages of the newspapers, with the same allegations about the rape. Further inquiries were conducted at the scene and it was found that a PVO officer, an enemy of Thakin Tin's, had hatched the plot to discredit the minister. Thakin Nu no longer considered it an important matter, but because the newspapers were making a big thing of it, it was deemed necessary to allay public concern. The chief justice of the Supreme Court and two others were appointed as a special commission to report on the matter. Their inquiries showed it was a trumped up charge, and some of the newspapers quieted down. But not all. Three newspapers closed their eyes and kept plugging away. What the effect of this perversity was on Thakin Tin could only be imagined. Thakin Nu himself found the situation intolerable.

On 12 March, Lord Listowel was being honoured at the City Hall when a crowd collected in the adjacent Bandoola[3] (formerly Fytche) Square and began shouting through loudspeakers. The reception guests, Thakin Nu and Lord Listowel among them, went out on the veranda to see what the hubbub was about. The speeches and slogans were condemnatory of the press, and Thakin Nu, pleased that the Socialists were getting their own back, explained to Lord Listowel about the Thakin Tin incident. The wayward press, he said with a smile, was getting its comeuppance.

Fifteen minutes or so after his return home, U Kyaw Nyein joined him, and Thakin Nu greeted him with:

Hey, Kyaw Nyein, I'm so pleased the public has demonstrated against those newspaper sons of bitches. No more bowed heads before unjust criticism, what?

Mr. Prime Minister, I staged the demonstration.

Aw . . .

Not only that; I told them to break in and smash the presses.

What! What did you say?

I instructed them to destroy the printing machines.

Why you useless chap, this is a democracy—not an authoritarian state. You're supposed to be home minister. A demonstration would have been appropriate, but what right have you to smash up the machinery?

As U Kyaw Nyein fidgeted, the prime minister stormed on: "Get the commissioner of police straightaway. I'll deal with everyone who has broken the law." Thakin Nu was on the verge of saying that U Kyaw Nyein, as defendant number one, was fired, but fortunately he checked himself in time. For the Communist rebellion

3. Maha Bandoola was a famous general who fell in the First Anglo-Burmese War, in 1825.

was on its way, and Thakin Nu was soon rejoicing that he still had this able man by his side.

The police found that Members of Parliament, Parliamentary secretaries, labour and peasant leaders were involved in the wrecking of newspapers, and the prime minister ordered every one of them arrested. Some of the suspects evaded arrest for a time, but their leaders ordered them to surrender. Since the offence was a bailable one, they were later set free on bond.

Three days later, the prime minister made a public statement in Bandoola Square. He said the vandals had been taken to task. At the same time he warned the press they would not get away with it if they continued to misuse the freedom of the press. "I'm not afraid of you, or of your grandfather either," he said. The allusion to the grandfather was a figure of speech intended to mean that the prime minister was not afraid of any power above and beyond the press. The press, with diabolical cunning, exploited Thakin Nu's reference to "grandfather." It came out with screaming headlines that the prime minister had gratuitously insulted Thakin Kodaw Hmaing, the Grand Old Man of Burmese letters, who because of his age and eminence was embraced by journalists as their "grandfather." Four or five editors hurried to Thakin Kodaw Hmaing's side, won his sympathy, and led demonstrations in the streets castigating the prime minister. Thakin Nu, recalling what he had once done to Principal Sloss, could only grin and call it retribution.

THE COST OF INDECISION

While the skirmish with the press was going on, Thakin Nu called the AFPFL into executive session and notified it of the imminent threat of a Communist uprising. A number of those present advised him to hold peace talks with the Communists. Among these advisers, some were genuinely concerned with avoidance of bloodshed, but others, who leaned towards the Communists, were advocating discussions as a delaying tactic. Knowing this to be the case, the visionary in Thakin Nu yet made him pause. Besides being indecisive, and quite unlike U Kyaw Nyein in this respect, he felt he had rather the enemy struck him four or five times before he retaliated. So he accepted the suggestion to enter into discussions with the Communists. Duwa (Chief) Sinwa Nawng of Sima, the head of the Kachin State, was accordingly sent as an emissary to Communist headquarters, only to find the door shut in his face. Again, Deputy Prime Minister Bo Let Ya himself went with Sinwa Nawng, and they were refused admittance.

When 27 March arrived, the meeting with the Communists had not yet taken place. This day was being celebrated as Resistance Day against the Japanese, and public speeches were made, by Thakin Nu on Martyr's Hill, the rise near the Shwedagon Pagoda on which General Aung San lay buried, and by Thakin Than Tun in Bandoola Square. Thakin Nu stressed the need for peace and unity among the Communists, Socialists, and the PVO. He offered to resign, both as prime minister and as president of the AFPFL, in favour of a popular candidate acceptable to these major organisations. Thakin Than Tun, on the other hand, openly declared that he was resorting to arms to bring down the government. "With AFPFL corpses I will level the Bagaya pit,"[4] he announced.

As was to be expected, the threat of war filled the country with despair. It also rendered negotiations with the Communists impossible. Arrests were ordered, and the Rangoon police together with the Union Military Police (UMP) raided the Communist headquarters, but the birds had flown. Recriminations seized the prime minister. It was wasted effort on his part to open before the Communists the path of peace and unity, knowing they would never take it. He might have met with more success persuading a tiger to turn vegetarian. The poison dispensed by the Russians had done its work only too well. The Burmese Communists were too far gone. "If only I had been firm, if I had acted when Kyaw Nyein came to me, this could not have happened," he blamed himself.

THE COMMUNISTS STRIKE

The English have a saying "Trouble never comes singly." This has certainly been true of the vicissitudes that visited Burma in 1948 and 1949.

When Burma became independent on 4 January 1948 the Muja-

4. A very deep underpass where two roads cross beneath the railroad line in a quarter of Rangoon known as Bagaya.

hids[5] and the Red Flag Communists[6] had been in revolt for some time and had gathered a good deal of momentum. On 29 March 1948, seventy-six days after independence, the Communist Party of Burma, led by Thakin Than Tun, rebelled. As soon as this happened, Thakin Nu realised that his expectation of being able to quit politics by 4 July 1948 had disappeared in the blinking of an eye. Simultaneously, he foresaw government supporters and rebels in mortal combat. The picture conjured up in his mind of men shooting and killing one another, with blood streaming from their bodies, sickened him. He had recoiled from the prospect of being a ruler. Now he was to be a ruler with a gun in his hand. If Lord Buddha were present he would have liked to ask, "What *kan* in your disciple's life has wrought this?"

A moment later, however, his grumbling ceased. He had on Resistance Day publicly declared that the Communists, the Socialists, and the People's Volunteer Organisation had only to unify and he would give up the offices of prime minister of Burma and president of the AFPFL. Despite his willingness to step aside, the Communists were determined to force the issue. The die was now cast. He would meet force with force.

MAHAWTHADA THE MODEL

While he awaited his ministers, whom he had summoned to an emergency Cabinet meeting, U Nu took down a volume of the Ten Zat[7] and opened the page at Mahawthada. Among the myriad of *paya-alaung,* Mahawthada, the learned, was one of the most recent ones, with a *parami* that could be called ripe.[8] As one destined to become a Buddha, who had been through countless existences as an embryo-Buddha, he would have been the last to cause unnecessary pain to anyone. Nevertheless, in the defence of his sovereign, his country, and his race, he was never slow in circumventing and pun-

5. The Mujahids are Moslems. They were rebels who sought to establish a Moslem state in the Buthidaung and Maungdaw areas of the Akyab District in Arakan.
6. The Burmese Communist Party had split to form the Red Flag Communist Party and the White Flag Communist Party.
7. The ten life stories of the future Buddha.
8. The concepts of paya-alaung and parami are discussed in Chapter 1; see especially note 16.

ishing the enemy. He personally seized Kinwut Ponna, the enemy
king's adviser, banged the man's forehead against the floor, and
flung him off into the distance. When his sovereign's capital was
besieged by the enemy, Mahawthada had his Anukinwut Ponna
infiltrate the opposite camp as a spy. It was this agent who, under
Mahawthada's guidance, lured the enemy troops through a moat
for an assault on the city walls. The moat was full of crocodiles and
those who escaped the reptiles were cut down in an ambush.
Through the use of this and various other strategems the superior
investing army was put to the rout.

Having failed on the field of battle, the enemy king put up his
daughter as bait for Mahawthada's sovereign. The latter was very
much smitten with the princess and, disregarding Mahawthada's
advice, would have fallen into the trap but for the fact that Mahawthada was able to abduct the princess and capture her father. Having the adversary king as captive, Mahawthada could have executed
him; instead he set him free. This action evoked the praise of his
king, who said, "Oh wise one, replete with strength of arm and
virtues of heart, how is it that you have not taken control of the
entire island continent called the world?" To which Mahawthada
replied that if he wished to be king he could indeed conquer the
world, but he had no such ambition. He made it clear that, while
he would wage war in defence of the realm and its people, it was
to protect them against harm and not for self-aggrandisement. To
seek worldly gain at the expense of another was to incur the displeasure of the Buddha, the gods, and holy men. "I wish to do what
is praiseworthy in their sight," Mahawthada explained, "not what
is detestable to them."

The law is impartial. It is not one thing for the great, another
for the common. Mahawthada could not exculpate himself by
claiming he was the Buddha-to-be and that in any case those he slew
were the enemy. Whether done by a paya-alaung or an ordinary
mortal, killing is sinful. To kill a foe or a friend or anyone else is
a sin. Whether it is in defence or on the offensive that killing occurs,
sin is committed and must be atoned for in hell. That Mahawthada,
in full knowledge of the implications of his actions, did what he
had to do to save king and country fully satisfied Thakin Nu's
scruples. That Mahawthada, for self-glory, would never do what in

the eyes of the Buddha, the gods, and holy men would be reprehensible struck a satisfying chord in Thakin Nu's mind. As he went in to confer with his ministers he vowed to abide by what he had been reading.

The Communists put everything into the rebellion from their vantage points in the Pegu, Toungoo, Pyinmana, and Delta areas. They attacked police stations to seize firearms. They overran towns and villages and stole grain from rice mills and warehouses. Bridges were blown up, the railway track destroyed. At that time they had ten thousand seasoned fighters under arms, supplemented by twenty thousand auxiliaries armed with weapons less lethal than guns.

LEFTIST UNITY PROVES FUTILE

The government, being totally unprepared for armed revolt, had to deal with immediate threats to its seat, ignoring the more distant ones. The result was like throwing bait only in the spots where the fish had risen. During this sporadic fighting with makeshift methods, the People's Volunteer Organisation (PVO), in May, offered to mediate between the government and the rebels.

The diehards among the PVO next proposed that Burma should declare war on Britain and the United States. Prime Minister Thakin Nu, when he heard the proposal, had to make an effort to contain himself. Had he not been anxious to avoid a quarrel with the PVO, he would have laughed out loud. Instead, he patiently explained to the PVO why their suggestion was impracticable.

"Then make a token declaration of war," the PVO urged. This left Thakin Nu speechless. It took him a long time to convince the extremists that even the Soviet Union did not dare to declare war on Britain and the United States, token or otherwise.

Nothing daunted, the PVO next demanded that "Leftist Unity" be forged among the Communists, the Socialists, and themselves. An organisation comprising some leaders of the Socialist Party and the PVO was therefore formed. In it were Budalin U Thein Pe and Prime Minister Thakin Nu himself. This organisation drew up a fifteen-point Leftist Unity Programme and this was presented at a public meeting at the Aung San Stadium on 25 May 1948.

Great expectations prompted Thakin Nu to publicise the Leftist

Unity Programme, but it made no impression on the Communists. What did happen was that the attention of the West, particularly the newspapers and some individuals in England, was drawn to the last point of the fifteen-point declaration. This was to the effect that an institution for the propagation of Marxism would be established. This led newspapers in Britain and the United States to conclude that Burma had adopted communism. In England, the foreign secretary, Mr. Ernest Bevin, called in the Burmese ambassador and demanded an explanation. It was also stated in the British Parliament that, if in fact Burma had turned communist, British policy in regard to it would have to be changed.

Mr. Bevin was well intentioned towards Burma and had been among the front rank of those friends assisting it towards independence. Wishing to repay his goodness in some way, Thakin Nu had once suggested sending a Burmese practitioner of native medicine to treat Mr. Bevin, who was suffering with haemorrhoids. Mr. Bevin had agreed to such an arrangement, but back in Burma friends told Thakin Nu that the native doctor's "cure" was an extremely harsh method involving the use of arsenic. If something were to happen to Mr. Bevin, they cautioned him, not only Thakin Nu but Burma would be disgraced. As for Mr. Bevin's strictures in the British Parliament, Thakin Nu understood too well the motivation behind them. The whole episode put him in mind of a domestic issue that arose early in his married life.

Thakin Nu's first child was a month old when he fell ill. The doctor was called in but the baby did not improve. Under a friend's advice a native "doctor" was consulted but his medicine sent the child into convulsions. The next "doctor" suggested was a *sandala,* and this immediately raised a problem. Prior to independence the group called sandala and pagoda slaves were outcasts, sandala being undertakers, who lived near cemeteries and either buried or cremated the dead. The word itself is perhaps derived from the Hindi *chandala.* As for pagoda slaves, they tended ancient shrines and pagodas, kept the precincts clean and were entitled to eat the food offerings. The pagoda slaves were descended from those the Burmese kings had willed into servitude.

In this context it can easily be understood how much of a problem was caused by the proposal to bring in a sandala. When Thakin

Nu consulted his wife she said that her father would object. He, on his part, was more concerned about saving his child's life. If because of a social taboo the infant should be allowed to perish, he would be haunted by this thought for the rest of his life. A woman visitor, overhearing the discussion, was constrained to point out that once a sandala was admitted into the house no other guests would call. In some exasperation Thakin Nu said the sandala doctor would be called; everybody else could stay away, but he was not going to let his son die.

This incident remained imbedded in Thakin Nu's memory. In fact, fifteen years after it took place, Thakin Nu, as prime minister, saw to it that the Declaration of Independence read by the president of the Union of Burma released the sandala and pagoda slaves from bondage and from the position of an oppressed class and made them equal in status with all other citizens.

To come back to the original theme, Thakin Nu's first-born was already in extremis and the sandala could not save his life. Similarly, the Burmese Communists, because they had become too badly infected with outside influences, could not be brought back into the fold. The appeal for leftist unity proved unavailing. Not only did the Communists not respond to its appeal, but on 16 June a whole battalion of Burma Army troops stationed in Pegu deserted to the Communists.

In July the government resigned *en bloc* and had to be reformed two or three times. Foreign observers and even uninformed Burmese felt that these changes were taking place because of dissension among the ministers. Actually there was no conflict of any kind. Certain ministers who in travail should have placed their faith in the Three Gems (the Buddha, the Law, and the Assembly) forgot them entirely and had recourse to fortune-tellers instead. If the fortune-teller ordained that there should be resignations the ministers complied. If it was reckoned that a more propitious period had dawned, they came back into the Cabinet.

A NARROW ESCAPE FOR THE GOVERNMENT

Some two weeks later, Home Minister U Kyaw Nyein came to see Thakin Nu.

Mr. Prime Minister, a serious situation has arisen.

What serious situation?

It has been demanded that you appoint either Bo Ne Win or Bo Ze Ya as defence minister.[9]

Who has made this demand?

Both of them.

Is it proper for army officers to take advantage of the difficulties we are having with the enemy?

The leaders of the Socialist Party knew what Thakin Nu's reaction would be to what was virtually blackmail. But they knew also that, in the existing situation, refusal to appoint either Bo Ne Win or Bo Ze Ya would be attended with dreadful consequences. Accordingly, in place of a delegation, they had sent U Kyaw Nyein alone. Thakin Nu could be difficult on occasion. If handled wrong, he was capable of obstinate action bordering on the reckless. U Kyaw Nyein alone, a friend of his youth, was believed to have the right touch, as the following illustration will show.

At the end of the school strikes in 1936, it was arranged to convene a general assembly of an All-Burma Students' Union. Ko Nu would be chairman, but he was asked to go to Moulmeingyun until the day of the assembly. The plan was for him to return to Rangoon on the opening day, be met by the delegates at the wharf, and be led in procession once round the town. Ko Nu agreed and left his chairman's speech to be printed, with strict instructions that it was not to be altered in any way. In his absence, the Rangoon University Students' Union read the speech and detected one paragraph which they considered inappropriate. In view of Ko Nu's injunctions, there was no way by which the offending paragraph could be deleted. Ko Kyaw Nyein, regarded as Ko Nu's "handler," was therefore sent to see him in Moulmeingyun. He went, taking Ko Tha Hla[10] with him.

---

9. Bo Ne Win later became the Armed Forces chief of staff and overthrew the government twice, in 1958 and in 1962. He is presently the head of the Burmese government. Bo Ze Ya became a member of the politburo of the Communist Party of Burma. He was later killed in action.

10. After independence U Tha Hla became dean of University College.

When the two arrived at about 8:00 A.M. in Moulmeingyun, Ko Nu asked them why they had followed him. Ko Kyaw Nyein said there was no particular reason; they just felt bored. So they sat there all day, reminiscing about old times. Ko Kyaw Nyein, as was his wont, kept the conversation going, interspersed with humorous anecdotes. Then, around 3:00 P.M., apropos of nothing, Ko Kyaw Nyein mentioned the controversial paragraph in the chairman's speech and casually asked if its inclusion was really necessary. By then, Ko Nu, honeyed up as he was, was feeling no pain. He had also forgotten that he had forbidden any part of his speech to be changed. So he said he did not think he had to be consulted. "You all go ahead and make any alterations you wish," he said.

Now, in another ticklish situation, the "handler" was back at work. To Thakin Nu's irate complaint that the army was taking advantage of the country's difficulties, U Kyaw Nyein offered no immediate comment. He stared at the floor awhile and finally came up with: "Of course it's a cavalier thing to do, but the fact is they're applying the pressure and a solution will have to be found. My duty is to present the facts. You can decide any way you wish."

I will not tolerate this squeeze. I hate it in my guts, in my liver and the marrow of my bones. I won't appoint anyone. They can do their worst.

Mr. Prime Minister, you're our leader. Please feel free to do as you wish.

All right, I won't appoint anyone. Let them do as they please. We're not without hands and feet. You Socialists, get busy with the systematic organisation of your party to gain mass support. I will organise my own support. We'll retaliate with the strength of the people.

In that case, can you spare a moment to see them?

I have no wish to see them.

Tears streamed down from U Kyaw Nyein's face. Perhaps he felt as if there were robbers at the gate, and the householder was thinking of getting a gun license. A prime minister who talked of organising mass support when the army was at his door must have struck him as asinine. Or was he using an effective means of applying the brake to Thakin Nu's runaway outburst?

Thakin Nu treated U Kyaw Nyein as a confidant and loved him. There were many reasons for such special affection, and they stemmed from a study by Thakin Nu of the men around him—in the political arena as well as in the administration—since the Communist insurrection. Some people, viewed from a distance, seemed courageous. At close quarters, however, they were revealed to be weak and cowardly beyond pretence. Others, opportunists, had one arm around the government, the other outstretched towards the rebels. Then there were still others who found it impossible to understand a simple thesis: that here was a situation in which those who regarded power as flowing from the people, and exercisable as a mandate thereof, were locked in combat against those who viewed power as emanating from the barrel of a gun. In point of fact, this last class of people understood the issues only too well. Generally, they were persons of intelligence and perspicacity. But, like a man pretending to be asleep, it was impossible to wake them. They might even inwardly hanker after democracy, but they were afraid to espouse it openly because just now democracy seemed to be in its death throes. Their immediate problem was what to do in case democracy was vanquished and Communism came into the ascendency. Not for them the people's court, the gibbet, and the disembowelling. Far better to avoid getting scalded. If the conge[11] comes steaming out of the pot, avert the tongue! The main thing was to stay out of trouble. Invent the excuse that the AFPFL buffalo was locking horns with the Communist buffalo, and the grass beneath them was likely to be trampled. So keep away from both, as far as possible!

U Kyaw Nyein, however, was not among those already enumerated. He had courage. He did not ride with the tide. He was not an opportunist nor a double-dealer. He faced the enemy and fought him decisively. He was consequently hated by the enemy—probably more so even than Prime Minister Thakin Nu. If he were to be caught, the enemy would dispense with a people's court and string him up immediately. They would split him open and eat him raw.

11. The boiling liquid in which rice is cooked.

U Kyaw Nyein knew the dangers but disregarded them. There was no doubt in his mind as to the basic nature of the fight between those who believed in the sovereignty of the people, and the idea that power comes out of the barrel of a gun. For this reason, the sight and presence of his home minister filled Thakin Nu with a sense of well-being. Now, when he saw the tears flow, he became greatly concerned. "Look, Kyaw Nyein, if that's the way you feel, send your fellows and I'll see them," he conceded. The moment he said this, U Kyaw Nyein found the opening he was looking for. He pointed out that the only battalion the government could rely on was Bo Ne Win's Fourth Burma Rifles, which being so, he urged that Thakin Nu should not only see the two officers but should appoint Bo Ne Win as defence minister. U Kyaw Nyein of course was being quite truthful about the Fourth Burma Rifles. Other than the Chin and Kachin battalions, it was the only dependable unit of the army. Thakin Nu, who by this time had calmed down considerably, could only say, "Yes, we'll see about it."

That same afternoon Bo Ne Win and Bo Ze Ya arrived. They were not alone. Accompanying them were two or three army officers, Budalin U Thein Pe, and some Socialist leaders, along with U Kyaw Nyein. As Thakin Nu entered, the company rose in their seats. In an instant Thakin Nu noticed one of the officers was wearing sidearms. Most probably it was worn as part of his uniform, with no intent of threat to the prime minister, but the immediate effect was to upset him sufficiently so that he directed his stare at Bo Ne Win and Bo Ze Ya and asked tersely, "What's on your minds?" Those officers said nothing, but Budalin U Thein Pe, acting as spokesman said, "Mr. Prime Minister, please choose between Bo Ne Win and Bo Ze Ya for the post of defence minister." If he had stopped there all might have been well. The prime minister had more or less agreed with U Kyaw Nyein that Bo Ne Win should have the appointment, but Budalin U Thein Pe went further and gave him three days in which to make his choice. Stung to the quick, Thakin Nu forgot his promise to U Kyaw Nyein. The threat of consequences to his government and country was overridden by the provocative thought that here was an ultimatum backed by a revolver in a holster. Sputtering with rage, he said,

"Thein Pe, I don't need three days—not even three minutes. I've already decided. I'm appointing nobody. If you're dissatisfied, pull that gun and start shooting." The group left silently.

Some time elapsed, but Thakin Nu was still pacing the floor when the telephone rang.

Who's there?

Kogyi[12] Nu? It's me—Bo Let Ya.

What do you want?

Bo Ze Ya requests an interview.

I don't wish to see him.

This is a time of great emergency. Let me plead with you. Please give Bo Ze Ya a hearing. He has something important to say.

(*There was a pause.*) Send him along, then.

When Bo Ze Ya arrived, he found two chairs had been placed at the bottom of the stairs. He was greeted by the prime minister with:

Well?

Kogyi Nu, give me the job of defence minister?

I thought we had exhausted that subject. I thought I had made it clear neither of you gets that job.

Kogyi Nu, I . . .

Look, Bo Ze Ya, I'm in no mood to talk. I'm all upset. You'd better go.

Back in his room, Thakin Nu thought for a while. Then he reached for the telephone.

Kyaw Nyein, Bo Ze Ya has just been here.

Oh, on what errand?

He wants to be defence minister.

What did you tell him?

That I was appointing nobody.

12. A term of address meaning "elder brother." Many of Thakin Nu's friends called him this.

Victory!

What are you celebrating, Kyaw Nyein?

Mr. Prime Minister, you won't understand. I'll come and explain it to you.

As soon as he had put the telephone down, U Kyaw Nyein sent for Bo Ne Win and told him what had transpired. Bo Ne Win, as expected, felt he had been double-crossed. He called Bo Ze Ya who did not deny what he had done. Bo Ne Win and Bo Ze Ya had come to the parting of ways.

That very night, officers of the Third Burma Rifles held a meeting. This battalion, stationed at Mingaladon, was charged with the task of defending Rangoon. Its commanding officer was Bo Ye Htut, with Bo Chit Myaing second in command. Bo Ye Htut had thrown in his lot with Bo Ze Ya and determined to rebel. Bo Chit Myaing, not being a politician, was loyal to the government. After a full discussion, they arrived at a curious decision. Those in favour of rebellion would pick up their rifles and follow their commanding officer. This arrangement included officers, NCOs and all other ranks. Those who opposed rebellion would also arm themselves but would stay behind with Bo Chit Myaing. There would be a period of thirty-six hours during which there would be an armistice. Thereafter the soldiers would obey the orders of their superior officers.

It goes without saying that if Bo Chit Myaing had joined the rebels there would have been frightful consequences. The Third Battalion had merely to enter Rangoon, seize the prime minister and his Cabinet, and proclaim themselves the new government. Thakin Nu had a platoon of Union Military Police and a section of Chin soldiers guarding him. The prime minister, who, over quite trivial matters, often allowed himself to go off the deep end, would have been powerless to act. He would have been like a cock in a basket bound for the noodle shop. He would have been yanked out and his neck put on the block.

Consequent on the breakup of the meeting over rival claims to the defence ministership, and the desertion to the enemy of the Third Burma Rifles, U Kyaw Nyein came to report to the prime minister:

Thein Pe has not gone underground with the Third Rifles. He's still in Rangoon.

Is that so?

Yes, and I've arranged to take him in.

When will he be arrested?

This very day.

Is he involved in the army desertion? If it's only the matter of the generals wanting office, he should not be arrested.

He is one of those who instigated the battalion desertion.

In that case it's very serious. He will have to be apprehended.

I've asked him to come and see me. The police will arrest him at the gate.

I'll say that's very neat.

Budalin Thein Pe was accordingly arrested and imprisoned. Some time later the prime minister received a letter from him asking to be released. If not, he would go on a hunger strike, he threatened.

Kyaw Nyein, this fellow is not going to go hungry. But if you think he's had enough you may let him go.

Outside, he's going to give more trouble.

If he doesn't keep still—if he continues to meddle—you do as you please.

What I've done is nothing to what he would do if he were in power. When the Japanese came and we were in the underground in Kabaing I peeked into his diary. He had me marked for killing.

I remember your telling me this when I first escaped from Mandalay Jail. But let him go this time, please.

Thakin Nu had long felt an attachment to U Thein Pe. Since university days, when Ko Ohn had first brought them together, along with Ko Aung San and Ko Kyaw Nyein, they had become very close. Ko Thein Pe was a master in the art of inflicting hurt. In dealing with an adversary one man might rely on his choice of words, another on his mode of delivery, a third on facial expression to emphasise his point. Ko Thein Pe had all three weapons in his armoury, and he could make the enemy squirm. Among those who had come off second best in encounters with Ko Thein Pe were the lecturers and tutors in the Burmese Literature Department at Rangoon University. Because Ko Thein Pe was such an effective speaker Ko Nu always went to hear him. Whenever Ko Nu went into the city Ko Thein Pe was with him. When they left the university both found employment at the *Deedok Journal*. The friendship had ripened over the years, hence Thakin Nu's compassionate desire to spring him from jail.

U Kyaw Nyein wanted him detained on the ground that he would be a disruptive influence outside. There might possibly be another reason: U Thein Pe was the one who had upset the applecart after U Kyaw Nyein had made it all neat and tidy for General Ne Win to become defence minister. At any rate, U Kyaw Nyein heeded the premier's request and released the detainee.

A part of the Third Burma Rifles having deserted, the First Burma Rifles stationed in Thayet became restive. They were convinced that the Thakin Nu government was heavily beset and that they had merely to go down to Rangoon and seize it. They therefore served notice that they had revolted and began their march on Rangoon. They were so confident of success that they had accompanying them many villagers in large buses who were to share in the loot after victory. At that time the only reliable forces with the government, the Fourth Burma Rifles and the half of the Third that remained loyal, had been dispatched to Bassein, Maubin, and Pyapon, where the situation was said to be deteriorating. Small detachments from here and there were ordered to bar the enemy approach, and civilians who wished to take a crack at rebels were given musketry training and rushed into the breach with whatever weapons were available. The Burmese air force had two, perhaps three fighter aircraft. But they caught the rebels in the open at Kyungale, north of Tharrawaddy, and strafed them with machine guns and cannon. Almost the entire vanguard of the First Rifles became casualties. It was afterwards reported they had time to take cover after hearing the sound of aircraft engines, but they believed

Rangoon had already fallen and the planes had come to greet them, so they simply stood in the open and were killed.

BO SEIN HMAN THE LIONHEARTED

On the ground the hero of this action was Bo Sein Hman, a native of Tharrawaddy, who led the ambush against the enemy forces coming down from Thayetmyo. At the first sign of danger he had gone to U Kyaw Nyein and volunteered to defend Tharrawaddy. He could muster only five other men to go with him and even then the government could not find every man a gun. When the prime minister heard of this he forbade Bo Sein Hman to go. An added reason was that the rebel group from the Third Rifles was astride the highway at Wanetchaung and Bo Sein Hman was too well-known and too valuable a man to be exposed to the risk of capture. But he insisted on going and would not rest until U Kyaw Nyein had secured an interview with the prime minister, at which Bo Sein Hman declared that while he lived he would not permit Tharrawaddy to be occupied by rebels. The emotion-charged interview ended only when Thakin Nu reluctantly gave his blessing. Bo Sein Hman made a *shikhoe* to the prime minister and was last seen driving away in his stationwagon. Among the five followers in the vehicle, one had a Bren gun.

Nearing his hometown Bo Sein Hman recruited volunteers and took up positions to the north only minutes before the rebel troops from Thayet arrived. In fact Bo Sein Hman had just set a wooden bridge on fire and it was while the enemy was rushing to save it that the lone Bren started to bark.

Between the air force and Bo Sein Hman they managed to halt the rebels and remove the threat to Rangoon. Bo Sein Hman himself fell in action. He was in an aircraft on a mission to spot the enemy when a bullet fired from below penetrated into his seat. His death was a severe loss to the country.

As the First Burma Rifles advanced from Thayetmyo, the rebels of the former Third Burma Rifles left their Wanetchaung redoubt in an attempt to join forces. But the air force was again on the scene and the meeting never took place. The First Burma Rifles turned tail and returned to Thayetmyo which they occupied. The Third swung into Prome which they also occupied. Both these battalions had been under Communist influence and now they joined the Communists openly.

THE PVO GOES UNDERGROUND

These troubles had hardly been contained when elements of the People's Volunteer Organisation joined with the Union Military Police to loot government treasuries of some twelve million rupees. The military police deserters were made up of irregulars who had fought in the underground against the Japanese. All those who robbed the treasuries went underground.

Seeing regular army units in revolt, the People's Volunteer Organisation began to get restive. Ultimately some 65 percent of the PVO, under the command of Bo Po Kun and Bo La Yaung, donned white bands around their caps, called themselves the White PVO, and revealed their leanings towards the Communists, going into armed insurrection on 29 July 1948. The remaining PVOs, styled the Yellow Band and led by Major Aung and Bo Sein Hman (until his death), remained loyal to the government.

After the PVO defections, Brigadier Kyaw Zaw went to see the prime minister with the alarming report that the White PVO was concentrated between Syriam and Thongwa. They had dug bunkers to the east of Syriam whence they intended to attack the town, seize the guns in the police station, and loot the treasury. If their strength then permitted they would cross the river and attack Rangoon. The brigadier wanted the navy to shell the PVO positions from the frigate *Mayu*. Thakin Nu said:

Bo Kyaw Zaw, the White PVO's are wicked, but do they have to be killed off with shell fire?

Mr. Prime Minister, they're going to seize Syriam. We have no government forces there. The police are not going to lay down their lives. Whoever comes, they will open the police station and put down their arms. I have precise information after Syriam they'll come here.

I'm certain if we fire big guns at them they'll run away. Can't we fire above their bunkers to frighten them? Then they won't get to Syriam.

That could be done.

How are you going to control your fire?

There will be a spotter plane over the bunkers. It will signal the position to the *Mayu* and the sights will be raised slightly above the bunkers.

That's good. Please do accordingly.

7

Pulling Through

Misfortune continued to plague the Burmese government. Communist forces, army forces, the Union Military Police (UMP), the civilian police, and the People's Volunteer Organisation, all had aided the rebellion. By the time the PVO went underground, Thakin Nu's government had taken on the appearance of an old house with rotted supports. And now, seeing this, the Karen National Union (KNU) and its affiliated groups became visibly restive.

To put this new development into perspective, it should first be pointed out that, up to the outbreak of the Second World War in Europe, there had never been such a thing as a Karen-Burman problem in this country. The Burman was by nature officious and meddlesome; the Karen was a cool customer who minded his own business. The element necessary to bring them into conflict was missing.

The peaceful ways of the Karens were testified to by the crime statistics of the prewar years. The great majority of those accused of rape, assault, knifings, murder, picking pockets, robbery, and dacoity were Burmans; the incidence of such crimes among the Karens was extremely low—almost negligible. The Karens seemed to abhor courthouses and police stations. Even when transgressed against by others, or taken advantage of, they would try to compromise or cover up rather than go to court.

To say that before the war there was an absence of strife between the Burmans and the Karens would be only to bring out the negative aspect. On the positive side, there was a very real amity and neighbourliness. Friendships of the kind that encouraged Burmans and Karens to stay in one another's homes were the rule rather than the exception.

Thakin Nu himself had played among Karen children since he was in the infant standard in school. Among his closest friends were Tha Aye,[1] Sein Kho, and Ma Pu Sein, Karens from Thanbyuzu village. The village was a mile distant from Wakèma and Maung Nu would go there on holidays to hunt birds and to play with his Karen friends. On Sundays Maung Nu would often accompany his Karen playmates to the Christian Church.[2] He did not understand the religious service, but he followed the responses the others made and obtained much satisfaction from the experience. It was also profitable because of the candy and holy pictures that were doled out.

Later, Maung Nu was to find himself among adult Karens with whom also he felt much rapport. Two hours' journey by steamer from Wakèma to Kyonmangay were the twin Karen villages of Shanzu and Maungdee, where Maung Nu's father had a few plots of paddy. At reaping time, Maung Nu would be among the Karen sharecroppers, who took him to their homes and fed him some of the most delectable food he had ever eaten. On his return home, his boat would be laden with bananas, dried fish, gourds, pumpkins, and sticky rice. Yet, when the Karens came to Wakèma, they could not be prevailed upon to visit Maung Nu's home. They went about their business without inconveniencing anybody and departed quietly. Maung Nu had to take his gifts with him when next he went to visit the Karen villages. This was not an isolated case; friendly intercourse of this kind was widespread in the country.

Tragically for both peoples, however, Karen-Burmese relations were to be disrupted. The problem arose in this way: There was a period in 1942 between the British withdrawal and the occupation of the country by the Japanese. The Burmans at this time formed

1. After a separation lasting forty years U Nu and U Tha Aye were to meet again. By that time U Tha Aye had married a Buddhist woman (also a Karen), a friend of U Nu's. Under her influence he forsook Christianity and became a Buddhist. She prevailed upon U Nu first to sponsor U Tha Aye's entry into the monkhood and again to enter the Meditation Centre.

2. About 15 percent of the Karens in Burma are Christian.

local military units which were to become the Burma Independence Army (BIA). In doing so, the Burmans seized guns, money, motor vehicles, and jewellery. When the BIA in Myaungmya went to seize Karen guns, the Karens refused to deliver. The Karens' refusal was understandable, but the BIA insisted and fighting broke out sporadically. The fighting spread from Myaungmya District to Bassein and from Bassein to Maubin. Wherever the Karens outnumbered the Burmans, the latter got the worst of the exchanges, and vice versa. The edifice of friendship was damaged almost beyond repair.

During this interregnum Thakin Nu was in Mandalay Jail, and he knew nothing of what was happening. After his release, Thakin Nu spent some time with Ko Kyaw Nyein, Ko Tha Khin,[3] and Ko Thein Pe in Kabaing, so by the time he got to Rangoon the Karen-Burman imbroglio had assumed serious proportions.

With the formation of an administrative committee under Dr. Ba Maw, some Karen leaders headed by Dr. San C. Po responded to the invitation to come to Rangoon for consultations. The Burman reception committee, representing both the administration and political parties, comprised Dr. Ba Maw, General Aung San, Thakins Mya, Than Tun, and Nu. Many meetings were held, and these led to a mission of reconciliation, headed by Thakin Nu, which visited the delta areas with mixed Karen-Burman populations. Up to one month before the war ended Thakin Nu and Henzada[4] U Mya continued their pacification tours of the affected areas.

ATTEMPTS AT RECONCILIATION

Since Thakin Nu was very conscious of the problem, and since he was constantly haunted by the thought of innocent women and children being hurt in any kind of internecine strife, he kept on the pacification trail after he became prime minister. Arguing for unity, he used the analogy of two bale fruits hitting against each other, both breaking up in the process. Repeatedly he sought the counsel of such respected Karen leaders as Saw Ba U Gyi, Mahn

3. Ko Tha Khin was a student leader; he later became a minister in U Nu's Cabinet.
4. Henzada was the town from which U Mya came.

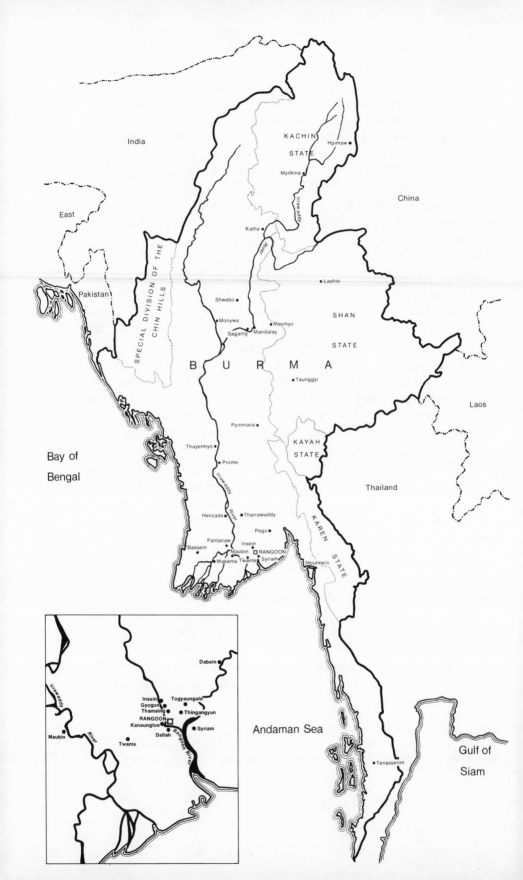

India

KACHIN
STATE

Hpimaw •

Myitkina •

China

Irrawaddy

Katha •

East

Pakistan

SPECIAL DIVISION OF THE CHIN HILLS

Shwebo •

Lashio •

SHAN

STATE

Monywa •
• Maymyo

Sagaing Mandalay

B U R M A

• Taunggyi

Laos

Pyinmana •

KAYAH
STATE

Bay of
Bengal

Thayetmyo •

• Prome

Irrawaddy River

Thailand

Henzada •
• Tharrawaddy

Pantanaw
Insein
Bassein •
Maubin RANGOON
Wakema Twante Syriam

Pegu •

KAREN
STATE

Moulmein •

Andaman Sea

Gulf of
Siam

Tenasserim •

Dabein •

Irrawaddy

Insein • Togyaungale
Gyogon •
Thamaing • • Thingangyun
RANGOON
Kanaungtoe •
Dallah
River

Rangoon River

• Syriam

Maubin •

Twante •

James Tun Aung, and Thra Tha Hto in keeping tensions down and preventing fresh incidents. He made frequent tours of the trouble spots in the delta.

Because the cancer of past animosities was too far advanced, however, the open clash that Thakin Nu feared proved unpreventable. But the unremitting efforts made by him and such people as Saw Ba U Gyi did not prove vain. Even after hostilities broke out, there was an influential section among the Karens that continued to support the Burmese government and its sincere attempts at reconciliation. Although the KNU and the AFPFL might differ in policy, at the leadership level there remained much personal goodwill.

For example, towards the end of June 1948, when a portion of the Third Burma Rifles had deserted, and the First Burma Rifles from Thayet were rolling down to seize Rangoon—when the government was helpless and unprotected—Saw Ba U Gyi and some friends asked to see the prime minister. At this meeting, Mahn James Tun Aung said that, if the Communists ever entered Rangoon, they would hide Thakin Nu in a place of safety and defend him against his enemies. Knowing as he did that this was a time when some within his own party were making overtures to the Communists, and that some police officers had given orders to their men to surrender, Thakin Nu was greatly touched by the Karens' solicitude.

Thakin Nu did not stop at conferences or making conciliatory gestures in public speeches. He set about making a Karen State a reality. On 6 April he appointed the Kawthoolei Boundary Demarcation Commission under Sections 199[5] and 200[6] of the Constitution.

Again, on 20 October the prime minister appointed the Statehood Inquiry Commission. This was headed by Dr. Ba U, chief justice of the Union, with full representation from the Chamber

5. "The Parliament may by an Act admit to the Union a new State upon such terms and conditions including the extent of representation of the State in the Parliament as may be specified in the Act."
6. "The Parliament may by an Act, with the consent of the Council of every State whose boundaries are affected thereby: (a) establish a new unit; (b) increase the area of any unit; (c) diminish the area of any unit; (d) alter the boundaries of any unit; and may, with the like consent, make such supplemental, incidental and consequential provisions as the Parliament may deem necessary or proper."

of Nationalities. At the first meeting of this commission, Thakin Nu himself was present, and he urged that the just aspirations of the Mons, Karens, and Arakanese be ascertained and that recommendations be made for speedy implementation of its conclusions. At that moment, Thakin Nu had fully made up his mind to grant to the Mons, Karens, and Arakanese statehood within the Union.

But although Thakin Nu had appointed the Boundary Demarcation Commission, in regard to the burning problem of Karen-Burman relations, he did not believe that it would suffice to bring lasting relief. The Karens had guns in their possession and this fact made for pessimism. In 1947, even prior to the assassination of General Aung San, the Karens had begun to arm themselves—for their own defence, it was claimed. They called the armed units the Karen National Defence Organisation (KNDO).

In a sense, it was inevitable that they should do this, because the times were unsettled and the Communists as well as the PVO had also armed their troops. The Thakin Nu government, its strength depleted, was unable to disband these irregular forces or to disarm them. A situation was thereby created which invited conflict.

The Karen National Union's demands were: (1) a Karen State, (2) the right to secede from the Union at will, and (3) incorporation into the Karen State of areas of the Pegu, Tenasserim, and Irrawaddy Divisions, or nearly one half of Burma. Of the three demands, Thakin Nu was agreeable to the first one. He was adamantly opposed to the second, and, as for the third, his Cabinet had already determined to abide by the recommendations of the Boundary Commission. The policy differences between the AFPFL and the KNU were a second cause for pessimism.

The third and decisive factor was the spread of the insurrection throughout the country and the palpable weakness of the government in meeting the threats to its existence. In July and August of 1948, a large number of Karens in the Union Military Police deserted with their arms to the KNDO.

At the same time the KNDO attacked the government forces in Papun and in Kayah State. The KNDO seized and for a time held Thaton and Moulmein, headquarters towns of two districts. This, coming on top of the Communist and PVO insurrections, rendered the government's situation desperate.

The question arises, Why did the government not raise more troops? With 60 percent of its troops gone over to the enemy, it would have been pointless to recruit new men because the deserters had taken their weapons with them, and there were no new ones available.

A government on the verge of collapse has the greatest difficulty procuring guns from abroad. Countries that have guns and are in a position to give aid do not believe in throwing water down the drain. In these circumstances the only recourse open to Thakin Nu was to meet frequently with Saw Ba U Gyi and other Karen leaders and to plead with them to put a curb on their followers.

The situation continued to deteriorate, and on 4 December 1948 the prime minister made a public statement that reports from every state of the Union showed a major crisis had developed.

As a last resort, Thakin Nu called in Saw Ba U Gyi and his associates and expressed his wish to appeal to the KNDO leaders directly, and Saw Ba U Gyi undertook to make, the arrangements for the premier to meet them. As soon as Thakin Nu's friends discovered he intended to journey to the KNDO headquarters in Insein they raised objections, his wife, Daw Mya Yee, being the most insistent among them. But he went, nevertheless, riding in Saw Ba U Gyi's car, with only his aide-de-camp, Captain Soe Myint with him. They were unarmed.

Saw Ba U Gyi's father-in-law, U Zan, did the honours in Insein. After eating his food—noodles cooked in coconut milk—Thakin Nu met the KNDO leaders. They listened in respectful silence while he drove home the point that Karens and Burmans were members of the same family who must settle their differences without resort to violence. It was evident from their expressions that little dent was made on whatever views they already held.

The next day, hearing that a clash was imminent between Karens and Burmans in Bassein, the prime minister hurried there to spread the message of peace to the contending groups. The motor gunboat that Thakin Nu travelled in was commanded by Lieutenant Saw Jack, a Karen naval officer.

January 1949 shattered Thakin Nu's fond hopes, for the end of that month saw a KNDO attack by land, while Saw Jack, now turned mutineer, shelled Bassein from his gunboat. However, as soon as danger threatened, the Fourth Burma Rifles were deployed around Maubin and Bassein in company strength, and these troops gave such a good account of themselves that the KNDO had to retreat. Saw Jack's fleeing boat was detected from the air and strafed. The boat was damaged and its crew severely punished. Saw Jack and four sailors barely escaped with their lives.

Following this engagement, Thakin Nu quickly got on the scene and attempted once more to undo the harm that had been done. He met with both Burman and Karen leaders and ordered relief supplies to be rushed down from Rangoon. He handed over sufficient funds to a son of Dr. San C. Po to repair the tomb of his father, which had been damaged by the Burmans. He also donated money to the Burmans to restore an image of the Buddha that had been defiled by the Karens.

As Thakin Nu boarded the steamer for his return home a friend dashed up the gangway.

Mr. Prime Minister, are there Karens on this boat?

I don't know.

You ought to be more careful when you travel.

What makes you say that?

Don't you realise you were on Saw Jack's gunboat on your last trip, and that this man has turned mutineer? A good job he didn't seize you when he had you in his power!

THE KNU REBELLION

About the middle of January 1949, Karens from KNDO headquarters in Insein began disarming government officials stationed in Insein, Gyogon, and Thamaing. Since this was taking place only seven miles out of Rangoon, government troops were dispatched to restrain the Karens. On 31 January fighting broke out and the KNDO overran Insein. The gates of Insein Jail were opened and two thousand prisoners set free, and all the money in the Insein treasury was looted.

This swift turn of events, taking place at the gateway to Rangoon, caused panic which can be better imagined than described. A KNU-led KNDO insurrection was in full swing.

The KNDO rebellion could not have come at a worse time. The black clouds had started to lower four or five days before the Insein debacle. Fifty miles from Rangoon the Karens raided a small Burman village, took all valuables, and executed six men in public. After the KNDO raiders had left, the villagers saw a steamer, with an empty cargo boat in tow, passing by, and frantically signalled it to stop. The steamer had discharged its cargo in Bassein and was returning to Rangoon. There was a police escort on board. Learning of their terrible misfortune, the police brought the villagers to Rangoon. The following morning, a full account of the atrocities appeared in exaggerated form in the newspapers. The prime minister at once went on the air with a five-point statement:

1. All Karens should not be condemned out of hand; it was wrong to say Karens were killing Burmans.

2. There were many good Karens not involved in the killings; the correct thing to say was that some criminals had killed good Burmans.

3. If the roles had been reversed, and if some Burmans had killed some Karens, there would be many Burmans not involved in the killings; then they would expect the Karens to regard the atrocities as being perpetrated by the bad against the good.

4. The government, in dealing with the criminals according to law, would make no distinction between "the child it carried in its arms and the child carried on its back."

5. Since a very serious state of affairs prevailed, the public was requested to cooperate with the government to prevent further deterioration.

If through such use of press and radio the prime minister hoped for an easing of tensions, he was sadly disappointed. There was a tremendous wave of anger, most of it directed against Thakin Nu. This was the fellow who had handed Twante over to the Karens; it was he who said nothing when the Karens attacked Burmans in Bassein but who hurried there to restrain the Burmans when they retaliated; he was the man who appointed the Karen Saw San Po Thin as special commissioner of the Irrawaddy Division, knowing full well the Karens planned to attack Bassein; and now with

Karens exposed as murderers he was trying to hoodwink the people. This fellow, they said, could not be a pure Burman. He must have Karen blood in him. Look at his jaw![7]

The fire of the people's rage was fanned by a prominent newspaper which dubbed Thakin Nu "Karen Nu" and called for his arrest. Then, the paper suggested, he should be led before the president[8] and compelled to sign a letter of resignation.

The usually brittle "Karen Nu" somehow maintained his composure. People in the mass, he told himself, tended to be irresponsible. They were confused and angry and the press had aggravated their condition, hence greater irresponsibility than ever was to be expected. They would speak irresponsibly, act irresponsibly.

Their charge that Twante had been made over to the Karens was substantially true. There were no Burman troops available, and while there was no dearth of volunteers there were no weapons with which they could be armed. Knowing the KNDO to be unreliable, knowing that Twante was a sensitive spot, the government had no option but to caution the KNDO to respect the trust of the people and protect their lives.

As for Saw San Po Thin, he was appointed special commissioner because he was a Karen who would not take orders from the KNU. Since there were others like him who owed no allegiance to the KNU and KNDO, his task was to prevent this substantial section of the Karen population from joining the rebellion even if they did not wish to support the government.

Likewise, it was true that "Karen Nu" had hurried to Bassein after the engagement with the Karen rebels. But it was not to restrain the hands of Burmans in retaliation. There were no Karen rebels to retaliate against; they had been driven off, leaving behind only the permanent residents, who were not involved in the fighting. The prime minister could not permit the innocent to be harmed for offences committed by others who were guilty but absent. Revenge must not be sought against the innocent, whether they be Karen or Burman.

If Thakin Nu had delayed going to Bassein, the local Burman

---

7. Karens generally have more pronounced jaw bones than Burmans.

8. The constitution of the Union of Burma provided for a president as well as a prime minister.

population, which was greater than the Karen, would have taken reprisals and the Karens would assuredly have suffered. But there were other places where the Karens outnumbered the Burmans and if the reprisals spread all over the country blood would flow freely. Not every Karen wanted to kill Burmans, and vice versa. It was the government's duty to protect its citizens wherever they might be, but circumstances were such that it could scarcely breathe, let alone embark upon punitive action against law-breakers. The only course left open was to get to the scene of the fire, each time there was an outbreak, and use all means to prevent its spread.

The people, however, were too inflamed to think of anything except that the Karens were on the warpath. When the newspapers reported Karen atrocities in a Maubin village, they vented their anger and frustration on the prime minister.

While Rangoon was seething with unrest, Thakin Nu's telephone rang.

Mr. Prime Minister?

Yes.

One hundred men, women, and children of the Karen quarter in Ahlone have been seized by Burmans and are held prisoner in the Christian Church near Mission Road. They intend to pour petrol on the building and set it ablaze. I thought you who make no distinction between races, but only between good and bad people, ought to know.

The prime minister called Bo Aung Gyi on the telephone, relayed the message, and ordered him to take immediate action. Fortunately, the people were released unharmed. Early the next morning, Thakin Nu, accompanied by Bo Ne Win and the commissioner of police, was on the scene.

At that time Major-General Smith Dun, the army chief of staff, was on leave,[9] and his place was being taken temporarily by Bo Ne

---

9. General Smith Dun, a Karen and a loyal and faithful regular army officer, found his position untenable when the KNU revolted. He thus took leave preparatory to retirement. The government did not force him to go on leave. On the contrary, the defence minister, on the instructions of the premier, tried to persuade him to return to active duty.

Win. The latter had been at his post just a day or two. The whole of Ahlone quarter was under police guard.

The prime minister held on-the-spot discussions with the Karen leaders. He remembered his friends, after whom he enquired. Mahn James Tun Aung was probably at the KNU headquarters in Insein, because he was not available, but Thra Tha Hto was present, and he and Thakin Nu visited each Karen household in turn. In about half an hour, the official party saw coming towards them two Burmans, one with a chicken in his hand. He had been caught by the other stealing the bird from a Karen home. Bo Ne Win struck him soundly with his fists.

After talking with the Karen leaders, Thakin Nu turned to the police commissioner and said, "I trust your men, but I don't want Burmans patrolling this area. I'd like you to recruit a special police force of Sino-Burmans from the Lanmadaw precinct and station them here. Would you give this your immediate attention?"

Later, as he prepared to leave, Thakin Nu became concerned over Thra Tha Hto. He persuaded his friend to leave together with him, promising to send him back after the trouble subsided. Thra Tha Hto thus became the prime minister's guest for a time. That very evening the police commissioner reported that he had raised a special force of Sino-Burman volunteers.

When the Karen rebellion broke out, certain Burman leaders, such as Sir U Thwin and Henzada U Mya, proposed that an offer be made to the PVO to return to the legal fold or—as they put it— "come into the light." The prime minister was not enthusiastic. He did not consider the PVO capable of fighting bravely; they would be more of a hindrance than a help to the government. But with the Karen threat so near, the Burman elders were frightened and they kept on pressing until Thakin Nu, more to mollify them than because he had any great expectations from the PVO, gave his assent.

The PVO from Syriam, Kyauktan, and Thongwa thus made their reappearance. They came to Rangoon chanting, "We want to eat Karen flesh," adding to Thakin Nu's misgivings. The first thing he had to do was to get the PVO returnees to stop making such provocative sounds.

ADDING FUEL TO THE FIRE

Bad tidings on the military front were matched by bad news on the economic front. The finance minister read a report in the Cabinet which said that because of the insurrections (1) export trade had greatly declined, (2) revenue and taxes could not be collected, and (3) civil war expenditure had soared. In order to reduce spending the Cabinet agreed that ministers should take a 30 percent cut in salary, and all government servants a 15 percent cut. Two days after the decision was made, the civil and ministerial services association declared they would not abide by it. The Cabinet went into emergency session and reaffirmed their decision as the only way out. When Thakin Nu proposed to explain to the president and leaders of the association the government's difficulties, his colleagues tried to dissuade him. They told him the association was not amenable to reason, and that in any case the finance and home ministers could more properly serve as channels of communication. The prime minister nevertheless insisted on seeing the officials concerned and making his bid for cooperation. As expected, his attempt failed, and he had to report back to the Cabinet that the association was unyielding. The Cabinet held firm: let the association strike.

The Cabinet secretary, U Win Pe, stayed behind after the ministers had gone. He was an exemplary civil servant, a hard worker and a man of few words. He was lugubrious over the certainty of the civil services strike and hazarded the opinion it would be a hard blow to take on top of the many ills in the country. Thakin Nu said the Cabinet had taken into account the implications of the threat; if the civil servants were so devoid of patriotism as to carry out their threat, the government would not flinch.

On 7 February the government found itself in the grip of a civil servants' strike. This was followed five days later by the Rangoon University students of the communist persuasion going underground.

On 16 February the Railway Workers' Union struck. The main communications system, a key factor in the fight against the rebels, was thus paralised.

More disasters followed. The remaining Karens in the civilian police and the Union Military Police deserted to the KNDO. The Third Karen Rifles revolted.

Beset by multicoloured insurgents—white PVO, red- and white-flag Communists—the government had nonetheless succeeded in raising a force of irregulars called *sitwundan* (levies). However, within days of their being armed with whatever weapons came to hand, whole companies deserted to the enemy. Of those that remained, not a single unit could claim that it had no defectors. Guns were being lost as fast as they could be procured.

By this time, more than half of the country had been overrun or occupied by the insurgents and every treasury looted. Rangoon was isolated. On the east, vanguards of the enemy held Togyaungale, Dabein, Thingangyun, and Syriam.[10] On the south, Dallah, Pyaw-bwègyi, and Kanaungtoe[11] had fallen; on the west, the insurgents held territory up to E-ywa;[12] and to the north, Insein and areas up to seven miles of Rangoon were under enemy occupation.

In the capital itself, the administration wobbled. There were daylight robberies in the heart of town. Of the offences against the people's person and property, about one-third were committed by dacoits and robbers, the remainder by the multicoloured insurgents.

Pressed on all sides was an expression the prime minister had heard. Now he was experiencing it. It was a most apt description of weights pushing against his sides and his chest until he was like to asphyxiate. His normal reaction was to go before the altar and find release through ritual recitation of the *payeik*. But so sunk in depression was he that his legs buckled and sent him tottering back into his chair. Only for an instant, though. In a flash it came to him that many another man in his position would bow the knee in surrender or bolt the scene.

"I refuse to kneel, and I refuse to run away," he declared to himself. Then, suffused with joy and rejuvenated in every limb, he prepared to begin his sacred incantations.

10. All these towns are within a radius of ten miles from Rangoon.
11. Dallah and Kanaungtoe are directly across the river from Rangoon.
12. E-ywa and Kemmendine face each other across the Rangoon River.

THE INSURRECTIONS GAIN MOMENTUM

It never rains but it pours, it is often said. This aphorism has proved apt in relating the history of postindependence Burma. Events have been described as, and shown to be, tragic. Unlike the rains, and the monsoons in Burma, they would not cease.

The Third Karen Rifles advanced along the Prome-Rangoon road with the obvious purpose of linking up with the KNDO in Insein and seizing the capital. It was a bold move and, in the circumstances, an eminently feasible one. It failed of its purpose because of one crippling factor—the Karens brought their women and children with them. It might have been overconfidence that led them to do this; more probably they thought the families would be safer with them than in the disturbed countryside. But the fact remains that the Burman defenders of Tharrawaddy caught them at a disadvantage, and the air force once again played havoc with an enemy caught in the open in mass formation.

After the Karens had scattered, the PVO, who had taken no part in the fighting, began grabbing the arms and ammunition abandoned by the soldiers. Government forces radioed Rangoon to inquire what they should do about the PVO. The only reply possible was to stop the looting, but not at the risk of having to fight it out with them.

Meanwhile, in Insein, the KNDO had fortified the buildings fronting on Rangoon and from their bunkers kept up a steady fire against the advancing Burma Army troops. The Karens fought well and kept the troops pinned down behind locomotives and railway wagons at the Insein workshops two hundred yards away. The days lengthened into weeks, with neither side able to advance.

One day an object came trundling down the road that made the Burman troops gape with amazement. It was a derelict British tank which the Karens had somehow patched up and made to run. It had advanced three miles into government held territory before it could be stopped with a suicidal attack at close range by commandos. Trapped inside were the bodies of two Karens—the driver and a machine-gunner.

This sudden appearance of a tank proved most unsettling to the Burman troops. Was it the only one the Karens had managed to repair? What if they had four—five—others, similarly reconditioned? Four tanks would give adequate cover to infantry soldiers in their advance into Rangoon itself.

The next morning, Brigadier Kyaw Zaw, commanding the South Burma District, brought a military proposal to the prime minister. He wanted every available aircraft to spray petrol over Karen positions, then ignite them with incendiaries.

Although every instinct told him the brigadier's strategy was sound, and that delay would be dangerous, Thakin Nu found himself unable to utter the two words "Go ahead." He could picture to himself Insein burning. But how did one burn only the enemy and not the innocent people around him? Buildings of all kinds— religious edifices—would go up in smoke. He fidgeted for five minutes and finally pleaded, "Please, Bo Kyaw Zaw, think up something else."

So Brigadier Kyaw Zaw conferred with other officers and came up with another plan. With experts from the British Services Mission he fashioned homemade bombs, and these were dropped over Insein. Much later, when peace talks were initiated and Saw Ba U Gyi came to see the prime minister, he brought up the subject of these bombs, lightheartedly, in after-dinner conversation. He said the Karens were delighted with these bombs because they did not explode and thus provided the KNDO with gelignite. This of course was not entirely true; some of the bombs did go off.

The Burmans then played the Karens at their own game. They, too, salvaged a World War II British tank and went into the attack. The Karens in Insein stood their ground and fired heavy calibre bullets into the caterpillar treads. Their own experience of these rusted machines had perhaps taught them how to find vulnerable spots. At any rate, the tank stopped astride the road and had to be abandoned.

AN EXCITING INCIDENT

Both sides displayed ingenuity in obtaining military hardware. They traced Japanese army caches, dug up old rifles and ammunition, and scoured the jungle for other discarded weapons.

Not long after the commencement of the KNU insurrection,

their armed forces, the KNDO, planned to overrun Henzada. There were about two hundred armed troops but they also had three hundred civilians to help carry substantial quantities of loot. The KNDO attack was spearheaded by a single armoured car, another reconditioned vehicle of World War II vintage. It had two Brens mounted on it.

The Burman police, Union Military Police, and sitwundan in Henzada were outnumbered and outgunned, but they had their own "secret weapon," a six-pound field gun, also salvaged out of the scrap heap. Burman mechanics said the gun would fire, but they had only one shell. Their strategy was to get out of town with the gun and wait for the marauders. So it was armoured car against cannon, and the issue was in doubt until the unsuspecting vehicle got within point-blank range and the gun disgorged its lone shell. Luckily for the Burmans it scored a hit, and the day was theirs.

Government officials from Henzada arrived in Rangoon to report the good news and to invite the prime minister to honour with his presence the relief of the town. Thakin Nu readily responded, carrying a Sacred Bodhi (pipal) sapling with him. Since the stretch between Maubin and Yandoon was infested with KNDO insurgents, the usual motor launch was accompanied by the gunboat *Inle*. The outward journey was performed without incident.

In Henzada, the sacred sapling was personally planted by the prime minister in Payagyi Monastery. A team of payeik masters chanted incantations. Thakin Nu visited the scene of battle and paid tribute to the defenders of the town.

On his return, the prime minister's convoy was ambushed from the shore at the mouth of the Pantanaw River. A running fight ensued and the Karen positions were heavily shelled. There were no casualties on the government side, except for a naval officer slightly wounded.

THE FALL OF MANDALAY

Despite the effectiveness of defensive warfare with improvised weapons, the overall situation remained extremely grave. In February 1949, the First Kachin Rifles stationed in Pyinmana became disaffected. These troops were there to contend with the Communists in the area; instead, Captain Naw Seng revolted with some of his men. Next, Naw Seng joined forces with the First Karen Rifles and the rebel battalion marched north, occupying one town after another. Maymyo fell into their hands, and the Karen officers and men interned there were incorporated into their army. On 13 March the rebels took Mandalay.

Mandalay was the capital of northern Burma and the second largest city in the country. Its loss was a severe blow to the government and an already anguished prime minister. Filled with an uncontrollable desire to see what progress was being made in the relief of Mandalay, Thakin Nu insisted on going north. The farthest he could fly was to Shwebo, where there was a disused airstrip, abandoned since the war and now overgrown with weeds. After landing there in a Dakota, he learnt that Special Commissioner U Win of Mandalay and some remnants of the armed forces had withdrawn to Sagaing and were outfitting there for a counterattack. Thakin Nu accordingly sped overland to Sagaing, a distance of some sixty miles.

The prime minister found the townspeople in a state of alarm. His coming posed a security problem because Sagaing town was within rifle range of the Ava Bridge, from whence a sniper could pick him out. After conferring with his staff, U Win took Thakin Nu to the range of hills north of Sagaing and together they lodged in a monastery. Since the prime minister was ignorant of military tactics he was of no help at all in the campaign to retake Mandalay. All he could do was to sit outside the Ponnyashin Pagoda and recite ritual verses. As often as his duties permitted, U Win, another firm believer in the efficacy of payeik, would join him in the incantations. The Sagaing hills were extremely pleasant by night. Their devotions held them in the open, one at each end of the platform. They prayed until they fell asleep.

A few days passed and the prime minister was restless for news of northern Burma. He made a quick trip back to Shwebo, to find little in the way of comforting news; but he found among the group of government officials one who was to make a lasting impression upon him—a superior type of civil servant whose loyalty, integrity, and courage had been put to the test, and who had come through with honour. He was John Shircore, an Anglo-Burman who served as district superintendent of police in Monywa. This district, which adjoins Shwebo, was a PVO stronghold. When the insurrection began, Shircore realised that the PVO by seizing one town after another—from his point of view, one police station after another— would be able to demoralise the headquarters town into submission. He therefore withdrew all police outposts and concentrated his force in Monywa. Soon afterwards the PVO sent three emissaries to demand the town's surrender. The district commissioner was for complying, but Shircore stood firm. He said he had no orders to surrender. The PVO told him they were giving the orders because Thakin Nu's government had fallen. "That's not true," Shircore told them, "I hear the voice of the government every day over the radio." Although, as expected, the PVO were able to seize guns and loot treasuries elsewhere, they could not shake Shircore and had to give up on Monywa.

Well pleased with this example of civil service probity, Thakin Nu returned to Sagaing and to U Win, and they were engaged in discussing plans for Mandalay when, towards the end of March, a telegram was received from U Kyaw Nyein asking the prime minister to return immediately to Rangoon. Since the Sagaing-Shwebo road was unsafe, Major Kyin went ahead of the prime minister in a pilot jeep. At one point the major spied two men with rifles who took cover in a paddy field, so he held up the convoy and gave chase. After he had seized the suspicious characters the journey was resumed, but because of the delay the DC-3[13] sent for the prime minister had already returned to Rangoon. The prime minister therefore had to mark time in Shwebo until the following day. Shwebo itself was under threat so the treasury boxes were emptied of cash and the money sent to the bank in the premier's plane.

THE SOCIALISTS LEAVE THE CABINET

Because he arrived a day late, the announcement that the Socialist members of the Cabinet had resigned had already appeared in the papers by the time U Nu reached Rangoon. An hour later one of them called, and reported to him.

We have tendered our resignations from the Cabinet.

13. At this time there were no Burman pilots qualified to fly, so British pilots had to be hired.

So I've read in the paper. What was your reason?

Bo Ne Win was constantly at us, saying the army were not watchdogs for ministers, and that they could not go on protecting us. Because he was forever egging us on to invite the rebels into a new government, we thought we should resign.

In an important decision of this kind you might have waited for my return.

We gave the matter serious thought. We knew you would not agree to our leaving, so we resigned while you were away. But we did very firmly insist that, when the new government was formed together with the rebels, you would remain prime minister.

That is beside the point. The Communists, PVO, and KNU have rebelled. The army has revolted, and now ministers leave the Cabinet. If the people judge this to mean the government has collapsed, it will be impossible to govern.

Although we've left the government, we still support you in the AFPFL.

Nevertheless, it was a damaging move on your part.

Mr. Prime Minister, we were in a most difficult position. If we did not resign we'd be accused of wanting to hang on to power.

When he first heard of the resignations, Thakin Nu had felt bitter about what he considered to be the Socialists' cowardice and desertion in the face of the enemy. He had wanted to fire them instead of accepting their resignations. Now he felt sorry for them.

When he was alone, he muttered: "The PVO have left the AFPFL, the police and the Union Military Police have quit the force, soldiers have deserted from the army, sitwundan have run away, and civil servants have gone on strike. Now the ministers are leaving. Who is still with me?" As on other such occasions, he sought solace in his payeik incantations.

Early the following morning U Kyaw Nyein arrived with General Ne Win. The general said nothing, but U Kyaw Nyein explained that circumstances had compelled the Socialists to resign. The purpose of his visit was to tell the prime minister that, if he wished, he was free to form a government with rebel participation.

Thakin Nu's decision was that under no circumstances would he include the rebels in his government. He agreed to take General Ne Win as deputy prime minister. He appointed only one new minister—Dr. E Maung, a justice of the Supreme Court. The other portfolios formerly held by the Socialists would be redistributed among the remaining ministers.

THE HEIGHT OF RUDENESS

Through the new foreign minister, Dr. E Maung, the ambassadors of Great Britain, Ceylon, India, and Pakistan asked for and obtained an interview with the prime minister. Dr. E Maung had apprised him beforehand that the Commonwealth countries would offer to loan Burma six million pounds, or roughly eighty-five million kyats. Burma at this time was virtually bankrupt. In fact, Thakin Nu caught himself saying wryly that it was just as well the government servants were on strike because he could not pay them salaries. In these circumstances, the Cabinet viewed the British loan with great anticipation.

Mr. E. Bowker, the British ambassador, acted as spokesman for the Commonwealth group. Thakin Nu had Dr. E Maung by his side. Greetings and pleasantries over, Mr. Bowker announced that, with the concurrence of the Commonwealth countries, Great Britain was pleased to offer to loan Burma a sum of six million pounds. Thakin Nu received this intelligence with a smile, but it soon faded when the British ambassador laid down, as a condition of the loan, that the government of the Union of Burma was expected to negotiate peace with the Karen National Union.

The prime minister began to think furiously. He had enough to contend with in his search for an accommodation with the Karen rebels. Surely he did not need interlopers to come and mind his business. Ambassador Bowker, who was warming up to his task, was cut short in the middle of a sentence by the prime minister suddenly asking him, "Have you finished?" There was an awkward silence which Thakin Nu broke by turning to Dr. E Maung and saying in Burmese, "Tell the ambassadors to leave." The foreign minister was thunderstruck but recovered himself sufficiently to be able to dismiss the envoys in diplomatic parlance.

Thakin Nu realised, of course, that he had committed a first-class faux pas. That evening he was so distracted he could scarcely pray. At dinner, too, he had been distraught and was beginning to mutter to himself when a thoroughly alarmed Daw Mya Yee brought him back to his senses by demanding to know what on earth was the matter with him.

Shortly thereafter, when the Cabinet met, Thakin Nu made no secret of the fact that the loan offer had been made, but that he had spoilt it all with a display of bad temper and bad manners. The ministers had already been briefed by Dr. E Maung so, instead of labouring the point, they guided the discussions into a constructive channel. They pointed out that, apart from making the government solvent once more, the British loan would also have an important psychological impact on the insurgents. The opportunity (to show that foreign governments reposed confidence in the Burma government) was too good to be missed. The prime minister, it was suggested, should make another attempt. As Thakin Nu sat silent and shame-faced, Dr. E Maung expressed the opinion that they must allow a little time to pass, to keep up appearances, and that he would resume the negotiations at an appropriate moment. When that moment arrived, the prime minister was still too embarrassed to attend. In June 1950, the British government granted their loan of six million pounds, with no strings attached.

A DISPLAY OF EXEMPLARY LOYALTY

It was not long after this that a delegation consisting of the heads of the Shan, Kayah, and Kachin States and the Chin Hills Special Division, and several members of Parliament waited on the prime minister. They spoke plainly and to the point: the situation as they saw it was critical, and they feared Thakin Nu might be compelled to leave Rangoon. In that event they wished to be told so that they might make a fighting withdrawal into the Kayah State. If the enemy then continued to press, they would fight in the Shan State, then in the Kachin State, then in the Chin Hills. "Find us the guns," they said, "and we will fight. We will never betray the government; we will never surrender."

Sao Hkun Hkio, head of the Shan State, made this solemn pledge and the prime minister was quite overcome. He decided the least he could do was to be equally frank and confiding. Yes, he told them, the crisis had deepened to such an extent that it was possible the city of Rangoon would fall. Only the night before he had received information that Naw Seng and his Kachins, supported by the First Karen Rifles, had begun their march from Mandalay to Rangoon, and the government had no means of stopping the advance. They were gathering together such forces as still remained available to make a last ditch stand.

Did it mean that the government might have to evacuate Rangoon? No, Thakin Nu said, he had decided to stand and fight whatever the odds.

Mr. Prime Minister, is it not possible to obtain arms from abroad?

The state we're in, that is going to be difficult.

But you've a friend in Mr. Nehru. Surely you could get some aid from him.

We got some arms from Mr. Nehru quite recently. But no sooner did the rifles arrive than our troops went underground with them.

We don't have any time to waste. Please get more guns and as quickly as possible.

Thakin Nu, on whom the urgency of the appeal was not lost, promised that if and when Naw Seng's threat was contained, he would personally go to India.

ENEMIES AT THE DOOR

As the ethnic leaders left the house, the telephone rang. It was the Pegu district superintendent of police calling. He apologised saying he realised he ought to be reporting to the inspector general of police, but the situation was extremely serious. Pegu was unprotected against Naw Seng, so unless reinforcements arrived in time, the town would be lost. The superintendent added, "Of course we have some PVO men, but you know what they are like." There was nothing Thakin Nu could do except to order the superintendent to hold fast. In desperation the superintendent begged for guns, saying the villagers would give up their lives, but the prime minister could not even give him a promise. He hung up sadly with the words ringing in his ears: "At least send us two thousand rounds of ammunition."

The next day Brigadier Kyaw Zaw came to report that every gun, every soldier he could find had been sent to Pegu with orders to fight to the death. But, he continued, there was a company of Chins giving trouble. Their commanding officer had bluntly refused to fight, saying they had had enough and were returning to the Chin Hills.

As Bo Kyaw Zaw explained, the recent history of this Chin company was as follows: They were bivouacked in the Kayah State when their positions were overrun by the KNDO insurgents. The prime minister had sent Brigadier Kya Doe, a loyalist, to prevail upon the KNDO to release the Chins. The KNDO had agreed to set the Chins free but had confiscated their rifles. This then was the company that had been hastily refitted in Rangoon and thrown into the breach in Pegu.

Thakin Nu did not hesitate. Together with a Chin parliamentary secretary, Captain Mang Tung Nung, and Brigadier Kyaw Zaw, he boarded a military aircraft and landed at an airstrip fifteen miles from Pegu. The airstrip, although unused since World War II, was preferable to the road, which was infested with PVO and Communist insurgents throughout its length. The dispirited Chin officer was at the forward position and all those at battle stations could see him. The prime minister made an earnest appeal to his patriotism and loyalty. Captain Mang Tung Nung reinforced this appeal in the Chin language. Thakin Nu pointed out that the Chins had established a well-deserved reputation for gallantry. He did not believe that the present company could return home and tarnish the record of great campaigns and great victories. The Union expected the officer to do his duty in its hour of need. To this the Chin officer said, "We won't let you down. We will stay and fight."

The prime minister became so emotional at this that he did something he was to regret later. He sanctioned a bounty of five thousand kyats to the Chins on the spot, thus greatly upsetting the Gurkhas and other loyal non-Burmans in the defence forces who were also ready to fight and die. Long afterwards, the commanding officer, Bo Chit Myaing, was to confess to the prime minister that in his annoyance he had put tea in a broken cup and offered it to

Thakin Nu. The latter needed no apology because in his eyes Bo Chit Myaing could do no wrong. He was the officer who had remained loyal when elements of the Third Burma Rifles went underground.

For the first time in his life Thakin Nu was to witness the scene of battle. There was a rise topped by a pagoda, from which a panoramic view could be obtained. At the suggestion of a Gurkha officer, Thakin Nu made a dash for the hillock immediately after a three-inch mortar had been fired to keep the enemy close to the ground. The prime minister had no stomach for bloody warfare, but the men understandably wished to display their zeal, and he thought his compliance might be good for morale.

The enemy, he discovered, had left the main highway and was fanning out through the paddy fields. The government defenders manned the roadblock, but in the main they were dispersed on either side of the highway. The prime minister could not be exposed too long on high ground because he was within rifle range of the enemy. But he saw enough to know the enemy was attempting to break through to the rear of the defence, and the government troops were trying to trim his flanks.

The enemy had boasted he would be in Rangoon on 26 April, but the defenders of Pegu gave such a good account of themselves that he broke and retreated. On 1 May Naw Seng and the KNDO withdrew towards Toungoo. Rangoon was safe!

TO THE RESCUE OF A FRIEND

In keeping with his promise to the hill people, the prime minister flew to New Delhi, to seek assistance from the Indian government. Pandit Nehru treated him with great considerateness and Thakin Nu returned pleased.

One day, soon after his return from India, the prime minister received a message from his friend John Shircore, in Monywa. Since their last meeting the PVO had gathered strength and now had Monywa surrounded. The road to Shwebo was cut and it was no longer possible for the district superintendent of police to get to Shwebo by car. In fact, there were no means of communication at all, and the message had to be smuggled (in the filter of a cheroot) through the district commissioner of Shwebo. Shircore urgently requested two thousand rounds of ammunition. The premier could not find even two hundred!

Since he could not supply the ammunition, the prime minister decided he would go to Shwebo to show himself. Shircore must not feel he had been abandoned. This time, however, the travel arrangements were slightly different. Thakin Nu was not flying in a DC-3 but in a Catalina.

The British pilots flying the Dakotas had been a great trial to the government. They were sticklers for rules and regulations. They maintained they were on civilian contracts and would not fly combat missions. Soldiers in uniform, carrying arms, constituted military cargo. To overcome the pilots' scruples, Burma Army troops had to wear civies and hide their rifles in gunny bags. Then, after the plane landed, the soldiers changed into uniform and assembled their rifles. The government had very few troops and these were being constantly shuttled about from place to place, to meet enemy threats as they arose. The charades about changing into and out of uniform had become ridiculous. Even when these measures were taken, some British pilots continued to protest. The government was compelled to seek out less scrupulous flyers, and that was how Catalina flying boats came to be chartered.

The American pilots who flew them were veterans who had been flying over the Hump in World War II, and their aircraft were a great asset because of their ability to land on rivers. The Americans did not make any fuss over who or what they carried or where. Thakin Nu flew frequently with a Captain Chet Brown and grew to like him. On this trip to Shwebo, Captain Brown was again at the controls. With Thakin Nu were a section of Chin soldiers commanded by Major Khap Za Htang.

At Shwebo, Thakin Nu's arrival filled the senior government officials with anxiety. They heard with dismay the prime minister's explanation that he had come to see whether he could dig up something for John Shircore. The district commissioner said that far from being able to help Shircore he could not even guarantee the prime minister's safety. Under questioning, the district commissioner revealed that he had received from Rangoon a wireless transmitting set for Monywa, but there was no means of delivering it. Thakin Nu conceived the idea of flying into Monywa, but the district officers would not hear of it. In the end, it was decided that the Catalina should deposit Thakin Nu in Myitkyina, then fly back with Khap Za Htang to Monywa.

The prime minister reached Myitkyina in safety but as the plane circled above Monywa it was anybody's guess who was in control on the ground. As it happened, John Shircore was still in command, and his men came on the street with a large Union flag to demonstrate this fact, but the PVO occupied the west bank of the Chindwin River, and the police had to fight a skirmish with the rebels before the plane could land. After the major had given Mr. Shircore his transmitter he emplaned for Myitkyina. There he reported to the prime minister that a platoon of Chin soldiers, dispirited because they believed Rangoon had fallen, were encamped in Monywa. These troops were posted in Pakokku, but they had left their posts to return to the Chin Hills. It would be a great boost to their morale if the prime minister would talk to them. Major Khap Za Htang also said the men had no shoes and no mosquito nets.

While preparations were being made for a return to Monywa it was discovered that there was no fuel for the aircraft. Captain Brown had understood he was flying to Shwebo and back; he was not fueled for the extra runs to Myitkyina and Monywa. Myitkyina had been without aviation fuel for some time past, and it was the practice for all planes to carry enough in their tanks for 1,500 miles. Brown's Catalina would normally have been grounded in Myitkyina, but the pilot expressed his willingness to fly on kerosene. This was an unheard-of thing, but he assured the prime minister he was dead serious. He had sufficient gas for the take off; once in the air he would switch to kerosene; he said he had done it in Australia. A search was thus organised through the town and its environs, but there was no kerosene to be found. During this time a Dakota arrived from Rangoon and left on its scheduled flight. The pilot had no aviation fuel to spare; also its British captain had never heard of kerosene being used, even in an emergency. As far as the prime minister was concerned, Captain Brown was the expert. If he thought he could get the amphibian to fly on kerosene, Thakin Nu was ready to go with him. Fortunately for them, the experiment was not made. Instead of kerosene, the searchers came up with some petrol that the police had hidden.

Next an appeal went out from the prime minister to all security forces that they should make what sacrifices they could so that the brave people of Monywa might know they were not friendless. A Bren, a grenade launcher, ten hand grenades, and two thousand rounds of .303 ammunition were obtained in this way. Thakin Nu detailed his officers to go from door to door to beg for old shoes, but eventually the local police gave up their mosquito nets and tennis shoes, and all was in readiness for the flight to beleaguered Monywa.

OFFICERS LOOT THE GOVERNMENT TREASURY

At this stage a development took place which greatly angered the prime minister and delayed his trip to central Burma. The district commissioner reported that all the administrative officers of Katha had left their charges and come to Myitkyina. The excuse they gave was that the Communist rebels had converged on the town, forcing them to flee. Thakin Nu immediately ordered the district commissioner to have a special train made ready to take the deserters back to Katha. The superintendent of police volunteered to escort them with a section of Union Military Police (UMP) men, but the prime minister said he would go himself. There would be a roll call on arrival at Katha and woe betide the men not present!

In spite of the district officers' plea that they be given a day to get a situation report on Katha, the prime minister ordered the train started at 10:00 P.M. that very night. He found no rebels in Katha, nor anywhere close by. Some senior officers had conspired to spread alarm, then opened the treasury and helped themselves to the money. Some of the loot was distributed among the staff, but they had the lion's share with them when they had the misfortune to run into the prime minister. Thakin Nu was furious and had some of the responsible officers put into jail.

A TOUGH LANDING

Back again in Myitkyina, the prime minister sent word to District Superintendent of Police Shircore that he was coming. Mr. Shircore tried to stop him with a wireless message warning that he would first have to clear the west bank of rebels, but before this could be delivered the prime minister had left. As the plane came down to land in the Chindwin River, Thakin Nu saw puffs of smoke everywhere, with a battle in progress. A breathless John Shircore arrived to inquire if the prime minister had not received his message cautioning delay. Thakin Nu said no, but it did not matter. In the motor boat taking them ashore Shircore proudly displayed a revolver and a Mills bomb he had just seized from the PVO.

THE FALL OF THE SHAN CAPITAL

After his setback near Pegu, Captain Naw Seng and his Kachin rebels backtracked towards Toungoo, whence they entered the Kayah State. Then they wheeled north and struck at Taunggyi, the capital of the Shan State, which they captured. Then, racing northeast over hills via Loilem, they fell on Lashio, the principal town in the Northern Shan State. The Shan head of state, Sao (lord) Hkun Hkio, was in Lashio at the time, and for a time after the fall of Lashio there was no news of him. His disappearance caused much anxiety to the prime minister, who did not know whether he had been captured or put to death. Orders accordingly went out to Brigadier Lazum Tang, an intrepid Kachin loyalist, to mount an immediate offensive against Lashio and to search for and rescue Sao Hkun Hkio.

Lazum Tang gathered together what forces he could muster and counterattacked from Maymyo. Naw Seng elected not to engage Lazum Tang in positional warfare and instead withdrew to Namkham on the Shweli River, where he took up strong positions. Lazum Tang pursued the rebels and threw a ring round them at Namkham. As soon as Thakin Nu heard of the relief of Lashio, he hopped on a plane in quest of Sao Hkun Hkio. While the pilot encircled the airfield, the prime minister's aide-de-camp scanned the area below and, not seeing any sign of life, was filled with doubt and suspicion. What if Naw Seng had returned in the night? Thakin Nu's decision was to land but to keep the engines running. They were greatly relieved when they saw government officials appear on the tarmac.

The cold season had set in, and Lazum Tang was in Lashio in

search of warm clothing for the troops when he met the prime minister. He also brought the glad news that Sao Hkun Hkio was safe in Mongmit. The prime minister dispatched a message to him: "Hkio, your worries are over. Come to me in Lashio." Sao Hkun Hkio responded immediately and there was a happy reunion. But Namkham was still in rebel hands, and the prime minister felt compelled to return to Rangoon to find the clothing for the troops that was not available in Lashio. The cotton uniform was insufficient protection against the cold, and if the soldiers built fires they were easy targets for rebel snipers.

Neither the War Office nor Police Supplies could meet the demand for woollens. The British Army, however, had left woollen blankets for the hospital and these were requisitioned. Likewise about five hundred hospital uniforms for patients were packed into bundles and conveyed by the prime minister to Lashio. Road transport to Namkham was slow and uncertain, so Sao Hkun Hkio and the prime minister flew over Namkham and lowered the bundles in a free drop.

THE TIDE TURNS

True to his word, Pandit Nehru sent several shipments of arms, without which Burma might never have recovered. Now the unserviceable guns of the combat troops were replaced, and new units were raised and equipped. By November 1949, the army, civilian police, and UMP felt strong enough to retake towns and villages under rebel occupation.

The travails through which Burma was passing made Thakin Nu more bitter than ever about Russian involvement and perfidy. He noticed that in this same year, when total victory was within sight of the Chinese Communists, Stalin had advised Chinese leaders in Moscow to carry the fight up to the Yangtse River and leave Chiang Kai-shek in occupation of the south. This was an imperialist scheme to prevent the Chinese Communists from becoming too powerful. The Chinese, however, saw through his game, and with the conquest of the whole of China and the expulsion of Chiang, Stalin's plan was flushed down the toilet.

Thakin Nu saw Stalin's hand in the Zhdanov Plan, which brought so much tribulation to Burma. It was a Cold War strate-

The Cabinet Room at No. 10, Downing Street, when the prime ministers of Britain and Burma signed the treaty regulating the future relations between the two countries, 17 October 1947. *Left to right (sitting):* U Tin Tut, Bo Let Ya, U Nu, Prime Minister Attlee, Lord Listowel, Foreign Minister Bevin, Sir Stafford Cripps. *The Times* (London)

U Nu and Pandit Nehru with a Naga Chief, March 1953. *Courtesy of Nehru Memorial Institute, New Delhi*

U Nu and his wife are met by Vice President and Mrs. Nixon on their arrival on a state visit to the United States in 1955. *Left to right:* Mrs. Nixon, Daw Mya Yee, U Nu, Vice President Nixon, Secretary of State Dulles.

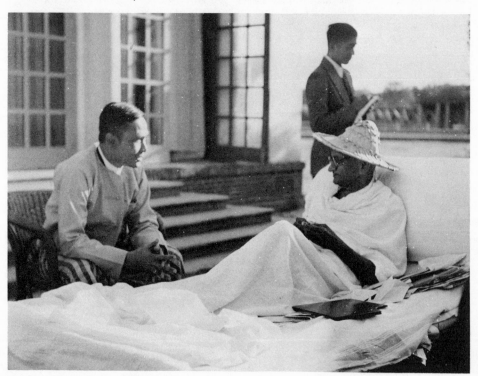

U Nu and Mahatma Gandhi.

U Nu with Premier Khrushchev and Prime Minister Nehru in India, 1960. *Courtesy of Nehru Memorial Institute, New Delhi*

At the Bandung Conference, April 1955. *Left to right:* U Nu, Sir John Kotelawala (premier of Ceylon), and Pandit Nehru.

Left to right: U Nu, Daw Mya Yee, Chou En-lai, Mao Tse-tung, Chu-teh, Liu Shao-chi.
Courtesy of Direk Davies, Chief Editor, Far Eastern Economic Review (Hong Kong)

U Nu addresses a mass rally in Peking to commemorate the signing of the Sino-Burmese Border Agreement, October 1960. *Wide World Photos*

gem, typical of the postwar period, when the Anglo-American powers found themselves ranged against Russia. Stalin had calculated that the Congress government in India and the AFPFL government in Burma would, after independence, join the Anglo-American bloc. His prime objective therefore was to sponsor communist regimes that would join the Russian bloc. Failing this, the AFPFL and Congress governments, which Stalin considered to be lackeys of Anglo-American imperialism, must be impeded and incommoded through Communist rebellions.

It occurred to Thakin Nu that if the Burmese Communists, following the example of their Chinese counterparts, had flushed the Zhdanov Plan down the drain, great damage and destruction[14] to Burma would have been avoided. Furthermore, the Communists, by placing their faith in Stalin, forfeited their opportunity to organise their political party systematically and the almost certain prospect of winning power from the AFPFL in the next democratically held general election.

During the period from the end of March 1948 to the end of 1949, Burma was in danger of being destroyed. The following elements, in combination, helped to avert this danger.

1. The army, police, UMP, and sitwundan forces that remained loyal despite the defections from each of these military units and acquitted themselves in a praiseworthy manner. No government minister or political leader could claim that his life was threatened for more than a fortnight during the year. Even when they stood at the forefront of battle they were in jeopardy perhaps three or four hours at a time, whereas all loyalist troops, because in their depleted numbers they were exposed to combat throughout, could claim they faced death without respite, twenty-four hours a day.

---

14. The record of destruction caused by the insurgents is impressive; it includes: (1) money looted from government treasuries; (2) buildings and property damaged or destroyed; (3) taxes and revenues forfeited; (4) private homes, jewellery, and private property destroyed or lost (whole villages, such as Pantanaw, were gutted). In 1949 Prime Minister U Nu made a statement announced to the public that the loss to the people, in movable and immovable property, was three billion kyats. This is exclusive of the government's military expenditures, and it also does not take into account the adverse long-range effects upon the nation of its being drained of capital investments and growth funds.

Needless to say, in terms of deaths and personal injuries, the losses to the government, the insurgents, and the people of Burma were enormous.

In terms of other sacrifices, however deprived the leaders might have been, they still had silks and fancy clothing, whereas most of the soldiers had only the uniform they stood up in; in the majority of cases they had nothing to change into, and no blankets in cold weather. They risked their lives in order that the Union might not go down in defeat to authoritarianism.

2. The hill people representing the Shan, Chin, Kachin, and Kayah States, who gave themselves body and mind to the defence of the Union and made a most important contribution to its survival.

3. The existence of a section of the Karen population that remained loyal to the Union, and whose loyalty was publicly acknowledged by the prime minister at the height of the insurrection.

4. The substantial strength contributed by the Socialist Party, headed by U Ba Swe, U Kyaw Nyein, and Thakin Tin, and the Yellow Band PVO headed by Bohmu Aung and Bo Sein Hman, without which Thakin Nu simply could not have stood alone.

5. The press which, though on occasion a source of annoyance and a severe trial to the government, generally supported the government effort against the insurgents.

6. The great majority of the population, urban and rural, which showed their preference, based on firsthand experience and an innate sense of right and wrong, for the rule of law over injustice and the cult of the gun.

The plight of the people in all insurgent-held areas was deplorable. They lived under a reign of terror and owned nothing except that which was rejected by the terrorists. They were subject to arbitrary arrest and punishment.

Because of this experience, the importance of free speech, free associations, freedom from fear and from unjust use of power was brought home to them in a unique, personal manner. The insurgency opened the eyes of the people to the fact that, whereas under the rule of law they had their dignity if nothing else, now they were reduced to the condition of cattle. And since it was the gun pointed at them that compelled them to obey, they came to detest the cult of the gun.

What the people felt, they whispered. Their abhorrence of gun-induced injustice and their longing for law and order found secret expression in tea shops, at religious initiations and ordination ceremonies, at weddings and funerals. In sum this constituted public opinion, a force that went into the preservation of the Union.

7. The Christian religion, which lays down as a commandment: Thou shalt not kill. All through the crisis Christian bishops and pastors came to give their blessings to Thakin Nu and to assure him that they would continue to preach to all who believed in Christ that they must keep His commandments. The prime minister was convinced that such religious instruction had a beneficent effect.

Also invaluable was the restraining influence of the Buddhist monks, who continued to live in insurgent areas and who never failed to speak out against killing, robbery, adultery, and drunkenness.[15]

Last but not least was the implicit faith of the people in the incorruptibility of their prime minister, U Nu. U Nu strongly believed that corruption among those in power repelled rather than attracted the masses. Without the active support of the masses, guns alone would prove useless, he believed, in meeting the threat of communism. U Nu used to admonish his colleagues that, if there was one thing in the world that would open the way to communism, it was corruption among those in power.

THE PREMIER GOES TO MEDITATE

In 1950 the situation eased sufficiently to enable the government to breathe freely. Cabinet members meeting in early June heard the prime minister announce: "My friends, I go to the Meditation Centre tomorrow. I have a vow to keep to attain the *thin-khar-ru-pek-kha nyan*.[16] Until then do not send for me, even if the whole country is enveloped in flames. If there are fires, you must put them out yourselves."

Fortunately, however, during the period of Thakin Nu's meditation no situation that could be called alarming arose in any part of the country. Thakin Nu fulfilled his vow on 20 July.

15. It is a matter of great regret to the writer that a proper history of crucial events during this period cannot be compressed into the narrow confines of this book. The parts played by various individuals and the influence they brought to bear should be viewed in a world historical context and are deserving of a serious research project.

16. An important stage in Buddhist meditation.

8

Plans for Progress

In 1950 the prime minister left the Dobama Asi-ayone, shed the prefix thakin, and became simply U Nu.

When political events gave him a chance to breathe freely, U Nu began to think again about Buddhism, in which he was very interested. He had learnt that the attainment of Buddhahood was a very rare phenomenon. Many worlds ended without witnessing a Buddha, though in some cases, there had been a Buddha to each world. No one world had produced more than five Buddhas. The doctrine of deliverance from endless rebirths and the attendant suffering, resulting from old age, disease, death, separation, and so on, is preached whenever there is a Buddha. It is not heard when a Buddha does not exist. U Nu very much wanted the Buddhists to take advantage of the Buddha's teachings while they had the opportunity to do so. U Nu felt very unhappy when he found that the great majority of Buddhists had betrayed the privilege and opportunity to free themselves of endless suffering. With this thought he decided to (a) encourage interest in Buddhism, (b) disseminate the Law of Deliverance from suffering, (c) provide the facilities to achieve such deliverance through the practice of the prescribed disciplines. These objectives took form in the following policies and programs:

1. Pali universities were established in monasteries.
2. Examinations in religious knowledge were held for monks and

laymen. Religious instruction in jails proved immensely popular; those who passed tests were given remission of their sentences.

The *Pitaka-da-ra,* the highest examinations for monks, took place in Rangoon at the height of the KNDO insurrection. As the name implies, these examinations comprise three branches of the Buddha's teachings, *Thok, Wini,* and *Abidhamma,* which together are referred to as the *Tripitaka.* The subject matter is contained in over fifty volumes, each with over four hundred pages. The examinations are both oral and written, and of course it is impossible to complete them in one session. Thus the Pitaka-da-ra examinations are taken in instalments with intervening periods of rest, and the entire process extends over four years. A yearly examination held in Mandalay, called the *Setkya Thiha,* is somewhat less exhausting, and yet monks have been known to die during the period of rigorous preparation. Therefore, it was thought that with the more exacting Pitaka-da-ra examinations, and the pressure of political events, the casualty rate of examinees would be unduly high. The battle was uncomfortably close and religious leaders asked for a postponement, but it was not granted. The Rangoon monks decided to picket, but there were police guards to see that there was no interference in the halls.

The examinations proved to be exceptionally difficult, so much so that only one monk, the Reverend U Wiseitta, passed with honours. All other monks failed at least once, either in the oral or written paper, and had to reappear again and again. But there were no deaths recorded.

3. Prime Minister U Nu had never been properly instructed by a teacher in religious subjects, although he had done some reading and listened to lay preachers as well as learned monks. With what little knowledge he had, U Nu took every opportunity to preach to audiences large and small. If his text was needed for distribution he defrayed the printing costs as an act of charity.

4. The Tripitaka were translated into Burmese, enabling those Buddhists who did not read Pali to understand them.

5. Encouragement was given to the spread of Buddhism in the faraway hill tracts.

6. A Buddhist Missionary Society was formed and government aid was granted to promote its activities.

7. Religious instruction on Buddhism was provided in all schools and at Rangoon University.

8. In the nineteenth century, during the reign of King Mindon, the Tripitaka were inscribed on stone. With the advent of the printing press, the stone inscriptions were committed to print. Mistakes were subsequently discovered, made both in the original tablets by sculptors and in published works by compositors and proofreaders. Since the danger of such errors corrupting practices was real, both learned monks and lay authorities advised a revision of the texts. Towards this end, Prime Minister U Nu convened the Sixth Buddhist Synod.[1]

9. In Buddhism, without right conduct, the truth of the religion cannot be discovered. Right conduct consists of (a) self-restraint in regard to speech and action, (b) concentration to induce calm and prevent distraction, and (c) total elimination of the passions of greed, anger, and ignorance. In order to provide a place for the observance of these necessary disciplines, the prime minister, for a start, established a Meditation Centre in Rangoon which he himself often visited, as we have read above. Soon its instructors were able to report that the results were astonishing. With the attainment of *Thawtapatti Megga,* the primary plane of spiritual experience, the minds of the devotees seemed to undergo a change. U Nu, wishing to experiment, sent a friend to the centre. This was a notorious person of whom the people went in dread, because he drank, lied, stole, fornicated, and would not have stopped at murder. On completion of the retreat at the centre he emerged a reformed character. He himself was so impressed by the religious experience that he brought his wife to share in the experience.

With such evidence before him, the prime minister felt encouraged to erect meditation centres throughout the country.

At this stage, U Nu was advised by his colleagues and friends that it would be unwise to involve himself further with religious

1. The first Buddhist Synod was convened by King Azadathat in 543 B.C. in Rajagriha, the Second by King Kalathawka in 443 B.C. in Wethali (modern Oudh), the Third by King Athawka (Asoka) in 241 B.C. in Pataliputra, and the Fourth circa 25 B.C. in Ceylon where for the first time the Tripitaka were committed to writing. The Fifth Buddhist Synod was convened in Mandalay by King Mindon in 1871.

matters. But U Nu's contention was that the people had voted the government into office so that it might bring them benefits. Religion was a beneficial institution and those who would gainsay it were wrong. If the government could provide for a life of one hundred years on earth, why should it feel deterred from providing for countless existences afterwards? He would not deviate even slightly from his path.

EQUAL TREATMENT FOR OTHER RELIGIONS

Living in Burma were Buddhists, Moslems, Christians, Hindus, and animists. U Nu did not interest himself with Buddhism only. Since he found great peace of mind from the influence of Buddhism, he felt that other religionists should also be able to find solace from their respective religions. The help that he gave to the Buddhists, he also extended to the others; for example:

1. In regard to religious grants, the total amount once having been determined, they were distributed proportionately among the various denominations on a population basis.

2. U Nu brought sacred relics of the Buddha from India, and of his saints from Ceylon, and exhibited them in Burma for public worship. After a visit with Pope Pius XII at the Vatican, U Nu brought back for the Catholics of Burma holy pictures, religious books, and medallions of the pope. On his return from Israel U Nu brought crucifixes and water from the Jordan for the Christians.

3. A Roman Catholic mission was sent to Rome at government expense, to pay their respects to the pope. Similarly, a Moslem organisation was set up and a mission sent to Mecca at government expense.

4. Just as the Tripitaka had been translated from the Pali into Burmese, so also a fund was set up for translating the Koran from Arabic to Burmese. Moslem leaders also received a promise of government assistance to convene a council of religious scholars to revise the new text.

Since a Christian Bible had existed in Burmese from the time of Dr. Adoniram Judson, there was no need for a translation. At a Protestant convention in Rangoon, the prime minister presented each delegate with a copy of the Bible.

5. Insofar as religious functions were concerned, the prime minister never refused invitations, whether they were from Moslems, Christians, or Hindus. He went to mosques, churches, and temples. He attended conferences and made speeches or sent messages on request.

6. When religious instruction on Buddhism was introduced in state schools, the prime minister did not forget to make provisions for the teaching of Islam and Christianity. This produced the repercussions described below.

A CLASH WITH BUDDHIST MONKS

In 1954 three representatives of a most prestigious organisation of Buddhist monks called on the prime minister.

Dagagyi,[2] we've come to object to Islam and Christianity being taught in state schools. We want this stopped immediately.

Monks, why do you dislike those subjects?

Because they are heresies.

Only Moslems study Islam, and Christians Christianity. Buddhist students do not study them.

Don't have them taught in state schools. If they want to study these subjects, let them go elsewhere.

Please refrain from injustice. King Mindon was a great patron of the Buddhist religion. During his reign he gave considerable aid to the Christian and Moslem faiths in his capital, Mandalay.

We were not there in Mindon's reign. Had we been present we would have prevented such aid.

State schools are run not only with money provided by the Buddhists, but with taxes paid also by Moslems and Christians. If therefore Buddhism is to be taught in these schools, equal opportunity must be given Islam and Christianity.

We most strongly object. These subjects shall not be taught.

2. Literally, *dagagyi* means "donor" or "benefactor" of the Buddhist faith. It is customary for monks to address others and to be addressed in the third person.

The prime minister lost his temper. "You may go now," he told the monks, "If Islam and Christianity are not to be taught in state schools, no other religious subjects will be taught either."

Actually, there was no need to make a big thing out of this interview. Had it been any other minister, he would have heard the monks out, entered into no arguments, and played for time to "consult the Cabinet." There were ministers like U Kyaw Nyein, Thakin Tha Khin, and Bo Khin Maung Gale who could have been deputed to resolve the matter with the monks. These Socialist leaders had worked hand in hand with the monks during the Second World War, in the resistance first against the British and then against the Japanese. With this association behind them, the Socialists and the monks were able to exercise much influence on each other. It just so happened, however, that the prime minister had taken an intense dislike to one of the three monks and had in fact refused to see him at all. If the Socialists had not repeatedly asked for his inclusion he would not have been there. On the other hand, if the Socialists had been allowed to handle the situation they would probably have succeeded in getting the monks to withdraw their objections or, alternatively, in arriving at a compromise solution that would have been acceptable to U Nu. As matters stood, the prime minister was convinced that here was a majority group coldbloodedly trying to suppress minority groups, and his ire had risen.

At the next Monday Cabinet meeting, U Nu made a fleeting reference to the interview he had had with the three monks. Then, turning to the education minister, he issued an order that the teaching of any kind of religious subject was to cease. The education minister, being a man of discretion, delayed putting this order into execution. At the next Cabinet meeting, the prime minister came back to the subject and asked if his order had been put into effect. The answer he received was that the minister intended to implement it. This did not prove satisfactory to U Nu, whose instructions to the minister were that, as soon as he reached his office that day, the order should go out as his first item of business. The newspapers carried the story and there was an uproar in both religious and lay circles. The prime minister made no public statement or explanation. His attitude was, "If they don't like it, they can jolly well get rid of me."

But a few days later the prime minister had a speech to deliver before the Military Academy in Maymyo. On his way up, he asked the Mandalay officials to invite the leading monks to meet him. Expecting to hear from him an explanation of his order discontinuing religious instruction in state schools, a large number of monks responded. As soon as they were assembled, the prime minister read out a prepared statement, the salient point of which was that he was and had ever been a humble and obedient member of the congregation, but that the monks in dealing with him had spoken with the roar of a lion. These same monks, he pointed out, maintained a strange silence in the face of misconduct and breaches of the discipline on the part of the religious themselves. U Nu said, "I will not be browbeaten by anyone. In no circumstances will I withdraw my order."

The words they heard, being completely different from what they had been led to expect, caused a commotion. Reporters on the spot asked for copies of the prepared statement but were frustrated by a cautious commissioner. There was a momentary pause which U Nu broke by saying, "Let them have the statement." After one reporter had succeeded in getting his copy, the commissioner made a determined appeal to have it recovered. He said bluntly that if that statement appeared in print he would not hold himself responsible for what might happen in Mandalay.

Although a verbatim report was thus prevented, the fact remained that all the monks and newspapermen present had heard the words. The entire proceedings were written up and published and spread like brushfire through the whole of Mandalay, from Mandalay to Rangoon, and thence throughout the country. All religious and lay communities, including those that before the speech had supported U Nu, or lain neutral, now combined to oppose him.

After his speech at the Military Academy, U Nu did not return directly to Rangoon. He took a steamer down the Irrawaddy from Mandalay to Rangoon and spent a week on the journey. The moment the steamer berthed, a secretary ran up to tell the prime minister that some Moslem leaders had requested an interview at his earliest convenience. From the ministers who came to meet him, U Nu learned that so much tension had built up that there was an imminent danger of riots breaking out between Buddhists and

Moslems. When the meeting that had been requested took place that evening, the Moslem leaders opened with:

We waited for your return in fear and trembling.

Why were you so alarmed?

We have reason to fear an open clash. Moslems have been stocking up on rice, oil, chillies, and onions.

But why should you be concerned? I'm the one who issued the order. If they don't like it, I'm the one they should harm. Why should there be riots?

It's true the order is yours, but there are rumours that you were instigated by us. There is great ill-feeling against us.

That's no problem. I'll call a press conference tomorrow and accept full responsibility. I shall say I acted on my own.

No, Mr. Prime Minister, please don't do that. A press conference would be powerless to help. Rumours have moved things too far. The robbers and looters are inciting the people to riot. Only this afternoon, a group of monks and their followers entered our street and threatened us. They called us pork-eating mother-fornicators and proclaimed we would be turned into corpses.

Then what do you expect me to do?

Please withdraw your order and meet the monks' demands. It is of no great importance that we cannot teach Islam in state schools. We can make other arrangements.

After the Moslem leaders' departure, U Nu was torn by conflicting emotions. On the one hand, if the monks resorted to force he would not be able to look on with unconcern. Action would have to be taken, and if shooting became necessary it would have to be ordered. This was a frightful prospect. On the other hand, if the majority were permitted to bully the minorities, it would be surrendering a principle. He put the authorities concerned on the alert against rioters, and went in to pray.

U Nu did not sleep that night. He well remembered that, before the Second World War, there had been Moslem-Buddhist riots over a book that one Shwe Hpi had written. In his mind's eye he saw the Buddhist monk again being attacked by a Moslem with a sword.

There had been many casualties at the time. Now, if rioting were to break out, the damage would be far more severe. He was reminded of the facetious Burmese saying "(Everything was going all right) till the mayor came to help; then I landed in jail." He did not want to hear this paraphrased: things were all right with the Moslems until the prime minister went to help; then they found themselves bathing in blood. He would withdraw his order and accept the demands of the monks. He announced this decision over the radio. He made a secret vow and surrendered.

BUDDHISM BECOMES THE STATE RELIGION

Out of his abundant religious zeal, U Nu had for a long time been desirous of making Buddhism the state religion. He knew that if he did so Burma would not be the only country in the world where the religion professed by the majority was made the state religion.[3] Moreover, he sincerely believed that equitable adjustments could be made in order to ensure that the state religion did not become an instrument for imposing a tyranny of the majority. As a result, during the campaign for the 1960 general elections, U Nu made a commitment that if his party won he would make Buddhism the state religion. His party won more than a two-thirds majority in that election, and U Nu was aware that even among the Opposition there were many who would support his State Religion Bill, so there was no question about its passage. Nonetheless, because of his respect for the rights of minorities, U Nu first appointed an Enquiry Commission to sound out public opinion. In the Kachin State capital of Myitkyina, the commission was given a rough reception by the Kachin Christians, but elsewhere conditions were peaceful. In Rangoon, the prime minister met with leaders of the Moslem, Christian, and Hindu faiths. They objected to Buddhism being made the state religion, but there was no one among them who claimed that the bill in any way infringed their constitutional rights. Freedom of worship was safeguarded by the Constitution as follows:

3. About 85 percent of the population in Burma is Buddhist. Among the major national minorities, such as the Karen, the Shan, the Arakanese, and the Mon, a majority profess Buddhism.

21. (3) The State shall not impose any disabilities or make any
discrimination on the ground of religious faith or belief.

The above had been an important plank in the laying of founda-
tions for national unity and it was common knowledge that the
prime minister would not disturb it under any circumstances.

The proposed bill did not do any violence to existing guarantees.
These guarantees had in fact been reinforced with government aid
each year to all religions on a pro rata basis.

What some Christian leaders pointed out was that, although Section 20 conferred upon them the right to practise their religion,
it did not specifically mention the right to teach, and this they
wanted done. The relevant wording is as follows:

20. All persons are equally entitled to freedom of conscience and
the right freely to profess and teach religion subject to law,
public order, and morality.

The prime minister would have thought that what the Christians
demanded was already covered by Section 17 (1) under the heading
Rights of Freedom; it reads:

17. There shall be liberty for the exercise of the following rights
subject to law, public order, and morality:—

(1) The right of the citizens to express freely their convictions
and opinions.

However, because the Christian leaders were insistent that the
right to teach their religion should be written into the Constitution,
the prime minister promised to do so.

When the newspapers came out with this story the monks again
became agitated. They demanded that the constitutional amendment in regard to the teaching of other religions should not be made
in the current session of Parliament, but that the bill should be held
over for a report by an Inquiry Commission. Since he had already
promised the Christian leaders that the amendment would be introduced immediately following the enactment of the legislation making Buddhism the state religion, U Nu would not permit the postponement. The result was that the monks staged demonstrations
and planned to bar Members of Parliament from approaching Parliament Building. Several lines of police cordoned off the Parlia-

ment and prevented the monks from coming closer than half a mile from the building. The prime minister himself had to enter by stealth.

Three days after the amendment was passed, Duwa (chief) Zau Lawn, former head of the Kachin State, came to express his gratification. He invited the prime minister to a Christian conference in Myitkyina, and U Nu gladly accepted. At Myitkyina, he was greeted by Colonel Lun Tin, the brigade commander, the district commissioner, and the district superintendent of police, all of whom reported that the state religion issue had created serious misunderstanding which no amount of explanation could eliminate. But the amendment safeguarding the rights of those of all other religions to teach their respective religions had made for universal satisfaction.

Kachin Christian leaders, when they were received by the prime minister, admitted that they had been deeply offended by the state religion measure and felt very great anger at the time. But the constitutional amendment in regard to their own religion had cleared all doubts and resentment. To the prime minister they all looked relaxed and pleased.

SHORTCUTS TO EDUCATION AND HEALTH

Throughout 1948 and 1949, whenever he could get to the people by breaking through the ring of insurgents, Thakin Nu made it a point to inquire what it was that they most wanted of the government. Everywhere in the country the answer boiled down to two things: primary school teachers and doctors. Many were the times he made a note of such requests, which were then transmitted to the departments concerned. But he had never had the opportunity to follow up on what he had initiated. By the time he got back to Rangoon he had generally forgotten about these matters. However, when 1950 arrived, and with it a considerable easing of the insurgent problem, Thakin Nu, again receiving pleas for more primary schools and physicians, decided to do something about them. Calling together the minister, the education secretary and the director of education, he put the question to them why there were insufficient primary schools.

Because we don't have sufficient teachers.

How many primary school teachers do you need, up to the village level?

Over ten thousand.

How many teacher training schools have we?

We've opened them in Rangoon, Mandalay, Moulmein, Bassein, Kyaukpyu, and Meiktila.

How long does it take to train a teacher?

One year.

And in one year how many new teachers do you train?

We turn out over one thousand.

At that rate we must wait ten years to get the required ten thousand. That's too long. Can't we double and triple the number of training schools? I'll find the money.

We don't have the manpower to serve in these schools.

This was a problem with which he could not immediately contend. He told the educational authorities they were the experts and must devise one means or another to get ten thousand teachers quickly. He would give them the powers they needed in addition to the funds. He urged them to renew their efforts, and not to give up too easily. They promised they would do their best.

☆ ☆ ☆ ☆ ☆

The health minister, his secretary, and his directors were next called and asked to explain why the rural hospitals had no doctors. The answer was that there were not sufficient doctors to go round.

How many doctors do we need for the country?

For a start, about three hundred.

How many do we qualify from Medical College?

About forty a year.

(*Sighing*) We cannot wait until we produce all we need. It's disgraceful having hospitals with no staff. Please hire doctors from India and Pakistan immediately, and send them to the districts.

We will do that.

Can't we open another medical school?

We shall discuss the possibility and report back.

How long does it take to be a doctor, after high school?

Seven years.

That's too long. Can't we reduce the period to five years?

We'll need to look into it. We shall submit a report.

The health ministry was able to report in a short time that it would be possible to open a Medical College in Mandalay. However, the leading physicians and surgeons were opposed to the shortening of the training period from seven to five years. They said graduates of a rapid course would tend to kill more than they would cure. The prime minister was not convinced. He said he would like them to reconsider. Subsequently they recommended that, physics and chemistry being already popular, such premedical courses as biology and botany also be taught in high school. Then when they entered the university the qualified medical students could expect to graduate in six instead of seven years. The prime minister accepted their suggestions, and stipends were given to would-be doctors in high schools.

U Nu continued to be troubled about the uneven distribution of the health and medical services. Qualified doctors with the Bachelor of Medicine and Bachelor of Surgery degrees were falling over one another in the few large towns. To provide equal facilities to the countryside would take twenty years, an intolerable state of affairs.

The prime minister's heart went out to the people living in villages who, in lieu of medicine, had to have recourse to fetishes, charms, and sorcery. Some resorted to animal sacrifices, others to fortune-tellers and magicians. Even such native doctors and herbalists as existed had a range of four or five remedies for common ailments. Outside of these, the treatment was experimental or sheer quackery. Whenever there was an outbreak of an epidemic, such as plague, cholera, or smallpox, the villagers blamed it on the supernatural and drove out the evil spirits by beating on tin cans and creating a din. The belief was that the apparitions could be frightened into leaving the village and going into the jungle. In this deplorable state of affairs, U Nu felt frustrated that he could not provide qualified doctors in areas where they were most needed. Rather than stand and wait, he preferred to make use of men and women with practical experience in public health services, even if they were not medical baccalaureates.

After anguishing over his problem, U Nu suddenly thought of Dr. Gordon Seagrave of the Namkham Hospital in the Northern Shan State, who was systematically turning out male and female nurses. The Namkham Hospital had both in-patient and out-patient services; furthermore, Dr. Seagrave's nurses responded to sick calls from distant villages. They were competent to deal with colds and coughs, bronchial ailments, malaria, stomach and intestinal complaints, and other common illnesses. They dressed sores and lanced boils and swellings, gave intravenous and intramuscular injections, and delivered babies. Only serious cases went to Dr. Seagrave and his assistants.

U Nu had long heard about Dr. Seagrave and been greatly intrigued with his training methods. So he called him down to Rangoon and asked:

I want the sort of nurses you have. How long does it take to train them?

Six months.

What sort of educational qualification must they possess?

Sufficient if they can read and write. In some cases, if they have a brain, they needn't be literate.

The prime minister was most enthusiastic about Dr. Seagrave's training programme. He summoned his medical advisers and had them confer with the American surgeon. But the Burmese doctors vetoed the plan, again maintaining that quickly trained personnel would be apt to kill their patients.

U Nu, possessing no medical knowledge, was not prepared to ride roughshod over the Burmese doctors. But he told them he was disappointed they had rejected the Seagrave plan. It was up to them now to devise a suitable plan that would bring quick relief to sufferers in the villages. He was tired of looking on with folded arms.

The urge to unfold arms and wade into a problem was characteristic of U Nu. He recalled how, when he was a schoolmaster in Thongwa, he had come upon a man urinating on the street. When shouted at, the man had trembled and pleaded that he was ill. So he was taken to hospital, where "Saya" Nu offered to pay for his treatment. However, the doctor told him the man was a diabetic and beyond cure. Relatives were so informed, and Saya Nu decided to take the man home and try to help him with native medicine. Although the doctor had advised against sugar, the patient craved bread sprinkled with sugar and, since he was taken for a terminal case, Saya Nu let him eat what he wanted.

Next, Saya Nu read an advertisement in the paper for a native remedy for diabetes. He bought the medicine which proved ineffective. He went to apothecaries and had herbs compounded. Finally, he found two potent drugs. The first, obtained from the headmaster of Okkanwa School in Thongwa, was not a prescription for diabetes but a medicine for eye disease, to be taken internally. Saya Nu's father, U San Tun, arriving in Thongwa about this time, diagnosed the case as one of "heat blockage," and he suggested a compound of six drugs as an antipyretic. The cataract medicine, on the assumption that diabetes often manifested itself in that condition, was administered in the morning, and the antipyretic last thing at night. In ten days the patient picked up strength and took regular baths. In three more days he was eating a normal diet and, at Saya Nu's request, gave up bread and sugar. Two months later, when school reopened, he went to report to "Doctor" Nu that he was not going to die.

Another incident, which also occurred in Thongwa, concerned an unusual case of parturation. A woman had been in great pain because the child was about to be born feet foremost, and she had been screaming so loud a crowd had collected at the hospital. Saya Nu, attracted by the crowd, found out that the doctor was away giving evidence in a court case, and that the nurse did not know what to do. To Saya Nu's suggestion that several midwives from the town should be fetched to massage the woman's stomach and squeeze the child out, the nurse said she could not take the responsibility in the doctor's absence. Meanwhile the woman was standing, propping herself against the wall with hands and forehead. Someone from the crowd said the child must already be dead. There was a good hospital maintained by the Burmah Oil Company in Syriam, thirty miles away, and Saya Nu resolved to save the mother's life. But there were no motor cars to be got at that late hour, and Saya Nu was lucky to find a bus, which he paid for. The woman was stretched out on the floor and the driver told to go as fast as she could tolerate. The road was full of potholes and Saya Nu wondered how the woman would fare. Late that night, the husband came to report that a stillborn child had been delivered but that the mother was well. Saya Nu asked if the Syriam doctors had been very good and was told they had not had to do anything. The rough ride had done the trick at the gateway into Syriam.

To return to the problem of the lack of doctors, the health minister and his team of medical experts responded to the proddings of the prime minister by laying before him their plan, which was that they would agree to the establishment of a School of Public Health if (1) the graduates of the school would limit themselves to treating well-defined diseases within their capability, (2) instead of being "doctors" they were styled "health assistants," (3) they were able to satisfy their examiners at the end of two years of study, and (4) they possessed a high school certificate. The prime minister readily agreed to the conditions laid down, except that he urged the committee to reduce residency from two years to eighteen months and added the stipulation that, with seniority, health assistants might proceed to a medical degree and receive full pay while going through medical college.

☆ ☆ ☆ ☆ ☆

With the arrival of doctors hired in India and Pakistan, rural hospitals got their staff, and complaints on this score ceased. But the clamour for primary schools continued unabated.

U Nu, pondering this problem in a country rest house, had a flash of inspiration and quickly returned to Rangoon with it. He told the education minister and his directors that the answer to the teacher shortage was to be found in the summer schools. During the long vacation, teachers already in service would be induced to teach a crash course to qualify the senior students as primary school teachers. Not only those who had passed the seventh standard but also those who had reached that class would be admissible. Naturally, there would not be a high level of excellence, but at least the new crop of teachers would be sufficiently proficient to teach the 3-Rs and the national anthem. From being waifs and strays, the children in the villages would find uplift in rudimentary education. The idea was to produce ten thousand new teachers in two years. Thereafter the teachers themselves could qualify by attending the regular teacher training schools on full pay. This plan was adopted and the results came up to expectations.

The prime minister's obsession with health and education was to take many shapes and forms. In regard to the country's health, it was a well-known fact that the staple foods of 90 percent of the population consisted of rice, *ngapi* (pressed fish), and a vegetable. This unvarying fare could not be expected to provide sufficient protein, especially in view of the fact that the rice was milled, polished grain. Consequently life expectancy was low, and the rate of infant mortality excessively high.

Doctors and health assistants were necessary, of course, but the crux of the matter was nourishing food. To be able to eat wholesome food, or a more balanced diet, the average villager would have to earn more money. U Nu had no ready means of improving the economic power of the people, but he could introduce measures to increase the protein content of the food available. With this end in view, the prime minister spearheaded a vigorous campaign for the consumption of hand-pounded unpolished rice, with a public speech in City Hall. Books, brochures, and pamphlets were distributed in abundance, extolling the virtues of unpolished rice and depicting the Burmese men of old, who grew to great stature on a diet of unpolished rice and possessed the strength and energy to lift and lay the huge slabs of stone in the building of pagodas. But the campaign proved a flop. The people were used to eating their milled, white rice and refused to eat any other kind. Hand-milled rice might contain more protein, but it smelled. U Nu himself, the great advocate of hand-pounded rice, found himself burping at the smell of bran and went back to white rice.

But he had not given up on his project. If the people would not eat the bran in their rice, he would give it to them separately in the form of vitamin tablets. He would put up a factory that would yield millions of tablets and these would be distributed free. He called into session his Economic and Social Council and subsequently sent the council's consultant, Mr. J. S. Furnivall, and two others to England to have the factory started. As a result of this mission, Burma Pharmaceutical Industries came into being near Rangoon. It was to manufacture various drugs, the profits from which would subsidise the free distribution of vitamin tablets.

Unfortunately for the originator of these plans, the government was twice overthrown by a military coup d'état,[4] and the free vitamins scheme did not come to fruition. The prime minister scarcely had time to review his project.

Concurrently with dietary deficiencies, the physical shortcomings of the Burmese people became apparent to U Nu, who therefore hit upon a plan to promote physical fitness, an ideal which at the time found appeal with only a limited few. With the establishment of a National Fitness Council, health improvement was sought through physical exercises and competitions, athletic meets and sports.

BEQUEATHING A ROCK OF LEARNING

Turning again to the subject of education, Prime Minister U Nu, when he was young, had not been fond of reading. Consequently, among Burmese political leaders, he was extremely deficient in learning. He realised to his regret when he was nearing forty that he had failed to acquire sufficient knowledge. After becoming prime minister he could be heard muttering from time to time that a strong body and strong limbs were not enough; a sound mind stocked with knowledge was also necessary. This was a form of self-criticism, as was also the phrase "Mr. Zero" which he coined in self-deprecation because of his failure to gather knowledge while he had the time.

To blame oneself after the event is as unrewarding as "putting down the plough after the rains have ceased." When U Nu therefore cast around to see what could be done that would be timely

4. These coups are described in detail in Chapters 11 and 12.

and profitable, he saw as clearly as the tracks of an elephant in a paddy field that Burmese experience in the modern world was extremely limited, and that in order to widen it access would have to be provided to a storehouse of knowledge. As a first step, he founded the Burma Translation Society. This society did not particularly want U Nu's brain, but it wanted his patronage, so it made him its president.

The world's great books were acquired by the society which, after selection, translated them into Burmese and distributed them free of cost to schools and libraries. Among the society's achievements, that most prized by U Nu was the compilation of the *Encyclopaedia Burmannica* in fourteen volumes. Great difficulties were encountered in publishing these books, the first two volumes having to be printed in Europe. When they arrived in Burma, U Nu and his council received them at the wharf and put them on display on decorated floats. U Nu was heard to boast that he was bequeathing to the nation a rock of learning.

A POPULAR PLAN FOR EDUCATION

A National Education Scheme also fell within the range of U Nu's ambitions. Accordingly he formed a commission to study the educational needs of the country and to underwrite a project for their fulfillment. The commission was made up of Burma's leading authorities in the field of education. In this field U Nu's goodwill exceeded his abilities. He became chairman of the commission.

Since it would have been improper to make frequent changes in the education system, it was deemed inadvisable to draw up a scheme hastily. It would be necessary to send out questionnaires and to study the replies; as a second step, the commission would separate into two groups and tour upper and lower Burma respectively, eliciting public opinion; as a third step, it would invite educators from America, China, England, India, and Russia, and seek their advice. The commission was already at the fourth stage—that of writing up its findings—when the first coup d'état took place in 1958. U Nu has not given up on the National Education Scheme, however. He waits for the day when he can present it to the country, and for the opportunity to confer once more with interested persons, so that, with omissions repaired and emendations made, it may be adopted as the new system of modern education.

In regard to health and education, U Nu had been gratified by being able to discover some shortcuts to success. He now sought a shortcut to rehabilitation. During the Second World War, Burma sustained considerable damage to roads, bridges, embankments, and buildings. After independence the insurrections resulted in more damage and also prevented the government from carrying out repairs. When the situation eased somewhat in 1950, the government had no funds for reconstruction. Members of Parliament demanded government aid for their constituencies, either in Parliament or directly from the ministries concerned. The answer that they received year after year was that the government was in financial stringency.

Then came the day when the prime minister introduced a Rehabilitation Plan which was devoid of esoteric overtones. It was based simply on the saying, "Heaven helps those who help themselves." People in each locality who wished to rehabilitate the country were enjoined to come forward with money or materials or labour, and the government would match the effort with money and engineering or technical skill. From all parts of the country came response. A bridge that would ordinarily have cost K.1,000 was built for K.250, with the government putting up K.100 and the local community contributing timber and labour and K.150 in cash.

By this means embankments were filled throughout the country, bridges and roads repaired, wells dug, and schools and reading rooms constructed. Using normal procedures the reconstruction would have taken five years and cost five times as much. In the 1953 budget session of Parliament, the finance minister described the success of the rehabilitation scheme: for the year 1952-53 the government spent K.11,000,000, whereas the public contributed in money and materials about K.20,000,000.

On Martyrs' Day in 1952, Prime Minister U Nu made a speech in which he said that Burma was a rich agricultural country, the largest exporter of rice in the world. It had teak and other forests, mines and minerals and oil. The mighty Irrawaddy provided equal irrigation to the eastern and western halves of Burma. The rainfall and climate were good, the population within reasonable bounds. It was a country that had the means of providing each family with a house, a car, and a monthly income of K.800 to K.1,000.

Facetious newspapermen reported this story as U Nu's having made a promise he would give each family a house, a car, and a monthly income of K.800 to K.1,000.

At any rate, if this speech had been made five years later, he would have been bound to say that the country was rich enough to provide the facilities listed, but that, in order to do so, in addition to the natural wealth, other conditions would have to be met: (1) there must be a sound economic system; (2) there must be sufficient managerial and technical personnel; and (3) there must be a code of morality from the president of the country down to the workers, peasants, and traders.

Following independence, U Nu's government had nationalised various industries. In doing so, U Nu did not appear to have studied all its implications. The nationalised projects soon showed the effects of poor management, corruption, and bad accounting. A case in point was the State Agricultural Marketing Board, the largest of the nationalised concerns.

One day the Bureau of Special Investigation (BSI) conducted a raid of a ship in harbour and found it loaded with good rice which the State Agricultural Marketing Board (SAMB) had sold abroad as damaged rice. The SAMB had the authority to sell rice at regular prices, but whenever they sold damaged rice at reduced prices they had first to get Cabinet sanction. The prime minister remembered that such sanction had been requested and granted just a short time before.

The BSI subsequently recommended to the prime minister that the SAMB be required to furnish an inventory of old and damaged rice. It said that there were no such lists extant because the corrupt officers of the SAMB found it easier to operate without documents that could convict them.

The Cabinet acted on this report and called on the minister of commerce to take appropriate action, but a year passed and still there were no stock lists. In the end, the prime minister lost patience and called in the BSI. He told them the "white ants" in the SAMB and all government departments must be exposed and punished. He was taking personal charge of the BSI with the purpose of putting teeth into its investigations. He admonished the BSI not to look too far afield, but to narrow its gaze to Windermere Court (the residences of Cabinet ministers), where termites might also be found.

Notwithstanding pressure from the prime minister, the SAMB was unable to provide the figures for rice leftover from previous years. The BSI therefore had to appoint a committee of experienced officers to compile the stock lists, and, when they were received, orders went out to dispose of them at the best prices obtainable.

In further discussions concerning the SAMB the following was discovered:

1. The SAMB was not only cheating in regard to old rice but was selling new gunny bags as old.

2. SAMB officials did not pay cash for paddy purchases but issued receipts which the peasants were compelled to encash at a discount of 5 percent.

3. SAMB officials posted at rice mills conspired with the millers and passed rice of lower quality than the specifications. Foreign governments inspecting the Burmese rice sometimes refused to accept certain consignments which they said did not meet the standards set in the agreement. The delay in shipments resulting from such protests used to irritate the prime minister until he learnt from the BSI that wholesale irregularities in the SAMB had damaged Burma's reputation in the international market.

4. SAMB officials embezzled funds by falsely claiming they had bought and stored paddy in warehouses. When milling time came, they set fire to the warehouses and reported that the insurgents had done it.

5. Burma spent, on an average, K.20 million on the purchase of gunny bags. There was considerable fluctuation in the jute market, but Burma never seemed to be able to buy when the market was down. It was only when shipping schedules had to be met that orders for the gunnies were placed and always at the highest

prices. The BSI reported collusion between the SAMB and the Indian jute merchants.

With similar reports in regard to other nationalised industries coming in, the prime minister was reminded of the frequent accusations made in Parliament by the Opposition that government departments were inept and corrupt and that accounts were missing. He had thought these criticisms to be the usual carps emanating from a party whose function was to oppose, but he now realised only too painfully that the state of affairs was even worse than the Opposition had alleged.

U Nu began to tackle the problem by having the BSI go all out after the guilty officials, but gradually it was borne in upon him that, no matter how sternly he dealt with the offenders, the crimes and irregularities in the boards and corporations continued unabated. U Nu became disenchanted with nationalisation. The whole policy would have to be changed, for these reasons:

1.   Nationalisation of an industry brought it under the control of the government. The Cabinet, which exercised ultimate authority over it, was composed of ministers—politicians whose lifelong preoccupation was with power, not with economics. Ignorance of economics put ministers at a distinct disadvantage in dealing with entrepreneurs acting in collusion with corrupt officials.

Whenever reports and recommendations came up from the boards or corporations, through the ministry concerned, they invariably involved Cabinet sanction in regard to funds, or approval of action taken, or delegation of authority. The prime minister, not fully understanding the minutes, would refer to his council of ministers, who understood as little as he did, and the funds and the authority asked for would be granted. The Cabinet was thereby reduced to being a rubber stamp.

Poor management of nationalised industries did not begin at the lowest level. It was in evidence at the topmost Cabinet level.

2.   Although the actual management of the industries was in the hands of secretaries and departmental heads, they too, as lifelong civil servants, were no match for the economic manipulators.

The highest ranking secretaries received a maximum salary of K.1,600, whereas privately owned enterprises could pay bonuses, gratuities, and house, car, and entertainment allowances. Government officials, in addition to lacking proper interest, often succumbed to bribery.

Perhaps the prime minister, in inviting BSI attention to high misdemeanours taking place "nearest to home," was conscious of the risk that he himself ran in respect to the nationalised industries.

3. One way out of the impasse might have been to take control of the nationalised projects away from the Cabinet and place it under economic experts with a clearer understanding of the profit motive, but the snag here was that in the eyes of the politicians private businessmen were exploiters and profiteers.

Besides, bona fide businessmen were scarce in Burma because from the time of King Mindon up to the end of British rule the Burmese had never had an opportunity to develop or manage large-scale enterprises.

Therefore there were hardly any business executives, managers, or directors. So, if the best among the existing businessmen were selected, their supervision would still be largely experimental for the first ten years or so.

It was one thing to bribe officials for import licenses, or to plot the sale of good rice as the damaged article, and quite another to restructure nationalised industries so as to render them viable and competitive in the modern world.

In point of fact, U Nu had selected the best and most trustworthy among Burman businessmen and given them responsibility in certain government concerns. These men he trusted had gone the way of all flesh, making him hesitant about employing other businessmen. He could not see himself giving a carte blanche to a panel of businessmen.

U Nu's intention undoubtedly was to uproot the entire system of nationalisation, but up to the time of the second military coup d'état, in 1962, a new system to supplant the old had not yet been devised. Appointment of new staff, changes in management methods, and other administrative improvements were stop-gap measures, but for the time being the prime minister had to be satisfied with these.

But in the hard school of experience, U Nu had learnt the following lessons:

1. Politicians should be kept out of the business world; otherwise business affairs will be damaged.

2. Businessmen should keep to their own sphere. If they interfere in political matters they will ruin the country.

3. Politicians must make use of political power to encourage private business to the fullest extent.

4. Businessmen must concentrate on improving the economy to such an extent as to provide the country with the means the politicians need for improving living standards, education, and public health.

WILL DEMOCRACY WORK IN BURMA?

Western observers never tired of asking U Nu if he thought democracy could take firm hold in Burma, and U Nu's answer has always been that there was no reason why it should not.

Even to turn a mango seed into a tree required time and patience. The task of raising the tree of democracy was incomparably more demanding. There were no instances, either in the West or in the East, where democracy just simply happened. Much effort and patience would be needed.

In promoting the ideal of democracy, two things were essential: first, to identify the natural enemies of democracy; and, second, to educate the leaders as well as the masses in the value of moral cleanliness, self-restraint, the spirit of compromise, and willingness to accept the verdict of the people as expressed at the polls, and to imbue them with such a spirit that they would be willing to die in defence of democracy.

The enemies of democracy, such as have surfaced in countries in which democracy is just putting down roots, fall into three categories:

1. Some politicians begin in the approved fashion, with victory at the polls. But later, because of either moral turpitude or incompetence (or both) on their parts, public confidence is forfeited, and they find themselves facing electoral defeat. In such a situation

they may delay elections or rig them.[5] If despite their unfair practices they should still lose, these men will cling to power by suspending the people's rights and by outright seizure of the government by unlawful military means.

2. Some politicians are tools of foreign powers. They know full well that they do not command the respect of their people. They also know full well that, lacking this respect, they have little or no chance of winning votes in a free election. So they take the offensive against the democratic system and denounce all free elections. Finally they beg for assistance from foreign governments likely to support them, and they go into rebellion against their own government.

3. Some military officers, being only human, begin to covet the power of the politicians. And since they have the weapons, they are tempted to use them as a readier and surer means of gaining political control, rather than to risk defeat in free elections.

In a newly independent country, the leaders as well as the masses are inadequately informed about democracy. They do not know the real value of this political system, in the absence of which the people are made to suffer greatly. They cannot be expected to have advance knowledge of the evils of government established by arms seizure. The longer a military dictatorship endures, the greater the people's hardships. They cannot understand how demeaning it is to become henchmen to foreign powers, nor how uplifting it is to feel pride of race and pride of one's own country. Most of all, in a democracy in the making, they do not appreciate the need to keep the army free of politics, and the need for the army to subordinate its role to civilian authority. These are the manifold dangers that a new democracy confronts.

To be able to isolate the elements that militate against democracy, and to apply corrective measures, is more difficult perhaps

5. U Nu had no patience with corruption among politicians in power, for he believed that these corrupt politicians could become the greatest enemy of democracy. Therefore, as head of the Bureau of Special Investigation, Prime Minister U Nu publicly admonished it to keep a close watch over the members of the Cabinet, including himself. And, in fact, during his tenure of office, one minister was jailed, another escaped imprisonment only by going underground, and many high officials, including a government secretary in one of the ministries and an ambassador, were also tried and imprisoned for corruption.

than the task of educating the people so that they may take democracy to heart and defend it with their lives. But because the problem is difficult, there can be no thought of delay or hesitancy in tackling it. The forces of democracy must go to work with grit, courage, and ingenuity. By faith and example, by practising what they preach, they can expose destructive elements. At the same time, attempts must be made to convert those individuals who are susceptible to outside influences by sending them abroad at government expense, to examine the government of a foreign country and thus find out (1) how the government conducts its administration; (2) what the fundamental rights of the people are; (3) what recourse is open to the people when these fundamental rights are infringed; (4) how high or low the living standard of the people is; and (5) in what way the system of government affects the lives and minds of the people.

Through such exposure to the conditions prevailing elsewhere, the selectees would be bound to discover that in a democracy politicians in power have as restraining influences the opposition, the press, the courts, and the rule of law. If they lose power these same politicians are not left helpless and unprotected against reprisals by the party in power, because they still have the press, the law, and the courts to defend them.

In authoritarian states, politicians who rise to power can exercise that power as they please. They can use every dirty and immoral trick. Dictators, both the grand and the petty, may possess nothing to start with, but overnight they can amass fortunes, large or slightly less so. There are no laws or courts, press or opposition, to deny them. But once let them lose power and they are reduced to degradation and despair without the protecting arm of the law, or the courts, or the press.

Some time before the second coup d'état took place, the chairman of the British Council visited Burma and extended an invitation for a group of politicians to visit Britain. Included in this mission were government supporters as well as some of the politicians most critical of the government. From this one visit alone, the prime minister found most beneficial results.

After the coup, General Ne Win's government selected a university lecturer who was a great admirer of the communist ideology and sent him on deputation to the Soviet Union. After spending three years in Moscow he decided to come home. On his return journey, he met in London a former pupil, to whom he made a profound statement: "If a man forms too deep an attachment to the communists, just send him to Moscow. There's no need to do anything else."

As for the education of the masses, so that they might learn to love democracy to the point of being willing to die for it, various people have various methods. As far as U Nu was concerned, he had a seven-point thesis which he expounded everywhere he went, even at the height of the insurrections:

1. This country is not the private property of a select few; it is held in joint ownership by all its people.

2. Because of such ownership, only that person or that party which is freely and willingly elected by a majority of the people has the right to govern.

3. In addition to exercising the free and willing mandate of the people, the person or party elected to office must govern in accordance with laws made by the duly elected legislators.

4. There must be adequate laws to safeguard the fundamental rights of the people to live in human dignity, to speak, worship, work, and organise freely.

5. Everyone of age must have the right to vote.

6. Upon losing the support or confidence of the people the government must resign.

7. The above conditions when met make the government of a country legal and equitable. They bring it into harmony with the equitable principles of liberty, equality, and justice. These are the essence of democracy, without which a human being is no different from a castrated bull. Accordingly, all who would destroy democracy must be resisted by all the people.

In lectures and public speeches, in books and pamphlets, the prime minister disseminated his views on democracy. He wrote a play[6] based on these seven principles, which became a textbook in schools. The play was made into a movie which was shown free of charge all over the country. A Burmese newspaper reproduced U Nu's play in cartoon form and the series ran into several editions

6. *The People Win Through,* which was staged by the Pasadena Playhouse in 1955.

in picture books. There were also collateral activities that suggested themselves to U Nu which could promote his seven principles of democracy, such as meetings and seminars, art, poetry, cartoon exhibits, and so on.

The efforts of the prime minister and all lovers of democracy were not in vain. During the 1948-49 rebellions, the country gave proof positive that when democracy was threatened and endangered the people would rise up to save it, by peaceful means if possible, by force if necessary.

U Nu by himself could not have withstood the assaults of the multicoloured insurgents; in fact, it was freely predicted that the country would collapse. In the government's climb back down from the edge of the precipice, and in the final deliverance from the clutches of the enemy, the lovers of democracy all over the country played a crucial and preponderant part.

In 1954, with his faith in democracy immeasurably strengthened and fortified, the prime minister declared at the opening of the Military Academy in Maymyo that the thesis of the Marxists that the last war on earth would be fought between capitalists and the proletariat was false. Instead, he asserted, the last war would be between the masses who loved democracy and the despots who would reduce human beings to the level of castrated animals.

U Nu made two brave attempts to help democracy take root in his country. The first was the formation in 1950 of the Society for the Extension of Democratic Ideals. This was financed by public contributions and a grant from the prime minister's contingency fund. But the society had a serious shortcoming. Since it was a voluntary effort, nobody could apply himself full-time to its work. Only the most dedicated individuals could contribute their services, and that on an intermittent scale. Performance therefore lagged behind expectations.

The society was suppressed in 1958 when the first military coup d'état occurred. U Nu's second spirited effort to revive and promote the ideals of democracy, through an unassailable National Foundation, will be discussed in a later chapter.

9

Travel and Diplomacy

RELATIONS WITH INDIA

Throughout his political career U Nu made many trips abroad; it would be fitting to start with those to India, the country he most frequently visited.

U Nu Meets Pandit Nehru

While Ko Nu was still a student at the university, Pandit Jawaharlal Nehru paid his first visit to Burma. Ko Nu was not able to get close to him, so he had to look at him from a distance. Even before his arrival, Nehru's reputation had spread in Burma: he was well educated, handsome, courageous, and a man of integrity who had made sacrifices for his country and thereby earned universal respect.

As described in Chapter 6, in 1947, consequent on the assassination of General Aung San, Thakin Nu became prime minister of Burma. Shortly afterwards he visited India, accompanied by Socialist Party leader U Ba Swe and U Tin Tut, a Cabinet member. There he met Pandit Nehru for the first time. Since learning, courage, integrity, love of country, and willingness to make sacrifices were qualities which he most admired in others, it was inevitable that Thakin Nu should have formed an attachment to Pandit Nehru from the time of that first visit.

Consequently, U Nu took special delight in visiting India at least once a year. According to diplomatic practice, a president, prime minister, or Cabinet minister was required to give prior intimation of his visit and to obtain the approval of the host country. But in the case of India U Nu would merely write a letter telling Pandit Nehru the date of his arrival and the mode of travel. With the exception of his first visit, when he was lodged in Government House, U Nu stayed with Nehru whenever he went to India.

U Nu Meets Mahatma Gandhi

Mahatma Gandhi had been to Burma while Ko Nu was in high school. As in the case of Nehru, Ko Nu had been able to get only a distant view of Gandhi. Therefore, when he arrived in India as prime minister, U Nu asked to be allowed to pay his respects to the Mahatma. The meeting took place in Birla House at about nine in the morning. The old man sat in a deck chair in the sun, and the sight of U Nu reminded him of a Burmese law student who was a contemporary of his while they were both attending one of the Inns of Court in England. He said he had forgotten the name, because it was such a long time ago, but he recalled that the Burmese student was extremely plucky. Mahatma Gandhi was wearing a hat woven out of bamboo, which he said was a gift from the villagers of Noakali. This village, U Nu learnt, had been the scene of carnage as a result of serious Hindu-Moslem riots which were quelled only when Gandhi personally intervened.

U Nu told Mahatma Gandhi that it would give him great pleasure if he might be permitted to send a Burmese hat, and Mahatma Gandhi said he was willing to receive it as a gift and to wear it. Accordingly, when U Nu arrived home, he sent for a variety of hats and finally picked a Shan hat which adviser U Ohn was deputed to deliver to the Mahatma. U Ohn's plane was over New Delhi when an assassin's bullet stilled Mahatma Gandhi's heart.

On the day following Mahatma Gandhi's assassination U Nu convened a mass meeting in Bandoola Square and moved a condolence motion. Next he proposed that a fitting memorial to the great Indian leader be built, using public donations. A committee was appointed to which U Nu made a personal contribution. When its funds reached K.500,000 a building that formerly housed the British-owned *Rangoon Times* was purchased, and renamed Gandhi

Memorial Hall. The building was then being used as a government warehouse, but U Nu had it immediately derequisitioned. When the Board of Trustees was about to be formed, the Indian ambassador approached U Nu and requested him to agree to be the patron for life; U Nu accepted the honour.

On 2 March 1962, after being overthrown in a military coup d'état,[1] U Nu was put into jail. He had been there less than two weeks when the Indian trustees of the Gandhi Memorial Hall, in a letter signed by their secretary, requested him to vacate his position as patron. Mahatma Gandhi had been a leader of exceptional courage, and it was to commemorate his bravery that the Gandhi Memorial Hall had been acquired in the first instance. Now, by contrast, the Indian Board of Trustees was proving to be cowardly. With a mirthless laugh, U Nu signed the letter of resignation.

A Friend in War and Peace

Burma had a brief moment of glory, lasting perhaps two months from the date of independence. Then, as we have seen in Chapters 6 and 7, came trouble and distress of a magnitude that can only be produced by armed insurrection and civil war. U Nu in his hour of need found in Premier Nehru a friend and saviour. Without the prompt support in arms and ammunition from India, Burma might have suffered the worst fate imaginable. As it turned out, from the middle of 1949, when Mr. Nehru's rifles began arriving, the enemy's threat was first contained, then eliminated.

Mr. Nehru was as staunch in peace as he was in war. When the government of the Union of Burma decided on land nationalisation it came face to face with the problem of what to do about the many Chettiar moneylenders, Indian immigrants who either owned or had foreclosed on more than half of all arable land in Burma. Simultaneously with the passage of legislation, U Nu wrote to Pandit Nehru explaining his action. Burma was likened to a stunted tree because it was being denuded of every tender shoot by the Chettiars. Generations of usurious money lending had enriched the Chettiars and impoverished the Burmans. Nationalisation of

1. See Chapter 12 for details.

land, without compensation, would cause the Chettiars no hardship.

The Chettiars launched a campaign of protest, but the backing they expected from the Indian government for their claim to compensation failed to materialise.

In 1956, with the general election approaching, the economic problem of rising costs and inflation began to trouble Prime Minister U Nu. It could turn into an election issue to the detriment of the AFPFL. To flood the country with consumer goods and bring down prices, two ministers were deputed to call on Pandit Nehru for help. The money was provided—on loan.

Dancing with the Nagas

In 1952, the Burmese press printed an Indian news dispatch that Naga tribesmen from Burma had crossed over into India and taken ninety heads. This raised apprehensions on U Nu's part lest the sanguinary sport of headhunting should mar Indo-Burmese friendship. But a month passed without complaint from the Indian government. There were no protests in the Indian Parliament, no agitation in the Indian press.

U Nu's inquiries revealed that of all the inhabitants in the Naga hill tracts the Sawlaw tribe of Nagas was particularly belligerent. They had armed themselves with World War II weapons and were a constant source of trouble to the Naga Hills Administration, raiding not only over the border in India, but on the Burmese side as well.

When U Nu flew to the Naga hills to make an on-the-spot investigation, he received petitions from Naga leaders that the government should curb the depredations of the Sawlaw. U Nu saw that if the cutting off of heads went unchecked, law and order would cease to be. Headhunting forays into India were bound to strain relations between the two countries.

The law and order situation in Burma proper being unsatisfactory at this time, it would have been impossible to detach troops from the regular army; the only course open was to send a platoon of Union Military Police (UMP) from the force guarding Rangoon.

The Sawlaw were nothing if not brave. With their superior knowledge of the terrain they fought from ambush and, in the first engagement, they drove back the UMP, who left one dead in the retreat. When the UMP counterattacked and recovered the body it was minus the head.

The UMP were no match for the Sawlaw in jungle warfare. So they isolated Sawlaw villages and lobbed three-inch mortar shells from a distance. The shelling caused heavy destruction, killing men, women, and children as well as pigs and cattle. The loud explosions completed the work of demoralisation. The Sawlaw sued for peace.

According to tribal custom the Sawlaw bound themselves, and generations coming after them, in allegiance to the government. A ceremony was conducted whereby tigers' teeth, bullets, daggers, and other weapons were soaked in a bucket and the oath water from it drunk.

Following the oath taking, all other Naga villagers who had suffered in the past at the hands of the headhunters, entered the Sawlaw village and cut off the heads of all those who had been killed by the shelling. These heads were then taken by them to their own villages and offered as human sacrifices to the spirits of their relatives slain by the Sawlaw, thus bringing the blood feuds to an end.

Towards the end of March 1953, U Nu invited Pandit Nehru to visit the Naga hill tracts in Burma. At Mr. Nehru's suggestion, the two first arranged to meet at Imphal in Manipur. From there, accompanied by Mrs. Indira Gandhi, they toured the Naga hills on the Indian side of the border. U Nu was able to draw a sharp distinction between the Nagas on opposite sides of the border. Many of the Indian Nagas were well educated and fluent in English; the men wore Western-style jackets and trousers; the women were fully and modestly clad. The Burmese Nagas, on the other hand, wore a string around the waist to which was tied a strip of cloth, fore and aft, the end piece in front hanging like a tassle over the private parts. A Naga who was better off than others might sport a miniature gong suspended over the same area as the tassle. In normal weather this was all the raiment he wore; in cold weather he covered himself with a blanket. The women, for their part, wore a piece of cloth from waist to knee. In the cold weather they too had blankets, but normally they went about topless. That was twenty years ago, and U Nu no doubt hopes that some change for the better may have come about since then. In stature, the men were tall and strong; the women short but well endowed.

After spending the night in Imphal, U Nu and his guests crossed over to Sinkaling Hkamti in Burma. There they found a large crowd of Naga tribesmen, with their wives and children, and Sawlaw leaders who had been got together for the occasion by the authorities. As soon as his name was called by the district commissioner, the chief of the Sawlaw tribe came through the crowd bearing a warrior's hat and a spear. Then, he made the speech according to the way he was tutored by the authorities, saying that he was sorry for having taken the heads of Indian Nagas, and begged for forgiveness. He then presented the hat and the spear to Pandit Nehru, who received them and was photographed wearing them.

At this or a subsequent function, a curious incident arose which discommoded U Nu. The Sawlaw chief had brought his two daughters with him. These girls stood out among the crowd because they were cleaner and fairer than the rest. The girls had been a week in Sinkaling Hkamti during which time they must have observed that, compared to the others, they were insufficiently clothed. In particular, they appeared to have become extremely self-conscious about their bare breasts since other townsfolk had theirs covered. To hide their embarrassment they untied the cloth around their waist and wrapped it around their breasts. Thus they were half-naked as before, except that it was now the lower portions that were exposed. The Sawlaw chief, who looked upon bare breasts as *de rigueur* and the act of covering them as a social affront to the distinguished visitors, ordered his daughters to readjust their dresses, but the girls averted their faces and would not obey. Infuriated, the father tore off the cloths in public and made them conform to tribal custom.

Lacking most other amenities of life, the villagers here customarily regaled themselves with rice wine, community singing, and dancing. The drinking of liquor was a recognised social custom. Another custom was the long house, or a large hut built at one end of the village, which was used by the young men and women as their sleeping quarters. As soon as a girl reached puberty she was no longer permitted to sleep in her parents' house but went into community living in the long house. As a prelude to the boys and girls sleeping with one another there was singing, drinking, and merrymaking. A boy and a girl thus got to know each other and to experiment as in a trial marriage. Since the begetting of children was the primary purpose of these unions, it was normally expected of the girl to conceive within a reasonable period; otherwise it was not unusual to see the partnerships dissolve and new ones entered into. If pregnancy should result the couple considered themselves married; then they had to leave the long house and begin a life of their own. Twins were greatly frowned upon, and their superstitious natures were such that some means was found to prevent twin children from growing up.

With such distinguished people in their midst, it was natural that the villagers should want to entertain them. The authorities facilitated the arrangements for a large party, and the customary drinking, singing, and dancing took place. Both the prime ministers and Mrs. Gandhi asked to be excused when the liquor was served, pleading slight indispositions, but they had no objection to joining in the revelry. With whoops and hunting cries the visitors joined hands with Naga girls and leaped about in the approved manner. Mrs. Gandhi afterwards told U Nu her father had seldom been in such fine spirits.

A Compromised Verdict

U Nu was at one with Pandit Nehru in the observance of the principles of peaceful coexistence. They believed in the democratic way of life and in the policy of strict neutrality. Except for the raids on Indian Naga villages, which were amicably settled before they could assume any kind of importance, there was nothing to disturb the good relations between the two countries that their leaders had worker hard to foster.

A problem that arose over the arrest of some Indian merchants might be taken as an example of the spirit of goodwill and compromise that prevailed at the time. The Bureau of Special Investigation (BSI) in Rangoon had a *prima facie* case against some Indian traders for contravening the foreign exchange regulations. It probably had to do with the sale of import licences by Burman traders to their Indian counterparts and the subsequent remittance of foreign exchange to exporters abroad. The worst aspect of such transactions was that very often waste paper or dried leaves were imported when the bills of lading showed real merchandise. At any rate, the BSI maintained they had a clear case against the Indians, while the latter charged victimisation.

The prime minister, who was the patron of the BSI, one day received the Indian ambassador, who confessed that he was very unhappy about the BSI arrests. He believed that the accused persons were innocent. U Nu said it was the first he had heard of the case and that he would look into the matter.

The BSI was a creation of the prime minister's. He had so instituted it that the officers of this special department would be controlled by a board whose members were drawn from among senior civil servants in honourable retirement and lawyers. In serious cases, such as those involving ministers or judges, the prime minister's sanction was necessary for arrest.

In the present case, the BSI committee with one accord held that the evidence they had against the Indians was sufficient for conviction. If therefore the prime minister yielded to the Indian ambassador, he would be impugning the credibility of his own officers. On the other hand, having received a representation, he wished to be less than severe in prosecuting the case. He therefore suggested to the BSI that its chairman and his deputy should meet with the Indian ambassador in the presence of the attorney general. Those attending the tripartite conference could be represented by counsel. The evidence could then be discussed and arguments made. What the prime minister expected was a compromise verdict that would satisfy all the three participants at this extraordinary pretrial session, and in fact a mutually satisfactory solution was reached.

A Reincarnation of Athawka

In the reign of Athawka (Asoka) a temple was built of stone in India in which to preserve the relics of Lord Sariputta and Lord Moggalana, two of the Buddha's disciples. During the British reign, these relics were removed to a museum in England. With independence, India was able to recover these sacred relics and arrangements were put in hand to enshrine them in Sanchi, not far from their original resting place. When an imposing structure had been raised, the Mahabodhi Society of India invited Pandit Nehru to place the relics in the tabernacle. Mr. Nehru in turn invited U Nu to the ceremony. From New Delhi the prime ministers flew to an airport forty miles from Sanchi. The rest of the journey was completed by car. Up to a few miles from the airport, large crowds of people lined the road on either side.

It struck U Nu that there was not a place in India that he visited with Pandit Nehru that was not crowded. There were crowds, he knew, that came out of a sense of obligation, but in the Indian masses that crowded upon Pandit Nehru there was a wild exhilaration as in a person suddenly placed within reach of a most desired object. They were not content with looking upon him; they must needs throw themselves upon him and shout themselves hoarse with delight. Bodies pressing upon and jostling one another made for confusion and disorder, and always the police and Congress officials were hard put to find any means of control.

In one such scene, near Benares, the crowd broke through the police cordon and U Nu, walking beside Mr. Nehru, was bodily lifted and swept along by a human river. The next thing he knew, Pandit Nehru was yelling out in alarm and pushing bodies aside in an effort to rescue him. Congress workers also charged in and were commanded by Mr. Nehru to "get U Nu out of here." U Nu went through the ordeal of fighting himself free with the help of the rescue squad. When last he saw Pandit Nehru, he too was being borne along by a human tide, a swagger stick in his hand. He took short jabs at those pressing against him and occasionally slowed down progress, but along would come the next wave and he was lost in the swirling crowd. He seemed none the worse for these demonstrations, however.

On another occasion, when U Nu was inspecting new steel mills with Pandit Nehru, they were told by the police at the airport that rival groups were waiting for them outside. One was the usual concourse of Indian villagers, who shouted their welcome and threw garlands and bouquets at Mr. Nehru's jeep. Then they came upon a separate group, carrying little white flags and led by a few communists. As Pandit Nehru came into view the communist leaders gave the cue but the crowd did not make the correct responses. Instead of shouting slogans they joined their hands in approved Hindu fashion to salute their prime minister. U Nu was told that the communists had paid them one rupee each for this demonstration.

Everywhere he went with Nehru, U Nu saw signs of love and

veneration of the people. They used every means to be associated
or identified with him. U Nu recalled that after he had given a talk
at the Hindu University, he was asked to dine with the chancellor.
As Pandit Nehru sat down, the servants could be noticed going
about their tasks with neat precision. As the last course was being
served, the servants quickly and silently lined up behind Pandit
Nehru and a flash bulb popped. Each one of the servants had made
sure he would be included in the photograph.

No one could go on shouldering such a heavy work load without
feeling the strain, and Pandit Nehru was, nothing if not human.
With advancing age he began to wilt and to tire, and he sometimes
went to sleep on the sofa when U Nu was around. Once, when at
U Nu's bidding the Burmese permanent secretary, James Barrington, was explaining to Pandit Nehru the details of the Sino-Burmese
Border Agreement, the Indian prime minister fell fast asleep. Barrington stopped in bewilderment and was told to take the rest of
his story to his counterpart in the Indian Foreign Office. Evidently,
Pandit Nehru had neither the time nor the inclination to rest up
on beaches and hill stations. He found his recreation in the people
and was beguiled by the music of their cries.

On the trip to Sanchi mentioned above, while they were in the
airplane between New Delhi and Sanchi, Pandit Nehru was so
fatigued that he dozed, and U Nu, in order that he might rest, re-
frained from speaking. But as soon as Sanchi was reached, Pandit
Nehru sprang to life. It was as though at the sound of a waiting
crowd all tiredness left him. The roof had been removed from their
jeep and U Nu and Mr. Nehru travelled standing up, each balanced
against an improvised iron railing. They were pelted with big
bunches of flowers, one of which hit Pandit Nehru squarely in the
eye. He had been catching the bouquets in the air and flinging
them back at the crowd, but now he ordered the jeep stopped. Then,
with one hand over his eye, he snapped at the girl, "Yay dastur hai?"
meaning, "Is it customary to do this?" Unabashed, the crowd
roared that it was indeed a good Hindu custom!

For U Nu, the privilege of conveying the sacred relics into the
new temple at Sanchi was a great religious experience. The ceremony entailed no more than that Pandit Nehru and he should
walk up the hill behind the casket, but U Nu, with the permission

of the Mahabodhi Society, reverentially placed the casket on his head and led the procession. The crowd this time was intimidating in size and not only the police but Mr. Nehru himself became anxious. As U Nu went up the slope, Pandit Nehru turned himself into a rearguard. He mounted the eastern steps backwards, facing the crowd. He shouted admonitions and waved his little stick like a baton orchestrating the cacophonous company below.

As for U Nu, his mind was filled with thoughts of Nehru and Athawka. Was the one an incarnation of the other? Athawka had built the first temple at Sanchi; Nehru was building its replica. The same relics of the disciples Sariputta and Moggalana that Athawka had venerated were being respectfully enshrined by Nehru. The flag of India bore Athawka's insignia—the wheel. The great love that the people had for Athawka they now showed to Nehru. So when Nehru in his previous existence lived as Athawka, he, U Nu, must have been somebody in close association with him. He wished most fervently that he possessed the insight to look into the past.

"Panditji, is it true you have no religion?" U Nu asked Mr. Nehru after the ceremonies. Mr. Nehru confirmed that that was true but he added, "I am inclined towards Buddhism," thus reinforcing U Nu's belief that Nehru was indeed a reincarnation of Athawka.

The Last Meeting

In January 1962 U Nu was again at Benares Hindu University to deliver two lectures on *Mingala* (virtue) and *Myitta* (genuine universal love). Again Pandit Nehru was in the chair. Afterwards they were alone in the Maharaja's residence. U Nu spoke:

Panditji, if you promise not to snap at me I'd like to say something personal.

Why should I snap at you? Go right ahead.

Every morning as you wake up, and every night, before you turn in, could you possibly repeat these words: *Buddhaṁ Saraṇaṁ Gacchāmi; Dhammaṁ Saraṇaṁ Gacchāmi; Saṅghaṁ Saraṇaṁ Gacchāmi.*[2] How would that be?

---

2. "I take refuge in the Buddha. I take refuge in His Law. I take refuge in His monk disciples."

U Nu resolved there and then that on his next trip to India he would bring an image of Buddha—in marble, or perhaps in copper —and leave it up to Pandit Nehru. But on 2 March U Nu was frog-marched into jail. He was still languishing there when word was brought to him that Pandit Nehru had passed away. Thus must brothers and sisters, husbands and wives, parents and children part. Death and separation—these were the common lot and the dearest of friends must part. The prisoner U Nu softly chanted over and over again the Memento of the Dead, a verse on the inevitability of old age, disease, death, and separation.

CHINA, BURMA'S NEIGHBOUR

In 1949, when the Chinese Communists were successful in ab-sorbing the whole of mainland China, friction with the United States was exacerbated and the world waited with bated breath to see if war between the two large nations would eventuate.

U Nu, as a citizen of the world, was necessarily among those who felt concern. In his particular case there was added cause for anxiety. In 1940, while World War II was being fought, U Nu was a mem-ber of a goodwill mission that visited Kunming, Chungking, and Chengtu in China. There he saw the results of bombing and shell-ing by fascist Japan. Photographs showed wholesale destruction of the Chinese populace, including the mass killing of children. When U Nu visited the nurseries, orphanages, and schools, their plight was so pitiful that it was all he could do to prevent himself from breaking down. Although many years elapsed this picture of misery, engraved in his heart, refused to fade. In fact, he became so ob-sessed with this subject that the spectre of innocent Chinese children being once again destroyed in the tens of thousands and in the mil-lions under a rain of bombs and shells, were war to be declared between China and America, haunted him like a ghost.

U Nu Meets Chou En-lai

Over the issue of war and peace between these big powers, U Nu felt his role to be insignificant. Yet, because his heart ruled his head, U Nu was not one to stand idly by. He was impelled by the desire to do something, even if it did not amount to more than seizing the

right opportunity to tell the Chinese and American leaders not to
be enemies but to be friends. Such an opportunity arose in 1954
when Chinese Premier Chou En-lai came to visit Rangoon. Before
the end of that year U Nu had agreed to respond to Chou's invitation to visit Peking: it filled him with gladness that he would then
have a chance to broach the subject of Sino-American friendship.

At the Cabinet meeting held on the eve of his visit to China,
U Nu was asked to discuss with Chou En-lai the problem of de-
marcating the border with China. Deputy Prime Minister U Kyaw
Nyein brought three or four reference books written by Westerners
and, reading chapter and verse from them, he urged that U Nu
should press for the return of the area called Shipsongpana over
which Burma had a claim to ownership. This course of action did
not appeal to U Nu. If the Burmese government placed its de-
pendence on books, documents, and treaties, the Chinese would
be bound to invoke the books, documents, and treaties in their possession. He recalled that when Chou En-lai came to Burma he had
complained of both Kuomintang and Communist maps showing all
the area north of Myitkyina as forming part of China. Chou had
explained that that had come about as a result of an agreement
between the Chinese and Burmese governments. In that treaty
drawn up with the Burmese king, Chinese ships were permitted to
sail up the Irrawaddy to Bhamo in order to facilitate their passage
to areas north of Myitkyina then under their administration. "But
these things don't matter; when the time comes to demarcate the
border, we will see that justice is done," Chou En-lai had said.
Consequently, if Burma chose to place reliance on papers, publications, and ancient treaties, the Chinese would be bound to do likewise, and the delimitation of the border would become a time-
consuming task. Delay would not be a problem to the Chinese; they
could afford to wait. The Burmese could not. Therefore, if it was
left to him, he would much rather try to cultivate the trust of the
Chinese Communist leaders. Once the AFPFL won this trust, the
border problem would become manageable. It would be quite
proper to place the subject of a border settlement on the agenda,
but he would not like to press the issue too hard at this time. Concurrently with the mention of a negotiated settlement, there should
be a total effort to win the friendship of the Chinese and thus to

win the confidence of the Chinese Communist leaders. If this were achieved 80 percent of the border problem would have been solved. This strategy was approved by the Cabinet.

U Nu Meets Mao Tse-tung

The moment U Nu's plane touched down at Peking in December 1954, Ambassador U Hla Maung entered bringing a balaclava hat. He said that it was cold outside and that it would not do to descend in his thin silk *gaungbaung*. U Nu resisted U Hla Maung's attempt to fasten the woollen headgear on him, saying that despite the cold he would prefer to appear in national garb. But the air outside was frigid and his body went taut as soon as it hit him. Consequently he could not deliver the speech he had prepared but was glad to enter a heated motor car after shaking hands hurriedly all round.

After an hour at the guest house, U Nu was conducted to Chairman Mao Tse-tung's residence. There he and his party were warmly greeted by Chairman Mao, President Liu Shao-chi, and a number of vice-presidents. The Burmese were then led into the parlour and ranged on one side of a long table, with the Chinese facing them on the other. U Nu was to meet with Mao Tse-tung on three separate occasions, and invariably the procedure was to start discussions across the long table as soon as the greetings and handshakes were over.

With each meeting, the deepest impression was to be made in U Nu's mind of a compassionate Chairman Mao. Benevolence was written on his expression. After the conversation, Mao told U Nu that during his visit he was welcome to go wherever he wished, and that the Chinese would afford him all the facilities. He added that the Chinese government had launched one hundred development projects and hoped that with their completion China would be placed in a position to assist Burma to a considerable extent.

On returning from Chairman Mao's residence, he went to dinner at Premier Chou En-lai's. Peking is full of grand houses, but Chou En-lai, with extreme modesty, lived in a small house within the compound of the former Chinese emperors. This small house might formerly have been allotted to a butler or someone of equivalent rank. U Nu recalled that a Western journalist had once laughingly remarked: "The Burmese prime minister's house in Windermere

Park is greatly inferior to a consul general's residence." He, as prime minister, had taken pride at this chance remark. Now, in China, it was borne in upon him that his lack of ostentation was as nothing compared to Chou En-lai's. An ailment of the nervous system kept Mrs. Chou confined to bed. But she emerged somewhat unsteadily for a brief moment to greet U Nu and Daw Mya Yee, and then retired.

An Undiplomatic Speech in Peking

At the time of U Nu's visit the entire Chinese public was incensed against the United States. The anti-American feeling found expression in frequent and continuous demonstrations. Because the population was so large, and because the various wards took to the streets at different times, the demonstrations went on throughout the day. Every time U Nu's party had occasion to go out, there were the omnipresent demonstrations, shouts and yells rending the air amidst clenched fists and waving arms. Even when they were within the guest house they could not escape the sounds of the never-ending protests.

In these circumstances many another state guest would have been inhibited from making any utterances advocating Chinese-American friendship. In U Nu's case, he had not yet reached the stage of easy intimacy with the Mao-Liu-Chou leadership. In fact, he had barely become acquainted with them. But U Nu had come determined to make his bid for understanding; the faculty to appraise what was inappropriate or undiplomatic was wanting in him. He had prepared his speech and he was resolved to deliver it, come what may. The only thing he knew was that if he discussed it ahead of time with anybody objections would be raised and he would be persuaded to withhold it. Consequently, he did not let anyone in on his decision—neither the members of his Cabinet, nor his delegation, nor the Burmese ambassador in Peking. He just went ahead and delivered his set piece, there in the heart of Peking.

The scene was the official dinner given in his honour. U Nu's prepared speech contained ten paragraphs, and it was delivered paragraph by paragraph, in Burmese, the same being translated into Chinese by a Chinese interpreter. The first half of the speech concerned itself with the fact of Burma being a small country, albeit one determined not to be the "walking stick" of any large power. It was stressed that Burma wished to win friends and that, having won them, it would never betray them; that it placed the greatest importance on the achievement and maintenance of peace. At the expression of each of these sentiments the distinguished audience showed approval by clapping loudly.

U Nu asserted that, "since we are a neutral nation, our view of these two countries (the United States and the People's Republic of China) is unclouded by prejudice." U Nu then described America and concluded that it was "a nation of great men and women capable of making the world a better world . . . heroes who saved the world from the scourge of Nazism and Fascism . . . playing the unprecedented role of benefactors showering the needy with billions' worth of free gifts, when most countries are indulging themselves instead of giving."[3]

The prime minister then delivered a much longer eulogy of the People's Republic of China, praising the "courage" of the regime and extolling its merits for what it was giving to the Chinese people. U Nu then concluded, "Therefore, we feel that as neutrals in power politics we ought to do something to enable both America and China to achieve their ends without resorting to bloody warfare."

After giving some very general and vague advice as to how these two great nations should conduct their affairs, he concluded as follows:

Hydrogen and atomic bombs will have one result. If these weapons are resorted to, of course countries will be laid waste. Out of the ashes will grow the inevitable hatred against the Anglo-Americans who wield the terrible weapon, and out of these same ashes will grow communism which thrives on destruction and poverty.

Therefore a Southeast Asian today requests that his voice be heard by those who are principally concerned, so that a worldwide conflagration may not break out.

3. At the time this was said Burma was no longer a recipient of American aid. In 1953, unable to find acceptance by the United States of a resolution before the United Nations declaring the Kuomintang intrusion into Burma an act of aggression, U Nu abruptly cut off American aid, which then totalled about $19 million.

I pray that the United States of America and the People's Republic of China may be able to work jointly and with understanding for world peace and progress.

Throughout this second half of his speech the audience observed a stony silence in marked contrast to the first half. No applause punctuated his translated speech. In this atmosphere, one might have heard a pin drop.

Intercession for Six Americans

During this period, the British were without an ambassador in Peking. The embassy was represented by a secretary or counsellor acting as chargé d'affaires. Presumably this official reported U Nu's speech by wireless to London, because two days later a wireless message was transmitted to U Nu from Sir Anthony Eden, the British foreign minister. It was a request that U Nu use his good offices to appeal to the Chinese authorities for the release of six American airmen held in China as prisoners of war. The moment this message was read, U Nu announced that he would approach Premier Chou En-lai. With the exception of Chief Justice U Myint Thein, who approved, the rest of the Burmese delegation objected, pointing out that the Chinese would be bound to misunderstand U Nu's purpose in registering an appeal in behalf of the Americans. But U Nu refused to be swayed. The mission was one for the relief of distress. He would do as much for the Chinese in a like circumstance. So he carried the appeal to Premier Chou, and the latter, out of a lofty spirit, promised that the airmen would be set free; furthermore, when it was done, U Nu would be the first to know. Soon after U Nu's return to Rangoon, the Chinese ambassador asked for an appointment which, due to pressure of work, U Nu set for three days later. When the ambassador duly appeared he brought word that the Chinese government had agreed to release the American airmen. U Nu immediately relayed the information through the Foreign Office to the American ambassador in Rangoon. The following day the release actually took place.

The Beginning of Sino-Burmese Friendship

Conditions seeming to be favourable during his 1954 visit to Peking, U Nu seized the opportunity to commence negotiations to fix the borders between Burma and China. But Chou En-lai pleaded that the Chinese needed time to study the question. He did say that the Burmese need not feel concern, and that the Chinese would not behave unfairly when the time came. As a result it was decided to leave it to a joint diplomatic commission to discuss the subject of the boundary in a friendly spirit and to arrive at a mutually satisfactory solution. A Trade and Diplomatic Communiqué was released on 12 December 1954, in which reference was made to the need "to settle the question (incomplete delimitation of the boundary line) in a friendly spirit at an appropriate time through normal diplomatic channels." Satisfied with this, U Nu returned to Burma.

Convinced as he was that Sino-Burmese friendship was the key to both countries' progress, welfare, and peace, U Nu, upon his return to Burma, strove to build it up into a substantial edifice. His plan consisted of inviting friendship and cultural missions from China and sending to China similar missions from Burma. In 1955 a Chinese Cultural Mission arrived, led by Vice-Premier Cheng Chen-to, followed by a Chinese Agricultural Delegation, a Chinese Buddhist Mission, and even a Peace Mission headed by President Kuo Mo-jo of the Peace Committee. In return, Burma sent a Cultural Mission under U Win, a Military Mission headed by General Ne Win, and a Buddhist Mission headed by Chief Justice of the Union U Thein Maung. This last brought back from Peking the Sacred Tooth of the Buddha.

U Nu gave strict instructions that whenever these Chinese missions visited Burma the hospitality accorded them should transcend the purely formal; in other words they were to be taken to the hearts of the Burmese as though they were blood relatives. He gave effect to these sentiments by personally involving himself. For example, not only the missions that came to Burma but also those that passed through Burma en route to other countries were invited to U Nu's home and given close attention. One of his guests was Vice-President Madame Sun Yat-sen, who came bearing a precious gift for U Nu—a sixty-year-old tree in a flower pot. The lady had apparently been apprised of U Nu's special efforts to foster friendship with China because, in presenting her gift, she expressed the hope that he would tend it with the same care with which he was building Sino-Burmese relations.

VISITS TO HANOI AND SAIGON

On his journey back to Burma in 1954, U Nu stopped briefly in Hanoi, the capital of North Vietnam. In the period between 1948 and 1954 the Vietnamese had been at war with the French. At the very start of this conflict, in 1948, Burma had achieved independence, but because of the civil war its government was reduced to penury. Although it was placed in the position of a beggar, however, Burma could not remain unmoved when in a neighbouring country nationalism found itself pitted against imperialism. It had accordingly dipped into its begging bowl and given what it could gather for the relief of the Vietnamese. This of course was detected by the French government, with the result that when Deputy Prime Minister U Kyaw Nyein, who was then visiting France after a trip to Britain, asked for an interview with the French foreign minister, he was snubbed.

But in Hanoi, as the Burmese delegation was entering the guest house, President Ho Chi Minh, who had playfully concealed himself behind a door, sprang out and without saying a word embraced U Nu and kissed him on the cheek. If U Nu had not seen photographs of Ho Chi Minh he would not even have known who was kissing him.

That day, Ho Chi Minh was wearing a khaki shirt and khaki trousers. The shirt was not new and the trousers lacked a crease. His clothes were not merely unpressed but looked as though he had been wearing them for two or three days. The way he walked, the way he comported himself, his manner of looking at others, and his choice of words were duly observed by U Nu. He noted that Ho Chi Minh was so free of cant and pretence that it was as though he was totally oblivious of the fact that he was president. Seeing him so patently honest, so wanting in pride, and so unpretentious, U Nu was filled with reverence.

A singularly uninformed person, U Nu did not know that Ho Chi Minh was a bachelor. Therefore, when he inquired after the president's family, asking how many sons and daughters he had, Ho replied with a smile that he had many. Not understanding the significance of the answer, U Nu asked, "But how many?" A laughing

Ho Chi Minh had to tell him that all the people of Vietnam were his children.

U Nu was lodged in a residence that appeared to have been the home of the French governor. The war having only recently ended, there was no one living there at the time and the place seemed to have been swept and tidied up in a hurry. U Nu slept in it only one night. In the morning, before leaving for the airport, he visited the toilet. To his dismay he found a nest of ants in the bowl. If he were to discharge his business atop them the ants would perish. On the other hand, he could no longer contain himself. In this crisis he had to have recourse to an adjoining contrivance which he understood to be a bidet. Afterwards he tried to flush it out with water, but the outlet was small and soon clogged up. He left the place in a mess.

All the way to the airport U Nu felt distressed. He could picture the servants at the guest house saying to one another what a washout the Burmese prime minister was not to be able to differentiate between the conveniences for a short business and a long business, and guffawing with laughter. Even after he got back to Rangoon, this thought often troubled him.

When President Ho Chi Minh died, U Nu was in London. He went at once to the residence of the North Vietnamese representative, laid a wreath, and signed the book of condolences. He also conveyed them in a written message to Premier Pham Van Dong.

In 1956, after U Nu had demitted office as premier, he responded to an invitation by President Ngo Dinh Diem to visit Saigon. Before he left Rangoon, he learnt that Ngo Dinh Diem was a fast walker. This suited U Nu perfectly. When eventually both of them took the road, the others had to come after them at a trot.

Diem, in European clothes, was struck by U Nu and his party appearing in their national dress. He issued a directive that all the members of his Cabinet should wear the traditional Vietnamese attire throughout U Nu's stay. He himself wore it also.

President Ngo Dinh Diem was desirous of Burmese recognition of his country, but this created a problem for U Nu, who felt that recognising one half of the country would antagonise the other. Recognition must go to both the halves or none at all.

U Nu met Ngo Dinh Nhu, the president's brother, and Madame

Nhu, whom he found to be a lady of considerable charm. Later, when he heard that Ngo Dinh Diem and his brother had been robbed of power and murdered by robbers in a church, he was gravely affected.

THE BOGOR CONFERENCE

Soon after his return from China, U Nu went to Indonesia to attend the Bogor Conference of the five Colombo Powers. Being in Indonesia was a poignant experience for U Nu. In December 1948, in violation of the Renville Agreement, the Dutch had bombed the airport of Jogjakarta, occupied the city, and captured Sukarno, Mohammad Hatta, Sutan Sjahrir, and half of the Indonesian Cabinet. At that time, Burma was also in great distress due to the general insurrection throughout the country. However, in response to the Indonesian plea for help, Burma dispatched a planeload of arms. Accompanying the arms in the plane was Thakin Tha Khin, U Nu's minister of home affairs. A Royal Dutch Air Force fighter pursued the C-47 as it neared Jakarta but turned back when it discovered the Union of Burma Airways markings on it. Soon after this, at the suggestion of U Nu, Prime Minister Nehru had convened a conference in New Delhi. Many Asian governments that were sympathetic to the Indonesian independence struggle were represented at the conference. A resolution lending moral support to the Indonesian people in their heroic fight for freedom was unanimously passed. Also sanctions against the Dutch were approved by the conference whereby participating nations refused fly-over and landing privileges to Dutch military and civil aircraft.

The Bogor Conference lasted for two days, 28-29 December 1954. With U Nu were Prime Ministers Ali Sastroamidjojo of Indonesia, Pandit Nehru of India, Sir John Kotelawala of Ceylon, and Mohamed Ali of Pakistan. Dr. Sastroamidjojo proposed the convening of a conference of Asian and African nations in April 1955.

In the days when the world was under imperialist rule, such a meeting would have been out of the question. Asian leaders could not meet other Asian leaders, nor could Africans meet among themselves. Therefore the idea of bringing Asian and African leaders together was an appealing one and it was quickly approved, but a difficulty arose when participants were being considered. Dr. Sastroamidjojo did not want Israel. U Nu wished to know the reason why, since Israel was an Asian country. Dr. Sastroamidjojo explained that the situation in Indonesia was such that were Israel to be invited, he would have a rebellion on his hands. He requested U Nu not to insist on Israel's inclusion and U Nu did not press the issue. Next, Mr. Mohamed Ali moved that the People's Republic of China not be invited, but this motion was withdrawn when U Nu said that in that case Burma would leave the five-nation association of Colombo Powers.

Bogor was an extremely pleasant city. It had a world-famous botanical garden in which U Nu was intrigued to find a peculiar flower whose petals closed upon marauding flies and insects. With the permission of the keeper, U Nu spent much time prying the flowers open and releasing the trapped insects.

THE BANDUNG CONFERENCE

The Asian-African Conference took place at Bandung, Indonesia, in April 1955. The governments concerned sent large delegations. The views expressed and the differences exposed were correspondingly numerous. To reconcile them in an acceptable joint statement at the end of the conference was a challenging task.

Overall, the speeches made, the subjects discussed, and the communiqués issued were not of absorbing interest, but the delegates, through propinquity, got to know one another and to establish lasting friendships. This gave the leaders concerned much satisfaction and contributed to the success of the conference.

In the art of winning friends Premier Chou En-lai was worthy of emulation. He brought with him excellent cooks and a number of interpreters proficient in the use of English and Arabic. Throughout the conference he threw luncheon and dinner parties every day. U Nu recalled the evening he was invited to dinner and found his host missing. The place was full of guests and each was told with an apology by the Chinese officials present that Mr. Chou had gone to attend someone else's dinner but would be back very shortly. U Nu learnt that this was a daily occurrence. He never turned down an invitation. He at least showed his face and made his presence felt before he hurried back to his own guests.

On one occasion during a reception at Prime Minister Nehru's guest house in Bandung, Prime Ministers Mohamed Ali (Pakistan), Chou En-lai (China), Sir John Kotelawala (Ceylon), Nehru (India) and U Nu (Burma) were present, among others. While they were joking and laughing, Mohamed Ali asked Chou En-lai if it would be difficult for China to make Chiang Kai-Shek the viceroy of Taiwan. Chou En-lai replied that it should not be difficult. Then Mohamed Ali added that if China could do so the Taiwan problem would be solved amicably and world tensions would be appreciably reduced.

President Sukarno was also a most affable host. He had a high popularity rating, accounted for in part by his insistence that friends and citizens alike call him *Bung,* or "Brother," Karno rather than Mr. President.

MEETINGS WITH BEN-GURION, TITO, AND CHURCHILL

In mid-1955 U Nu visited Israel, Yugoslavia, England, the United States, and Japan. In both Israel and Yugoslavia U Nu was given many opportunities to meet the people, who, he found, were glad to be friends with the Burmese. They gave many manifestations of this sentiment. Ben-Gurion of Israel and Marshal Tito of Yugoslavia were outstanding personalities, their faces filled with determination and honesty of purpose. It was impossible for anyone who had close personal relations with them not to be disposed in their favour.

In England, Winston Churchill had resigned and been succeeded by Sir Anthony Eden. Upon U Nu's request, the British government arranged for him to meet Sir Winston at the latter's residence. By that time Sir Winston had slowed down considerably. He walked with some difficulty, and his gait as he descended the stairs was awkward and unsteady. Sir Winston was also hard of hearing, which compelled U Nu to shout his words. As they sat at a table, there was a bottle of liquor on it. A single glass reposed beside it. A private secretary came to fill it for Sir Winston, who asked, "Where's the glass for U Nu?" The secretary told him U Nu did not drink. Half an hour later, host and guest appeared outside the house to be photographed. As he shook U Nu's hand, Sir Winston said, "Let us bury our old animosities." "Yes! we must, Sir Winston," was U Nu's eager reply.

FREE RICE FOR ASIA

U Nu's arrival in the United States coincided with a period during which there was a difference of opinion between President Eisenhower's secretary of state and his agriculture secretary over the exports of free rice to Asian countries. In the secretary of state's view, such an arrangement in regard to the traditional rice markets of Burma and Thailand would tend to hurt American influence in those countries. On the other hand, the secretary of agriculture considered that American prestige would increase as a result of rice supports to needy Asian nations, especially since American farmers were holding surplus stocks of grain.

Arrived at the White House, U Nu was waiting for President Eisenhower to appear when Assistant Secretary of State Walter Robertson came to converse with the premier's secretary, U Thant.[4] U Thant conveyed to U Nu Robertson's request which was that the latter should protest to the president against the free gifts of rice. U Nu said nothing, but he shook his head and U Thant withdrew.

When the president appeared, U Nu's first words were a vote of thanks for the American war effort in freeing Asia from the fascist Japanese. As a token of Burma's gratitude U Nu presented to the president a cheque for $10,000, to be donated to the "brave American soldiers" concerned.[5] For himself, President Eisenhower received a dinner gong suspended between two elephant tusks. U Nu found that Eisenhower did not behave at all like a general but rather like a lovable college professor.

4. U Thant later became Burma's permanent representative to the United Nations. While serving in this position he was elected secretary general of the United Nations, to succeed the late Dag Hammarskjöld.

5. U Nu made a similar gesture in England, where he attended a memorial service at Westminster Abbey for British soldiers who died in World War II and then met Lord Mountbatten, who was the Supreme Commander in Southeast Asia during the war. After expressing heartfelt thanks on behalf of the Burmese government and people, U Nu presented to Lord Mountbatten, as a token of Burma's gratitude, a cheque for £5,000 to be used for the brave British soldiers concerned.

After about half an hour, it was the president who asked U Nu whether the Burmese government objected to the free exports of rice to Asia. When U Nu said it did not, Eisenhower stared at him in disbelief.

Why don't you object?

The feeding of starving Asians is a laudable act. If I resist a good work I render myself punishable with hell. I would rather avoid this sort of involvement.

Eisenhower looked at U Nu intently for a while but dropped the subject of rice. The conversation was general until luncheon, after which the president invited his guest upstairs. There U Nu surveyed an assortment of gifts from kings, presidents, and prime ministers. Among them was a television set. The president explained that it was colour television, that it was new and not yet on the open market.

While in Washington, U Nu was invited to speak before the National Press Club. In introducing him, the moderator brought up the analogy of dog biting man (not news) and man biting dog (news). Foreign governments coming to America with their palms open and outstretched were a commonplace, but a government that came expecting nothing, bringing a monetary gift to American veterans, was a piece of exceptional news.

U Nu's speech was devoted to neutrality and nonalignment. When question time came, he was asked whether he believed the Chinese Communists to be sincere in their protestations of peace. U Nu answered yes. He believed that the People's Republic of China wanted peace, that its leaders were sincere, and that these men were primarily interested in China's internal problems. He added that it was the Burmese who had much to lose in the event that he was wrong in his estimate of Chinese designs, and that it was "in full realisation of this that I say I sincerely believe that the present government of China truly wants peace."

A CURIOUS INCIDENT

A curious incident occurred while U Nu was in Washington. An appointment had been set up for him to see the secretary of agriculture. The intention of the Burmese Foreign Office was apparently for U Nu to be able to voice his objections to the shipments of rice to Asia. But when U Nu arrived in Ezra Taft Benson's office he was kept waiting. After about ten minutes, U Nu's permanent secretary went to inquire about the delay and was told by Mr. Benson's secretary that no appointment with U Nu had been scheduled. The Burmese party thereupon returned home. However, when President Eisenhower heard about the matter, he ordered his secretary of agriculture to make amends. Mrs. Benson, who was not implicated in any way, accompanied her husband and the couple came to Blair House to apologise, arriving at a time when U Nu and his party were not in. When the Burmese returned two hours later, the Bensons were still waiting. U Nu told them there was no need for apologies. He readily appreciated that Mr. Benson's secretary was new at her job; similar incidents had occurred with embarrassing frequency in his own office in Rangoon. Mr. Benson waited for U Nu to protest about the rice exports, but the subject was not mentioned. In the end, Mr. Benson, as patron of the 4-H Club, pinned a tie clasp on U Nu's lapel and said he would receive the courtesies of the club wherever he went. U Nu and Daw Mya Yee then saw the Bensons to their car.

ENCOURAGING SINO-AMERICAN DETENTE

When the day arrived for U Nu to leave Washington, Secretary of State John Foster Dulles came to say goodbye. After about fifteen minutes, Mr. Dulles volunteered the information that recognition of the People's Republic of China could not be withheld forever. Sooner or later American recognition must be granted. In fact, if truth must be told, the United States government had had every intention of recognising the People's Republic of China, but the slapping and humiliation of the American consul general had caused it to change its mind.

"We do not harbour any spirit of revenge," Mr. Dulles said to U Nu. "When you see your Chinese friends, we should like you to tell them so."

In those days, the only contact the Americans had with the Chinese was through their respective consuls general in Poland.

Prior to U Nu's talk with Mr. Dulles, James Barrington, the Burmese ambassador in Washington, had conceived the idea that these talks were too low-level and that the conversations, to be meaningful, should be conducted by delegates at the ambassadorial level. U Nu found the idea greatly to his liking. When it was suggested to Mr. Dulles, the latter said it was a good idea. Not long after U Nu's return to Burma he had the satisfaction of knowing that the status of the conferees in Poland had been raised, as suggested by him to Mr. Dulles.

The membership of the Overseas Press Club in New York is made up of foreign correspondents and representatives of the various news services. In addressing this club during his Washington visit, U Nu reiterated much of what he had said in China on the subject of Sino-American friendship. The occasion gave him immense satisfaction. It was not that he expected amity and understanding to become an accomplished fact on his say-so. He was well aware of the difficulties that lay in the path of detente. But the mere fact that he had been able to reach both the Chinese and American leaders on a subject close to his heart filled him with euphoria.

On 27 September 1957, back in Burma U Nu was to devote over four hours in the Chamber of Deputies (the lower house of Parliament) to a statement on foreign policy. In summing up his impressions of the countries visited and the leaders with whom he had earnest conversations, he said, "The reception accorded me in China and America was most heartening and spoke volumes for the deep-seated desires of their people for peace. I cannot and do not claim to have performed wonders. In any event the attitudes of both sides have hardened to such an extent that it would be unrealistic to expect spectacular results. But this does not absolve us from the responsibility of doing all that is humanly possible to reduce these dangerous world tensions, and even if I have achieved nothing I have the satisfaction of knowing that the Union of Burma has done all that lies in her power to save mankind from the threat of extinction, and to this cause I shall devote all my energies."[6]

6. U Nu was especially gratified at the eventual improvement in Sino-American relations following President Nixon's February 1972 visit to China.

A VISIT TO JAPAN

On his trip home from the United States, Prime Minister U Nu visited Japan. At that time Mr. Ichiro Hatoyama was prime minister, and Mr. Mamoru Shigemitsu foreign minister. Mr. Hatoyama had been stricken with illness and was far from well. Nonetheless he kept doggedly at his job although he moved with difficulty. On the two occasions U Nu met with him, once in his office and again at the Imperial Palace, he took Mr. Hatoyama's arm and assisted him into and out of his chair.

Foreign Minister Shigemitsu had lost a leg in Korea and was on crutches. U Nu, when he visited him, found that the foreign minister had aged a good deal and was being tenderly cared for by his daughter Hana, who went with him everywhere. One night, coming to a reception given by the Burmese ambassador, Shigemitsu was let out of his car some distance away, besides which he had to negotiate some stone steps. When U Nu hurried to his side the foreign minister was perspiring profusely and trying to recover his breath.

It was the month of July and the weather was unusually warm; nevertheless, when U Nu went for an audience at the Palace, the emperor and the Palace secretaries were in traditional tailcoats and striped trousers. The cares and ravages of World War II had obviously had their effect on His Majesty's health. U Nu was much struck by the grace and serenity of the empress and the princess Chichibu.

THE BURMA-CHINA BORDER PROBLEM

The Burma-China border problem, having been tabled in 1954, was again taken up by U Nu with Premier Chou En-lai towards the end of October 1956. The discussions continued until agreement was reached and signed in January 1960 by Chou En-lai and General Ne Win, then in charge of the caretaker government. Because the negotiations appear to have been protracted, there has been much criticism in the press alleging delaying tactics on the part of the Chinese and suggesting that the Chinese had stepped up their demands with each successive meeting. The truth was as follows.

In June 1956 U Nu resigned and was succeeded as prime minister by U Ba Swe. About a month later, U Ba Swe informed U Nu of the bad news that Red Army troops had entered the Wa State in Burma and were entrenched there. Even before U Nu resigned, there had been two earlier clashes in that area between Burmese and Chinese soldiers. The first incident occurred in November 1955, the second in April 1956. In the first incident, with some thirty men on each side involved, the Burmese suffered one killed and three wounded; the Chinese one killed and seven wounded. In the second incident, also involving the same number of troops on each side, the Burmese suffered no losses, but the Chinese lost an officer and ten others. Following the second clash, the Chinese had poured in troops, and about fifteen hundred Red Army men were now entrenched in the Wa State. After U Nu had conferred with U Ba Swe, they both decided the matter should not be made public. In the meantime, U Ba Swe wrote to Chou En-lai requesting a withdrawal of the Chinese troops, and U Nu also wrote to Pandit Nehru in India.

U Nu's Speech before the Consultative Committee

Not long afterwards, the Chinese Government invited U Nu to Peking. It also expressly asked that U Nu should bring his wife and children with him. When the two leaders met in Peking in October 1956, U Nu reminded Chou En-lai that, as long as the border between China and Burma remained undemarcated, so long would such incidents as the Wa affair continue to occur. Chou En-lai agreeing with this contention, U Nu requested that the Red Army troops in the Wa State be withdrawn. Premier Chou's reply was that the Chinese central government was ignorant of what was happening in the Wa State, and he believed it was the outcome of a misunderstanding between the Chinese troops stationed at the border and the Burmese army. In any case, he said that he would see to it the matter was cleared up before the conclusion of U Nu's visit.

At U Nu's request, he was given the opportunity to address the Political Consultative Committee of China, a five-hundred-member body. Premier Chou made the arrangements and himself presided over the meeting. In his address, U Nu laid heavy stress on Sino-Burmese friendship as the *sine qua non* of Burmese foreign policy. The official transcript bore the following observations:

> . . . The impression may arise that there are difficulties hindering the growth of a sincere and lasting friendship. The basis for such a conclusion may be the fact that China is a Communist country while Burma is not, and that differences in ideology would keep the people apart.

> But . . . the cultivation of friendship should be based on common factors which mark the characteristics of the two peoples. . . . The Chinese are entitled to decide for themselves what is best for them, and they are free to adopt the kind of ideology that is best suited for themselves, just as the Burmese are entitled to make their decision for themselves. . . . Thus, the Chinese, considering all that is relevant, have decided it is for their good and to their advantage to adopt Communism, and the Burmese should have no quarrel with what the Chinese have decided for themselves. Similarly the Chinese should not quarrel with the Burmese for adopting the form of democracy, which they consider is best suited for them.

> Let me explain the first principle: mutual respect for each other's territorial integrity and sovereignty . . . To put it candidly, the Burmese dislike intensely any kind of subjugation or control, direct or indirect, and any attempt to control or subjugate us would be resisted. I know that, like us, the Chinese would similarly repel any attempt to fetter their freedom. Such control would be accepted only by lackeys. . . .

> Having dealt with the first principle, I proceed to the second, the principle of nonaggression. If we look at the history of China and Burma, we find evidence that there were times when the Chinese committed aggression in the territories of Burma. . . . What has happened in the past was bad. If it should happen again it will also be bad. . . .

> The Chinese and Burmese travel in the same boat. It was but yesterday that we managed to shake off the shackles that fettered our freedom. . . . The two of us have neither the inclination

nor the time to quarrel or to fight or to commit aggression on each other's land. Thus from this rostrum I declare plainly that the second principle also has the wholehearted support of the Burmese.

. . . Now the third principle, the principle of noninterference in each other's internal affairs. . . . It need hardly be emphasised that a mere declaration of acceptance of a principle is not enough. Both our countries must make a special effort, doing their utmost to see that the principle is strictly observed. . . . Apart from ties of friendship with China we have similar ties with other great countries. In her relations with the big and mighty countries it is not Burma's intention merely to receive. The thought is ever present in her that she will repay the many kindnesses whenever the opportunity should occur and I assure you that we are always ready to render such help or aid.

I now come to the fourth principle, that of equality and mutual benefit. . . . Both from the point of view of area and population and also wealth of natural resources, China is in fact one of the greatest countries in Asia and also in the world, and it would be lamentable if pride in her greatness should cloud her perspective.

Burma is one of the smallest countries. We would like to be friends with all countries but we would not like to be merely the appendage of the mightiest countries in the world. Therefore, the fourth principle, which eliminates distinctions between big country and a small country, is one that appeals to us and one that we accept without reservation.

I come now to the fifth principle, the principle of coexistence. Does anybody doubt that in this age of atomic and hydrogen bombs, if peace should end, the world would be converted into a huge ash heap? It is said that even with this realisation, because of distrust and suspicion, the idea of coexistence unfortunately is not universally accepted. Apart from four or five countries no country has even seriously considered its acceptance. . . . Some wonder with dread if the talk for peace is but a facade, and whether the aim of the other party is to breed fifth columnists and lackeys. All this is lamentable and should be eradicated. . . .

If we practise these principles honestly with full sincerity in order to eradicate mistrust and suspicion, China and Burma will go down in history as the two countries which turned a world of turmoil, suspicion, and distrust into a world of peace and contentment.

U Nu was to learn subsequently that his speech before the Consultative Committee was reported in full to Chairman Mao Tse-tung. Ambassador U Hla Maung, in relaying this information to U Nu, also said that Chairman Mao had reminded his men that past history showed the Burmese had twice succeeded in repelling the Chinese from their territory.

Premier Chou's Proposals

When Prime Minister Chou En-lai sat down with U Nu to discuss specific details, he was brief and to the point. Substantially the Chinese proposals boiled down to these:

1. The Chinese government would accept the MacMahon Line as the northern boundary of Burma with China.

2. The Burmese government should agree to return to China three villages: Hpimaw, Gawlum, and Kangfang in the Kachin State. The Chinese contention was that these villages were seized by the British in 1913 and incorporated into Burma. It was also contended that at the time of such forcible incorporation there were protest demonstrations all over China, in which Chou En-lai as a student had participated.

3. In 1897, the Chinese alleged, the British seized and incorporated into Burma the area known as the Namwan Assigned Tract. But in this instance the British behaved with perfidy. They did not declare Namwan to be Burmese territory but said the area had been acquired by them on perpetual lease. The British offered an annual payment of R. 1,000 for this lease, which the Chinese government never accepted.

Such an arrangement as a "perpetual lease" was a matter of derision and did not accord with the principle of Sino-Burmese friendship. Therefore if Burma wanted this slice of territory, it should take it. If Burma did not want it, it should be restored to China.

Since the area was one over which the highway connecting the Kachin State with the Shan State had been built, it might be of importance to the Burmese government. If so, and the Burmese government wished to retain it, the Chinese would cede it in exchange for the Panhung and Panlao areas in the Wa State.

Mr. Chou En-lai's suggestion was that, if the Burmese government agreed to these substantive proposals, a preliminary agreement would be signed. Next the boundary would be delimited. Then would follow a final border agreement signed by the governments of Burma and China.

U Nu was in no mood to dissemble. He told Premier Chou that he considered the proposals fair and reasonable. If he thought them otherwise, he would have been equally quick to denounce the proposals and return home.

After expressing his personal accord with the proposals, however, U Nu pointed out that he was not at that time the prime minister of Burma. He would accordingly inform Prime Minister U Ba Swe and suggest that he accept the proposals. If and when U Ba Swe and his Cabinet gave their approval, Mr. Chou would be immediately notified.

Returning to the guest house, U Nu broke the news to Chief Justice U Myint Thein and Ambassador U Hla Maung. They were gratified and urged that prompt steps be taken to implement the agreement just reached. The first impulse was to send a wireless message to U Ba Swe, but since a detailed explanation was deemed essential, the proposals were defined in a written communication and taken by U Hla Maung to Rangoon. The Chinese government provided a special aircraft for this purpose.

Since in the proposed agreement with the Chinese three Kachin villages were involved, U Nu had suggested that Kachin leaders should accompany U Hla Maung on his return to China. U Ba Swe agreed and three leaders, U Zanhta Sin, the head of state, and two former heads, Duwa (chief) Zau Lawn and Sima Duwa Sinwa Nawng, answered the summons. U Hla Maung also brought back a written agreement to the Chinese proposals, backed by his Cabinet. All that remained was for U Ba Swe to follow up and put his signature to the preliminary agreement.

The Kachin Response

When the Kachin leaders were assembled before him in Peking,
U Nu went over the Chinese proposals with them and stated the
following as his reasons for thinking they were fair and honest:

1. In all existing maps of China, whether drawn up by the
Kuomintang or the Communists, all that territory bounded on the
east by the Burma-China frontier area, and on the west by the
India-Burma frontier area, in a straight line above Myitkyina, was
shown as being a part of China. U Nu and the Kachin leaders had
anguished over the prospect of having some day to straighten out
this claim in official negotiations. Now, with Chou En-lai ready to
recognise the MacMahon Line, the risk of having to dispute the
ownership of half of the Myitkyina District had disappeared. This
was therefore a special gain for the Kachin State.

2. From the time of the Burmese kings and throughout the British
regime, the border with China was never clearly defined and efforts
to delineate it had been unavailing. The need to accomplish this
was great and the time most propitious because Chairman Mao
and Premier Chou En-lai regarded the Burmese leaders as their
younger brothers. The Burmese might not be equally fortunate
with their successors in office. Therefore they must make hay while
the sun still shone. In short, the Kachin leaders were urged to agree
to giving up Hpimaw, Gawlum, and Kangfang.

To these suggestions Sima Duwa Sinwa Nawng and Duwa Zaw
Lawn had nothing to say. But Head of State U Zanhta Sin objected,
saying he could not agree to surrender them. U Nu, U Myint Thein,
and U Hla Maung took turns at trying to get reason to bear, but
U Zanhta Sin was adamant, and U Nu was greatly troubled because he considered that U Zanhta Sin had allowed the trivial to
becloud the larger issue.

The next morning, Premier Chou En-lai called at the guest
house where they were all staying. U Nu told him that a message
agreeing to the proposals had been received from Prime Minister
U Ba Swe, but that discussions were still continuing with the Kachin
leaders. U Nu promised to give an official reply to the Chinese by
5:00 P.M. Since the Kachin leaders were present, Mr. Chou En-lai
sat down to recapitulate the terms of his proposal as first explained

to U Nu. The latter said that if the Kachin leaders agreed to give up the three villages in principle, the exact area of the tracts would be clearly defined and illustrated on a map, and this would serve as an annex to the agreement signed. Premier Chou agreed to this arrangement and left. The Kachin leaders listened, but they said nothing.

After Chou En-lai's departure, U Nu, U Myint Thein, and U Hla Maung again tried to win acceptance from U Zanhta Sin and again they failed.

According to the Constitution of the Union of Burma, the prime minister was empowered to appoint an MP of his choice as Kachin head of state. In 1956, he had, as prime minister, appointed U Zanhta Sin, over the objections of some Kachin MPs that he was not a real Kachin, but a Hkanung.[7] To find this same man now acting as an obstacle to an understanding with China greatly distressed U Nu. One way of getting over the impasse would be to put the issue before the Kachin State Council. If U Zanhta Sin should lose the vote there, Prime Minister U Ba Swe would be justified in getting him to resign as head of state and appointing another in his place. The border problem in such an event would be settled smoothly. But U Nu was not disposed to go to such lengths to overcome U Zanhta Sin's objections. He preferred to keep the matter in abeyance until the next general election, when U Zanhta Sin's appointment would expire automatically.

A Diplomatic Interlude

In the afternoon, Mr. Yao Chung Ming, Chinese ambassador in Rangoon, who had preceded U Nu to Peking, came to invite the three Kachin leaders to the Foreign Office. There, when they were asked what the status of the discussions over the three Kachin villages was, Head of State U Zanhta Sin said that they were minor leaders and that they would leave it up to the principals, U Nu and Chou, to do what was right and proper; they were prepared to follow their leaders. The deputy foreign minister, when he heard this, concluded that all the obstacles had been removed, and reported to Premier Chou accordingly.

7. One of the tribes in the Kachin State.

When, therefore, U Nu went to keep his five o'clock appointment with Chou En-lai, the latter fully expected him to say everything was plain sailing. Instead U Nu reported:

1. U Ba Swe had officially confirmed that Premier Chou's proposals were acceptable to the Burmese government.

2. In regard to the three Kachin villages, however, the head of state had entered objections and agreement on this particular subject was still pending.

3. In these circumstances the preliminary signing could not be done, but efforts to bring it about would continue.

Had their roles been reversed, U Nu would have said, "Don't try to hoodwink me; the Kachins have already been to us to say they would take your lead." But Premier Chou, being a cultured man and not given to insulting others, showed his usual complacency.

After his brief meeting with Chou, U Nu, greatly depressed, was on his way home with Ambassador Yao Chung Ming when the latter suggested that they should take in the Russian circus. U Nu pleaded he was very sleepy, but the ambassador persisted:

Please do come. I've been instructed by Marshal Ho Lum to invite you.

All right, but I can't stay long. I am very sleepy.

I expect Premier Chou was disappointed when you told him about the hitch.

Why?

Because U Zanhta Sin told the deputy foreign minister today that he would abide by your decision. The deputy foreign minister had already reported this conversation to Mr. Chou; now, of course, he heard differently from you.

Did Zanhta Sin really tell your deputy foreign minister what you say he did?

Yes, exactly.

Then, the fellow is a liar.

Anyway, that was what he said. I know because I was present.

So Zanhta Sin had been playing fast and loose with him! The thought drove U Nu wild. He had lost face with the Chinese. He trembled with rage. When he sat down at the seat reserved for him at the circus, he found U Zanhta Sin adjacent to him. He sprang up to settle the issue beyond all question, but the curtain was going up and he had to control himself. He did not see a thing of what was going on on the stage, but waited for the intermission which, when it came, found U Nu face to face with U Zanhta Sin. The Chinese ambassador was immediately behind them.

Look here, fellow, what rubbish did you go and tell the deputy foreign minister?

What did I say?

To me you said the three Kachin villages would under no circumstances be ceded to the Chinese; to the deputy foreign minister you said you would abide by my decision. Why are you so shifty?

I didn't say any such thing to the deputy foreign minister.

You most certainly did.

No, I did not. If you give these three villages away I will get a gun and fight.

This heated exchange attracted the attention of the audience and caused a disturbance. The Chinese ambassador told U Nu he now understood the truth of the problem and led him away to a guest room, but even there U Nu found himself still boiling.

It is probable that any other man but U Nu would have avoided the confrontation and waited until he got home. But U Nu by acting on impulse had done both some damage and some good. The damage consisted in giving the appearance that Burmese leaders were childish and prone to flying at each other in public; the good that came of the encounter was in the proof demonstrated to the Chinese that U Nu was telling the truth, and not playing off U Zanhta Sin against Chou En-lai.

By a coincidence, while U Nu was controlling his impulse to fly at U Zanhta Sin, the Chinese deputy foreign minister was sitting next to Ambassador U Hla Maung telling him what he thought of U Nu. The Chinese said he had reason to believe U Zanhta Sin was agreeable to the proposal about the three villages, but that U Nu was playing fast and loose with Premier Chou. He said he had taken U Nu for an honest man, but now he knew differently. These personal attacks were galling to U Hla Maung, who tried patiently to explain the difficulties involved. But the deputy foreign minister had been so insulting that U Hla Maung felt he had to make an issue of it. Accordingly, when he joined U Nu on their way back from the circus, he repeated the conversation and demanded that he be transferred from Peking or, alternatively, permitted to resign.

When he saw U Hla Maung's tears of mortification, U Nu was touched to the quick. He gave U Hla Maung all the documents in the file relative to the border discussions and instructed him to demand an immediate interview with the deputy foreign minister. If the latter behaved correctly, U Hla Maung was to do likewise; but if there was any further insult, U Hla Maung was to strike back. "I shall take full responsibility for what you do," U Nu said.

It was then past 1:00 A.M. but the deputy foreign minister was still in his office with Ambassador Yao Chung Ming, with whom he had returned from the circus. He agreed to see U Hla Maung at once. As soon as they met, the deputy foreign minister told U Hla Maung that he had learnt the truth from Ambassador Yao and wished to offer an apology for his conduct at the circus.

Mao's Magnanimity Wins the Day

On the day preceding their departure from Peking, the Burmese mission was entertained to dinner by Chairman Mao. During his previous visit, U Nu had come as prime minister and according to protocol had been dined by Premier Chou. Now he was the president of the AFPFL and it was apparently thought that it would be more appropriate for Communist Party Chairman Mao Tse-tung to do the honours. An unusual feature of the reception was that U Nu's children and Ambassador U Hla Maung's children were also expressly invited.

Dinner being over, the whole company, including wives and children, moved into an adjoining room and sat facing one another across a long table. With Chairman Mao were President Liu Shao-chi, Premier Chou, and several vice-presidents. Mainly it was U Nu and Chairman Mao who did the talking; the others sat and listened. After about a half hour, during which only pleasantries were exchanged, U Nu blurted out his grievances about the Wa State. He called Chairman Mao's attention to the fact that the occupation of Wa territory by Chinese troops was an act of aggression and not consistent with Sino-Burmese friendship. He further complained that Burmese Communists, who had taken up arms against the government, had been given shelter in China, permitted to attend Chinese Communist Party conferences, and allowed to broadcast over the Chinese radio. These acts constituted interference in the internal affairs of another country and were also inconsistent with the professions of Sino-Burmese friendship.

U Nu had no sooner said this than Ambassador Yao Chung Ming was on his feet. He accused the Burmese government of being partial towards the Kuomintang in Burma, and this in the face of protestations of friendship for the People's Republic of China. Yao alleged that on 10 October of each year, the Kuomintang adherents bedecked their houses, offices, and party precincts with Nationalist flags, and that the Burmese government had turned a deaf ear to official Chinese protests. Furthermore, the ambassador said, the Kuomintang in Burma had displayed posters condemning Chairman Mao as a thief and a robber. The Chinese embassy had lodged protests, but the Burmese government had delayed about ten days before taking down the posters. He was warming to his subject when Chairman Mao held up his hand.

He addressed these remarks to U Nu: "You may continue. There must be openness among friends and such openness must not be misunderstood. We cannot have this sort of intercourse with the Americans. If they shoot one arrow at us, we shoot one arrow back. If they shoot two arrows, we return two arrows. U Nu knows how we deal with them at Panmunjom. However, you may continue." With this encouragement, U Nu was able to finish what he had set out to say.

Chairman Mao's answer was to the effect that the Chinese and Burmese had become good friends, which being so there was no need to maintain troops at the border. Chinese officers from the War Office would soon visit the frontier and order all Chinese soldiers to withdraw a minimum of twenty miles into the interior of China.

When the visit was over, Chairman Mao rose and made to accompany U Nu outside towards the waiting car. The guests pointed out that it was cold outside and begged to be allowed to say goodbye within the room. But no, Chairman Mao said, he would get his hat, muffler, and overcoat. Thus accoutred, he got to the car and only then shook hands.

Arrived at the guest house, U Nu had to accept blame from everyone that he had once again blotted his copybook by speaking out in the way he had at the reception. They said it was a good job that Mao was so forbearing, so calm and collected. Even Daw Mya Yee injected the remark that Chairman Mao was such a "perfect gentleman."

The Withdrawal of Chinese Troops

The following day the arrangement was for Premier Chou to come to the guest house, sign a joint communiqué with U Nu, and accompany him to the airport. By 8:00 A.M. a Chinese secretary had arrived to confer with U Myint Thein and U Hla Maung and draft the communiqué. The Chinese wanted the document so worded that the Chinese troops in the Wa State would be required to withdraw "gradually." U Myint Thein and U Hla Maung wanted a time limit of one month imposed on the Chinese. They remained deadlocked until U Nu stepped in and sided firmly with the Burmese advisers. He said that if the time limit of one month was not observed, he would not sign the communiqué. The secretary thereupon telephoned Premier Chou and was ordered to yield.

The communiqué having been signed, the leaders were en route to the airport when U Nu began with:

Premier Chou, was I wrong to speak to Chairman Mao as I did last night? As far as my people are concerned, they ganged up against me and sided with Chairman Mao.

U Nu, you and I are in the habit of meeting frequently. Instead of speaking to Chairman Mao, you might have brought your complaints to me.

I am very sorry.

That's all right. It's no matter.

The Water Festival in Yunnan

Learning that the Shan people living in the region of Shipsong-pana in Yunnan kept up the Thingyan Festival by water throwing as in Burma, U Nu, in February 1957, after he returned to office as prime minister, informed Premier Chou that he wished to go there.

The original arrangement was for the two premiers to meet in Kunming and to go from there by air to Shipsongpana. But U Nu was filled with a desire to see the Burma-China Road, along which he had once travelled during the war. So he prevailed upon the Chinese to let him fly to Paoshan in Yunnan, and from there to travel by car to Kunming. Marshal Chen Yi met U Nu at Paoshan and the two travelled together to within five hours of Kunming, where they found Premier Chou En-lai awaiting them near a hot spring. Chou was then just recovering from an illness and had repeatedly been cautioned in Peking against getting himself wet.

U Nu realised that there was really no need for either the Chinese premier or Foreign Minister Chen Yi to come out to Yunnan to welcome him. The governor of Yunnan would have met the dictates of protocol. But whenever Chou En-lai came to Burma, U Nu had made it a point to accompany him everywhere, and this was Chou's way of reciprocating the personal attention. U Nu felt badly about getting Mr. Chou out of his sick bed, but the latter expressed his readiness to make the planned trip.

While they were resting in Kunming, Premier Chou broached the subject of a Nonaggression Pact as well as a Sino-Burmese Friendship Pact. U Nu gave the matter consideration and replied that he was agreeable to concluding these pacts, but not during the pendency of the negotiations over the Border Agreement. Chou did not pursue the matter. The following day Premier Chou and Marshal Chen Yi accompanied U Nu and his family by air to Shipsongpana. During the water festival, Premier Chou insisted on going out with U Nu and, despite entreaties to the crowd not to get him wet because he was sick, he got completely drenched.

The Historic Border Agreement

At the beginning of 1958, the AFPFL held its general assembly. U Nu's opening speech was confined to the rejection of Marxism as an ideology by his party. In his closing speech he dwelt on the Sino-Burmese border negotiations which he described as eminently satisfactory in their progress. He stated that in presenting to Burma fair and reasonable proposals, Premier Chou had doubtless been influenced by his great regard for Socialist leaders U Ba Swe, U Kyaw Nyein, and Thakin Tin. It was intended as a morale booster for home consumption, but the upshot of the speech, which was on the radio as well as in the newspapers, was that Ambassador Yao Chung Ming called on the prime minister to set the record straight. He said Premier Chou had been motivated by his regard not for U Ba Swe, U Kyaw Nyein, and Thakin Tin but for U Nu alone. U Nu preferred to believe that no individual, or individuals, deserved the credit. Premier Chou's fairness was actuated by the sincerity he found in the wholehearted promotion of Sino-Burmese friendship by the AFPFL members of high and low level.

In January 1960, based upon Premier Chou En-lai's proposals of 1956, the Burmese and Chinese governments reached agreement on the border question. This agreement was signed in Peking by Premier Chou En-lai and Premier Ne Win, who had ousted U Nu in 1958. At that moment, neither from the east nor the west, from the north nor the south, nor from any of the four corners of the world, was there the sound of anyone taking up a gun over the loss of the three Kachin villages. There was not even a whimper or the whisper of a sound. The Burmese army had the power to say "Give," and even Prime Minister U Nu had had to yield. A man like U Zanhta Sin was muted by the thunder of the army's might and power. Only behind the army's back might one detect whispers!

In April 1960, prime minister once more, U Nu proposed to Premier Chou that: (1) the Chinese and Burmese governments appoint special boundary commissions; (2) these commissions complete the task of border demarcation before 1 October, the Chinese National Day; (3) on that day, 1 October, the Border Agreement, based on the findings of the commissions, be signed in Peking; and (4) the signing be repeated in Rangoon on Burmese Independence Day, 4 January 1961. Premier Chou agreed to these proposals.

It was no easy task to complete the inspections of all border points by 1 October. But U Nu was in a hurry and pledged the fullest financial support to the Boundary Commission. The amount of work put into the field surveys was phenomenal, but U Nu had his wish and by 1 October was in Peking accompanied by a Cultural Mission. After the signing he invited Premier Chou to bring a Chinese ballet troupe to Rangoon.

The Chinese ballet duly made its appearance and the hundred members of the troupe were put up at the Inya Lake Hotel and treated as members of the prime minister's family. U Nu and Daw Mya Yee were frequently at the hotel and constantly entertained the Chinese in their home. They made expeditions together to the Rangoon Zoo and otherwise treated one another with informality and friendship.

While the Chinese ballet was performing at the old Race Course, an American dance troupe arrived to perform in the Jubilee Hall compound. When the prime minister signified his desire to attend the American performance, a member of the reception committee came to dissuade him. He said it was a particularly poor show; the performers were ugly; their voices were bad and too loud; their songs were like those bawled out by Burmese cowherds out of sheer ennui. He said the dancing was as bad as the singing—all hands and feet in disharmony, like students learning to drill. "If you come, you'll be disappointed," U Nu was told.

U Nu thanked the committeeman for his tip. But, as he laughingly explained, he was under an obligation to see the show because of "strict neutrality." Having adopted this policy, he felt bound to attend the American performance since he had already been to the Chinese Ballet. Because he understood that attendance at the opening night had been poor, U Nu immediately issued instructions that several busloads of students should be sent to swell the audience.

The American show turned out not to be good, but it was not as bad as he had been led to expect. U Nu, while watching it, could not suppress the wish that the Americans had come up with better choreography when the Chinese were so evidently pleasing the crowd. The next day, U Nu asked the American troupe to luncheon. He put on a special performance of the Shweman Tin Maung Burmese musical troupe. As the guests were departing, the prime minister singled out U Law Yone, editor of *The Nation,* and said,

"When you see the Americans please tell them they have suffered by comparison. They should be able to do better when the Chinese are in town."

The signing of the Border Agreement with China was of such great historical significance—it was without precedent—that U Nu was determined to lend to it every pomp and ceremony. The dates of signing, 1 October 1960 and 4 January 1961, were the most auspicious in the several calendars. The cultural troupe that U Nu took with him to Peking was no scratch affair. It was rehearsed and trained to the highest pitch, and the officials were told to spare no expense. It was no accident that the Chinese also sent their showpiece to Burma. U Nu had expressly asked for it, to do full justice to the occasion. Also, in order that future generations might remember this great event, the Burmese distributed among Chinese residents along the border two thousand tons of rice and one thousand tons of salt. The Chinese reciprocated by distributing two and one half million yards of cloth and six hundred thousand pieces of china among those on the Burmese side of the border.

A Very Remarkable Person

In the course of his dealings with the Chinese prime minister, U Nu learnt to respect and admire him. His consideration for foreign guests had become a by-word, but his concern for and care of his own people, including the workers in his employ and the servitors who followed him everywhere, were equally great. He never showed condescension to anybody; he was long-suffering and tolerant of others. An incident occurred during the Bandung Conference that brought home to U Nu the extent to which Chou En-lai's patience could be stretched. During a lull in the main conference hall, Chou En-lai, U Nu, and Sir John Kotelawala of Ceylon found themselves discussing a problem in one corner. Evidently Sir John was fast losing his temper, aggravated all the more because Chou En-lai was as calm and poised as ever. The Ceylonese prime minister began using expletives that surprised U Nu, who warned him in English to take a grip on himself. But Sir John went on cursing and swearing, his "damns" and "bloodys" coming thick and fast.

This was an astonishing performance and one U Nu recalled because the other remained completely unperturbed and went on to clinch his argument. When a Burmese delegate heard of this episode he said that if he had been in Chou's place he would have knocked Kotelawala to the ground.

Chou En-lai's hospitality was proverbial. He attended to the minutest details for the comfort of his guests. U Nu recalled that in Peking, whenever there was no official function scheduled, the Burmese were provided with meals at the guest house. The food was of the highest quality, consisting of some well-known Chinese dishes, but the Burmese characteristically had to have a touch of home. They asked the butler if they could have rice and chillies. These were provided with their next meal and continued to appear on the table throughout their stay. When the Burmese mission visited a distant town, their hosts welcomed them with the tidings that Premier Chou had telephoned about rice and chillies, and these awaited their pleasure at the table!

One day U Nu happened to remark that chrysanthemum tea was greatly to his liking. Thereafter this new found delicacy was provided for him at lunch and at dinner. If U Nu prepared to leave the house, there was a cup of this tea ready for drinking; when he returned there was another cup awaiting him.

Another chance remark by U Nu, that on his trip to Peking he noticed that the hills were barren of trees, brought a deputy premier to his guest house. Premier Chou had sent him, complete with files and maps, to explain the government's reforestation programme.

Busy though he was, Mr. Chou found time during U Nu's 1956 visit to Peking to take him on an unscheduled tour of Peking's suburbia. Suddenly Chou remembered a restaurant to which he had once taken General George C. Marshall. There was a fish dish to which Mr. Chou was partial. It was cooked whole, and after the outside was eaten, the bones and head were boiled into a soup, which was then laced with lemon. After serving three small helpings of soup into U Nu's bowl, Premier Chou asked him whether he liked it. When U Nu said yes, Premier Chou added his own approval. Then, reaching for a small envelope in his pocket out of

which he extracted a toothpick made of duck fin, Premier Chou
gave it to U Nu.

HOW TO WIN THAI FRIENDSHIP

In August of 1948, the year Burma gained independence, diplomatic relations were established with Thailand. In furtherance of
his desire to be friendly with all neighbouring nations, Prime Minister U Nu was looking, during the next few years, for an opportunity to reach out to Thailand for closer contact when the Air Force
created an incident. In 1953, Burmese aircraft on a bombing mission against the Kuomintang intruders in the Shan State accidentally
bombed a village on the Thai side of the border, causing some
casualties and damaging Thai homes. This was not a very serious
matter and could have been settled with the Thai government. Unfortunately some Burmese Members of Parliament made speeches in
the Chamber of Deputies over the incident, which offended the Thai
government. Prime Minister Pibul Songgram was incensed, and he
ordered anti-aircraft guns mounted along the border and Thai
bombers flew provocatively into Burmese air space.

U Nu thereupon called his colleagues together and pointed out
that in the past Burmese kings had aggressed against Thailand and
got themselves embroiled in wars, and that his government must be
most careful not to repeat these mistakes. He admonished them to
do their best to gain the friendship and goodwill of the Thais. At
the same time, U Nu tendered an apology over the accidental bombing and offered to pay compensation. The affair then died down.

Then, towards the end of 1954, Pandit Nehru and U Nu were
en route to the Bogor Conference when they rested for a day in
Bangkok. The dinner given that evening by Premier Pibul Songgram presented to U Nu the opportunity to say how much he deplored the frequent wars of the past between the Burmese and the
Thais, and the attendant lootings and wanton destruction. As head
of the Burmese government and representative of the Burmese people he wished to apologise to the Thai people and their government.

Rapport between the leaders thus having been established, Premier Pibul Songgram visited Burma in 1955 to officiate at a ceremony in connection with the Sixth Buddhist Synod. The Burmese

government and the public gave Field Marshal Songgram and Madame Songgram and their retinue a fitting welcome. That same year U Nu went to Thailand and the two prime ministers toured Ayutthaya, the ancient Thai capital that was sacked by Burmese invaders. Both men there and then solemnly promised to rebuild and restore the damaged shrine and monastery, including the image of the Buddha. The Burmese government donated 400,000 baht for this purpose. Premier Pibul Songgram ordered the road leading to the holy places to be paved and a rest house was built for the accommodation of the two government leaders. Within the precincts of the pagoda built by the field marshal the two prime ministers, with mutual affection, planted a Bodhi tree.

Another opportunity to promote goodwill between Burma and Thailand came in 1954, when U Nu made his first trip to the People's Republic of China. Although it did not concern him, Prime Minister U Nu could not refrain from inquiring about the Thai Autonomous Region which had been set up the year before. Prime Minister Chou En-lai explained that the establishment of the region had no bearing on Thailand, being solely concerned with people of Thai origin living in Chinese territory. He said that if the Thai government felt any concern they could send a mission and the Chinese authorities would permit them to make an on-the-spot investigation. U Nu transmitted the message to Pibul Songgram, and a Thai mission was in fact sent.

One other advantage that accrued as a result of friendship with Thailand was the relative ease with which all outstanding matters were settled. During the Second World War, two Shan States, Kengtung and Mong Pan, were taken over by Thailand. For this, Burma had a claim to compensation which she now chose to forfeit. For the accidental bombing of Thai villages by the Burma Air Force, the Thais had compensation due them, but this was also waived. In addition, travel of Buddhist monks between the two countries was facilitated, and new friendships were established between the religious leaders of the Theravada communion.

In 1960 Their Royal Majesties of Thailand visited Burma, and there were exchanges of friendship and cultural missions. Never before in history had the two countries been so well disposed toward each other.

RELATIONS WITH PAKISTAN

As early as 1947 U Nu, accompanied by U Tin Tut, went on a visit to Karachi. They were received by Governor General Jinnah and his sister Fatimah. In 1949 U Nu was again in Karachi, this time to ask Prime Minister Liaquat Ali Khan for arms aid in his fight against the Burmese Communists. Then, in 1950 the Foreign Office reported to U Nu that the permanent secretary of the Pakistani Foreign Office had called in the Burmese chargé d'affaires in Karachi and warned him that Burma must stop oppressing the Moslems in her population; if this was not done, the government of Pakistan would not look on with folded arms.

Inquiries showed that this official protest stemmed from happenings in the Buthidaung and Maungdaw areas in Arakan. These areas were preponderantly Moslem and there was a militant group called Mujahids whose aim was to wrest these townships from Burma and become part of Pakistan. The common people, although Moslem by faith, were loyal Burmese citizens. They appealed to the government for protection against the Mujahids, and this appeal was answered. When the government forces arrived, the Mujahids broke and fled. Their leader, Cassim, crossed into Chittagong and spread tales of Burmese atrocities.

Since the action of the Pakistani permanent secretary could be construed as interference in the internal affairs of Burma, U Nu's first reaction was to put him right to mind his own business. However, Burma's internal situation was difficult enough as it was, and he did not want a quarrel with Pakistan. So he bethought himself of U Pe Kin, a Moslem who had been Burmese ambassador in Karachi for two years. U Pe Kin was a gregarious officer who counted the Pakistani foreign minister and the permanent secretary among his friends. He was then serving in another post but was quickly recalled to Burma. Before being sent again to Karachi, U Pe Kin was asked whether he had heard of atrocities being committed against the Moslem population. He told U Nu that he had not, nor did he believe the reports that were being fed to the Pakistan government. He carried his convictions to Karachi and no more threats were heard from that quarter.

In 1961 Pakistani President Ayub Khan came to Rangoon; before his departure he extracted a promise from U Nu to return his official visit. Ten days before U Nu was due to leave, however, Buddhist monks clashed with Moslems in the satellite town of South Okkala. The incident arose over the forcible seizure by the monks of a mosque in the new town. It transpired that when plots were being allocated for building purposes Buddhist monasteries were given sites on the outskirts whereas the mosque was in the middle of town. By taking the law into their own hands the monks had put themselves in the wrong. Fearing a conflagration if he moved precipitately, U Nu appealed to the monks to restore the mosque to the Moslems, adding that he would see that justice was done. But the monks would not, and some newspapers came out in their support. The situation deteriorated, and when a picture was published showing U Nu wearing a Moslem cap which Ayub Khan had given him the monks became more defiant than ever. There was a possibility of riots breaking out between the Buddhists and the Moslems, so Prime Minister U Nu's Karachi trip had to be reluctantly cancelled. U Nu then gave permission to the police to move in and the squatters were evicted. Force was used but fortunately no one was killed.

CAMBODIA, LAOS, AND BURMA

The holding of the Sixth Buddhist Synod in Rangoon in 1954 drew the leaders of Cambodia and Laos to Burma and opened friendly relations with these neighbouring countries. The crown prince of Laos (the present king) and Prince Sihanouk of Cambodia came to the opening ceremonies and both countries sent religious delegates who participated fully in the deliberations of the synod. Wherever the princes went in Burma the people responded to their charming personalities with rousing enthusiasm.

CEYLON AND BURMA

Prime Minister U Nu once went to worship at Buddhist shrines in Ceylon and on his return brought back relics of the Buddha and his disciples. These relics were carried with ceremony through the length and breadth of Burma, and everywhere the people flocked to kneel in adoration and to earn merit. Public morale, which had suffered because of the insurrections, received a tremendous lift.

It is a Buddhist belief that Gautama Buddha attained omniscience under a pipal tree in Bodh-Gaya in India. During the reign of Athawka, the king's son and daughter took Buddhism to Ceylon. They also took the southern branch of the Sacred Pipal Tree and planted it at Anurudha, where it flourishes up to the present time. Two aboriculturists and two Ceylonese Buddhist monks guard the tree jealously and only one or two selected monks may approach it, pilgrims being stopped at a distance. U Nu greatly yearned to reach up to the Sacred Tree and touch it with his forehead in veneration. He even appealed to the prime minister of Ceylon to obtain this privilege but the monks would not give permission. U Nu would not give up, however, and on his second visit he was permitted to go very close to the tree. But because the Sacred Pipal was very old, he was not permitted to touch it with his forehead in adoration.

Like those from Laos and Cambodia, Buddhist monks from Ceylon took a prominent part in the councils of the Sixth Buddhist Synod.

RELATIONS WITH THE SOVIET UNION

A Blunder on the First Day

In October 1955 U Nu went on an official visit to the Soviet Union. With him were a number of Burmese editors. On the very day of his arrival in Moscow, the unthinking, impetuous prime minister found himself doing something he ought not to have done.

Unknown to his entourage U Nu was carrying with him a letter which he had received in Rangoon from Premier Moshe Sharett of Israel. This letter was intended for Soviet Premier Bulganin, but U Nu was also requested to use his good offices with the Soviet leaders so that they might feel disposed to release those Jews in the Soviet Union who wished to resettle in Israel.

U Nu had met Moshe Sharett many years before when, as foreign minister, he came to attend the Asian Socialist Conference in Rangoon. U Nu realised, of course, that he ought to have discussed the letter with his own Foreign Office. The fact that he did not do so was prompted by his suspicion that the Foreign Office would have raised all sorts of objections. Also the humanitarian aspect of the mission with which he was entrusted appealed to him. So he told no one about the matter.

At the Moscow Airport U Nu was met by Bulganin, Malenkov, Mikoyan, Kaganovich, and others. The arrangement was for him to go to the Kremlin and officially call on the same group of leaders. He took with him Ambassador U Ohn, the Burmese ambassador to Britain, U Kyin, and his secretary, U Thant.

At the Kremlin, courtesies had hardly been exchanged when U Nu produced Sharett's letter and proffered it to Premier Bulganin. Not content with this, U Nu blurted out that he understood there were Jews in the Soviet Union who wished to go to Israel and could not, and that he hoped the Soviet government would be good enough to let them go. The Soviet leaders were speechless with surprise.

The reaction when it came was tinged with unconcealed annoyance. It was pointed out to U Nu that there was an Israeli embassy in Moscow which was the proper channel for communications which the Israeli government might wish to make with the Soviet government. But U Nu was not easily snubbed. He said that Premier Sharett was an old friend, and helping old friends was with him an obligation. If it was not too bothersome a problem, he said he would be obliged if the Soviet leaders would look with favour on the Israeli request.

No more was said on the subject by Bulganin, but he sat glumly, discouraging further appeal by U Nu. It was Kaganovich who finally cut off U Nu with, "Please tell Prime Minister Sharett to make use of his embassy." U Nu's mission had not prospered, but he was very pleased that he had discharged it.

As they left the Kremlin, the Burmese ambassadors with him reproached U Nu for having done what he did without consulting them. Had they known ahead of time, they said, they would have prevented him. "I was aware of that," U Nu told them with a smile.

U Nu's happy knack of rushing in where others feared to tread was revealed on yet another occasion. This too had something to do with Israel and a letter from Mr. Sharett. It was at a time when Israel was leaving no stone unturned to gain recognition from India.

U Nu was well aware of the fact that India had no reason to hate the Jews, but there were other inhibiting factors which stood in the way of a full diplomatic exchange. Anyway, U Nu very readily complied with Mr. Sharett's request and spoke earnestly with Pandit Nehru. Mr. Nehru was neither surprised nor annoyed. U Nu himself had not expected anything dramatic to happen. But he was relieved whenever he was able to get something off his chest.

Prudence was continually being outrun in U Nu's case by his good intentions. On another occasion, when Monsignor Provost, the Roman Catholic bishop of Rangoon, came to invite him to a pontifical high mass, U Nu gladly said yes, then added, "I think I'll bring my friend Bishop West to the ceremony." Bishop West was the Anglican bishop. The look of consternation on Bishop Provost's face was enough to convince U Nu that he had dropped a brick. He recovered with, "On second thought, I think I'll come alone." This gave Bishop Provost the opportunity to explain that there had been something of a rift between the two churches in ancient times and that it might be embarrassing for one bishop to assist at a ceremony conducted by the other. Many similar instances of U Nu's indiscretion could be cited.

U Nu Meets Khrushchev

Luncheon the following day was at Party First Secretary Nikita Khrushchev's, where the usual welcoming speech was made by the host. But when U Nu rose to respond, it was to plunge immediately into the history of the Communist rebellion in Burma. Right after the achievement of independence, U Nu recounted, "a certain foreign power" had instigated the Burmese Communists to rebel, and their bad example was copied by other political organisations until at one time nine-tenths of the total area of Burma was in rebel hands, and the whole world thought Burma might never recover.

"But from those inauspicious beginnings we fought back," U Nu said, "until today I can report the territory seized by the rebels has been recovered; the Communists and other rebels are on the run and being everywhere mopped up. We have broken the back of the Communist rebellion."

Back at the guest house, U Thant remarked:

Did you notice Khrushchev's face during your luncheon speech?

Why do you ask that? Of course I was looking at him all through lunch.

Then you must have seen how his expression changed.

I don't believe I did that. He seemed very quiet.

Brigadier Aung Gyi, who was also present, interposed that he agreed with U Thant that Khrushchev did not seem pleased.

Said U Nu, "I can't help that. It was because of these Russians that our country was reduced to dust and ashes. While I have the opportunity I should at least be permitted to say that. I think the Russians should thank me for not coming right out with the statement that they fomented the Communist rebellion in Burma."

The second evening was set apart for a civic reception by the mayor of Moscow. Speeches were exchanged in advance. In essence U Nu's speech was the same as the one he had delivered at Mr. Khrushchev's function, but he had had time to include more elaborate details in the second speech.

In the morning, U Thant, the prime minister's secretary, had a caller. He was Mr. Shiborin, the Soviet ambassador in Rangoon, who had come in advance of the Burmese mission to prepare for their visit. He called to explain to U Thant that U Nu had, since his arrival in the Soviet Union, promoted Burmese-Soviet friendship very well, but that the repetition of the speech that had upset Khrushchev would not be particularly helpful.

When U Thant relayed the ambassador's message, U Nu smiled and told the former to leave out whatever he considered unnecessary. U Thant missed the luncheon that day for having to rewrite the whole speech.

Special Prayers for Stalin

While in Moscow U Nu went to visit the mausoleum where the bodies of Lenin and Stalin were preserved for public display. U Nu was very disgruntled with Stalin for his interference in Burma's affairs, but when he looked upon Stalin's earthly remains he felt a change come into his heart. He reasoned that Stalin, who in life had oppressed, tortured, and murdered so many, could not possibly find happiness after death. He must have gone straight to hell and must at that very moment be suffering great torment. U Nu felt pity

for him and, according to Buddhist faith, wished him deliverance
by extending to him a share of the merit he himself had acquired
through alms giving and other spiritual and corporal works. The
efficacy of this merit sharing was such that even gods in their abode
could find added bliss, and if Stalin from the nether regions should
make the single response *"thadu"*[8] he would be delivered. In this
faith, therefore, U Nu invoked the name of Stalin and solemnly
diffused merit over him.

Again, while relaxing for a day in the pine woods ten miles from
Moscow, in the dacha which Stalin had occupied, U Nu prayed,
intoned the *payeik,* and offered alms food to the Buddha with the
single intention of obtaining deliverance for Stalin.

U Nu and his party travelled to many parts of the Soviet Union
and were everywhere received with great hospitality. At Yalta U Nu
was invited to dinner in Khrushchev's residence, and there he met
Mrs. Khrushchev and their daughter. Mikoyan was the only other
guest present.

A warm send-off awaited U Nu at Moscow Airport. All the leaders
of the Soviet government were present. U Nu shook hands with
them. However, when Kaganovich's turn came, U Nu went out of
his way and embraced him warmly to show that he bore him no ill
feeling, saying: "Comrade Kaganovich, I love you!"

Khrushchev and Bulganin Visit Burma

Shortly afterwards, in December 1955, Khrushchev and Bulganin
came to visit Burma. U Nu and his party gave them a rousing
welcome.

In Bulganin U Nu found an individual who spoke and comported himself with decorum. He commanded respect and attention.
Khrushchev was more forthright and in the habit of speaking his
mind. U Nu did not agree with everything he said, but his out-
spokenness was rather appealing. After he got to know them better,
U Nu concluded they were not like Stalin, in that they were well
disposed towards Burma.

At the banquet given by the president of Burma, Khrushchev
could not eat anything because he was suffering from indigestion.

8. An expression of joyful approval for a meritorious act.

U Nu offered to bring in a Burmese physician, but Khrushchev said that would not be necessary because he had brought a Russian doctor. But he added at the same time that he was not dependent upon drugs. The secret of good health he said was: (1) to keep your head cool, (2) keep your feet warm, and (3) keep your stomach hungry.

In one important respect, the visit of Bulganin and Khrushchev to Burma was beneficial. For seven years, since independence, the Communist Party and their followers had been agitating that the British through trickery had imposed a sham independence on Burma. They closed their eyes against the truth and kept on shouting their objections. They stated as the reason for armed insurrection the spurious independence that had been foisted on Burma and their determination to change it into a real independence. All the efforts made by the AFPFL to make them see the light had been in vain. But when Khrushchev and Bulganin came to visit Burma the Communists and their followers stopped shouting.

Mikoyan Tells an Inside Story

Four months after Khrushchev and Bulganin ended their Burma visit, Mikoyan arrived. U Nu noticed while he was in the Soviet Union that Mikoyan had a very close relationship with Khrushchev. As noted above, he had been the only Soviet guest at the private dinner that Khrushchev gave U Nu at Yalta. There was much to like in Mikoyan. He was such an attractive person that he could win over anyone in half an hour's conversation. He came to dine with U Nu and, afterwards, U Nu himself accompanied him to the president's house where the state guest was staying. Arrived at their destination, Mikoyan indicated that he would like to continue talking by asking U Nu if he was too sleepy. U Nu therefore went in with Mikoyan and sat in the hall below the staircase. The only other person present was the Russian interpreter, the same man who had assisted U Nu in the Soviet Union and again when Khrushchev and Bulganin were in Burma.

In the course of the conversation U Nu said he wanted to know more about Stalin. What was he really like? Mikoyan said that Stalin was a frightful person and that if he had lived three months longer both Khrushchev and Mikoyan himself would have been liquidated.

When Mikoyan was asked what had led to this conclusion he said first, with respect to himself, that it was because he was such a close friend of Khrushchev's. As to the latter, it was because his disregard of Stalin bordered on defiance. During the war, Mikoyan explained, Khrushchev, then at the front, had occasion to call Stalin on the telephone. Malenkov, who was in Stalin's room, answered the telephone. Khrushchev told Malenkov he did not want to speak with him, but only with Stalin, and asked to be put through. Malenkov repeated the conversation to Stalin, who directed that if Khrushchev had anything to say he should say it to Malenkov. So Malenkov told Khrushchev and Khrushchev banged down the telephone. Mikoyan said Stalin took a dim view of such behaviour and that nobody but Khrushchev would have dared to do what he did.

The talk then went to Beria, who, Mikoyan explained, was a wicked man who had conspired to liquidate Malenkov and all others who might be in Beria's way, and to seize power. U Nu asked how the Soviet leaders were able to deal with Beria in time, and Mikoyan related that it was Khrushchev who had taken the principal role in the drama that ended with the downfall of Beria. First, Khrushchev confided in Marshal Bulganin and Marshal Zhukov and made sure that the army would be in readiness if the secret police should want to take action against them. Then Khrushchev went to see Malenkov, who was the prime minister; before discussing his plan, he asked Malenkov to tell him what he thought of Beria. When Malenkov said Beria was a dangerous person, Khrushchev revealed that when the Presidium met the following day he would prefer charges against Beria and have him arrested. If he resisted, the army would step in. Malenkov was pointedly asked where he would stand in case this plan was carried out, and he said he would side with Khrushchev.

As soon as the proceedings started at the Presidium meeting the next day, Khrushchev announced that he had certain charges to prefer against Beria. The latter replied that he would be ready to receive the charges as soon as the other important business on the agenda had been gone through with. So saying, he reached for a leather attache case lying on the table before him. Suspecting that Beria was about to extract a pistol from the case, Khrushchev swept it off the table. He then commanded Beria to stand up and the latter rose unsteadily to his feet. The whole Presidium could see that he was trembling. Khrushchev strode up to him and pinioned his arms from behind. This was the signal for the soldiers lying in wait to enter the room and take Beria into custody.

Marshal Zhukov Visits Burma

In 1956, at a time when U Nu had resigned as prime minister and was engaged in party reorganisation as president of the AFPFL, Marshal Zhukov came to Burma and asked him for an interview. At this meeting, Zhukov asked,

U Nu, do you think there will be a third world war?

No, I do not.

For what reasons?

Because the third would not be like the first and second wars. There would not be any victor or vanquished, since the whole world would go up in flames due to the atom bomb. The people who make wars would be afraid, I think. What do you think?

I don't agree with you.

And why not?

On this earth wars were fought in the beginning with knives and spears, then bows and arrows, then guns and cannon. Later there were aircraft and bombs. From one era to another the engines of destruction became progressively more frightening. But men were not deterred. They used the improved weapons and they made war. It cannot be denied that the atom bomb is vastly more destructive than previous weapons, but men intent on war will not be afraid to use it. That is why we are equipping ourselves with atomic weapons as fast as we can, so that we may be ready when war comes.

After some time the conversation turned to Stalin.

I understand Stalin did not like you. Is that true?

Yes.

I am told Stalin got rid of those he disliked by imprisoning them, or sending them to Siberia, or liquidating them. How is it that you escaped?

He was afraid of my troops.

Khrushchev Not Overthrown

After the general election of 1960, Khrushchev was again in Burma. He told U Nu that he had planned to go on to Calcutta and suggested that U Nu should join him there. Taking his adviser U Ohn with him, U Nu complied with this request and met both Khrushchev and Pandit Nehru in Calcutta. This was to prove to be his last meeting with the Soviet prime minister.

In 1962 U Nu was overthrown and imprisoned. Sometime in October 1964, some of his colleagues and fellow-prisoners came to his cell and informed him that Khrushchev had been deposed. U Nu had known Khrushchev well. He made a detailed study of the circumstances leading to the overthrow and arrived at the conclusion that Khrushchev had left office voluntarily and was not evicted. His reasoning was as follows:

1. It would be no easy task to overthrow Khrushchev because of his courage. It would not be wrong to say that courage had propelled him from the lowest rung of the ladder to the topmost. In 1953 Khrushchev took on Beria, the most feared man. In 1957, when the Presidium deposed him, Khrushchev refused to give in, but called the Central Committee into action and brought down his opponents in the Presidium. This is the only instance in the history of the Soviet Union when a leader dared to fight the Presidium. Stalin the dictator did not dare to tangle with Marshal Zhukov, but Khrushchev fired Zhukov from his post as defence minister as well as from the Presidium.

2. Mikoyan's name was among those reported as having ganged up against Khrushchev. But he was Khrushchev's closest friend. Also, just as Malenkov and Beria were Stalin's handpicked lieutenants, Brezhnev, Kosygin, and Podgorny happened to be Khrushchev's trusted supporters. It might be argued that in a power struggle ambition often smothered loyalty. U Nu was not prepared to enter into a controversy over Brezhnev, Kosygin, and Podgorny, men whom he had not met; but he would go to any length to defend Mikoyan. Whatever else Mikoyan might do, he was not capable of disgracing Khrushchev. Although there were friends capable of

turning into enemies, there were also friends incapable of betrayal. U Nu believed unswervingly that in regard to Khrushchev Mikoyan was such a friend.

3. Khrushchev might or might not have been an able administrator in the government of his country. But in party organisation there were no two men like him. Stalin had served as the party first secretary, but he took scant notice of party men of whatever degree. At night he was in his cups; during the day he was often asleep. Khrushchev, on the other hand, met with every party leader and took a personal interest in them. When Stalin was alive, such leaders as Bulganin and Voroshilov stood in awe of him. It was quite different with Khrushchev. The man who thumped his shoe before the United Nations might be considered a boor, but he was politeness itself when it came to Russian workers or peasants or the man in the street. Khrushchev was forever cracking jokes; he laughed when others poked fun at him. When he came to Burma and was met by the Russian community, he greeted everyone down to the lowliest worker as a long-lost relative. Every Burman onlooker was struck by this spectacle. This was a great contrast to what U Nu had seen in a documentary in Russia. There was a scene of Stalin, complete with pipe, walking out of a garden. When a worker saw him he became frightened and ran away. Stalin's men had to run after him to assure him he would suffer no harm.

4. Being such a good organiser, Khrushchev had the Central Committee practically in his pocket. If he had chosen to carry the fight there, Mikoyan, Brezhnev, Kosygin, and Podgorny would have been sent flying. They were scarcely of the same status as Bulganin, Molotov, and Zhukov; they represented nothing so formidable as the de-Stalinisation that Khrushchev carried through at the Twentieth Party Congress. Even banishing Stalin's embalmed body from the mausoleum to an obscure corner would have been a more difficult task.

5. Consider what happened to Bulganin, Molotov, and Kaganovich after they were sacked from the Presidium. Even Marshal Zhukov had to go into obscurity. Khrushchev, on the other hand, was able to relax in Stalin's arbour twenty miles from Moscow. Whenever he came to Moscow he was given a good house, a car, and a chauffeur. He was also given a security guard. Moreover,

Khrushchev appeared on American television. Dismissed leaders in the Soviet Union were seldom, if ever, seen again.

6. In dictatorships the usual pattern was for the dictator to die or to be overthrown. He did not resign voluntarily. Therefore, when Khrushchev went, nobody believed the statement released by the Communist Party that he had resigned office voluntarily. He was believed to have been ousted for adventurism, for his hare-brained schemes and for reviving the personality cult. If indeed he had been expelled, there was no reason why the Communist Party could not have said so, instead of announcing his resignation on grounds of ill health. U Nu remained convinced that the Party's explanation was true.

7. Although Khrushchev demitted office, the party line he laid down did not change, either in its attitude towards the Chinese Communist Party or in its policy of peaceful coexistence with capitalism. Brezhnev and company continued to follow the same party line, reinforcing U Nu's belief regarding Khrushchev.

8. The Communist Party had learnt from experience that their system had a built-in defect in that changes in leadership were apt to precipitate a bloodbath. Khrushchev and his group realised that it would not always be possible to get rid of persons like Beria without incurring grave risks. They therefore must have searched for a better arrangement and come up with the formula whereby top-ranking leaders like the party first secretary or prime minister would cease to be permanent fixtures; they would retire as Khrushchev did and the offices would rotate. U Nu had reason to believe that a proper system of resignations at the top and promotions from below had been adopted and would continue to operate in the future.

THE BELGRADE CONFERENCE

A conference of nonaligned nations was held in Belgrade in 1961. At that time tension between the Soviet Union and the United States was almost at a breaking point, so it became the main preoccupation of the Belgrade Conference to attempt to ease it. The conference took the step of deputing Prime Minister Nehru and President Nkrumah to carry an appeal for restraint to the Soviet

Union, and President Sukarno and Emperor Haile Selassie went on a similar mission to the United States.

Before the conference's joint communiqué was issued, a drafting committee was appointed. James Barrington and U Thant, who served on this committee, reported to U Nu that the draft likely to come before the conference for approval was unacceptable to Burma because of the strictures it contained against Israel. They told their prime minister that a more balanced version had been drafted by Krishna Menon of India, but that he had been outvoted in committee by the Arab bloc.

When the draft resolution came up for approval, the majority of the delegates expressed their satisfaction with it. But U Nu stated that since Israel, a country with which Burma had friendly relations, was attacked, it would be difficult for him to accept the offending paragraph. If the roles were reversed, if for the sake of argument, it was Egypt that was being condemned in absentia, Burma, as a nation friendly towards Egypt, could never countenance it. On the contrary, Burma would have sprung to the defence of Egypt. In these circumstances, he urged that the draft resolution submitted by Krishna Menon be considered for adoption, rather than the other. U Nu was supported by Mrs. Bandaranaike of Ceylon and the delegate of Nepal.

The conference accordingly took up Krishna Menon's draft and adopted it unanimously. In the aftermath of this conference, President Nasser invited U Nu to Egypt and King Hassan invited him to Morocco. Towards the end of 1961 U Nu was able to accept both these invitations. When President Nasser died, his friend U Nu was in exile raising an army to oust the military dictatorship in Burma. But for this he would have been at the funeral.

10

A Private View

The record of U Nu's political career reveals only part of the man, leaving many aspects of his more private self obscure. What manner of husband is he? How is he as a father? What kind of a family is his? The answers to these and other such questions will be explored in this chapter.

THE FIRST QUARREL

As already related, Ko Nu was a schoolmaster when he married Ma Mya Yee. After their marriage he took her home to Thongwa. Within the first month they had their first quarrel. It began innocently enough. He came into the kitchen and began teasing her. There were laughs and giggles as he acted the clown. Then there was some light banter, and suddenly he pushed her by the shoulder, shouted "Go!" and flung himself out of the room.

This outburst of temper was brief enough, but when he reentered the kitchen she was nowhere to be found. He called to her, then searched the house and inquired of the neighbours. Finally he found a pupil and together they conducted an aimless search in town. An hour later he returned home in a state of considerable alarm to find Ma Mya Yee packing her things. He at once went to seize her hand but she pushed him aside. He told her he was in the wrong, that he was sorry and begged her to forgive him. She said nothing but the flood of tears spoke eloquently of the hurt a gentle, sensitive girl felt when ill-used by a man for whom she had left a loving family and a sheltered life.

Genuinely contrite at having made her cry he tried to comfort her, but she was still angry. "I'm going home," she announced.

He looked at her in surprise, then recovered himself and tried to bluff his way out. "You know," he told her, "You remind me of Po Saung the oil vendor. The slightest thing would set him off, and the moment he was displeased he would grab his little catch-all and threaten to go home to upper Burma." The tears had stopped but she was still sullen. So he gently put his arms around her and said, "All right Shwe[1] Mya, since you're determined to go I'll take you back to Pantanaw." Then as she looked up at him he added, "But don't do like the woman in the play who quarrelled with her husband and threatened to leave. He tried coaxing her to no avail, so in despair he produced the five kyats she needed to pay her passage. 'But I need five kyats more,' she said, 'It's five kyats to go and five kyats to come back.' "

Ma Mya Yee did not laugh. But she smiled. "This opium eater certainly knows how to make his wife ecstatic," she remarked and allowed herself to be led back into the kitchen. There they found the cat had eaten their dinner!

A SPECK OF DIRT

U Nu was well aware of this ugly streak in his character which made him flare up and do or say things which he was to regret later. Like a speck of dirt in a pot of curry, it spoilt what would otherwise be wholesome. But try as he might, he could not overcome the failing. It was with him when he was a child running half-naked behind a hoop. It was to plague him when he was well past sixty and approaching seventy.

U Nu's outbursts came as a shock to Daw Mya Yee in the beginning. But gradually she learnt to put up with them and to adopt certain tactics of her own as a defence mechanism. If her husband yelled at her she covered her head with a blanket and emerged from it only when he came to apologise. If he was tardy with his apology she refused to eat her meals. Or she would lock herself in the room and refuse to lift the bolt until he had abjectly surrendered. The

1. Literally, *shwe* means gold. When used before a name between husband and wife or other intimates, it is a term of endearment.

years passed, but the pattern remained the same: a sudden show of bad temper on his part, accompanied by sound and fury, a retreat into ominous silence on her part, then the gentle coaxing and the making up. It had become only too familiar to the participants in the household drama, but at least on one occasion their younger daughter, Than Than Nu, was moved to protest. "You're behaving like a couple of children," she scolded them. "One moment you're bringing down the house; the next moment you're billing and cooing like lovebirds. I wish you would grow up."

There was an occasion when U Nu, living alone in his annex, was visited by his wife and eldest daughter, San San Nu. They were having fun, trading light banter and teasing one another when all of a sudden U Nu went off the deep end. There was so much ferocity behind his words ordering his wife out of the room that for a moment mother and daughter were dumbfounded. Then Daw Mya Yee hurried out in such evident distress that San San Nu was alarmed. She asked her father to do something quickly and, getting no response, decided to waste no more words. She went after her mother only to return with the information that something terrible had happened. This took U Nu to his wife's bedside to find her prostrate and moaning in anguish. Her blood pressure was normally below one hundred, but now it was found to have risen to one hundred and forty, so a tranquilizer was at once given. U Nu, now thoroughly repentant, rubbed his wife's hands tenderly while his daughters upbraided him. Long after Daw Mya Yee had calmed down, U Nu lingered by her side feeding her Ovaltine with a teaspoon.

Then, since the daughters continued to pull long faces, U Nu spoke facetiously. "You girls blame me for upsetting your mother, but in fact she's not put out at all. She's quite used to being yelled at. The old woman just wants me to fuss over her." Both the daughters sided with the mother. They said this was not the time for levity, but Daw Mya Yee could be seen smiling.

DOMESTIC BLISS

In over forty years of marriage, these explosions on U Nu's part, although of unfortunate frequency, were the only incidents that marred domestic bliss. There was no clash of temperaments between husband and wife. In regard to domestic economy there was perfect understanding. There were times when there was sufficient money in the house. Then they donated to charity or spent with each other's approval. There were other times of financial insufficiency but it never caused distress. There was not a single occasion on which husband and wife quarrelled over money. Frankly speaking, U Nu never knew how much money they had and he never interfered with his wife's management of the family finances.

In regard to political affairs, there could be no question of dissension in the house because Daw Mya Yee was singularly free of political opinions.

Could it be then that the missing ingredient was love? In answer to this it would have to be asserted that love was not only present but expressed in pronounced fashion. U Nu found in Daw Mya Yee a woman who returned in full measure the affection he entertained towards her. Early in their marriage he was so overcome one day that he seized her and bit her on the forehead. It was such a sudden passion that she screamed in alarm and pain. "What did you do that for?" she asked, and U Nu answered, "Because I love you." The bruise would not go away for days and Ma Mya Yee had to lie to neighbours, saying that she had slipped and fallen.

This then was the woman, among all in the world, he most cherished and in whom he felt fulfilled. Love there was without question. Except for those interludes when both were rendered unhappy by his sudden outbursts, the U Nu menage was blissful. Husband and wife treated each other as friends. There was light banter and clowning on his part and some gay repartee on hers. On all occasions each showed great consideration for the other. Ma Mya Yee was partial to liver and gizzard and these bits U Nu would retrieve out of the curry and heap on her plate. She would transfer them back onto his and this would occasion from the children such remarks as, "If you don't eat it quickly, there're hawks ready to snatch."

Whenever Ko Nu, as he then was called, was in funds his first thought would be to stop at the bazaar and pick up a choice delicacy for his wife. Whenever she fell ill he gave her his personal care, praying and reciting incantations, invoking a religious cure if a medical one got delayed in the process.

CAUSES OF DISSENSION

With this evidence in support of the theory that all the ingredients were present for a successful partnership, one would have to look for causes of dissension other than those that might be attributed to a nagging wife or a suspicious husband. If one were to analyse a total of perhaps two hundred occasions on which, in the course of their marriage, U Nu violently lost his temper, it would be shown that some such incident as those about to be related almost invariably provided the spark.

In the early period of their marriage Ko Nu had to leave home early for work and did not return until two o'clock in the afternoon. Invariably he found Ma Mya Yee had not eaten breakfast because she did not wish to eat without him. He remonstrated with her, pointing out that she was liable to make herself ill. Thereafter, when she continued to go hungry, he exploded.

Papers and files were also a perennial source of trouble. Ma Mya Yee was always mislaying them. When he was in a good mood U Nu did not seem to mind, even if the document involved was an important one. But now and again, the loss of a file or a sheet of paper would set him off.

First impressions never registered as deeply with Ma Mya Yee as they did with Ko Nu. Ko Nu would sing the praises of a man he had met for the first time, and if Ma Mya Yee should ask how long he had known the man or caution him about appearances being deceptive Ko Nu would be likely to fly into a rage.

Ko Nu was extremely receptive to suggestions about wonder drugs and medicines. He collected herbs and formulae and compounded and dispensed the drugs to others besides experimenting with them himself. Generally, Ma Mya Yee, although disapproving, was able to contain herself, but when a woman enthusiast helped herself to an overdose of Ko Nu's concoction and made herself ill, Ma Mya Yee scolded her husband for being an ignoramus and a potential killer. He felt greatly wronged and expressed his feelings in no uncertain terms.

There was a man with whom Ko Nu was greatly taken. Given to feats of piety and meditation, this friend continued fast in Ko Nu's affection until Ma Mya Yee told him the man was a faker and a secret drinker. To shatter his illusions was to provoke Ko Nu to wrath.

Out of the two hundred known cases of frenzy or seizures put up for analysis, one hundred and ninety or more must fall into one or another of the above-mentioned categories.

At first, Ma Mya Yee must have found herself wondering what manner of man she had chosen for a husband. But as a year passed, she grew accustomed to his bouts of distemper. At first he succeeded only in putting her on her mettle, but gradually she began to show it. She would seek to distract him at work and get a rise out of him in various ways. One of her favourite poses was to sit on the arm of his chair and assume a patronizing air, saying, for example, "Hey, Maung Nu, are you sure you can write this? If you're in any kind of difficulty don't feel ashamed to tell me." And if he should appear meek and say "Yes, ma'am," she would thrill with laughter.

At other times she interrupted his work out of sheer boredom. If he pleaded with her to go to sleep on the couch and let him finish his writing she might comply, but again she might not. "I want to talk," she would sometimes insist, and he would have to put everything aside. A tactic or two that he used to make her angry enough to leave the room boomeranged on him, as when he said, "You chatter just like a fishwoman. If I had known you were a fishmonger I would never have married you," and she came back at him with, "Ko Shwe Nu, you can thank your lucky stars you got this fishwoman. Who else do you imagine would have married you?" This sort of jibe would hit home and he would expostulate with, "You bitch! I was only playing the fool with you. You clip me with a foul blow." This would be greeted with giggles and an accusing finger sometimes poked into his cheek. "You're not exactly a good sport," she would say. "You like to dish it out but can't take it with a smile." Oftentimes he saw she was in the right and acknowledged it in silence.

FACING LIFE WITH EQUANIMITY

After they were wedded Ko Nu and Ma Mya Yee lived together for a year. Then he was transferred to the Pantanaw school, as we have seen above, and they spent another year together, in his new

job. But when Ko Nu went off to law school in Rangoon he had
to leave his wife behind with her parents, seeing her only during
holidays. When the 1936 student strike was called off and Ko Nu
left law school, he became so preoccupied with the national university project that he still did not get around to sending for his
wife. Only once was he able to take a few days off and pay her a
flying visit. When the time came for him to return to Rangoon
she made ready to accompany him, but he gently dissuaded her. He
left, promising to come back for her, but she never understood why
she could not go with him.

The national university work paid a pittance of forty rupees a
month, of which ten rupees went towards renting a single room.
On the thirty rupees that remained Ko Nu and his co-workers, Ko
Hla Pe and Ko Tun Ohn, led a frugal existence. Every day Ko Nu
had to walk eight miles to work and back. It was impossible to provide rice and curry on their budget, so they generally ate a hash
made of fried lentils, which they could buy cheaply at a roadside
Indian stall. Ko Nu knew Ma Mya Yee could not possibly eat hash
every day. Even they, eating merely to keep alive as they did, could
not long endure this unvarying fare. The moment there was a slight
improvement in their fortunes—when at length a number of Ko
Nu's articles got published—the trio bought a primus cooker, an
aluminium pot, and a frying pan. They could now afford rice, peas,
and duck eggs, but their joy was short-lived. Ko Hla Pe amateurishly
overheated the cooking oil and, rather than see the little room go
up in flames, found a stick and scooped the burning mess out the
window. The next day Ma Mya Yee was sent for. She came at once
and set to work, but it was an impossible situation. She collapsed
and had to return home to her parents. Soon, however, Ko Nu's
Nagani Book Club got off to a good start and Ko Nu was earning
eighty rupees a month. He could now maintain a wife.

In their over forty years of marriage, Ma Mya Yee has seen her
husband change roles often in his stormy career. He was a strike
leader as far back as 1936, an entrepreneur starting a national university, a book publisher, an early member of the Thakin movement
and a two-term prisoner before he became prominent in politics
and headed the AFPFL. As a prime minister he was to be twice
overturned by a military coup d'état, to suffer long imprisonment,

and to stage a revolution. Ma Mya Yee must have found the going rough at times, but she never once complained, neither did she pause to inquire what the struggle and turmoil were in aid of. Wherever her husband led, she followed. Hers was not to reason why but to keep her man replenished.

As a political agitator Thakin Nu frequently found himself caught in the police dragnet. The British were strict about law and order but liberal with detainees. Food, for instance, could be brought in from outside. The moment Thakin Nu landed in jail Ma Mya Yee would be ready to provide home cooking for as long as might be necessary. During one period of detention she was pregnant but nothing—not even the fact that it made her husband very cross— could prevent her from carrying food to the jail, twice a day.

After the second 1962 coup, the long confinement in jail of nearly five years told on U Nu's health. He returned home with high blood pressure. It almost broke Daw Mya Yee's heart to see him turn away in disgust from some of her best cooking.

A VOW OF CELIBACY

As we know, U Nu had for some time been considering taking the vow of celibacy. In January 1948, with Burmese independence achieved, he finally judged his purpose to be firm enough and his determination sufficiently advanced. Consequently, about the middle of July of that year, he told Ma Mya Yee of his intention to adopt the celibate way of life. Ma Mya Yee's reaction was the same as before: "Ko Ko Nu, a man takes a wife and a woman a husband for the very purpose you are renouncing. But if you feel very strongly about it, I shall not stand in your way. I will help you fulfill your parami."

During the time of Lord Buddha, a rich man in the capital city of Yazagyo, Withakha by name, hearing a sermon preached by the Buddha, was uplifted spiritually to the state of *anagam*. In this state sexuality was uprooted and it became impossible for him to have intercourse with any woman. Calling his wife, Dhamma Deinna, before him, he said, "Behold I have become an anagam. Between us there can no longer be a husband and wife relationship. Therefore you may dwell in this house and care for me as a sister would an elder brother. Since you are still young, you may, if you wish, take another man to be your husband and continue to live with him here. Or, if you prefer, you may take whatever you wish of my property and go from hence."

Thus the legend. U Nu was not an anagam. He had not even reached the lowest, the elementary stage of meditation. Nevertheless, Withakha's words to Dhamma Deinna were seared in his memory. Calling Ma Mya Yee before him he said, "Ma Mya Yee, I've made my vow. From this moment onwards you must regard me as your elder brother as I do you as my younger sister. Since you're still young, you may, if you wish, enter into marriage with another man. You may continue to live in this house, or go whenever you please." Tears were the only sign she gave that she had heard. That day U Nu left his wife's bed and went to live alone in a small house adjoining theirs.

U Nu was able to keep his vow, but Ma Mya Yee took it hard. The damage to her was psychological. In three months, having lost interest in food and drink, she began to waste away and had to be assisted in and out of bed. The family physician diagnosed a breakdown and ordered absolute quiet. She was accordingly moved into new premises and received constant medical care. By and by the family doctor became anxious and called in a physician from the Rangoon General Hospital for a second opinion. The patient did not improve, however. She was now rejecting her medicine and had an attack of nerves even if the noise she heard was no louder than the sound of crockery over plates.

A MIRACULOUS CURE

Daw Mya Yee seemed ready to die. She asked that she be allowed to die in her own home and she was moved back immediately. U Nu then decided that the doctors were powerless to help her and that only the power of religion remained. He asked that he might have recourse to the Three Noble Gems and find a cure through spiritual means. When Daw Mya Yee hesitated, he reminded her of the time they were on board a steamer to Hlaingbon when she fell ill and he had to resort to a religious cure because there was no medicine of any kind. He had recited payeik stanzas over a cup of water which she drank and soon was made well again. All other means having failed, he would like to try the same incantations again. Daw Mya Yee nodded her head in agreement and the religious "doctor" went to work. The family doctor was told he should keep up his visits but he must prescribe no more drugs and stop giving his patient injections. In the seclusion of his prayer room U Nu performed his religious devotions and prepared the payeik water. He needed a placebo to induce faith in Ma Mya Yee, so he obtained a bottle of bisurated magnesia and administered it diluted with boiled water, a few drops at a time. This was followed by the real faith cure, the payeik water, also fed to her in droplets. While she drank he sat by her side and prayed.

After two days of the new treatment Daw Mya Yee expressed hunger and was given chicken soup. A week later she could eat solids, and after another week was able to walk in 'the room. In a month she was up and about.

U Nu was very pleased with his effort. As they sat down to a meal together he asked his wife as a favour in return for restoring her to health that she would be tolerant with him when next he shouted at her.

"That, doctor," she replied, "is a fee I am not prepared to pay."

A FEW MINOR PROBLEMS

Having taken the vow of perpetual celibacy, U Nu found there were a few minor problems remaining. The way he looked at it, adultery or sexual intercourse of any kind consisted not only in the act itself but in thinking and planning it in the mind. The act might be called the greater impurity, and the thought the lesser impurity. The lesser kind would include fondling, embracing, or kissing. The complication arose because of the possibility of contacts with foreigners with a different social background. Because under his new guidelines touching the hand of a Burmese woman might be improper, should this prohibition extend also to foreign women, with whom shaking hands was the proper and expected thing to do? If handshaking was all right, what about the more familiar form of salutation, the kiss? And to project it one step further, ballroom dancing? He resolved it all in his mind. He would avoid the physical contact of dancing. If ever circumstances were such that it could not be avoided he would recite the burial service to himself while dancing.

A FACE FROM THE PAST

Towards the end of 1960 U Nu and Daw Mya Yee went to visit Kyaukpyu, where a curious incident took place. One morning, while the district commissioner was with him at the Circuit House, U Nu, apropos of nothing, mentioned that he had once met a Kyaukpyu girl in college who, although of gentle disposition, was a fearless debater, and who he understood had unfortunately been cut off in her prime by tuberculosis.

You don't mean Cissy Aung Gyi, do you?

Yes, I do.

She's not dead; she's alive and well.

Oh! They told me definitely she'd succumbed to TB.

She's alive, she's here and I can bring her to see you.

I'd like to meet her very much. But let's do it this way. You invite her to dine with us here at seven. At six o'clock Ma Mya Yee and I shall call on her and bring her back with us.

Casting back in his memory, U Nu could see Cissy Aung Gyi, a slim, seemingly sickly, little girl. Now she must be over fifty. Had age been kind to her? Would they be able to recognise each other?

When U Nu and Daw Mya Yee arrived at her house, Cissy Aung Gyi came forward to greet them. She was indeed the real Cissy, but how different from what she had been. Then she had been thin, emaciated; now she was firm and full. Then she had been like a peachick, still scraggy and unattractive; now the grown-up Cissy was a peahen in plumage, who lent an air of grace everywhere with her presence.

"How are you, Cissy?" were U Nu's first words. On the instant he realised he had never spoken to or with her before. He had admired her, but always from a distance. Now she was close beside him, smiling and looking twenty years younger than her age. Yes, she was beautiful, and when she spoke she struck a note that vibrated between compassion and passion, a split tone that transcended the one and just fell short of the other. U Nu was able to maintain his composure but only with the greatest of difficulty. He was able to brace his mind, but beneath it his heart danced a little jig with his liver.[2] He was over fifty and regarded as an old man. But he knew better.

In addition to Daw Mya Yee, Cissy's sister was present. Throughout the hour of conversation they held together, it was on the tip of his tongue to ask Cissy if she ever received those three love letters he had written her. But he judged the moment to be not quite right. Perhaps after he had seen her three or four times . . .

Six months went by, and then at a Cabinet meeting the presence of U Ba Saw, who hailed from Kyaukpyu, reminded him again of Cissy Aung Gyi. He inquired:

Do you know Cissy Aung Gyi in your town?

Yes, but she's no longer among us. She died here in Rangoon five days ago. There are stories in the news about her because after she was buried her grave was defiled by robbers.

U Nu was pensive for a while. What a strange fate! Cissy the girl was reported dead, but she was alive. Now she was really dead. It would not be true. He wished that it was not true. He wished she were alive.

A WORD ABOUT THE CHILDREN

U Nu and Daw Mya Yee had five children: San San, Thaung Htike, Maung Aung, Than Than, and Cho Cho. It was lucky for the parents that San San was not a boy. Even the name was not one they had chosen: she named herself San San after a movie actress who always played the part of heavy.

From the age of two, San San was a wilful, wayward child. At home she drank milk but not coffee, which she found bitter to the

---

2. It is only in recent years, with open heart surgery, that the sentimental role of the heart has been denigrated in the West. However, the Burmese, and perhaps the Chinese as well, have always given to the liver rather than the heart pride of place and a dictionary definition as the seat of emotions.

taste. But if she was in somebody else's home and coffee was brought for her parents she would snatch the cups away and force herself to drink. If she saw a baby in the crib she was apt to turn it out and take its place. Consequently her parents took to leaving her at home when they went out to pay calls.

One year, while Ko Nu was president of the Rangoon University Students' Union, Ma Mya Yee was invited to come down and present the trophies for the sports events. Ma Mya Yee and San San put up with Ko Khant and Ma Saw Yin, old family friends. They had a son about San San's age and the children played together. The boy gave half of his toys to San San, but she grabbed all of them and finally beat him on the head with a toy pistol.

The next year, San San and her mother again went to Rangoon and Ko Nu took them to the cinema. After entering the theatre, the child said she wanted to go outside. When she got out, she wanted to go in. She asked for lemonade, but when it was brought refused to drink. She again and again demanded to be led out and was fast becoming an annoyance to the other people. So when she began screaming, Ko Nu whisked her outside, followed by a distraught Ma Mya Yee. There was a scene in the lobby when Ko Nu gave his daughter a good spanking.

Another year passed, and then a letter came from Moulmeingyun to inform Ko Nu that San San had become naughtier than ever. Ma Mya Yee said she was compelled to take a cane to the child, but the latter had snatched it out of her hand and beaten her with it. Ko Nu replied that he did not believe a child five years old could do that. But when, after a few months, he went to visit them in Moulmeingyun, Ko Nu discovered that San San had not forgiven him for the spanking at the cinema. When he went forward to take her in his arms she pushed him away. When he told her, after the visit, that he was returning to Rangoon, she just said, "Go away."

San San at the time was going to school. One day her father saw her come home, drop her bag, and run out again. Curious as to what was going on, Ko Nu looked out in the street to find that his daughter had pounced on two other girls, each with an ice cone in her hand. San San had already got possession of one cone when the others put up a fight. When Ko Nu reached the scene at a bound,

San San had one of the girls by the ear. It took a struggle to free the ear before San San bit it clean off.

But this same child grew up to be a good, responsible girl. When she was sixteen San San went with her father to the Meditation Centre. She came out of it loving and obedient to her parents. The grudge she held against her father for beating her was forgotten; she was no longer capable of being rude to her mother. When eventually she married, she found a man who was good-natured, upright, and kind.

During World War II, Thakin Nu was on trial before a British court when his son Thaung Htike was born. After two years of confinement Thakin Nu came home to find a thin, sickly child who still had not learnt to sit. When he was not lying down, he was being carried about. A steady diet of milk, eggs, and orange juice and plenty of sunshine saved him from an early death.

Thaung Htike was not wild like San San, but he was stubborn. When he was six and his younger brother Maung Aung four, they ran a race together. Because the father exhorted him to run faster, Thaung Htike stopped in midfield. He received a scolding and a beating, but he would not run at his father's bidding. He was a boy determined to do everything his own way, and at his own pace. During the holidays, the boys were required to rest in the afternoon. Maung Aung used to go obediently to sleep, but Thaung Htike simply refused to do so, and would not yield even when he was caned. At thirty, Thaung Htike developed gastric trouble and U Nu obtained some special medicine which he left for his son, with directions how to take it. Discovering later that Thaung Htike had not taken his daily dosage, U Nu raised his voice at him and was promptly told, "Father, if you keep ordering me about like this, I promise I will never take your medicine." U Nu realised only then that at the first hint of compulsion this boy was apt to dig in his heels.

Thaung Htike was a little withdrawn from the rest of the family. With strangers he was usually stiff and reserved. In an age when kings, presidents, and ministers had to put so much effort into public relations, U Nu often wondered what sort of an image his son intended to create—whether he would ever care enough to think of such things.

Maung Aung, the younger son, was short-tempered and quarrel-some. If he did not have to fight with another boy, he fought his brother. U Nu once took him to the zoo and showed him a black panther. Unlike the lion, the tiger, and the bear, which had learnt to behave in captivity, the black panther never ceased to be resent-ful and aggressive. It growled constantly and seemed frustrated be-cause it could not get at the spectators. U Nu told Maung Aung that if he did not mend his ways he would have his name changed to Black Panther.

When he got to the university, Maung Aung did undergo a change. Instead of defiance and truculence, he began to display a latent suavity, and to take a keen interest in politics.

The middle girl, Than Than, grew up gentle and timid. Where the rest of the family was self-reliant, Than Than was dependent and helpless. She was always obedient to her teachers and submis-sive to authority. For years she was bullied and ill-treated by a maid who was supposed to be looking after her in school, but although she was frequently pinched and slapped she never once let her parents know. Unlike her father when he was in school, Than Than proved to be a very good student and generally passed at the head of her class. In twenty-five years of life under the parental roof, Than Than never once merited chastisement but was an exem-plary daughter in every way.

Cho Cho, the youngest daughter, was the apple of her father's eye. She resembled him in his childhood in many ways. She was of course spoilt by everyone in the family, just as her father had been. In fact she reminded U Nu so much of himself that he had reconciled himself to being shouted at, saying to himself that was how his own father must have felt. Cho Cho, like Than Than, was bright in school; but there all resemblance ended.

FIVE-MINUTE FATHER

U Nu was never a good family man. In the beginning he had to live apart from his wife and children because he could not afford to have them with him. Later, when he could afford them, he either was too preoccupied with politics or was in jail. During the period after the assassination of General Aung San and especially the protracted period of insurrections, he very often forgot he had a family. Then, after conditions returned to normal, at a time when many other men might have tried to make up for lost time, he took the vow of celibacy and removed himself to a separate establishment. Thus, although they lived practically next door to each other, the children felt they had never really been close to him. No wonder they referred to him as their "five-minute father."

TAMING THE CHILDREN

In the midst of his official duties, U Nu did make efforts from time to time to give as much of himself as possible to his growing family. Daw Mya Yee had her hands full because of the two spirited boys who soon got to the stage of pummelling one another. She once appealed to her husband to get them to pay more attention to books, and his way of doing this was to warn them that at the rate they were going they would become street cleaners and garbage men. He laid down the hour from seven to eight every night as study time.

One night, emerging from the conference room, U Nu asked San San where the boys were and was told they had gone to bed. Without checking the time, U Nu had them up and laid it across them with a belt. The following day, the boys followed him to work and demanded to know why they had been punished. The upshot of this confrontation was that U Nu had to admit he had been so busy he did not realise it was long past eight when he took it into his head to look into their homework. As on all such occasions he had to make it up to them in some tangible form.

The boys were not above playing one parent off against the other. They once complained to U Nu that their request to Daw Mya Yee for permission to go to the cinema had been turned down. U Nu therefore approached his wife on their behalf and learned that they had already been to the cinema the night before but were determined to go again because there was a new Bob Hope picture in town. Since U Nu had more or less promised the sons he would wheedle the money out of Daw Mya Yee, she had to pay for the tickets, but she complained that he was spoiling them.

His sons were perhaps eleven and eight years old when U Nu

heard that they had been drinking some liquor. He spoke sharply
to them, saying there was nothing good about liquor. It had a bad
taste when drunk, and afterwards it led to quarrels and fights.
Nobody had any respect for a drunk and when he died he went to
hell.

From talking about liquor he went on to the subject of women.
The boys were told when they were old enough they could have
any woman they loved, though she might be a beggar maid. But
they must never go to a prostitute because of the possibility of contracting venereal disease. They were also warned against exploiting
good girls. "You wouldn't want other people to take advantage of
your sisters," he said to them.

On the subject of misconduct, U Nu laid stress on some people's
propensity to get something for nothing, and to incur debts which
they had no intention of repaying. Cards, horse racing, and other
forms of gambling were to be avoided at all costs.

Finally he warned his sons that the punishment for any of these
major infractions would be severe. The offender would be tied to
the post on the tennis court and given fifteen lashes with a rattan.
A second offence would drive the offender from the house, "and
even after I'm dead you shall not defile its shadow."

One might have thought U Nu's homily would have a dampen-
ing effect on the children. But almost immediately after it was
delivered, friends arrived in large numbers and stereo music blared
out as usual. When U Nu requested that it be toned down, loud discordant singing was the result. He had to go out and work elsewhere.

U Nu had an entertainment hall built next to his official residence in Windermere Court. On one occasion a diplomatic party
had been invited to a Burmese musical recital and secretaries were
in attendance to supervise the seating arrangements. U Nu's sons
arrived early and seated their friends in the front row. When a
secretary remonstrated, he was told it was all right because there
were other seats vacant. U Nu, upon arrival, was told about the
squatters and he went to his sons and added his plea, saying that
some ambassadors had been invited and that the boys should be
polite enough to go to the rear. Their reaction was to gather up
their friends and stomp out of the hall. U Nu consoled himself

with the thought that insofar as major infractions were concerned his adjurations would not go unheeded.

Although the boys were in the habit of playing rough and hitting one another, they took good care not to tangle with San San. They called her "Ma Ma San" and treated her with the respect due to an elder sister whose reflexes were extremely quick. One day, when Thaung Htike was thirteen, all the children were with their parents coming down the Chindwin on a steamer. At Pakokku, the parents went ashore. For some undisclosed reason, San San suddenly slapped Thaung Htike's cheek and he punched her in the face. The next moment, while the other siblings looked on, the two combatants staged a knock-down drag-out fight up and down the main deck. The town of Pakokku knew about this, but not the parents. None of the children sneaked.

A MATTER OF CONSCIENCE

Other aspects of U Nu's character are revealed in his actions in what he considered matters of conscience. One such matter concerned Mr. Sloss, the Englishman who was principal of University College during U Nu's student days. It might be recalled that Ko Nu, while at the university, had repaid good with evil insofar as Principal Sloss, the Englishman, was concerned. In 1936, the year of the strike, Ko Nu's ingratitude towards Mr. Sloss was at its worst, but the enormity of his wrong was not then apparent to the wrongdoer. Later, when he fully realised that a teacher ranked with the Buddha, the Law, the Assembly, and one's own parents, Ko Nu was overcome with remorse. Principal Sloss had left Burma to take up another appointment, but Thakin Nu had him on his conscience. In 1940, as he sat in Ward Four of the Rangoon Central Jail, the thought of how deeply he had injured his teacher came to him again and again until, with the clanging of the door and the departure of the turnkey for the night, Thakin Nu found his guilt almost insupportable. Finally, he knelt on the floor, and with his hands joined in obeisance he asked forgiveness of Mr. Sloss, wherever he might be.

In 1950, as soon as he found a breathing space from the insurrec-

tions, Thakin Nu sent an official invitation to England so that Mr.
Sloss might return to Burma and receive at least a token of his
contrition. Thakin Nu was disconsolate when he heard from the
Burmese ambassador in London that Mr. Sloss had aged, and that
because of a heart condition he was under doctor's orders not to
attempt the long flight to Burma.

Fate was to deny Thakin Nu an opportunity to meet with Mr.
Sloss even when he went to England. Hearing that Mr. Sloss was
in Oxford, the Burmese ambassador arranged a tea party in a lecturer's residence, where U Nu was to see his former principal so
that he might at last find the forgiveness he so much craved. As
they neared the lecturer's residence, Thakin Nu removed his shoes
in the car, with the intention of making his *shikhoe* in true Buddhist fashion. But, although host and tea were in readiness, Mr.
Sloss was not there. When the ambassador inquired about Mr. Sloss,
the lecturer stared at the ambassador and replied that he did not
know anything about it.

Thakin Nu could no longer remain silent. He wrote a humble
letter to Mr. Sloss, saying how false and ungrateful he had been and
asking for pardon. The principal replied at once and in the kindest
manner gave absolution to his former pupil. Both Thakin Nu's
letter and Mr. Sloss's reply were released to the press.

Another serious matter on Nu's conscience was the destruction
of bird and animal life he had been responsible for in the past. His
Buddhist beliefs gave rise to fears that he would be made to suffer
in future existences because of the suffering he had caused in this
one. He took to buying fish, crab, prawns, chickens, and ducks in
large quantities and setting them free. As mentioned before the
thoughtless destruction of insects weighed so heavily on him that
he took to walking with his eyes riveted to the ground, so that he
might avoid stamping on animal life.

In 1951, the World Peace Pagoda having been built near Rangoon, the date approached when the consecration of the finial was
to take place. For seven days there was great feasting, with all-night
performances of song and dance troupes, magic shows, circuses, and
boxing matches. Because of the large crowds that came without cessation and the refuse that was dumped, millions of flies appeared.
As the prime minister arrived one morning he found municipal

workers going to work with DDT sprayers. Crying out like a
wounded animal, U Nu leaped from his car and sent the workers
away. Then he got together a group of ex-monks who were translating the *Tripitaka,* and set them to work, chanting the *Yadana thok
payeik,* in which he himself joined. They did this for two hours a
day. On the third day a storm arose and the flies were blown away.
Then the rain fell and the air was cleansed.

The lake at Meiktila has surrounding it a pleasant walk which
the prime minister used whenever he was in the vicinity. One day
he noticed with dismay that fish was being caught in traps in large
numbers and loaded onto boats for sale. He called the district commissioner and said, "This lake was constructed by King Anawrahta
for agricultural and drinking purposes. Fishing in it is prohibited."
The district commissioner could have told him that not only the
townsfolk but the people for miles around depended on the lake
for their food, but apparently he did not wish to enter into what
he knew would be a fruitless argument, so he did issue the order.
But as far as the people were concerned, no sooner did the prime
minister leave than they were back with their nets. Furthermore,
the government servants would not lift a finger to prevent them.
In 1958, however, with the first military coup d'état, U Nu's order
was automatically superseded.

In 1955, as described in Chapter 9, U Nu was in Bandung for the
Asian-African Conference. At its conclusion he surprised everyone
by insisting that he would travel by road to Jakarta. The Indonesian
government pointed out in vain that it was a long drive and that
everybody else was travelling by air. Three months before, U Nu
had seen the strange flowers in Bogor which closed their petals over
flies and insects, and he was eager to stop by and free as many crea-
tures as possible.

Similarly, when travelling by the frigate *Mayu* from Kyaukpyu,
U Nu saw two baskets filled with poultry which the Navy officer
was carrying for his men. He immediately begged for their lives and
the owner had no option but to surrender them. The chickens were
taken to Rangoon and set free in the zoo.

As prime minister, U Nu realised that there were occasions when
his administration had to arrest, imprison, and even kill human
beings. These things might be inevitable, but he never was able to

view this aspect of government except with the greatest of distaste. Where he profited was in the satisfaction he drew from the holding of the Sixth Buddhist Synod, the revision of the *Tripitaka,* and the publication of the *Encyclopaedia Burmannica.*

He got a special thrill out of being prime minister when he was able to stop the killing of cattle. The reason he gave the country at the time was that the cattle population had been depleted by the Second World War and that the need had arisen to conserve draft animals for ploughing purposes. Actually, the slaughterhouse rules established by the British ensured that bullocks and buffalo would not be killed. Only those animals which could not be put to agricultural use or were too old to work were turned into meat. This seemed to U Nu to be a grossly wicked arrangement—that man should sweat an animal until it could no longer work, and then eat it, when by rights he should be treating it with the consideration due to a benefactor. In his opinion, a better case could be made out for killing a human being who had oppressed or harmed another. Therefore, knowing that the reason he gave out publicly— that there was a shortage of draft animals—was inadequate, he persisted in barring the slaughter of cattle as long as he was prime minister.

As soon as U Nu was deposed in 1958, his ban on the slaughter of cattle was lifted. But the moment he won the general election in 1960, U Nu determined to reimpose it. Three days before he was scheduled to take the oath of office as prime minister, U Nu ordered Secretary U Win Pe to have a proclamation ready. As Parliament met to elect U Nu prime minister, an officer was sent to telephone U Win Pe, who immediately proclaimed the slaughter of cattle to be an indictable offence.

ATTITUDE TOWARDS ASTROLOGY

No biography of U Nu would be complete without a reference to fortune-telling and *nat* worship. The Burmese as a race are addicted to fortune-telling. As soon as a child is born, the year, month, and day as well as the hour of his birth are taken to an astrologer to have his horoscope cast. Before a house is built an auspicious day has to be chosen; before a new job is taken the astrologer must calculate whether it is suitable and if so, at what particular time. Astrologers are consulted for weddings, to see if the planets are in the proper conjunction; if a man is ill the astrologer finds out what spell has caused it and what remedy will counteract it; if a husband quarrels with his wife the fortune-teller gets to know about it; in short, the astrologer is in evidence at every stage of life.

As a Burman, Maung Nu was no different from others in his general acceptance of astrology. When he was at the university he kept an English-Burmese diary that listed auspicious and inauspicious or harmful days. He was careful on *pyatthada* or *warameiktu* days[3] because of the likelihood of fights and quarrels.

Since he was a boy he had heeded the warning not to have his hair cut on the day of his birth, on Mondays, or on Fridays. If through forgetfulness he went to the barber's on these days he was bound to fall ill or feel uneasy.

In common with other students, Maung Nu went to the Shwedagon Pagoda on holidays to worship and then consulted the fortune-tellers in the precincts. One of his favourite fortune-tellers wasted no time on dates and days. He looked at his clock and said things like: On your way here you met a woman who had "Sein" in her name, didn't you? Three days ago you had stomach pains because you ate duck eggs. Don't eat them on Sundays. The thief who stole your ring has "Ohn" or "Aung" in his name. At nine on Thursday, sit under a palm tree, look directly East and eat three pieces of jaggery; you will get your ring back. If you wish to pass your examination eat *pilau* and mutton curry; pour an ablution over a statue in this pagoda, and you will pass. For these predictions the fortune-teller charged one rupee and one anna. The rupees he spent; the annas he saved until he could buy a cow at the slaughterhouse and set it free, for he too respected animal life.

Later, when Maung Nu worked at the *Deedok Journal,* he met and was much impressed with a "seer" who was called *Deikbasekkhu* ("ESP") Saya Kyaw. When consulted, he would shut his eyes for five minutes, then reopen them and launch into his predictions.

However, two years' serious study of religious literature confirmed him in his belief in the Three Noble Gems—the Buddha,

3. Some Burmans avoid engaging in business activities on these days.

the Law, and the Assembly. His reading of the *Pokbanna thok,* one of the Buddha's sermons, gave him an insight into what was clearly intended to be a revelation: a certain merchant had completed arrangements to have his son married to the daughter of a friend in another village. On the day of the wedding the local astrologer divined that the planets were not auspiciously juxtaposed and forbade the journey. The friend in the next village, angered by what he took to be a breach of promise, found another man to marry his daughter. When the merchant's son arrived, he found the girl already wed to another. In that sermon, the Buddha categorically declared that the inanimate planets could have no influence whatsoever on the lives of human beings and that anytime in which one was doing good deeds, saying good words, and conceiving good thoughts was an auspicious time.

This thok brought about a noticeable change in Ko Nu. He became disenchanted with astrologers and discarded his diary of predictions. He ignored the warning about haircuts, choosing any day he pleased and being none the worse on that account. However, he did not oppose anybody who had faith in astrology. For instance, when his eldest daughter wanted to consult an astrologer to choose a suitable day for her wedding, he did not intervene. But before the ceremony on the wedding day he took her and the bridegroom into his shrine room and asked them to shikhoe the Three Noble Gems and to recite certain stanzas from the payeik.

When U Nu became prime minister, friends induced him on some occasions to meet astrologers, which he did to oblige them, but at least on one occasion U Nu offended the astrologer by betraying his skepticism. It was not that he looked down upon or underrated the science of astrology, which he did not understand. After all, he had been a willing and eager subject at one time. But having received the word of the Buddha in the *Pokbanna thok* he was convinced that he did not have to go outside of the Buddhist law to arrive at the truth.

There have been three occasions in U Nu's political career on which the influence of astrologers has been imputed. Could U Nu deny that he accepted the prediction of astrologers that independence should be declared at twenty minutes past four o'clock in the morning of 4 January 1948? Would he deny that, following the demise of General Aung San, his Cabinet was reshuffled two or three times after consultation with astrologers? And could he dispute that, immediately preceding the second military coup d'état, he had sand pagodas built all over the country on the advice of astrologers?

U Nu has maintained that in regard to the date of independence he neither consulted a fortune-teller nor instructed anyone else to do so. While he was in London for the signing of the Nu-Attlee Agreement, Deputy Premier Bo Let Ya and Henzada U Mya cabled him saying that according to astrology the most propitious days were 4 and 6 January. Since he was given the choice of these two days, he had selected 4 January because that brought independence two days earlier than the other.

Again, in regard to the several resignations and reappointments of ministers in his Cabinet, U Nu was able to say that no astrologer ever advised him or was besought by him to have the Cabinet reshuffled. But there were three or four ministers who placed greater reliance upon astrologers than upon the Three Noble Gems. They maintained an establishment of astrologers, according to whose reading of their fortunes they asked to leave or to return to the Cabinet at certain times. U Nu had indulged them, but he himself had no traffic with the astrologers.

As far as the sand pagodas were concerned, the first U Nu heard about them was at the end of 1961, when he was in a railway train returning from Popa. At Pyawbwè station, a Member of Parliament, U Thein Maung, told him that he was on his way to a finial-raising ceremony. Discovering that the pagoda in question was little more than a pile of sand, U Nu expressed surprise that brick and mortar had not been used but was told that the order for the sand pagodas had been issued by the minister of religious affairs. This was confirmed by the minister concerned at the next Cabinet meeting in Rangoon, and U Nu immediately told the ministers never to build sand pagodas since they were susceptible of being desecrated or stamped out of recognition by human feet.

Daw Mya Yee did not share U Nu's distaste for astrologers. Whether U Nu approved or not, she was ever willing to consult such fortune-tellers as came her way. The astrologers she particularly favoured were those whose calculations showed that U Nu became a prime minister solely because her horoscope was exceptionally transcendent.

ATTITUDE TOWARDS *Nat* WORSHIP

To what extent would it be true to say that U Nu came very much under the influence of *nat*?[4] To put this matter in perspective, facts must be recorded as they existed. On the first day of the Buddhist New Year, the president, the prime minister, the minister of religious affairs, and others regularly conducted a *bali natsar* ceremony—an offering of food fit for the nat. The object was to obtain protection from danger and ensure the physical and mental well-being of the residents of Burma as well as the world.

During the Second World War U Nu witnessed a bali natsar ceremony, but as a mere bystander. When he became prime minister and went to pay his respects to the senior abbots in Mandalay, it was the famous monk Hanthawaddy Sayadaw who put him wise in regard to the bali natsar ceremony. He explained that the Buddha in the *Ah-pri-har-ni-ya thok* prescribed seven methods of preventing loss or degeneration. One of these methods was the offering of bali natsar. If possible, there should be an offering of food and drink to the gods. If not, after worshipping the Buddha, or reciting the payeik, or the performance of any good work, one should invite the gods to share in the merits. This would have the same effect as the offering of food to the gods.

Returning to Rangoon, the prime minister stated these facts to U Win, minister of religious affairs, and the latter asked for a ruling from the State Theological Board. The presiding abbots of this advisory body gave their finding in writing, and this was printed by the government as the *Balinatsar Winisaya Manual*. In it they declared that the bali natsar offering conformed with the Buddha's wishes.

In the bali natsar ceremony, a special blessing is invoked for the peace and well-being of the people of the world. If this invocation

---

4. Explained above, Chapter 1, "An Inquiry into Buddhism."

can be made to accord with true *Myitta* (genuine universal love), the merit exceeds the mere offering of food and drink to the gods.

As for himself, whether he felt joy or distress, whether he was beset by insurgents or had overcome their threat, U Nu, from the time he became a true believer in Buddhism, and except for periods of serious illness, observed the following routine: He went to bed not later than nine in the evening. He rose at four and, entering the altar room, worshipped the Three Noble Gems; then he took the Five (or Eight) Precepts and recited the payeik. At five he made an offering of alms food with the Three Noble Gems as his intention. On Saturdays he also offered bali natsar to the gods. At six thirty his devotions ended with the diffusion of merit.

In offerings to the Buddha and to the gods, meat was excluded. Rice was the principal *swun* (food for the Buddha, monks, and nat), to which were added cakes and fruit, coffee and water. Wax candles were lit despite the presence of electric lighting.

In offering food to the Three Noble Gems, these words are intoned: I make this in thanksgiving to the Buddha, who preached the Law of Deliverance whereby men, nat, and *byamma*[5] might be freed from the sufferings, and to the Buddha's Law, and to the Assembly, monk followers of the Buddha.

In offering bali natsar, the words intoned are: "To the nat and byamma who are superior to me in age, wisdom, and moral conduct, I, their humble servitor, make this offering."

Whenever he went abroad, U Nu took with him a wooden case with another, smaller one enclosed in it. These boxes opened out as tables. The larger of the folding tables was used for the daily offerings to the Three Noble Gems, the smaller for the bali natsar offering. The plates and cups and candles needed for the ceremony were also carried in the travelling cases.

Friends advised him against lugging around this cumbersome contraption, pointing out that there were tables and cups and saucers everywhere, but U Nu would have no part of tables and utensils that had been used for the serving or drinking of liquor. His box was one specially designed by the ministry of forests.

At home, bali natsar was offered only on Saturdays. But on his

5. Explained above, Chapter 1, "An Inquiry into Buddhism."

peregrinations, he made daily offerings just as he did to the Three Noble Gems. He offered such alms food in Pandit Nehru's home, and in Stalin's dacha in the pine woods of Moscow. Rice was not always available in Europe, but it was readily forthcoming in Moscow. The same ceremonies were held at the Ritz in London, at Blair House in Washington, and at the guest house in Peking.

At night, U Nu recited the payeik from eight to nine o'clock. If he had engagements to keep during this hour, he made sure of saying his prayers ahead of time. He had kept up these practices for very many years.

11

The AFPFL: His Life, His League

No account of U Nu's life would be complete without a full reference to the Anti-Fascist People's Freedom League. U Nu first became president of the AFPFL in July 1947 following the assassination of General Aung San. Eleven years later, in mid-1958, the AFPFL split into two. When this occurred, politicians being what they are, the leaders of both factions took to the housetops and traded insults and vituperation. This gave journalists and writers, foreign as well as domestic, the opportunity to interview the leaders. What they reported in print often contained half-truths and exaggerations—even manipulated or slanted news.

Articles and books, based as they were on the heat generated at the time, with the leaders vying with one another in abuse and invective, were bound to contain errors, besides giving prominence to less important factors, while much of the truth remained submerged. The fault of course did not lie with the writers—foreigners and natives alike—but with the AFPFL leaders shouting out their differences and their resentments for the world to hear.

In order to get to the fundamentals of the split situation it is necessary to recount some historical facts. When Thakin Nu became president, the executive committee of the AFPFL contained some individuals with no parties of their own. There were also representatives of organisations, such as the Asian Youth Association, the Karen Youth Organisation, the People's Volunteer Organisation, and the Socialist Party. Up till the time he became president of the

313

league, U Nu was relatively unknown. Since he had no organisational support of any kind, he could not have survived for long as president of the AFPFL or as prime minister if, in the beginning, the Socialists had offered strong resistance to his leadership. However, the key figures in the Socialist Party, U Ba Swe and U Kyaw Nyein, had accepted his leadership since student days at the university, and were personally attached to him as to an elder brother. To add to this fact, Thakin Tin, head of the Peasants' Organisation, had thrown his support behind U Nu, thus giving his presidency and premiership strength of tenure. In these circumstances, beyond the fact that he was secure in office, it remains to be seen whether he was installed as a puppet, or what if any influence he wielded in party and government.

In both executive committee (party) meetings and in the Cabinet (government), the pattern was set whereby most important matters were discussed among U Nu, U Kyaw Nyein, and Thakin Tin. U Ba Swe, although a top leader of the Socialist Party, was generally not interested in political matters and had only entered the government under compulsion by the premier. It was seldom he made any kind of contribution to Cabinet deliberations, his attitude being that there were others who could involve themselves with competence. On most issues, U Nu, U Kyaw Nyein, and Thakin Tin were in agreement. And if they should ever disagree, U Kyaw Nyein and Thakin Tin generally left it up to U Nu, saying, "These are our views, but you're our leader and we'll abide by your decision."

One matter over which U Nu and U Kyaw Nyein were sharply divided concerned the Moslem population. U Kyaw Nyein was concerned lest the Moslems take control over Burma. U Nu on many occasions tried to explain why these fears were groundless but U Kyaw Nyein remained unconvinced. He would point to Indonesia, a Buddhist country at one time but now a Moslem state. According to his religion a Moslem male could take up to four wives. There was thus scarcely any need for them to proselytize; they merely had to propagate. They could flood the country with Moslems by taking Burmese Buddhist wives.

Arising out of this deep concern, there was placed before the AFPFL executive committee a bill drafted by U Kyaw Nyein which made for easy divorce in Moslem marriages.[1] He wished to have the bill presented in Parliament and passed into law. U Nu tried to dissuade him in vain. He had become so obsessed with his cause that U Nu's continued opposition to it drove him to tears. Finally U Nu gave in. The significant thing was that, even when he felt very strongly about a policy matter, U Kyaw Nyein would rather drown his frustration with tears than try to frustrate U Nu in open conflict.

THE FIRST SIGN OF A CRACK

In this atmosphere of unity the first sign of a crack in the AFPFL developed at the end of 1954. U Nu was on a China visit, had completed his round of consultations, and was about to return home when it occurred to him to induce Premier Chou En-lai to buy a quantity of old rice held in Burma. When Mr. Chou agreed to do so, U Nu suggested that a Chinese mission should come to Burma and inspect the rice. Then if it were too badly spoilt the Chinese would be under no obligation to buy. Mr. Chou En-lai approved of this arrangement also. U Nu accordingly cabled Rangoon telling his government about the rice deal and asking that everything be held in readiness for the Chinese mission. As it happened, the Rice Marketing Subcommittee in the Cabinet had sold the rice on the very day U Nu's cable was dispatched.

Here it must be remembered that in the Cabinet of ministers there were three or four subcommittees with specific duties to perform. In dealing with these duties the subcommittees were invested with the powers of the full Cabinet, and this had been duly sanctioned by U Nu. There was therefore nothing improper in the sale of the old rice by the Cabinet, especially as the price realised had been a fair one. But knowing U Nu as he did (U Nu had only to open his mouth and U Kyaw Nyein could anticipate his words) U Kyaw Nyein could not remain composed. He met U Nu's plane and, after the other ministers had left, accompanied the premier home. There he explained about the subcommittee's action over the rice deal. Any other prime minister would have been pleased

1. After her divorce, the Burmese wife of a Muslim would probably revert to Buddhism.

that the old stock had been got rid of and that the price had been right. He would have congratulated the subcommittee and expressed regret to the Chinese premier. But the emotional being that was U Nu, with heart transcendent over mind, exploded. All he thought about was his promise to Chou En-lai and how he would lose face because "the sons of bitches" would not wait for him to return, despite the cable sent. It was fortunate for U Kyaw Nyein that the powers of the subcommittee were so clearly defined, for in his vile mood the blind old fool was capable of dismissing all the ministers concerned.

Three or four days later, U Kyaw Nyein came to apologise once more, this time bringing some Socialist ministers with him. By this time the tide of resentment had ebbed somewhat and U Nu did not behave as unreasonably as he did before. However, the incident was to remain with U Kyaw Nyein, and to enter into his calculations when U Nu next betrayed the perverse streak in his nature.

RESIGNATION AND ITS AFTERMATH

U Nu had been toying with the idea of quitting politics for a long time. In 1948 and 1949 the insurrections made it impracticable. Since 1950 his colleagues had systematically restrained his impulse and succeeded in keeping him going, year by year. In 1954, disenchanted with some of the monks, U Nu suddenly stopped religious teaching in all government schools.[2] One result of this action was a confrontation between the Buddhists and the Moslems. The crisis mounted and was resolved only when U Nu gave in to the extent of restoring religious instruction on Buddhism in government schools. At the same time teaching of the Christian and Islam faiths was forbidden. U Nu felt so depressed over being compelled to make these decisions that in other circumstances he would have stood firm and resigned from office. But the Sixth Buddhist Synod then in progress gave him no option but to yield.

To a Buddhist there could be no more important event than this ecumenical council. U Nu had been the prime mover for its convocation and he had a most ardent desire to see its work completed

2. See above, Chapter 8.

to the glorification of the teachings of the Buddha. But he vowed that at its termination he would give up the premiership.

The synod ended successfully in May 1956 and U Nu continued to meditate in the Sacred Cave. There he recalled his vow and proceeded to fulfil it. U Kyaw Nyein, the first to be told, implored him in many ways not to disrupt the AFPFL and the government, but the vow had been made and must be kept. At the next weekly meeting of the AFPFL, held on Saturday, U Nu made known his decision. He had bound himself to resign as prime minister and this he would do straightaway. He would continue to serve the party as president for one more year, at the end of which he would leave politics altogether. Everyone protested, but U Nu stood firm and the committee reluctantly gave in. But the moment the resolution was passed, one of the committee members, Thakin Tha Khin, got up to move that U Nu be required to return to the premiership within a year after resigning. This motion too was carried, despite the realisation on U Nu's part, as he sat on silently, that it was vitiated by his earlier intention to quit politics.

In the middle of July, U Nu attended the graduation ceremony at the School of Journalism, held under the auspices of the Burma Translation Society, and announced that he would cease to be president of the AFPFL in January 1957. This was his method of serving notice to the public that he was giving up politics.

To resign from the premiership was U Nu's privilege and no blame could attach to this act. There was nothing irregular either in U Nu's proposing U Ba Swe to succeed him in the government. Although U Ba Swe was less than the complete politician, he had seniority among the leaders of the Socialist Party and was the obvious choice for the post of prime minister. Where U Nu acted arbitrarily was in determining that Thakin Kyaw Dun should resign from the Cabinet and follow him to AFPFL headquarters as secretary general of the party, while U Kyaw Nyein, then the secretary general, moved up to vice-president. The normal procedure would have been for U Nu, as a member of the party executive committee, to embody these proposals in a resolution and have it passed by the committee, but now he simply ordered the move on the pattern of a chief secretary transferring divisional and district commissioners. Actually, his highhandedness stemmed not from any wish to denigrate U Kyaw Nyein but from his ingrained habit of taking U Kyaw Nyein for granted.

Of course it was wrong to effect changes in a political organisation —especially one based upon democracy—in the manner characteristic of government services. Because it was wrong in principle, those affected by it, both U Kyaw Nyein and Thakin Kyaw Dun, felt the situation very keenly. But neither protested, preferring to carry out U Nu's orders.

Within three days, though, information was brought to U Nu that U Kyaw Nyein was greatly disgruntled over having to give up the secretary generalship. If this was a problem, it was amenable to reasonable solution in a calm and objective manner. If U Nu had chosen to explain that holding a government portfolio tended to reduce the effectiveness of a party executive committee member, and that the changes had been necessitated by a falling off in party organisation, U Kyaw Nyein would have understood and been pacified. But U Nu's immediate reaction was to summon U Kyaw Nyein and fling at him the words: "I hear you're fed up about something. Let me know in writing what you're dissatisfied with. Then we'll meet and talk."

U Kyaw Nyein was greatly troubled. U Nu had vented his spleen on him over the rice deal, although he had been proved blameless. U Nu was obviously holding a grudge against him, hence his removal at the first opportunity from the post of secretary general. Now he was being asked to commit something to writing as a prelude to hostile action.

A chain of events was thus set in motion, the tragedy of errors culminating in the AFPFL split. U Nu, through impulsiveness rather than any conscious thought of hurting U Kyaw Nyein, committed wrongs, accentuating the fears of a naturally apprehensive and suspicious U Kyaw Nyein. Proof of vindictiveness in U Nu was wanting. On the contrary, the evidence is strong of continuing goodwill in a number of ways.

Among the AFPFL leaders, each headed an organisation that might be considered his power base. Thus U Ba Swe had the Trades Union Congress of Burma, Thakins Tin and Kyaw Dun the Peasants' Organisation, Thakin Pan Myaing the Retailers. At the very meeting where he relieved himself of the premiership, U Nu had proposed a Women's Organisation to be headed by his friend U Kyaw Nyein, and a Youth Organisation under Thakin Tha Khin, U Kyaw Nyein's right-hand man. U Kyaw Nyein had not wanted the Women's Organisation and asked for Youth instead, and this was approved by U Nu over some objections.

Anyway, about three days later, U Nu went to U Kyaw Nyein and delivered himself of some thoughts that had occurred to him regarding the youth movement. "Teach them socialism by all means," he urged, "But instil iron-clad discipline at the same time." Because discipline was slack some Socialists had earned the opprobrium of the people. The old leaders of the AFPFL would be making way for the rising generation and they must through exemplary conduct help reverse the swing in public sentiment. He pointed out that the Communists had won nearly 50 percent of the popular vote in the last general election because the people had become disenchanted and the Socialist Party itself was falling into disrepute. He offered to go out and solicit funds for the establishment of a sound youth organisation.

As he listened to these admonitions U Kyaw Nyein wore a strange expression. He had already written a long letter preferring charges against U Nu. Noticing that the usual note of frivolity was lacking in U Kyaw Nyein's speech, U Nu said, "You're behaving very odd today. Anything the matter?" U Kyaw Nyein replied that, as desired by the other, he had already dispatched a letter. "If I have committed any wrongs in that letter, forgive me," he said. U Nu told him not to worry. But when he reached home and read U Kyaw Nyein's letter he was very angry.

There were no charges of misconduct, or of errors and omissions on the part of U Nu, either as president of the AFPFL or as prime minister. Of the accusations made the most severe were that U Nu was dictatorial and fond of flattery, honours, and titles. It was alleged that he hated U Kyaw Nyein for standing up to him.

Most leaders are accused sooner or later of being autocratic. Those with strong convictions or passions have to bear the charge more frequently than others. U Nu was such a wilful person. Unyielding as a boy, he was no less obstinate as president of the Rangoon University Students' Union. Despite his outbursts, U Kyaw Nyein, U Ba Swe, and Thakin Tin had been able to put up with him, rain and shine, for ten years. They and the country would not have tolerated a boorish dictator.

That he was fond of respect or flattery was a wide charge. Who was not fond of respect? Men liked it, gods and monks expected it. Men and women, young and old, students and politicians, even those approaching sainthood wanted it. U Nu could hardly be an exception. As for love of honours and titles, it might be revealed that when eminent leaders such as Marshal Tito and Premier Pibul Songgram arrived, they were invested with the highest orders and decorations in Burma. In return they were eager to confer upon U Nu such honours as were commensurate with his rank, but U Nu declined them, although the president of the Union and his Cabinet ministers were permitted to receive and wear Yugoslav and Thai decorations.

There remains the charge that U Kyaw Nyein was being victimized because he had had the temerity to challenge U Nu. From the time he wrote his long diatribe he could claim to have opposed U Nu, but prior to that the record spoke differently. On every occasion it was U Kyaw Nyein who supported U Nu against criticism. Fledgling Socialists who tried to belittle U Nu in his absence were brought to order by U Kyaw Nyein with the stock phrase, "Not for nothing is he our leader." He resisted U Nu's attempt to resign and brought up Socialist reinforcements to make such resistance effective.

Since there was nothing irretrievable about the letter, U Nu had only to say "Kyaw Nyein, you son of a bitch, what are you rambling about? You don't bother me with your wild swings—a tyro with eyes closed flailing the air. Here, take your letter and go," and the matter would have ended there. The split in the AFPFL would not have occurred.

However, U Nu, with that strange perversity that impelled him sometimes to make light of serious matters but on other occasions to magnify trivial matters out of all proportion, took the course of answering U Kyaw Nyein in kind. He then had copies made of the charges and his own rejoinder and those documents were distributed to members of the AFPFL executive committee. They would have been given to the press as well, but the executive committee wisely applied an embargo. An attempt was made to bring about a reconciliation but the unity that had marked the AFPFL was already shattered. Two groups emerged: one supporting U Nu, the other U Kyaw Nyein. U Ba Swe alone remained on good terms with both.

Those orderly meetings of the executive committee, where quiet and decorum prevailed, were now a thing of the past. Voices began to be raised in anger and on several occasions the factions almost came to blows. With the masters quarreling and exchanging insults in the room, the danger arose of the bodyguards outside becoming involved. U Nu had to issue an order that the security men must not carry guns in AFPFL premises. Within a month the realisation came to U Nu that the course he had followed had been wrong, and that a situation susceptible of peaceful solution had been turned into a perilous one. He could only hope that when he retired from politics in a year the dissensions would die a natural death. In the meantime he would keep a hold on himself and his followers.

CAUSE FOR ANOTHER STORM

While U Nu was reining in his impetuosity, U Kyaw Nyein was running true to form. His was an excessively cautious nature. He reminded one of a species of plover that exists in Burma called *tit-tee-doo*. Easily alarmed, it sleeps with its feet pointing at the sky. The sky was not likely to fall, but just in case . . . And so the story goes. Vigilance was U Kyaw Nyein's forte.

During the university strike of 1936 Ko Kyaw Nyein had taken charge of security. He deplored Ko Nu's habit of seeing all and sundry. He formed a committee to vet all callers because he was convinced there were police spies and informers among them. Ko Nu had bodyguards to protect him from assassins and also to field questions for him when he met interviewers or reporters. The whole thing was overdone, but U Kyaw Nyein took his responsibilities very seriously. He was the subject of much raillery on the part of the students. Now, grown to maturity and no longer friends, U Nu the impulsive and U Kyaw Nyein the wary were to play out their parts in another act of the political drama.

At the end of December 1956 U Nu returned from Ceylon where he had gone to attend the celebration marking twenty-five hundred

years of the teachings of the Buddha. As his aircraft came to a stop
at Mingaladon, his secretary general came aboard. He said he had
an urgent message from Thakin Tin.

What is it, Thakin Kyaw Dun? Anything alarming?

Thakin Tin is in the hospital. Last night General Ne Win and
U Ba Swe went to see him. They asked him to dissuade you from
rejoining the government. Thakin Tin also said U Ba Swe and
General Ne Win would be coming to see you.

I don't understand this. Have I been telling anyone I wish to
form the Government again? The idea has not crossed my mind.

We have not heard of any such thing.

I think I know what's at the bottom of this.

In the seclusion of his home he wondered about the plot. He
had publicly stated he was retiring from politics in January 1957.
Why then had they done this to him? And why had the army been
brought in if not as a threat? He felt insulted. His ire rose.

The next day General Ne Win arrived alone, without U Ba Swe.
His suggestion was that it would be best for U Nu to remain presi-
dent of the AFPFL and hold the strings of government. He gave
Chairman Mao Tse-tung of China as a model.

U Nu said he resented the way he was being coerced. He had
already announced his withdrawal from politics in 1957 but because of the new development he had decided on the previous day
to reenter the government. He would fight for his reelection, once
in the party and again in Parliament. At both stages he would
encounter strong Socialist opposition and was bound to lose. But
it was better that way than to surrender without a fight.

There was really no need to force a showdown in this manner.
He might have remained calm, attended the Saturday meeting of
the executive committee and reassured them about his retirement
in 1957. U Kyaw Nyein, after all, did not hate U Nu. He looked
to him for leadership. It was just that U Kyaw Nyein felt threatened.
Remove this shadow and all would have been well. But the threat
inherent in the use of the army drove U Nu to throw caution to
the winds. Those who imagined that he attained to eminence in

the party and in the government because of virtue unsullied by faults were wrong. U Nu had many failings, among which was intolerance.

Still suffering from a sense of injustice, U Nu announced at the Saturday meeting that he would again form the government. An un-ruffled U Ba Swe reminded him that nobody had wanted him to leave in the first instance, and that he himself had not wanted to be premier. It was U Nu who had forced him into the job. Now that U Nu wanted it back, he would be glad to resign. U Ba Swe said this without a trace of emotion. U Kyaw Nyein, being out of town, was not at the meeting. There being no objectors, it was resolved that U Nu should return to the government.

The following Saturday, U Kyaw Nyein, having returned from his trip, was present at the meeting. He must have felt that U Nu's reelection constituted a threat to him. Had he been in Rangoon when that decision was being made he would have objected, and he said so before the committee. He could have demanded a review of the proceedings, but, though this was a right which neither U Nu nor the committee could dispute, he chose not to exercise it. From that time U Nu felt a reluctance to tangle with U Kyaw Nyein. He took extra care to avoid conflict with all his colleagues. Calm returned to the AFPFL sea where there had been so much strife before. It lasted about a year after U Nu returned as prime minister.

THE SPLIT

In March 1958 the National Defence Council met to consider a report from the army. This charged that criminals were being protected by influential politicians and led to U Nu's ruling that nobody was above the law, and that if politicians were involved he would himself deal with them upon complaint. Under his orders the army and the Home Ministry jointly made a number of arrests. Among them were followers of Thakin Tin, Thakin Kyaw Dun, and U Kyaw Nyein. Thakins Tin and Kyaw Dun charged that many more of their men were being seized than U Kyaw Nyein's because the latter was using his influence with the army and the home minister. The storm had returned to ravage the AFPFL sea. *The Nation* commented, "There is a strong belief that the arrests are not merely a purge of bad elements but an elimination contest between warring factions of the AFPFL in a secret struggle to the death."

A serious problem had arisen and the prime minister found himself without a solution. To correct the imbalance complained of by Thakins Tin and Kyaw Dun, would more arrests of U Kyaw Nyein's men be in order? Or should the followers of the Thakins be released? That of course would demoralise the law enforcement services and impair their effectiveness in the future.

Gravely disturbed in mind, U Nu took a group of children, including his daughter Than Than Nu, and went to Moulmein for the Water Festival. On his return he found on his desk a newspaper open at a page flagged and sidelined in red. His attention thus directed, he read the report of a conference of the AFPFL Youth in Insein, attended by leaders from party headquarters, who denounced Thakin Kyaw Dun's group as dacoits, kidnappers, and assassins.

Insein was Thakin Kyaw Dun's stronghold and its invasion by U Kyaw Nyein's followers was tantamount to a public declaration of war. An already confused situation had become compounded. U Nu realised that he could no longer delay a decision; furthermore, the decision would have to be his alone. When it arrived it brought dangers with it but it was the only possible answer and he would enforce it unflinchingly.

Meeting the Thakin Tin group, U Nu pointed out that at the rate they were going the AFPFL was bound to crack, with resultant shedding of blood. The constant bickering had to stop. Under the motto "Limit words: end strife," he had devised a three-point formula:

1. The factions would agree to a parting of the ways before it was too late.

2. If Thakin Tin's group wished to retain his leadership U Nu would insist on pledges against liquor, bribery and corruption, womanizing, and gambling. Such pledges would be enforceable in the central executive committee on pain of expulsion.

3. After partition the two factions would compete in Parliament for power to form the government, and for this Parliament would be called into session.

This formula proved acceptable to Thakin Tin's faction and U Nu agreed to join it. Thakin Tin's group had been one of his main supports in the past. Added to this bond was U Nu's proclivity for going to tĥe aid of the underdog. Had that newspaper article sidelined in red told of indignities suffered by U Kyaw Nyein's group, and had the Socialists subscribed to his three-point formula, his decision might well have gone the other way.

U Nu also met with U Ba Swe and explained about his plan for the party split. U Ba Swe's reaction was to request him not to go through with partition.

When the partition eventually took place the U Nu-Thakin Tin group became the "Clean" AFPFL, and the U Ba Swe-U Kyaw Nyein group the "Stable" AFPFL. Within the AFPFL only one or two organisations supported the Clean, the rest siding with the Stable. Across the country the people by and large chose to stay Clean.

The campaigns for the control of Parliament were fought bitterly, with charges, countercharges, and vituperation hurled from the platform or splashed across the columns of newspapers. Members of Parliament were accosted like pilgrims by touts at jetties and railway stations, until onlookers were filled with disgust.

When the voting took place in the House of Deputies,[3] the Clean AFPFL squeaked through with an eight-vote majority, and this was made possible only by the extreme Left bloc—the National Unity Front (NUF)—which abandoned its Opposition role and supported U Nu for the first time. Following this it became necessary to dissolve Parliament and go to the people, but the Stable opposed an immediate dissolution, and in order to avoid violence and bloodshed the matter was kept in abeyance.

The First Coup d'État, 1958

U Nu did not wish to call Parliament into session for the budget deliberations in August. He was sick of hearing how MPs were wooed and solicited, besides which if he lost in the cut motions he would have to run the gamut of dissolution, protests, and threats

3. The Burmese Parliament is bicameral, consisting of the House of Deputies and the House of Nationalities. It is the House of Deputies that elects the prime minister, who forms the government.

of violence. So with the advice of Dr. U Ba Han, the attorney general, U Nu used the Emergency Provisions Act to pass the budget estimates.

The Stable AFPFL immediately set up a howl of protest. It appealed to the army to seize the government for acting *ultra vires* of the Constitution. The army agreed. While this was taking place U Nu was on a steamer between Mandalay and Rangoon. He was told of the conspiracy by Home Minister Bo Min Gaung as soon as he arrived back at the capital. An airplane was in readiness in case he wished to flee. U Nu refused to run away like a common criminal; instead he ordered Bo Min Gaung to seek out Brigadiers Aung Gyi and Maung Maung and bring them to him. The home minister reported back in the evening that the brigadiers could not be located. He also brought the intelligence that an army battalion from Mandalay had failed to arrive and that the coup would not take place that night. Next the prime minister noticed much activity in his compound and inquired of Captain Hla Myint, his security officer, what the young soldiers might be doing. He was told they were digging a bunker.

Whatever for?

When they come in the night, we'll fire on them.

How are they planning to get here?

The tanks will roll ahead. The men come behind.

How many men have you?

A platoon.[4]

What guns have you?

I've just been issued a Browning machine gun.

So the tank smashes it to smithereens.

I'll hide you elsewhere. Don't worry. I've made all the arrangements.

Captain Hla Myint, who had no politics and was faithful and brave, appeared puzzled when told he must stop the digging and

---

4. About thirty troops.

withdraw all rifles from the trigger-happy troops and that he himself must not shoot until ordered to do so.

Brigadiers Aung Gyi and Maung Maung presented themselves at nine o'clock the following morning and were told by U Nu without any preliminaries to call off the coup. It would only give the army and the country a bad name. He was prepared to hand over power to the army on condition that a general election, free and fair and conducted by the army, be held in six months. He himself would propose General Ne Win to be prime minister and would call Parliament into session for this purpose. Furthermore he put this in writing and handed the document to the brigadiers, who went off to consult the general. They returned in the afternoon and said General Ne Win agreed to the proposals.

When they had left, U Nu pondered what the effect of the changes would be. The army of course would rule over the country as over a military establishment. At the moment the people regarded soldiers as friends and protectors. After the takeover they would be looked upon with loathing. Politically, the party that had called in the army would suffer from the intervention. It was like putting a noose round one's own neck. It would be very difficult to recover from it.

The world being constantly plagued by military coups d'état, with attendant executions of ministers and military tribunals, U Nu wondered how his Cabinet ministers were going to take what he had improvised. As for himself, he not only sent out the summons for Parliament to meet but appointed an Inquiry Commission consisting of one judge each of the Supreme and High Courts and the chairman of the Public Service Commission to investigate him. The report of the Inquiry Commission was to be made public, and if any wrongdoing on his part was detected he was to be put on trial. While he was prime minister witnesses might have been reluctant to testify against him, but once he was out of office his accusers would be emboldened. He subsequently handed over power as planned, but afterward nothing more was heard of the commission.

U Nu announced his resignation in Parliament as he had promised. He proposed the name of General Ne Win to be the new prime minister and this was duly approved by Parliament.

THE *Ginga Bawga*

Shortly thereafter, a friend, U Kyaw Sein, came to see U Nu.

Mr. Prime Minister, have you heard about the *Ginga Bawga?*

No, what about it?

The newspapers are full of it. When this fishing vessel was leased to Bo Let Ya an agreement was drawn up that raised all sorts of suspicions. It is stated in the press that the caretaker government[5] is about to take action against U Kyaw Nyein as the minister responsible.

That's unfair. The responsible person is not U Kyaw Nyein but myself. I remember telling U Kyaw Nyein that people like Bo Let Ya and Bo Set Kya had risked their lives for the country, and ordering him to assist Bo Let Ya in the *Ginga Bawga* lease. I will have to testify accordingly when the case goes to court.

Wouldn't you be involving yourself?

I detest leaders who try to get underlings to take the rap for them. I can't dodge it. I did give the order.

But Mr. Prime Minister, you know the army has a down on you.

Don't worry about me. Just go to Kyaw Nyein and tell him I'll testify.

U Kyaw Sein said he did not think it would be advisable for him to go. He was known to be an U Nu man and the U Kyaw Nyein faction would think he was up to some form of trickery. But U Nu tried to reassure him as follows:

Regardless of the quarrel between us, Kyaw Nyein knows I won't let the innocent suffer. You will recall that as home minister he put a considerable number of people in jail under Section Five of the Public Order Preservation Act and became immensely unpopular. When an editor who had been imprisoned and released later organised a dinner, I attended and took Kyaw Nyein with me. At the dinner I publicly admitted all the arrests had been made under my orders.

5. I.e., General Ne Win's government.

Still U Kyaw Sein hesitated, and U Nu went on:

> Then there was the matter of Japanese reparations. When the
> mission was being selected, there were other ministers who wanted
> to go, but I selected Kyaw Nyein, who did not want to go at all.
> He said he would probably be blamed for whatever he did. In the
> event he did a very good job. He got everything I expected and
> secured another important advantage on his own. When he re-
> turned, five thousand AFPFL members went to cheer him at the
> airport. But, as luck would have it, he subsequently came in for
> unjust censure and I had to go on the air to set the record straight.

When, at the next meeting of the Clean AFPFL executive committee, U Nu repeated in detail what he had offered to do through
U Kyaw Sein, they could not at first believe him. Finally they dissuaded him from making his intention known in advance. If he
was called to testify in court he could do so. Two days later U Kyaw
Sein came to tell U Nu that although he did not wish to risk seeing
U Kyaw Nyein personally he had apprised him of U Nu's remarks,
through the mail. However, nothing more was made of the *Ginga
Bawga* affair by the caretaker government.

PREPARATIONS FOR CIVIL DISOBEDIENCE

General Ne Win's government failed to order elections in six
months but unjustly arrested many members of the Clean AFPFL.
There were also acts of oppression aimed at disrupting the AFPFL
organisation. The time had come for the Clean to offer resistance.
In accordance with a resolution that their civil disobedience should
be (1) nonviolent, (2) disciplined, and (3) structured in such a way
as to ensure continuity, indoctrination classes were opened so that
as one leader fell there would be another to step into his shoes.

In the midst of these preoccupations U Nu was visited by a group
of friends who, by giving some convincing reasons, almost changed
the course of events. They said that civil disobedience worked with
the British because of British liberalism. The British government
could not ignore Burmese public opinion, let alone world opinion
and the wishes of their own people. They had respect for law and
order. Except on one or two occasions when repression followed

protests in India and Burma, they showed great restraint in the face of provocation. With the present military dictatorship, however, there could be no expectation of anything less than outright slaughter. Perhaps a section of the people would be sufficiently aroused to fight the army, but the superior weapons of the soldiers would prevail. Before departing they made their point: If U Nu was determined to launch civil disobedience, they would not stand in his way. But they themselves had decided to wage armed insurrection. They needed guns for their purpose and hoped U Nu would assist them in any way possible. This led to inquiries being made by U Nu and a link established whereby the necessary weapons could be procured. But a general election did come on 6 February 1960, which rendered both violence and nonviolence unnecessary.

RECONCILIATION

The following were the results of the general election:

Party	Number of Seats Won
Clean AFPFL	159
Stable AFPFL	41
Arakanese	6
Mon	3
Chin	3
Kayah	2
Shan	23

This was a landslide for the Clean AFPFL. If army officers had not openly aided the Stable AFPFL, the latter would have suffered an even more crushing defeat. Burmese informed circles had a variety of explanations for these remarkable results. Some thought that Buddhism being made the state religion had ensured victory to the Clean AFPFL. Others said U Nu's photograph on the ballot boxes was what attracted the voters. Somewhat along these lines a Western writer published a report saying that the people looked upon U Nu as a future Buddha. U Nu's own analysis was that army involvement had damaged the Stable AFPFL. He had no reason to believe the people resented the army. As far as the rank-and-file were concerned, the soldiers were after all their own kith and kin, who, when the Union was threatened, had manned the ramparts and rescued the people, often at the risk of their own lives. There was general respect and admiration for the army. But they seemed to take strong exception to a group of army officers elevating themselves into being the government. The civilian population disliked being ordered about; they hated seeing military methods being applied by the caretaker government. Theirs was a protest vote.

Shortly after the new government was formed, U Nu one day found himself alone and sunk in reverie. The days of struggle in his early career passed through his mind; he recalled all too vividly his friends U Ba Swe and U Kyaw Nyein. Then came General Aung San's death, the comradeships in the AFPFL that won the country independence, then the appearance of the multicoloured insurgents and the months and years of peril when they carried their lives in their hands. His partners in the nation's defence loomed large in the panorama now unfolding before him. Suddenly his cheeks were wet with tears. He wiped them away, got up and headed for U Ba Swe's and U Kyaw Nyein's homes.

"You're my very own," he said. "Let us forget our quarrels."

12

Freedom with Fairness

FREE AND FAIR ELECTIONS

Among the election promises made by U Nu in 1960, the most important was the pledge to do all in his power to strengthen Burmese democracy. Accordingly, in his policy speech in Parliament on 5 April 1960, he took pains to reiterate that there was no alternative to democracy, and that efforts would be made to make it "native to our soil." He said that his Pyidaungsu Party,[1] despite its huge majority in Parliament, would operate in strict compliance with the true principles of democracy. It would respect and welcome constructive opposition in and out of Parliament. Above all, he pledged that the politicians would not interfere with the administration. He reviewed the many "undemocratic" mistakes that he and his party had made during the previous years of his government—mistakes he would endeavour to avoid making again. This meant among other things that in the economic sphere his government and party would act with restraint, and that there would be limits to the intrusion of the state in further developing a new Four-Year Plan for a balanced economy.

In the old days, U Nu had treated the politicians of the Opposition with distrust. With a one-track mind he discounted everything said and done by the Opposition. Whether in Parliament or out-

---

1. The Clean faction of the AFPFL was now renamed the Pyidaungsu Party, which in Burmese means the Union (of Burma) Party. The Stable faction of the AFPFL simply dropped Stable from its appellation.

side, the Opposition's views, demands, and criticisms were studiously disregarded by him. He considered the Opposition to be false and destructive.

But the general election of 1960 brought about a total change in U Nu's attitude. He saw the Opposition not as obstructionists but as the party that would assume political power on the day the people who reposed their trust in him and his party chose to withdraw it in an election. The change in U Nu was reflected in the following ways:

1. Previously only government MPs were chosen to serve on parliamentary select committees. Subsequent to 1960 Opposition MPs were also included, under U Nu's direction.

2. Previously, in all committees, from the village to the central levels, appointed by the government to implement national projects, only members of the ruling party could expect to serve. Subsequent to 1960 Opposition representatives were included.

3. Previously, national planning was an exclusive province of the government. Subsequent to 1960, the drawing up of plans and projects was thrown open to the Opposition, the ideal being a bipartisan plan, with the people as judges to determine which of the two parties was the better able to implement it.

4. In all previous elections the people had the right to choose freely. But were these elections actually fair? (a) The prime minister, members of the Cabinet, and parliamentary secretaries had the free use of the government radio. The Opposition was denied it. (b) The prime minister and other ministers and their parliamentary secretaries campaigned throughout the country with travel expenses paid by the government. The Opposition candidates, lacking funds, were restricted in their travels. (c) Government candidates, with armed protection, were able to visit and campaign in far-flung places. The Opposition lacked security arrangements. (d) The government party was in a position to misuse power, e.g., by transferring to their constituencies civil servants who would do their bidding, or providing public facilities that were calculated to win them votes.

This lopsided system being in need of correction, U Nu appointed a six-member committee to frame rules that would make future elections both free and fair. Two of these members were

Cabinet ministers, but the Opposition AFPFL and the NUF (National Unity Front) also sent two members each. The committee met many times and submitted a unanimous report incorporating six recommendations, all of which were accepted by U Nu.

The test came shortly afterwards when there was a by-election in the Budalin constituency in Monywa District. Following this by-election, a representative of the NUF came to tell the prime minister that they had met with much unfairness in the past, as a result of which the voters had begun to hate elections, but in the present instance they had nothing to complain about, and they hoped all future elections would be equally fair.

Despite these assurances, the prime minister was to learn of a patently unfair practice in the conduct of the same by-election. The minister managing the campaign for the government candidate was told by an influential monk that he would prevail upon all his pupils to vote for him if a new primary school could be opened in his parish. The minister thereupon telegraphed his colleague, the education minister, to do the necessary and the school was provided. U Nu was so upset when he received this information that he thought of dismissing both the ministers concerned and ordering a fresh election. Other ministers in his Cabinet argued against both steps, pointing out that democracy needed to be nurtured with patience and that other than succumbing to political influences in providing the new school the minister had done nothing meriting stricture. The prime minister reluctantly closed the proceedings, but he was to regret again and again his dereliction of duty.

5. However busy he might be, U Nu made it a point to attend meetings of Parliament. At question time he answered all pertinent questions, and he took personal action in matters arising out of Parliamentary debate.

6. The new respect in which he held the Opposition was demonstrated in various ways by Prime Minister U Nu. An incident arose in which an allegation of murder was made against an AFPFL Member of Parliament. After routine investigation the police came up with sufficient evidence to indict, but because the accused was an MP the prime minister was informed. Ordinarily, whether the accused belonged to the government party or the Opposition, an

order of arrest would have been issued. But in this instance U Nu took the Deputy Inspector General of Police with him and called on the leader of the Opposition. The latter was embarrassed when he learnt the purpose of the visit. He kept saying repeatedly he would have been ready to go to the prime minister instead. After the police officer had briefed him, the leader of the Opposition agreed that the accused MP should go on trial.

On another occasion, some NUF leaders came to complain to the prime minister that some of his followers in Shwebo had killed an NUF district leader. It so happened that, before the AFPFL split, there had been a similar case in Tharrawaddy and the NUF had raised a public outcry which was taken up by the newspapers. On that occasion, all U Nu had done was to call up the home minister and receive an assurance that the accusation was false. But now nothing so slipshod was possible. Immediate orders went out to the district authorities in Shwebo to act strictly according to law. This was followed up by U Nu personally with a visit to the wife and son of the deceased, and an assurance that justice would be done.

REHABILITATION OF THE ADMINISTRATION

As already mentioned, the structure of government in Burma was put out of joint during the Japanese occupation; it was further damaged by AFPFL politicians during the fight for independence and of course the insurrections tore it out of recognition. Then, when the split in the AFPFL occurred, the government servants ranged themselves on this side or that and did the bidding of others without regard for rules and regulations. After the 1960 general election, U Nu found the administrative machinery all but broken down.

Repair work was taken into hand with meetings at district headquarters to which all heads of departments were invited, along with the leaders of all the political parties. In addressing these meetings, U Nu stressed the point that political power was ephemeral: a political party exercised power at the pleasure of the people. This pleasure might be short; it was also transferable. But the administration was a permanent structure that must remain unaffected by shifts in political power. Civil servants owed no allegiance to politicians; their loyalty was to the administration. At the same time U Nu warned the politicians not to interfere with the civil service; if such interference went unchecked democracy would disappear.

Under the prime minister's encouragement, the civil servants aired their grievances, some of which U Nu settled on the spot; others he took to Rangoon for disposal after detailed study. A persistent complaint heard by the prime minister was over procedural difficulties in the withdrawal of allocated funds, and these were only resolved when the prime minister invited divisional commissioners to Rangoon and left them face to face with the finance secretary.

When U Nu first presided over the joint meetings of civil servants and politicians, there was apprehension on the part of some who had been guilty of misconduct in the past and feared that they were about to be taken to task. But the new atmosphere was friendly and forgiving. Reports began flowing in to the prime minister showing that the response from the civil servants was encouraging.

SOLVING A THORNY PROBLEM

After 1952, when the government could again breathe freely because of a decline in insurgent activities, U Nu received some bad news. It was nothing more nor less than that the minority races, principally the Shans, were hurt and displeased with the Burmans. Inquiries showed that some AFPFL politicians and some army officers had been highhanded in their dealings with the Shan people. In order to remove whatever misunderstanding had been created, U Nu made frequent visits to the states and spoke earnestly with the heads and other leaders. He pointed out that the many should not be blamed because of the misdeeds of a few. It was unfair to use blanket terms, such as "the army" or "the party" because everybody who served in the army was not born of the same mother and did not have the same identity. There were good and bad in any organisation. He would not deny that there might even be very bad soldiers, but everybody would have to concede there were very good ones who had served the country and suffered loss of life and limb in the process.

The prime minister made it a point to counsel and instruct army officers as well as civil servants that they should conduct themselves with propriety in dealing with the people of the various states. Everyone, from the head of state down, should be treated with respect and civility. He warned them that allegations of unfairness and injustice could lead to a dissolution of the Union.

While U Nu was touring the country and busily engaging himself in trying to remove racial misunderstandings, a Shan MP speaking in the Chamber of Deputies in 1958 severely criticised the budget appropriations for the Shan State. He claimed the grants from the central government were insufficient and inequitable and ended with the words, "For every kyat the Burman gets, the Shan expects one kyat."

U Nu could not pursue this matter at once because the coup d'état intervened. With the election of 1960 won, however, U Nu took up that complaint. The heads of the Shan, Kachin, Kayah, and Karen States were invited to meet with him and express any dissatisfaction they might feel over the annual budget grants. The complaint was that the finance minister had been distributing grants arbitrarily. They wanted a proper system laid down so that they might know what to expect. U Nu accordingly told them they themselves should draw up a scale and embody it in a system of future allocations so that everybody would be satisfied.

The heads of states went to work with the assistance of their secretaries and drew up their "system" in two weeks. This was presented before the very next Cabinet meeting with U Nu's instructions that it be adopted forthwith. When the time came for the grants to be made, calculations were based on the new system which produced some startling results. Under this scale, amounts equal to only two-thirds of the previous grants were payable to the Karen, Kayah, and Kachin States. Only in regard to the Shan State was there an increase, amounting to K.500,000. The heads of states, on discovering this, came back to the prime minister and requested that their system be kept in abeyance, and that the finance minister should instead follow precedent. U Nu's decision was that the Kachin, Kayah, and Karen States should continue to receive the larger grants as before, but that the Shan State should get the additional K.500,000 allocated under the new system. From that day onward the voice of "Burman one kyat—Shan one kyat" was heard no more.

TOWARDS NATIONAL SOLIDARITY

It had been U Nu's resolve, in the event that he won the 1960 general election, to consult with the leaders of the constituent states and to bring about constitutional reforms that would strengthen and solidify the Union. He put it to the Cabinet in these terms:

1. The government now had more than a two-thirds majority in both chambers of Parliament. It was therefore a most propitious time to make the necessary changes in the Constitution.

2. While the government held this position, he wished to inquire of the state governments what changes, if any, they desired in the Union Constitution.

3. On receipt of proposals from the state governments, a conference would be held to examine and discuss them in the widest possible terms. The conference would be attended by representatives of the Union and state governments as well as the Opposition parties.

4. A family spirit would permeate the conference. Wherever consensus was reached immediate steps would be taken to give it effect; wherever a problem eluded solution it would continue to be discussed until agreement was reached.

U Nu stated his conviction that the above measures would consolidate the Union. It was something he ardently hoped to accomplish before he retired from politics.

The Cabinet having approved his proposal, the four-point statement was circulated among the state governments. Their responses and the arrangements for the conference were placed in the hands of the minister of justice.

THE NATIONAL FOUNDATION

While the arrangements for constitutional reforms were going forward, the prime minister's overweening desire to see democracy take firm root in his time was also being translated into action. There had been an early attempt, before the 1958 coup, through the establishment of the Society for the Extension of Democratic Ideals. But this organisation failed to live up to its promise simply because it was composed of the prime minister and his colleagues, together with secretaries and other heads of departments, who could devote to it only part of their spare time. The society came alive from time to time, but mostly it slumbered.

Therefore, gathering together a group of prominent persons who shared his view that consolidation of democracy should be worked at full-time, the prime minister convened a meeting and presented a proposal for the establishment of a National Foundation. In order to place it beyond government interference and pressure and also to make it independent, the prime minister promised to endow it with ten million kyats.

The Rules Committee, which was appointed at the above meeting, went to work with great enthusiasm. Its members held many meetings among themselves and with the prime minister. In three months there was a draft constitution ready for approval by a provisional executive committee. Membership of this committee was carefully vetted by the prime minister, who judged that the time was ripe to announce the birth of the National Foundation. The members of the Rules Committee, the person who had been hand-picked to serve as the secretary general of the foundation, and other prominent persons were invited to a dinner on the night of 2 March 1962, where the prime minister would formally announce the birth of the National Foundation.

RUMOURS OF IMPENDING REBELLION

On receiving from the government an open invitation to put up proposals for constitutional reform, the states responded with a will. With the Shan State government acting as host, a conference was held in Taunggyi to which were invited the leaders of all constituent states of the Union, as well as those from Arakan and the contingent Mon state. It was widely held that the conferment of statehood on these two areas was imminent.[2]

2. Prime Minister U Nu had promised statehood to these two minority groups.

The main item on the agenda of this conference was what was to become known as the "Federal Principle." There was nothing sinister about this Federal Principle, which was an adaptation of the constitution of the United States. It had three main features:

1. Burma proper would be turned into a constituent state of the Union, bringing it into parity with all other existing states.

2. The two chambers of Parliament, namely, the House of Nationalities and the House of Deputies, would be invested with equal powers.

3. All constituent states of the Union (regardless of size and population) would have equal representation in the House of Nationalities.

The arrangements were for the Federal Principle to be proposed as a resolution and passed by the conference, following which it was to be laid before the prime minister's conference. The moment the resolution was passed with acclamation at the Taunggyi Conference, rumours became rife that if the prime minister's conference should reject the Federal Principle all the minority races would go into rebellion.

As far as the prime minister was concerned he refused to place any credence on these persistent rumours for the following good and sufficient reasons:

1. The proposal for constitutional amendment had been put forward at his bidding. Before he invited these proposals no one from the states, singly or collectively, had ever suggested an amendment. No heads of state had so much as brought a hint or a suggestion about it to him.

2. In his career as prime minister, U Nu had often been taken advantage of. But the offenders were always Burmans, never the minority races.

3. If the minority leaders wished to hold him in a vise they had had an opportunity when the multicoloured insurrection was at its worst, when his administration was confined to Rangoon, when his army consisted of one and a half Burmese battalions. At that time the minority leaders had clung to U Nu and the Union.

4. When the government's fortunes were low, and the rebels likely to win, it was Burman leaders who made secret overtures to the enemy. Only when the tide turned did the opportunists return

to the government's side. The leaders of the constituent states were not involved, directly or indirectly, with the rebels.

5. The leaders who authored the Federal Principle were not newcomers to the political game. They were men of experience and responsibility—not bloodthirsty incipient rebels.

6. With overwhelming support in Parliament, U Nu could afford to look with equanimity upon any piece of legislation. If he did not like it, he did not have to worry about hurting other people's feelings.

The only thing that U Nu could not disregard was Chapter 10 of the Constitution, which conferred upon the Shan and Kayah States the right of secession. If the Shan and Kayah leaders demanded to leave the Union, U Nu would be helpless to prevent them.

In view of these facts, if the state leaders were intent upon rebellion they would be unlikely to spend time and effort on their Federal Principle. This was an uncertain bird in the bush; they had in Chapter 10 of the Constitution their bird in the hand. No wonder U Nu looked upon the rumour of impending rebellion as a joke in poor taste.

MEETING WITH STATE LEADERS

The conference on constitutional reform opened on the evening of 1 March 1962. The delegates were welcomed by the prime minister in a short speech. The first day's programme called for opening speeches from the delegates which, at the close of the day's proceedings at 9:00 P.M., had not been completed. The delegates who had not spoken yet would do so on the following day and then the necessary resolutions would be moved.

As the prime minister left the lobby of the Broadcasting Station, where the conference was being held, he was joined by Sao Hkun Hkio, head of the Shan State, and Sao Wunna, head of the Kayah State, and together they went to the premier's residence in Windermere Park. Here, Sao Hkun Hkio asked:

Mr. Prime Minister, have you been hearing rumours about us? I've heard some.

I wouldn't like you to believe them.

You may set your mind at rest, Hkio. I don't believe them.

If we wanted to play rough we could have done it in 1948 and 1949. We've never taken advantage of anyone.

Hkio, I trust in you all.

Thank you, sir.

It seems to me the rumour mill is ignorant of the fact you are here at my invitation.

That's absolutely right. We're going to submit a resolution, but that doesn't mean you must give in to us. It is a proposal to be discussed. If something can be done about it, fine. If not, well, just throw it out. We'll abide by your decision.

Look, Hkio, I wonder who's spreading these rumours. I can't imagine what the purpose is.

We can't either.

THE SECOND COUP D'ETAT, 1962

It must have been 11:00 P.M. before the Shan and Kayah ministers left. Windermere was the prime minister's official residence, but he did not live in it. His family had a home in Pyidaungsu Lane, off Goodliffe Road, and he himself slept in a rented bungalow next to his own home. It was therefore to this place that he returned late that night.

U Ohn, the premier's adviser, rode in the car with him that night and walked with him to the door. Before he turned to go, he could not help saying, "Kogyi Nu, you say you are retiring from politics after the next general election, but I doubt that the army will let you go. They're bound to ask you to stay."

Captain Hla Myint, the security officer, chimed in with, "That's what I think, too." All the prime minister said was goodnight.

Inside his room, U Nu thought momentarily of the next day's function when he would be entertaining the members of the National Foundation. He found the speech he was to deliver then and read it once. Afterwards he went in to pray, as usual. It was past midnight when he went to bed.

About two o'clock there was a disturbance in his compound. He woke up with a start and saw a young army officer with a service revolver in his hand.

U Nu's first words were:

What d'you want?

Our Army has seized power.

So? What am I supposed to do?

You are to come with me.

The prime minister got up, put on a jacket, and opened the door to the bathroom.

Uncle, what are you going to do?

I'm going to pass urine.

He was not permitted to enter the room, but was led out to the front porch. There as they waited for the car, U Nu heard a soldier speak into a walkie-talkie, "We've got the maggot." This did not register immediately, but when the soldier kept repeating "We've caught the maggot" it dawned upon him that the man was reporting his capture to headquarters, and the word "maggot" was the code name assigned to him. It seemed a big drop, from prime minister to maggot. He smiled.

His captor took U Nu to Mingaladon and confined him in a small, two-storey house. It was four o'clock in the morning. U Nu's impression was that there had been a revolt by junior officers and that General Ne Win was in the dark as to what was going on. When his plight was known, he thought, General Ne Win was bound to come to him. He had no trouble going to sleep. He awoke once at eight but stayed in bed until ten, when a box containing his clothes was delivered to the room. He still felt confident General Ne Win would come to his rescue.

At 5:00 P.M. an army officer arrived to announce that the president of the Union, U Win Maung, awaited him downstairs. So, General Ne Win had found out and arranged for the president to take him home!

But as soon as U Nu came face to face with the president, the latter said:

Mr. Prime Minister, did you listen to General Ne Win's broadcast this morning?

No, Mr. President, what did he say?

It was very brief. He said the army had seized power because the country had gone to rack and ruin.

Almost involuntarily U Nu allowed the words "Aw! So that's the way it is" to escape his mouth. Then he stared straight ahead for a full minute.

Afterword:

An Exchange of Letters

From: U Nu
        Payagyi Road
        Wakèma
        Myaungmya District

To: Maung Nu
        42 Pyidaungsu Lane
        Goodliffe Road
        Rangoon

27 October 1966

My dear nephew Maung Nu:

Your aunt and I are overjoyed to hear you have been released from prison.

I enclose the manuscript of *U Nu—Saturday's Son,* the book of your life which I have completed writing. It covers the period from the day of your birth to 2 March 1962, when the second coup d'état took place.

I have tried my best to be factual in all things relating to you. If errors have inadvertently crept in, please forgive me.

As for what has happened during your incarceration and thereafter, I trust I may be able to put it into narrative form at an appropriate time.

Blessings on you and your family. May you find contentment of body and mind.

Sincerely,

U Nu

From: Maung Nu
        42 Pyidaungsu Lane
        Goodliffe Road
        Rangoon

To: U Nu
        Payagyi Road
        Wakèma
        Myaungmya District

4 January 1967

My dear uncle:

I acknowledge with thanks receipt of *U Nu—Saturday's Son*.

As author you have the right to freedom of expression, and I have no comments to make except in one respect.

It is said in a certain chapter that I am quick to believe others. This judgment and the inferences that would be drawn have come as a surprise.

Those who have had close relationships with me, in particular my wife and children, make the same charge against me.

The truth of course is that I know myself best. That you, or my friends, or my wife and children should have a better insight into my character is an impossibility.

If there is one person in this world who does not take anyone on trust, that person is me.

With best wishes to you, Auntie, and your family.

Sincerely,

Maung Nu

Index

Ahlone, 173–74

All-Burma Students' Union, proposed, 152

Animals, Buddhist objection to killing, 305–06

Anti-Fascist People's Freedom League (AFPFL), 88, 89, 114–15, 117–28, 138, 143, 145, 146, 228, 237, 279, 281, 292; Communists expelled from, 119–20, 137, 138; and independence of Burma, 121–25, 132; in *1947* election, 126–28; Communists oppose, 140, 141; and Karen insurrection, 167, 168, 182; Stalin's strategy on, 193; U Nu's speech, *1958*, 265–66; U Nu's career in, 313–31; split in, 313–16, 318–25; U Nu resigns from presidency, 316–22; U Nu resumes presidency, 322–23; "Clean" and "Stable" factions, 325–26, 329–30, 332n; in *1960* election, 330; after 1960 election, 334–36

Arakan, 339; Mujahids in, 147n, 272; Moslems in, 272

Arakanese, 168, 204n

Asian Youth Association, 313

Aspinall, Dr., 55

Astrology, 306–10

Athawka (Asoka), King, 198n, 232, 274; Nehru as incarnation of, 235

Attlee, Clement: statement on independence of Burma, 124; agreement with Aung San, 126, 130–31; U Nu confers with, 132–33; Nu-Attlee agreement, 139–41, 309

Aung, Major, 161

Aung, Maung, son of U Nu, 118, 297, 299–303

Aung Gyi, Bo (Brigadier), 173, 277, 326, 327

Aung Gyi, Cissy; U Nu's early interest in, 39–42; U Nu's reunion with, 296–97

Aung Nyein, U, 58, 66, 70

Aung San, General (Ko, Bo, or Thakin), 18n, 103, 105–08, 114–19, 138, 158, 165, 168, 300, 309, 313, 331; in student nationalist activities, 71, 73, 79–85; in Dobama Asi-ayone, 85–89; in Freedom Bloc, 99–101; resistance to Japanese rule, 110–11; disagreement with Than Tun, 115–17; in AFPFL, 118–19; Communists oppose his government, 119–20; and independence of Burma, 121–23, 125–26, 132; mission to Britain, 123, 126; agreement with Attlee, 126, 130–31; wants U Nu in Constituent Assembly, 126–27, 129–30; drafting of Constitution, 128–29; and minority groups, 130–31; prime minister, 133; assassinated, 133–34, 137n; burial place, 146

Aung Thin, 20

Aye Kyaw, Ma, 29–30

Aye Maung II, 21

Ayub Khan, Mohammed, 272–73

Ayutthaya, 271

Azadathat, King, 198n

Ba, Ko, 15

Ba Choe, Saya Deedok U, 18, 76, 80; and inn (oath water), 93–95; assassinated, 134n, 135

Ba Gyan, Pagan Ko, 41, 104

Ba Han, U, 326

Ba Khaing, Mahn, 134n

Ba Kyaw, Saya, 25–27

Ba Lwin, U, 28

Ba Maung, Kalama, 21

356 *Index*